Specialty Competencies
in Clinical Psychology

Series in Specialty Competencies in Professional Psychology

TITLES IN THE SERIES

Specialty Competencies in School Psychology
Rosemary Flanagan and Jeffrey A. Miller

Specialty Competencies in Organizational and Business Consulting Psychology
Jay C. Thomas

Specialty Competencies in Geropsychology
Victor Molinari (Ed.)

Specialty Competencies in Forensic Psychology
Ira K. Packer and Thomas Grisso

Specialty Competencies in Couple and Family Psychology
Mark Stanton and Robert Welsh

Specialty Competencies in Clinical Child and Adolescent Psychology
Alfred J. Finch, Jr., John E. Lochman, W. Michael Nelson III, and Michael C. Roberts

Specialty Competencies in Clinical Neuropsychology
Greg J. Lamberty and Nathaniel W. Nelson

Specialty Competencies in Counseling Psychology
Jairo N. Fuertes, Arnold Spokane, and Elizabeth Holloway

Specialty Competencies in Group Psychology
Sally H. Barlow

Specialty Competencies in Clinical Psychology
Robert A. DiTomasso, Stacey C. Cahn, Susan M. Panichelli-Mindel, and Roger K. McFillin

ROBERT A. DITOMASSO
STACEY C. CAHN
SUSAN M. PANICHELLI-MINDEL
ROGER K. MCFILLIN

Specialty Competencies in Clinical Psychology

OXFORD
UNIVERSITY PRESS

Oxford University Press is a department of the University of Oxford.
It furthers the University's objective of excellence in research, scholarship,
and education by publishing worldwide.

Oxford   New York
Auckland   Cape Town   Dar es Salaam   Hong Kong   Karachi
Kuala Lumpur   Madrid   Melbourne   Mexico City   Nairobi
New Delhi   Shanghai   Taipei   Toronto

With offices in
Argentina   Austria   Brazil   Chile   Czech Republic   France   Greece
Guatemala   Hungary   Italy   Japan   Poland   Portugal   Singapore
South Korea   Switzerland   Thailand   Turkey   Ukraine   Vietnam

Oxford is a registered trademark of Oxford University Press in
the UK and certain other countries.

Published in the United States of America by
Oxford University Press
198 Madison Avenue, New York, NY 10016

© Oxford University Press 2013

Library of Congress Cataloging-in-Publication Data
DiTomasso, Robert A.
Specialty competencies in clinical psychology / Robert A. DiTomasso,
Stacey C. Cahn, Susan M. Panichelli-Mindel, Roger K. McFillin.
   pages cm.—(Series in specialty competencies in professional psychology)
Includes bibliographical references and index.
ISBN 978-0-19-973756-7
1. Clinical psychology.   2. Clinical competence.   I. Cahn, Stacey C.   II. Panichelli-Mindel,
Susan M.   III. McFillin, Roger K.   IV. Title.
RC467.D57 2013
616.89—dc23
2013006568

9 8 7 6 5 4 3 2 1
Printed in the United States of America
on acid-free paper

DEDICATION

I dedicate this book in loving memory of my father, William DiTomasso, on the 53rd anniversary of his passing, Lucy DiTomasso, Robert DiGiovannantonio, and Rita Macera Vinci, all sadly missed. I also dedicate this volume to Deborah, my wife; Natalie Denise DiTomasso and Alexis Deborah DiTomasso, my daughters; and Bill DiTomasso, Teresa Maria Misko, and Josephine DiGiovannantonio for their ongoing love and support during these past many years. Dahlia Jade also deserves a special note of recognition for her unwavering loyalty.

—RAD

For Dave.

—SCC

This book is dedicated to my husband, Harvey; my three children, Rebecca, Arielle, and Jonathan; and my parents, Sherrie and Ernie, who have all been sources of constant support, love, and strength in encouraging me to follow my professional dreams.

—SPM

This book is dedicated to my loving and supportive family: my wife, Tracy, and our children, Madison, Alexa, and Shane. A special thanks also goes to my mentors and outstanding professors at Philadelphia College of Osteopathic Medicine.

—RKMcF

SELECTED EVENTS IN THE HISTORY OF CLINICAL PSYCHOLOGY

ca.350 BC Aristotle published *De Anima*, where he described mental processes and the relationship between mind and body

ca.900 Ahmed ibn Sahl al-Balkhi published on the concept of "mental hygiene"

1025 Avicenna published *The Canon of Medicine*, in which he described insomnia, melancholia, hallucinations, and mania

1792 Phillipe Pinel arrived at the Bicêtre hospital, where he initiated legendary reforms about the ethical treatment of patients in asylums

1806 Phillipe Pinel published *A Treatise on Insanity*, which espoused a five category classification of mental disorders

1812 Benjamin Rush wrote *Medical Inquiries and Observations Upon the Diseases of the Mind*, the first textbook on psychopathology published in the United States

1841 Dorothea Dix visited the East Cambridge Jailhouse, which inspired her career in reforming treatment conditions for the mentally ill

1883 Emil Kraepelin published *Compendium der Psychiatrie*, which called for research into the origins of mental illness

1895 Ivan Pavlov presented his work on the role of nervous system in digestion in animals

1898 Edward Thorndike described the Law of Effect

1890 James Cattell coined the term "mental tests"

1896 Lightner Witmer founded the first psychological clinic at the University of Pennsylvania; this event is often cited as the birth of clinical psychology

1900 Sigmund Freud published *The Interpretation of Dreams*, the first major work on psychoanalysis

1907 Lightner Witmer founded the first clinical psychology journal, *The Psychological Clinic*

1911 Alfred Adler formed his own school of psychotherapy and personality theory, Individual Psychology, after breaking from Freud

1912 Max Wertheimer published the founding article of Gestalt psychology, *Experimental Studies of the Perception of Movement*

1913	Carl Jung developed a new school of thought that became known as Analytical Psychology
1913	John B. Watson published *Psychology as the Behaviorist Views It*
1917–1918	The Army Alpha and Army Beta tests were developed as tests of ability for military personnel
1921	David Levy brought the Rorschach Inkblot Test to the United States
1938	B.F. Skinner published his first major work, *The Behavior of Organisms*
1939	David Wechsler developed the Wechsler Intelligence Test for Adults
1939	Starke R. Hathaway and J.C. McKinley developed the Minnesota Multiphasic Personality Inventory (MMPI)
1943	Abraham Maslow described his hierarchy of needs
1945	The APA formally recognized the field of clinical psychology by establishing Division 12
1946	Viktor Frankl published *Man's Search for Meaning*
1949	The Boulder Conference proposed the scientist-practitioner model of clinical psychology
1949	David Wechsler developed the Wechsler Intelligence Scale for Children (WISC)
1951	Carl Rogers published his major work, *Client-Centered Therapy*
1952	The *Diagnostic and Statistical Manual of Mental Disorders* (DSM) was published by APA. This publication represented the beginning of modern classification for mental illnesses
1952	Hans Eysenck published *The Effects of Psychotherapy: An Evaluation*, concluding that there is no evidence for the effectiveness of psychotherapy
1953	B.F. Skinner established behavioral therapy
1953	The Code of Ethics for Psychologists was developed by the APA
1953	Harry Stack Sullivan published *The Interpersonal Theory of Psychiatry*
1954	Abraham Maslow helped to found Humanistic Psychology
1959	Noam Chomsky published a review of Skinner's *Verbal Behavior*, which is viewed by many as the start of the Cognitive Revolution

1962   American psychologist Albert Ellis published *Reason and Emotion in Psychotherapy*, a foundational text for Rational Emotive Behavior Therapy

1967   Aaron Beck published his first major work on the cognitive theory of depression

1968   APA published DSM-II

1973   The Vail Conference proposed the practitioner-scholar model

1974   The U.S. National Register of Health Service Providers in Psychology was founded

1977   Albert Bandura published his book *Social Learning Theory* and an article on self-efficacy, "a unifying theory of behavioral change"

1977   Mary Lee Smith and Gene Glass published a meta-analysis that provided evidence for the efficacy of psychotherapy

1980   APA published DSM-III

1986   Stephen Hayes developed Acceptance and Commitment Therapy (ACT)

1987   APA published DSM-III-R

1992   Standards for training scientist-practitioners were proposed at the National Conference on Scientist–Practitioner Education and Training for the Professional Practice of Psychology

1993   Marsha Linehan developed Dialectical Behavior Therapy

1994   APA published DSM-IV

1994   The Trilateral Forum was established so that leaders in the field of psychology in the United States, Canada, and Mexico could meet annually to discuss the current state of professional psychology

1995   APA established the Commission on the Recognition of Specialties and Proficiencies in Professional Psychology

1996   APA offered accreditation to postdoctoral programs for the first time

1996   The Association of State and Provincial Psychology Boards (ASPPB) hosted the first International Congress on Licensure, Certification, and Credentialing in Professional Psychology

2000   APA published DSM-IV-TR

2001   Canada achieved consensus on competency-based rules, which allowed for psychologists who demonstrated all core competencies to have their licensure recognized in neighboring provinces

2002	APA co-sponsored the Competencies Conference: Future Directions in Education and Credentialing in Professional Psychology, where the cube model of competency was first developed
2002	The Association of Psychology Postdoctoral and Internship Centers (APPIC) hosted a Competencies Conference
2003	The National Council of Schools and Programs of Professional Psychology (NCSPP) conference emphasized identification of best practices in competency-based training and assessment of competence in graduate programs
2003	The APA Education Leadership Conference expanded on the findings of the Competencies Conference of 2002, and emphasized assessment of competency from undergraduate education to professional training
2006	APA published *Final Report of the APA Task Force on the Assessment of Competence in Professional Psychology*
2006	Based on the recommendations of the APA Task Force, the Assessment of Competency Benchmark Work Group was formed to develop guidelines for clinical training programs to assess competence
2007	APA published competency-based *APA Guidelines for the Undergraduate Psychology Major*
2011	APA published *Revised Competency Benchmarks for Professional Psychology*
2012	APA published *A Practical Guidebook for the Competency Benchmarks*

Compiled from King, Viney, and Woody (2009), Groth-Marnat (1997), and Rubin et al. (2007)

CONTENTS

ABOUT THE SERIES IN SPECIALTY COMPETENCIES IN PROFESSIONAL PSYCHOLOGY

This series is intended to describe state-of-the-art functional and foundational competencies in professional psychology across extant and emerging specialty areas. Each book in this series provides a guide to best practices across both core and specialty competencies as defined by a given professional psychology specialty.

The impetus for this series was created by various growing movements in professional psychology during the past 15 years. First, as an applied discipline, psychology is increasingly recognizing the unique and distinct nature among a variety of orientations, modalities, and approaches with regard to professional practice. These specialty areas represent distinct ways of practicing one's profession across various domains of activities that are based on distinct bodies of literature and often addressing differing populations or problems. For example, the American Psychological Association (APA) in 1995 established the Commission on the Recognition of Specialties and Proficiencies in Professional Psychology (CRSPPP) to define criteria by which a given specialty could be recognized. The Council of Credentialing Organizations in Professional Psychology (CCOPP), an interorganizational entity, was formed in reaction to the need to establish criteria and principles regarding the types of training programs related to the education, training, and professional development of individuals seeking such specialization. In addition, the Council on Specialties in Professional Psychology (COS) was formed in 1997, independent of APA, to foster communication among the established specialties, in order to offer a unified position to the pubic regarding specialty education and training, credentialing, and practice standards across specialty areas.

Simultaneously, efforts to actually define professional competence regarding psychological practice have also been growing significantly. For example, the APA-sponsored Task Force on Assessment of Competence in Professional Psychology put forth a series of guiding principles for the assessment of competence within professional psychology, based, in part, on a review of competency assessment models developed both within (e.g.,

Assessment of Competence Workgroup from Competencies Conference—Roberts et al., 2005) and outside (e.g., Accreditation Council for Graduate Medical Education and American Board of Medical Specialties, 2000) the profession of psychology (Kaslow et al., 2007).

Moreover, additional professional organizations in psychology have provided valuable input into this discussion, including various associations primarily interested in the credentialing of professional psychologists, such as the American Board of Professional Psychology (ABPP), the Association of State and Provincial Psychology Boards (ASPBB), and the National Register of Health Service Providers in Psychology. The widespread interest in and importance of the issue of competency in professional psychology can be especially appreciated given the attention and collaboration afforded to this effort by international groups, including the Canadian Psychological Association and the International Congress on Licensure, Certification, and Credentialing in Professional Psychology.

Each volume in the series is devoted to a specific specialty and provides a definition, description, and development timeline of that specialty, including its essential and characteristic pattern of activities, as well as its distinctive and unique features. Each set of authors, long-term experts and veterans of a given specialty, were asked to describe that specialty along the lines of both Functional and Foundational Competencies. *Functional Competencies* are those common practice activities provided at the specialty level of practice that include, for example, the application of its science base, assessment, intervention, consultation, and, where relevant, supervision, management, and teaching. *Foundational Competencies* represent core knowledge areas that are integrated and cut across all functional competencies to varying degrees and, depending on the specialty, in various ways. These include ethical and legal issues, individual and cultural diversity considerations, interpersonal interactions, and professional identification.

Although we realize that each specialty is likely to undergo changes in the future, we wanted to establish a baseline of basic knowledge and principles that make up a specialty, highlighting both its commonalities with other areas of professional psychology as well as its distinctiveness. We look forward to seeing the dynamics of such changes, as well as the emergence of new specialties in the future.

Robert DiTomasso and his co-authors were confronted with the significant challenge of surveying and consolidating the wide breadth of relevant competencies to present in the series volume focused on the specialty of clinical psychology. They have clearly met this challenge in this incredibly useful book in the series for professional psychology. Specifically, the authors provide a helpful and pragmatic guide for psychologists seeking to refine and improve their competencies across the various theoretical orientations to assessment and treatment; individual, family, and systems-based approaches; and the use of case formulation to synthesize an idiographic approach to treatment. The chapter that focuses on the therapeutic relationship competencies nicely underscores the importance of the interpersonal aspects of treatment that are required for competent practice. Similar to several other books in the series, but focused specifically on clinical psychology, DiTomasso and his colleagues provide an insightful and illustrative guide to ethical, multicultural, and professional competencies. This volume is unique, however, in that the authors have identified and conveyed the important aspects of other psychology specialties that are also important to and intersect with clinical psychology, as one of the original and comprehensive specialties.

Arthur M. Nezu
Christine Maguth Nezu

ACKNOWLEDGMENTS

We acknowledge the assistance and support of the faculty and staff of the Department of Psychology at Philadelphia College of Osteopathic Medicine (PCOM). We also recognize the contributions and efforts of our graduate students, Daniel Miranda, Hussain Alhashem, Victoria Limon, Robert Brecher, and Kerri Petro Garruba, with a special note of recognition and gratitude to Ashley Higgins.

PART I

Introduction

ONE

Introduction to Competencies in Clinical Psychology

In this chapter we introduce the reader to the burgeoning movement toward competence-based training, functioning, and credentialing. We trace the evolution of the competency movement from its beginnings, to current status, to future directions. The literature associated with the competency movement uses the term "professional psychology" as related disciplines such as counseling psychology are participating in the movement. While this book focuses on clinical psychology, we use the term "professional psychology" in this chapter in the interest of accuracy and consistency with the literature.

The services provided by clinical psychologists typically include (a) clinically relevant research and the application of scientific principles; (b) assessment (including evaluation, diagnosis, formal psychological testing); (c) interdisciplinary consultation; (d) supervision, teaching, and management activities (including administration and program development); and (e) evidence-based practice and intervention (within theoretical paradigms such as interpersonal therapy, cognitive-behavioral therapy, and psychodynamic therapy). Further, clinical psychologists exhibit and value professionalism, practice ethically, are interpersonally skilled, respect diversity, and advocate for change. Benchmarks of competency are defined within each of the individual competency domains. Within this volume, we define competence within these domains along a developmental continuum. We further address how competence in these domains can be evaluated and documented (i.e., credentialing).

WHAT IS COMPETENCY?

Competency has also been an area of keen interest within other health-related disciplines. For instance, in the field of medicine, Epstein and Hundert (2002) defined competence as "the habitual and judicious use of communication, knowledge, technical skills, clinical reasoning, emotions, values, and reflection in daily practice for the benefit of the individual and community being served" and is contingent upon "habits of mind, including attentiveness, critical curiosity, self-awareness, and presence" (p. 227). *Competency* in professional psychology has been defined as "an individual's capability and demonstrated ability to understand and do certain tasks in an appropriate and effective manner consistent with the expectations for a person qualified by education and training in a particular profession or specialty thereof" (Kaslow, 2004, p. 775). Competence is a reflection of one's knowledge, skills, and attitudes and is conceptualized as "developmental, incremental, and context dependent" (Rubin et al., 2007).

Not only is competence recognized as integral to the ethical practice of professional psychology and the protection of the public, it is an expectation of consumers, regulators, and legislators. The American Psychological Association (APA)'s Ethics code, amended in 2010, includes a specific standard on competence (Standard 2), which includes the following:

> Boundaries of Competence—2.01: (a) Psychologists provide services, teach, and conduct research with populations and in areas only within the boundaries of their competence, based on education, training, supervised experience, consultation, study or professional experience.
>
> Maintaining Competence—2.03: Psychologists undertake ongoing efforts to develop and maintain their competence.

Thus, the APA clearly defines practice within one's competence, and the maintenance of one's competence, as essential to the ethical practice of psychology (Rubin et al., 2007).

As an extension of this focus on competence, the field of clinical psychology has witnessed growing interest in competency-focused training and credentialing (e.g., Belar & Perry, 1992; Kaslow, 2004; Peterson, Peterson, Abrams, & Stricker, 1997; Sumerall, Lopez, & Oehlert, 2000). The discipline is increasingly evolving toward a "culture of competence" (see Kaslow et al., 2009; Roberts, Borden, Christiansen, & Lopez, 2005).

Brief History of Defining Competence in Professional Psychology

Historically, the marker of competence was the acquisition of knowledge and "time practiced," as evidenced by markers such as attainment of an advanced degree, number of required clinical hours, and successful completion of a national exam. For example, the Association of State and Provincial Psychology Boards recommends that independent practice require a scaled score of at least 500 on the national exam for psychologists, the Examination for Professional Practice of Psychology (EPPP). While most states adhere to this recommendation, state boards independently decide upon their own minimum requirements. Notably, this scaled score is an aggregate across a number of knowledge domains from wide areas as disparate as industrial psychology and development. Thus, an obvious limitation of using a passing score on the EPPP as a benchmark of competence is that one may achieve a passing score on the test while failing multiple content domains. It is possible, for example, to answer every question on the statistics or ethics portion of the exam incorrectly and pass the test by a wide margin. The use of the hours accrued in practice as a benchmark of competence has obvious limitations; hypothetically, one could spend every single hour practicing incompetently. While one may argue that this is precisely why such training hours are practiced under supervision, how does one establish a supervisor's competence? Traditionally, such "competence" has been established by hours accrued (e.g., until recently, Pennsylvania required only that a supervisor be licensed for at least two years). Thus, such an argument is circular. In sum, the use of the EPPP and "time practiced" as benchmarks of competency clearly highlighted the necessity for a better system of certifying competence.

COMPETENCY MOVEMENT IN PROFESSIONAL PSYCHOLOGY

The first widely disseminated model of competency in professional psychology was advanced by the National Council of Schools and Programs of Professional Psychology at its Mission Bay Mid-Winter conference in 1986 (see Peterson et al., 1997). Consensus was reached on six core areas of competency: relationship, intervention, assessment, research and evaluation, consultation and education, and management and supervision. This model marked a paradigm shift, a departure from the prevailing doctoral training model of accumulating extensive knowledge in particular aspects of psychology (Peterson et al., 1997). Building on this model, additional efforts focused on revising curricula to reflect "knowledge, skills, and attitudes" in these competencies, in addition to ethical practice and values (Fouad et al., 2009; Peterson et al., 1997). Following this initiative, the Committee on Accreditation of the APA modified its accreditation standards and required doctoral training programs to articulate their education and training goals vis-à-vis expected competencies, which, accordingly, must be congruent with the program's philosophy and training model (Fouad et al., 2009). As the competency movement gained further momentum, attention increasingly focused on how to (a) identify specific competencies, (b) train psychologists to be competent in these domains, and (c) assess and certify their competence. It was with these laudable aims that the "Competencies Conference: Future Directions in Education and Credentialing in Professional Psychology" was initiated.

THE 2002 CONFERENCE

This landmark conference to identify competencies in clinical psychology was held in Scottsdale, Arizona, in 2002 with 126 invited delegates. The Association of Psychology Postdoctoral and Internship Centers initiated and hosted the conference (Kaslow et al., 2004). Delegates represented undergraduate, graduate, internship, and postdoctoral training, as well as private practice. The conference was intended to identify the core competencies necessary for clinical practice (see Collins, Kaslow, & Illfelder-Kaye, 2004). Moreover, this conference was predicated on the following convictions: that "(a) core or foundational competencies can be identified, (b) individuals can be educated and trained to develop these core competencies, and (c) core competencies can be assessed" (Kaslow et al., 2004, p. 701). This conference marked the first time that people from a variety of professions, representing a wide range of organizations, collaborated to further "competency-based education, training, assessment, and credentialing in professional psychology" (Kaslow et al., 2004).

Expert consensus from the conference generated the following eight domains of "knowledge, skills, and attitudes" that were deemed integral to the training of ethical, and competent, professional psychologists: (a) scientific foundations of psychology and research methods; (b) ethical, legal, and public policy issues; (c) cultural and individual diversity; (d) interdisciplinary relationships and consultation; (e) intervention; (f) psychological assessment; (g) supervision; and (h) professional development issues (Kaslow et al., 2004; Rodolfa et al., 2005). These eight domains served to prescribe the Competence Conference's "work groups," which were charged with (a) defining each competency domain; (b) examining how these competencies are attained in education, and in what developmental sequence; and (c) determining how the respective competence should be assessed (Kaslow et al., 2004; Rodolfa et al., 2005). Two additional subgroups were charged with how attainment of the competencies could be assessed and how education and training could be reconfigured with respect to both the competencies and professional development (Kaslow et al., 2004; Rodolfa et al., 2005). One important product of the Competencies Conference was the "cube model" described by Rodolfa and colleagues (Rodolfa et al., 2005), which has garnered increasing acceptance from training groups in professional psychology.

Cube Model

This conceptual "cube model" uses the three-dimensional image of a cube to illustrate competencies in professional psychology and their development. The three orthogonal axes that make up the cube are *Foundational Competencies* (x-axis), *Functional Competencies* (y-axis), and *Stages of Professional Development* (z-axis; Rodolfa et al., 2005). The competencies are viewed as somewhat overlapping, with some, such as ethics and diversity, cutting across other competencies. Additionally, the underlying Foundational Competencies are seen as being intertwined, or embedded, within the Functional Competencies.

FOUNDATIONAL COMPETENCIES

The Foundational Competencies are the knowledge bases fundamentally underlying what professional psychologists do (Table 1.1). They include "(a) reflective practice/self-assessment, (b) scientific knowledge/methods, (c) ethical/legal standards/policy, (d) relationships, (e) individual/cultural diversity, and (f) interdisciplinary systems" (Rodolfa et al., 2005).

FUNCTIONAL COMPETENCIES

On the y-axis, Functional, or Core, Competencies refer to the knowledge, skills, and attitudes necessary to perform ethically and competently as a professional psychologist (Table 1.2). The model proposes that the foundational competencies are integrated into the skill-based, functional competencies.

TABLE 1.1 **Foundational Competencies**

DOMAIN	DESCRIPTION
Reflective practice/self-assessment	Practice within the scope of one's competence, commitment to lifelong learning, critical thinking, and scholarship
Scientific knowledge/methods	Ability to critically evaluate research, appreciation of evidence-based treatments, data collection and analysis, biopsychology, cognitive-affective bases of behavior, and human development
Relationships	Ability to effectively interact with individuals, groups, and communities
Ethical/legal standards/policy	Advocating for the profession, knowledge and application of ethics and legal standards
Individual/cultural diversity	Knowledge and sensitivity of cultural diversity among individuals and groups with diverse backgrounds
Interdisciplinary systems	Ability to collaborate with professionals in related disciplines, and an understanding of the important issues within those disciplines

TABLE 1.2 **Functional Competencies**

DOMAIN	DESCRIPTION
Assessment/diagnosis/case conceptualization	Assessment, diagnosis, and conceptualization of problems within individuals, families, and/or organizations
Intervention	Knowledge of interventions designed to ameliorate suffering, including empirically supported treatments
Consultation	Ability to seek or provide professional assistance or expert guidance toward meeting a client's needs or goals
Research/evaluation	Generates research that furthers knowledge base of profession; evaluates outcomes
Supervision/teaching	Supervision and training of profession's knowledge base
Management/administration	Overseeing provision of mental health services, administration of programs, organizations, and agencies

STAGES OF PROFESSIONAL DEVELOPMENT

The z-axis of this conceptual model represents the increasing levels of competence trainees should be attaining at stages throughout the continuum of professional training (i.e., graduate school, internship, postdoctoral training, lifelong learning). This may also include specialization, including board certification as a specialist through the American Board of Professional Psychology, for example, given that the Foundational and Functional Competencies are broadly applicable in all specialties of professional psychology. For example, the assessment competence will certainly look different for neuropsychologists than for industrial-organizational psychologists. Moreover, specialties such as forensics may have specific competencies in *addition* to those detailed above that are necessary for all professional psychologists (Rodolfa et al., 2005). One implication of this shift is that the EPPP can be reviewed and updated to be consistent with the core Foundational Competencies, thus maximizing face and content validity.

IMPLICATIONS OF THE CUBE MODEL

Practicum Training   After the cube model was introduced, the Council of Chairs of Training Councils (CCTC) made the identification of competencies an ongoing priority (Fouad et al., 2009). The CCTC is an association of chairs representing the major professional psychology education and training councils in the United States and Canada, such as the Council of University Directors of Clinical Psychology and the National Council of Schools and Programs of Professional Psychology, and is separate from APA. The CCTC provides comment and recommendations to various APA boards and committees, including the Board of Education Affairs (BEA) and Committee on Accreditation (COA). Utilizing the cube model, the CCTC is largely responsible for the Practicum Competencies Outline, which expanded upon earlier work by the Association of Directors of Psychology Training Clinics (Hatcher & Lassiter, 2007). This outline is developmentally based and conceptualizes the practicum students as progressing within competency domains from novice to intermediate to advanced. Descriptive benchmarks are provided for each of the three levels appropriate to the practicum stage of training. These progressive levels are conceptualized as successive steps building toward eventual expertise, which may ultimately be attained with future training (Fouad et al., 2009).

The APA's Board of Educational Affairs appointed a task force in 2003 to move beyond defining competencies to measuring them (Fouad et al., 2009). This group investigated models of competency assessment and produced the "guiding principles" for the assessment of competencies (Fouad et al., 2009; Kaslow et al., 2007). As consensus mounted for the competencies articulated in the cube model, the Board of Educational Affairs appointed a task force (the Assessment of Competency Benchmarks Work Group) in 2005 based upon a proposal from the CCTC. This work group was charged with the task of moving past defining such competencies to articulating how they should be operationalized and assessed (see Fouad et al., 2009).

Competency Benchmarks   The work group expanded on the cube model. Three new competency domains, which had previously been subsumed under other competencies, were added: professionalism, teaching, and advocacy (Fouad et al., 2009). The work group generated the "Competency Benchmarks Document" as a resource for those involved in training and assessing competence in professional psychology. Consistent with the cube model, the document categorizes the competencies as either *Foundational* or *Functional*.

The Foundational Competencies in the document include (a) professionalism, (b) reflective practice/self-assessment/self-care, (c) scientific knowledge and methods, (c) relationships, (d) individual and cultural diversity, (e) ethical/legal standards and policy, and (f) interdisciplinary systems. The Functional Competencies in the document include (a) assessment, (b) intervention, (c) consultation, (d) research/evaluation, (e) supervision, (f) teaching, (g) management/administration, and (h) advocacy.

Within the benchmark document, each Foundational and Functional Competency is defined and the specific subcomponents, or "essential components," of the competency are delineated. Behavioral anchors for the essential elements of the competency represent competent practice at that level of training for each essential component. The behavioral anchors are described for each of three sequential developmental levels: readiness for practicum, readiness for internship, and readiness for entry to practice (Fouad et al., 2009). For instance, the foundational competence of ethical/legal standards and policy is defined as "Application of ethical concepts and awareness of legal issues regarding professional activities with individuals, groups, and organizations." This competence has three essential elements, one of which is "knowledge of ethical, legal, and professional standards and guidelines." Behavioral anchors for this component of ethical legal standards and policy are provided for each of the three developmental levels. One behavioral anchor for this component demonstrating "readiness for internship" is "Identifies ethical dilemmas effectively."

In this way, the benchmarks document utilizes the cube model to operationalize the expected professional development within the competencies, across three stages of training. The interested reader is referred to the "Competency Benchmarks Document" by Fouad et al. (2009) for a comprehensive list of the benchmarks and behavioral anchors for all of the Foundational and Functional Competencies.

Assessing Benchmark Competencies   While the importance of articulating specific competencies in clinical psychology is clear, the assessment of competence, or specific competencies, is more complex. As Kaslow (2004) points out, "assessment of competence fosters learning, evaluates progress, assists in determining the effectiveness of the curriculum and training program, and protects the public" (p. 778). Yet until recently, there have not been widely disseminated competence assessment methods with consensual validity. The Assessment of Competence in Professional Psychology work group published a "Competency Assessment Toolkit for Professional Psychology" as a companion resource to the "Competency Benchmarks Document." The toolkit was informed by previous efforts to assess competence in medicine, namely the Accreditation Council for Graduate Medical Education and American Board of Medical Specialties Toolkit of Assessment Methods (Kaslow et al., 2009). The toolkit reviews a set of recommended evaluation methods and their administration, including the advantages and disadvantages to each, as well as their psychometric properties. Information is provided on how useful each method is for evaluating the essential elements of each foundational and functional competency. The toolkit also reviews the suitability of various assessment methods to evaluate competence at the three levels of professional training described in the benchmarks document. In addition, the toolkit includes a fourth level of professional training: advanced credentialing. The toolkit describes 15 tools for assessing competence: 360-degree evaluations, annual/rotation performance reviews, case presentation reviews, client/patient process and outcome data, competency evaluation rating forms, consumer surveys, live or recorded performance ratings, obstructive structured clinical examinations, portfolios, record reviews, self-assessment, simulation/role-plays, standardized client/patient interviews, structured oral examinations, and written examinations. For example, "structured oral examinations" is listed as being useful to assess both the scientific knowledge and methods, and the ethical and legal standards and policy competencies. The interested reader is referred to the actual toolkit for a comprehensive compilation of the assessment methods and their suitability for evaluating competence within all competencies across four levels of professional training and development.

Current Trends

Most recently the competencies have been simplified into six "clusters" (May, 2012) based upon feedback from training programs (see http://

www.apa.org/ed/graduate/benchmarks-evaluation-system.aspx). The six clusters and their components are listed below (APA, 2012):

Professionalism:
- Professional Values and Attitudes
- Individual and Cultural Diversity
- Ethical, Legal Standards and Policy
- Reflective Practice/Self-Assessment/Self-Care

Relational:
- Relationships

Science:
- Scientific Knowledge and Methods
- Research/Evaluation

Application:
- Evidence-Based Practice
- Assessment
- Intervention
- Consultation

Education:
- Teaching
- Supervision

Systems:
- Interdisciplinary Systems
- Management/Administration
- Advocacy

Along with these efforts to simplify the competencies, rating forms have been developed to identify benchmarks of competency across three levels: readiness for practicum, readiness for internship, and readiness for practice (see http://www.apa.org/ed/graduate/guide-benchmarks.pdf, July 2012).

Concluding Remarks

At this point in the competency movement, the initial goals of the 2002 Competency Conference have largely been met: competencies have been defined, competency benchmarks have been identified, and a toolkit of assessment methods has been compiled. Yet considerable work remains. While the competencies have been identified, only face validity and consensual validity have been established among experts in the field. The impact of the established competencies will be greater, for example, if predictive validity can be documented, and the utility and feasibility of products such as the Practicum Competencies Outline can be demonstrated. Similarly, progress in this area could provide greater standardization within the field of how competency is instilled and evaluated.

In the following chapters, we provide an introductory survey of the Functional Competencies of assessment and intervention (cognitive-behavioral, interpersonal therapy, relationship factors, systems-based, and contemporary psychodynamic). While not an independent competency, we discuss case formulation as a critical component of competent intervention. We also review the Functional Competencies of consultation; teaching, management, and supervision; and science-base and research. We also explore the Foundational Competencies of relationship competency, ethical and legal challenges, and individual and cultural considerations. Finally, while not a distinct Foundational Competency, we include "professional identification" as an important component of being a competent professional psychologist, as professional identity encompasses important competencies such as ethics, lifelong learning, and advocacy. To be a competent professional psychologist requires an understanding of what competencies are necessary and the expectation that one must be able to demonstrate competence in these areas. We hope this volume serves to inspire you and further your interest in the various competencies in clinical psychology. If so, we invite you to explore these areas in greater depth in the specialty volumes of this series.

PART II

Functional Competency: Assessment

TWO

Assessment Strategies

In this chapter we discuss the important role of psychological assessment as a critical competency of the clinical psychologist. Assessment may be defined as a higher-order, detailed, highly complex, and sophisticated process of integrating, synthesizing, and deriving meaning about a client from a number and variety of sources. Assessment can be used to infer characteristics and traits about an individual, develop a formal diagnosis, aid in the development of a case conceptualization, create a treatment plan, determine prognosis, make professional recommendations, and answer a referral question. Peterson, Peterson, Abrams and Stricker (1997) describe this competency as an "ongoing, interactive, and inclusive process that serves to describe, conceptualize, characterize, and predict relevant aspects of a client" (p. 380). Because assessment may dramatically affect the lives of those being assessed, clinical psychologists must use great caution when conducting assessments to ensure that they are conducted in a professional, empirical, ethical, and legal manner.

To conduct assessments effectively requires special competencies. These competencies involve (1) understanding of the relevant empirical knowledge base; (2) experience and skill in using specific instruments and tools with given populations; (3) understanding of the psychometric properties of the instruments and methods being used; (4) skill in selecting, administering, scoring, and interpreting instruments; and (5) a thorough grounding in the ethics of assessment.

Theoretical Orientation

Clinical psychologists often define and identify themselves by allegiance to a specific theoretical orientation. Different theoretical models, of course, may value one assessment domain over another and focus upon specific facets within each domain. For example, while behavioral clinicians place a premium on directly verifiable and observable behavior in defining problems, psychodynamically oriented clinicians see behavior as a sign or symptom of some underlying issue. Assessors operating from different models will typically emphasize one domain or aspect of a domain as more important in understanding and explaining a person. All told, however, the greatest challenge in psychological assessment is perhaps truly appreciating what the data mean about a given individual within a given context at a given time (Groth-Marnat, 1997). Groth-Marnat (1997) has described the process of assessment as entailing a number of critical components ranging from explicating one's role, identifying the referral question, selecting appropriate tools to answer the question, acknowledging factors that may adversely affect clinical judgment, recognizing contextual factors influencing the client, considering ethical/legal issues, and understanding factors that may bias the process and outcome. This process subsumes the requisite competencies for conducting assessments.

Function of Assessment

According to Freeman, Felgoise, and Davis (2008), assessment as a whole may serve different aims and functions based on whether it serves as a foundation for planning and implementing direct psychological services to a client, answering referral questions of a consultee, or monitoring instrumental or ultimate outcomes of treatment. Clinical psychologists must, then, be competent in using one or more of a variety of techniques to collect information about a client and to use this information to perform a number of clinical tasks. These tasks often include delineating the specific characteristics of a client, making a diagnosis using a formalized classification system, and predicting some future behavior (Freeman et al., 2008). In clinical practice, any attempt to separate these tasks is purely artificial and arbitrary at best as they mutually affect each other.

DESCRIBING CLIENTS

Providing a formal description of a client's attributes is often critical. The history of clinical psychology is based on the intensive study of the person, so capturing the uniqueness of a person is considered essential. When the aim is to understand the essential uniqueness of a person, a comprehensive assessment of one individual is all that is necessary.

INDIVIDUAL DIFFERENCES

Clinical psychology is based on the construct of individual differences. Individuals vary in an endless number of ways, and these differences often account for the differences in observable behaviors across individuals. Without developing an accurate description of a person, diagnosis and prediction would be virtually impossible. Gaining a thorough understanding of the uniqueness of a person is often rooted in the identification of key areas, including the biological, cognitive, affective, psychological, social, emotional, behavioral, and cultural components of a person. The clinical psychologist may, then, be likened to a highly skilled investigator whose job is to uncover specific aspects of the above domains that account for the behavior of a person.

DIAGNOSIS

Diagnostic classification provides a formal standardized means of communicating information about an individual. Clinical psychologists must be well versed in diagnostic criteria and the constellation of symptoms that constitute a particular disorder and that differentiate it from other disorders (see the American Psychological Association [APA], 1994). The entire process of diagnosis is embedded within a multi-axial system that requires the clinical psychologist to consider a number of important domains. The underlying notion is that a multi-axial system is more likely to comprehensively capture and describe the uniqueness of a given person.

To competently use any system of diagnosis, the clinical psychologist must be knowledgeable about the specific diagnostic criteria and be able to ask questions that allow a determination of whether specific diagnostic criteria are met or not met in an individual case. There are many advantages and disadvantages to this system, not the least of which has to do with failure to capture the unique aspects of an individual that are critical for informing treatment. DiTomasso and Gosch (2002a) have discussed this issue in the context of anxiety disorders and illustrate how in two instances individuals who met diagnostic criteria for social phobia had completely different historical causes that required different treatment targets. Diagnosis itself, then, does not necessarily inform treatment; if anything, it may fail to capture rather important aspects of an individual case. Failure to appreciate the differences that uniquely characterize a person with a given diagnosis undermines the very reasons psychological assessments are undertaken.

Simply stated, not all patients with the same diagnosis should be presumed to be the same (Kiesler, 1973). Moreover, studies of the diagnostic assessment process have revealed many important and relevant findings. For instance, Chorpita and his colleagues (Chorpita, Brown, & Barlow, 1998) have reported that diagnostic accuracy for anxiety disorders is affected by a number of variables, including the presence of comorbid problems, the severity level of the disorder being assessed, and the existence of behavioral markers of a disorder. Diagnostic reliability of anxiety disorders suffers when clinicians are confronted with comorbidities, less severe and subclinical variants of disorders, and the absence of behavioral indicators such as maladaptive avoidance patterns. Competent clinical psychologists must always apply careful scrutiny to the assessment process, but this is especially important in such instances.

PREDICTING BEHAVIOR

Finally, competence in predicting behavior is also important. While there is always error in prediction, clinical psychologists are often required to make some prediction about the behavior of a person. In the context of a specific case, a clinical psychologist may be asked to predict any number of important things that depend in large part on the context of the setting. These settings exert their influence by the nature of the decisions that must be rendered about individuals.

Clinical psychologists are employed in many different settings, including the private practice sector, inpatient hospitals, medical settings, correctional settings—the list is endless. Such predictions include, but are not limited to, forecasting the potential for risk of suicide; violence against others; homicidal risk; adjustment to incarceration; recidivism after release from incarceration; suitability of a treatment or treatment program; fitness for duty; ability to use discretion in legally carrying a weapon; risk for relapse and the like. More often than not, psychological assessments are used as a vehicle to render high-stakes decisions about individuals, the outcomes of which may result in serious consequences. For this reason, competency is necessary to carefully navigate through this difficult terrain.

Perhaps one of the most common tasks confronting clinical psychologists across settings is the prediction of suicide. Rudd and Bryan (2010) have provided a comprehensive overview of the number of factors that must be carefully weighed in a primary-care context. As is the case in predicting other behaviors, failure to comprehensively address all areas may have grave consequences for the patient as well as the psychologist. Undeniably, when compared to practitioners outside of psychology, assessment is a skill that is unique to clinical psychologists.

Assessment as a Skill Unique to Clinical Psychology

Clinical psychologists, as well as those in other specialty areas, routinely conduct assessments. The history of clinical psychology emerged in large part in response to the need for assessment in psychiatric hospitals and military settings. Given their training, psychologists were well positioned to provide these types of services. Psychologists often served in a consultative role to psychiatrists seeking answers to questions related to diagnosis of patients they were treating. Considering the training of psychologists in measurement, psychometrics, and statistical constructs and the absence of such training in psychiatrists and social workers, assessment has proven to be a distinct skill set for psychologists. Yet, today, despite the many benefits potentially accrued from assessment, managed-care companies often fail to reimburse for such services.

This unfortunate state of affairs has undermined the distinct skills psychologists bring to clinical situations. No other profession places the same emphasis on the use of psychological assessment. Clinical psychologists, through their training in scientific psychology and scientific aspects of professional practice, learn important skills that are critical to competency in this domain. Consideration of APA curriculum requirements underscores the critical importance of assessment to the definition of clinical psychology, training clinical psychologists, and competently practicing this craft (Groth-Marnat, 1997).

Unlike psychiatrists, social workers, general physicians, and counselors, the training of clinical psychologists is steeped in the relationship between measurement principles, psychological phenomena, and individual differences (Anastasi, 1996; Kline, 2005; Nunnally, 1994). A competent foundation in these areas includes tests and measurements; test theory and construction; statistical and research methods; psychopathology; the psychology of adjustment; the ability to generate, evaluate, and rule in and rule out hypotheses; and the ability to choose and utilize methods to obtain the requisite information (Groth-Marnat, 1997). Psychological assessment is built, in part, on the use of psychological tests. These instruments are carefully constructed standardized and objective measures of samples of behavior specifically developed to assess individual differences on a psychological construct of interest. However, test scores may be relatively meaningless without a comprehensive interview process coupled with behavioral observations (Groth-Marnat, 1997).

The key role of measurement in psychology and science in general is supported by the observation that major developments in psychology have been predated and associated with discoveries in measurement (Nunnally, 1994). The process of psychological assessment, however, is only as good as the quality of the components, many times psychological tests, on which it is built. Competent psychologists recognize the advantages of carefully derived assessments over subjective guesswork. Acceptable psychological tests are relatively objective, are subject to empirical validations, produce quantifiable results, facilitate professional communication, yield economy of time, provide consistent results, and measure what they intend to measure (Nunnally, 1994).

The development of assessment tools in clinical psychology is based in psychological theory, research, rationality, and/or experience (Aiken, 1996, 1997; Kline, 2005). Clinical psychologists have frequently sought new and improved methods for efficiently measuring and assessing constructs of relevance to clinical practice and research. These motivations led to the identification and operationalization of important constructs, item development, designing scoring response systems, data-collection strategies, establishment of reliability methods, and standards for establishing validity.

Assessment Procedures Unique to Clinical Psychology

There are a variety of assessment procedures that are unique to clinical psychology. More or less, each type is designed to provide a snapshot or sample of behavior or behaviors that are constructed to facilitate our understanding of a client. There are a variety of characteristics of psychological tests that are quite distinctive, and competent clinical psychologists possess critical knowledge and skills related to such measures. The competent clinician would be wise, however, to heed the following dictum in guiding clinical practice: "Testing is to assessment as skill is to wisdom" (Richard & Huprich, 2009).

BIOPSYCHOSOCIAL ASSESSMENT

The biopsychosocial model of assessment in the medical community was derived from the original ideas proposed by Engel (1977), who convincingly argued for a more comprehensive evaluation of patients in medical settings. This multimodal assessment approach addresses key components affecting patients, and without consideration of these, one cannot appreciate the fullest understanding of the patient and account for the patient's problems. Belar, Deardorff, and Kelly (1987) provide a thorough elucidation of the number and variety of factors that constitute a biopsychosocial assessment. Consideration of these key areas and their interaction is essential to competent practice.

When working with patients, clinical psychologists must assume a broad-based perspective in assessment. Failure to do so will likely cause them to ignore important components affecting patients and provide an incomplete picture. It is critical to consider the multifaceted nature of human beings. These domains include the biological or physical, cognitive, affective, social, behavioral, environmental/familial, and cultural aspects of the individual, and the many factors included within each domain. Assessment of biopsychosocial factors is in large part based on the growing evidence base delineating the significant role that these factors play in the onset, development, exacerbation, and maintenance of medical problems (DiTomasso, Golden, & Morris, 2010). The advantages of the biopsychosocial model over the traditional biomedical approach are clear, coupled with the diagnostic and predictive utility of psychological assessments in medical patients (Bruns & Disorbio, 2009; Hutton & Williams, 2001). For example, in the realm of forecasting the outcomes of spinal surgery, a comprehensive review of the literature reveals a host of important factors (psychological symptoms, environmental factors, cognitive variables, etc.) associated with negative outcomes.

BIOLOGICAL ASSESSMENT

The evaluation of physiological parameters was not traditionally tied to the role of the clinical psychologist. A number of forces within the field have contributed to the integration of physical measurements into the process of assessment. These forces include the emergence of biofeedback based on the pioneering work of Neal Miller (1975), behavioral medicine and health psychology, neuropsychology, and most recently the profound effects of integrated healthcare models (DiTomasso et al., 2010).

The early work of Miller (1975) opened up new avenues of investigation and a novel paradigm for understanding, testing, and applying concepts related to the role of learning on autonomic processes. Clinical psychologists may employ biofeedback as a primary treatment modality or as an auxiliary method to treatment by using electromyography, thermal, and electroencephalography assessments and measuring heart rate, blood pressure, or galvanic skin responses.

Even though dyssynchrony may exist between patient self-reports, biological indicators, and behavior, the use of physiological assessment coupled with psychological and behavioral measures can prove helpful to the practicing clinical psychologist.

THE CLINICAL INTERVIEW

Perhaps no other means of gathering and synthesizing information from clients is more critical than the clinical interview. The clinical interview may be considered a formalized professional interaction between a clinical psychologist and client that provides a context or backdrop within which other information about the client can be understood. While criticized for its subjectivity and related reliability and validity issues, the clinical interview remains a mainstay in the toolbox of the seasoned and competent practitioner. When implemented carefully and used effectively, it provides a rich source of information not otherwise available to the clinical psychologist.

Consider the hypothetical situation in which an interview is used exclusively as a basis for psychological assessment. Relying upon an interview alone has many disadvantages. The quality of the information derived from a clinical interview is likely to be a direct function of the individual conducting the interview, the rapport built between the participants, the expertise of the interviewer, the specific questions asked, the manner in which questions are posed, and the comprehensiveness and scope of the interview (Groth-Marnat, 1997; Summerfeldt & Antony, 2002).

By their very nature clinical interviews lack important features such as standardization, exact content, objectivity, scoring, and norms. While interviews are time-intensive, they do provide opportunities for things that most psychological tests preclude. Clinical interviews provide a great deal of latitude for seeking out meanings, probing and delving into further detail, and exploring a variety of important areas including, but not limited to, the thoughts, attitudes, beliefs, perceptions, and behaviors of the client. Most importantly, an interview allows the client to tell his or her own story and share idiosyncrasies. The psychologist gets the chance to directly observe the behavior and reactions of the client; this often keys the clinician into important discrepancies between verbal and nonverbal behaviors. For reasons already described, in conducting an assessment, relying solely on an interview can be problematic.

Exclusive reliance on psychological tests, however, would be just as disadvantageous for obvious reasons. While providing a great deal of useful information about a client, the data may overshadow important subtleties of the person that warrant consideration and that may beg for adjusting the meaning and interpretation of the derived data, providing a system of checks and balances. As Groth-Marnat (1997) has aptly noted, "Without interview data, most psychological tests are meaningless" (p. 67).

Overall, clinical interviews, while varying between interviewers and clients, are intended to achieve certain objectives. The traditional unstructured interview will likely remain a core, essential ingredient of a competently conducted psychological assessment. It essentially defines the interpersonal, rapport-building, and hypothesis-testing components of assessment. The marked observed variability in the reliability and validity of the clinical interview (Groth-Marnat, 1997), however, behooves the clinical psychologist to carefully consider and compensate for those factors that may undermine its usefulness. The interview provides a basis for observing the client's behavior firsthand, experiencing how the client relates, using one's reactions to the client as a means of understanding others' reactions to the client, understanding how the client processes information, validating the client's concerns, and the like. However, most importantly, it is the primary vehicle for formulating testable hypotheses to be validated by other independent information, including psychiatric and medical records, psychosocial history, reports of significant others and peers, and psychological test data.

Competent clinical psychologists approach the interview as a fallible process, subject to the questions the assessor chooses to ask (information variance) and the criteria one employs and integrates (criterion variance), to establish the existence of problems (Groth-Marnat, 1997; Summerfeldt & Antony, 2002;). The competent clinician practices assessment from a perspective that recognizes the contribution of both assessor and assessee in potentially undermining the stability and accuracy of diagnostic and related conclusions. Professional and ethical practice presupposes an awareness of these factors, with a keen eye toward evaluating the likely influence and impact of each within a given context.

Groth-Marnat (1997) has warned clinicians about a number of critical threats for consideration. In the realm of the assessor, this list includes halo effects, primacy effects (initial impressions), confirmatory biases, base rates, the role of salient characteristics, a focus on trait as opposed to situational determinants of behavior, and theoretical orientation. The list of client factors includes cognitive distortions, outright deceit, fixed ideation, frank delusions, confabulatory processes, and inaccuracies tied to memory decay. Taken together, the interaction of one or more of these factors across participants may bias the assessment process through the selection of certain hypotheses, exclusion of other viable hypotheses, choosing one line of questioning over some other, and inaccurately weighing the relative importance of selected information, thereby completely threatening the reliability and validity of clinical judgments. To overcome its limitations, clinical psychologists have standardized the interview process.

Structured Clinical Interviews   The challenge confronting clinical psychologists in arriving at diagnoses of mental disorders is well established. The impetus to develop structured and semistructured interviews actually emerged in large part from the disillusionment with traditional unstructured approaches. These approaches routinely yielded not only lack of congruence in assigned diagnosis but interdiagnostic agreement statistics that did not exceed minimum levels that would be expected on the basis of chance alone (Summerfeldt & Antony, 2002).

Structured interviews vary on a number of dimensions, including the skill required to appropriately administer them, the degree of structure of the questions, and the goals (overall functioning or given diagnoses) (Groth-Marnat, 1997). Regardless of these differences, efforts were then naturally directed toward developing approaches that would improve diagnostic reliability and validity. Improving reliability, for instance, necessitated a method that overcame sources of variation that had an adverse impact on the diagnostic process itself. As Summerfeldt and Antony (2002) have emphasized, content, form, and the sequence of questions are important in achieving diagnostic reliability and accuracy.

Careful consideration of the main sources of problems contributing to traditional open-ended interviews fueled the development of structured interviews. These problems were captured and corrected by addressing what was being asked, who was being asked, who was asking, and how the information was integrated. Through a process of standardization, structured interviews control for variability related to the exact questions included in the interview, the manner in which interviewees are asked to respond, how questions are asked by the interviewer, and criteria for decision-making (Groth-Marnat, 1997).

Yet even with structured interviews, careful considerations must be made when choosing one for use in the clinical setting. Clinical psychologists must address a number of important factors, such as the number of diagnoses to be considered in a given context, the stability of the diagnostic information yielded, and the degree to which the measure validity reflects the diagnosis in question (Summerfeldt & Antony, 2002). These factors reciprocally influence each other and affect the decision to choose a given structured interview.

The competent clinical psychologist must carefully weigh these issues. The question relating to the number of diagnoses to consider in a specific context has its roots in the very nature of the patients seen in clinical practice and practical considerations. In clinical research studies, structured interviews are used to rule out extraneous sources of diagnostic variability and to ultimately identify relatively homogenous groups of participants who share the same diagnosis, recognizing the existence of the patient uniformity myth (Kiesler, 1973). In the interest of achieving sound research methodology, clinical psychology researchers often seek to minimize individual differences. In clinical practice, however, psychologists have the opposite goal: the clinician is interested in describing the unique aspects of the client, and this usually entails consideration of multiple diagnoses and traits, with an emphasis on what makes an individual different. How else might one then truly capture the unique essence of a client?

In either case, however, issues of practicality prevail, for to consider all possible diagnoses in the DSM system would present a daunting task for any professional in terms of time, effort, and cost. While there is a positive relationship between the number of diagnoses one wishes to assess and the number of questions to be asked, there is an inverse relationship between the breadth of diagnostic coverage sought and the amount of detailed information one acquires about each possible diagnosis (Summerfeldt & Antony, 2002). While reconciling these issues is necessary, this task is fraught with many other problems as well. For example, in summarizing the psychometric status of structured interviews, Groth-Marnat (1997) has concluded that clinicians are more consistent in their clinical decisions when judging presence or absence of minimally inferential and directly observable attributes of less complicated cases. Nonetheless, competent clinicians must make important decisions about selecting specific structured interviews.

In choosing a structured diagnostic interview for clinical use, the competent clinician would be wise to consider a number of factors. These factors, conveniently summarized by Summerfeldt and Antony (2002), fall into several distinct areas: diagnoses included and disorder characteristics (e.g., severity); adequacy for populations of interest; reliability and validity characteristics; logistical issues; administration and scoring requirements; and availability of formalized sources of information for assistance (e.g., technical manual).

The reliability and validity of diagnostic interviews are critical characteristics worth highlighting here. *Reliability* refers to the stability of the diagnoses derived from these interviews by the same clinician over time (test–retest) and between clinicians (interrater reliability), and the overall homogeneity and internal consistency of the item pool. *Validity* refers to the extent to which these systems measure what they have been designed to measure. Types of validity of relevance include content validity (adequacy to which the content of the interviews represents the universe of the content domain); construct validity (degree to which the diagnosis is in fact a measure of the construct); and criterion-related (predictive and concurrent validity in that the diagnoses derived should be capable of differentiating patients from other patients with different diagnoses in the present or in the future on some criterion of interest). Validity studies have been hampered by the lack of an objective, independent criterion standard, as found in judgments by psychiatrists that could hardly considered as such (Groth-Marnat, 1997). Nonetheless, there appears to be benefit from providing more structure to the interview process.

There are currently a number of commonly available structured and semi-structured interviews for Axis I, Axis II, and specific disorders. For a comprehensive review and discussion of some of these instruments, the reader is referred to Groth-Marnat (1997) and Summerfeldt and Antony (2002). Two examples of structured interview scales include: the Anxiety Disorders Interview Schedule–Revised (ADIS-IV) (DiNardo, Brown & Barlow, 1994) and the Eating Disorders Examination (EDE) (Fairburn, Cooper, & O'Connor, 2008), The emergence of an interesting, alternative approach to assessment is found in behavioral assessment.

Behavioral Assessment   Behavioral assessment refers to a distinctive, empirically based assessment paradigm that has its roots in behavior therapy (Ascher & Esposito, 2005). This model grew out of dissatisfaction with traditional trait-based models of assessment that relied heavily on inference as opposed to directly observable and verifiable data; viewed the symptoms as emerging from some nonobservable underlying causative agent (e.g., unresolved conflict); and asserted that assessment data must be generalized to some criterion in the life of the client. In behavioral assessment there is minimal inference, direct observation, and verifiable data, and the test setting and the criteria are identical. Bellack and Hersen (1998) defined several critical and distinguishing components of behavioral assessment in that it is an empirical, multimodal, and after multimethod, multi-informant approach that places a premium on the specification of observable behavior and time-related causal factors.

The overarching goal of behavioral assessment is twofold: to provide a solid foundation for clinical decision-making and to facilitate the development and implementation of interventions for altering behavior (Haynes, Leisen & Blaine, 1997; Haynes & Williams, 2003). The process of behavioral assessment yields critical information for the clinical psychologist by carefully describing the problematic target behavior of the client; the situations under which it is reliably observed to occur; the frequency, intensity, and/or duration of the behavior; and the impact of the behavior on the client and his or her environment through what is contingently gained, avoided, or escaped as a result (Bellack & Hersen, 1998; DiTomasso & Gilman, 2005).

As DiTomasso and Gilman (2005) have noted, using a broad-based definition of behavior and sharing assumptions of the behavioral approach, behavioral assessment emphasizes (1) the primary role of learning in the precipitation, development, and maintenance of maladaptive behaviors; (2) the importance of directly observable and verifiable behaviors; (3) the value of a here-and-now, present-focused orientation; (4) the belief that the target behavior is the problem as opposed to some presumed underlying source; (5) learning as a key explanatory and therapeutic mechanism; and (6) fostering effective behavior change through a process of learning to replace problematic behaviors with incompatible, adaptive behaviors. Behavioral assessment may be combined with traditional forms of assessment to enhance the clinical picture of the client and to facilitate treatment planning.

To implement behavioral assessment effectively, the clinical psychologist must approach the assessment process with a number of key points in mind; to do otherwise undermines the process. We provide a fairly comprehensive list of recommendations described in detail below (Bellack & Hersen, 1998; DiTomasso & Colameco, 1982; DiTomasso & Gilman, 2005). These recommendations are based on the unique assumptions and characteristics of behaviorally based assessment processes. Behavioral assessors must carefully and precisely specify the target behavior in question, operationalize it in observable descriptions, facilitate its detection, differentiate it from other behaviors, and provide reliable recording. Observation opportunities are planned and scheduled (e.g., time sampling or event sampling) in such a manner as to obtain representative observations across a number and variety of situations. Multiple methods may be employed that are based on the specific problem and the nature of the problematic behavior.

Relevant dimensions such as frequency, intensity, and duration of behaviors are most often obtained in the natural environment and are collected by independent trained observers, the client, or other individuals in the client's natural environment. Moreover, reliance on different informants is utilized to provide perspectives from multiple sources, each employing behavioral assessment tools in which he or she has been adequately trained regarding when and how to collect the information.

In behavioral assessment, behavior is broadly construed to include more than the client's overt behavior, including cognitions, emotions, and physiological parameters, with the intent of making the typically unobservable more observable. Even when standardized self-report measures are employed, such as behavioral rating scales, they comprise explicitly defined behavioral descriptors that represent an adequate sampling of the universe of the content domain that defines the construct of interest. Also, specific stimulus conditions that represent circumstances under which the target behavior occurs must be identified. An analysis of differential situations under which the problem behavior is manifested may provide important clues to subtle precipitants. One must also identify comprehensive time-related and associated causal factors. These data include antecedent conditions; target behaviors; and client thoughts, images, and feelings as well as important consequential events that may be critical in reinforcing and maintaining the target behaviors (Sturmey, 2007). Here, the assessor is focused on what the client gains from the target behavior as well as what aversive circumstances the client is able to avoid or escape. In addition, one must collect repeated measurements as a function of time extending from baseline throughout treatment, with one or more follow-up points at periodic times.

In describing this process, DiTomasso and Gilman (2005) have noted that

> Assessment is therefore not a one-shot deal. Rather, the clinician obtains a series of integrated snapshots of the targets across a variety of relevant contexts...Baseline information provides a measure of the severity of the problem, useful information for performing a functional analysis, and a criterion against which to measure treatment efficacy. Ongoing data obtained during treatment further inform the case conceptualization, either supporting the selection of the treatment or necessitating the reanalysis of the problem and selection of another treatment...Follow-up data provide a measure of the stability of the behavior change. (p. 63)

Finally, scheduling of observations must be planned in such a manner as to avoid the risk of bias and must be designed to provide a cost-effective means of gathering representative data. Careful consideration of factors influencing the reliability of observations must be addressed, such as interobserver agreement, reactive effects of observations, and efforts to ensure the integrity of reliability checks. Implementation of these guidelines is likely to provide competent behavioral assessment.

Cognitive Assessment   Clinical psychology practitioners are frequently called upon to conduct cognitive assessments. Included within this domain are a number of characteristics that affect the functioning in the everyday lives of our clients. Freeman and colleagues (2008) have described several critical areas of focus in this domain, including "attention, perception, memory, schemas, learning (intelligence, achievement, aptitudes), cognitive development, creativity, language, problem-solving, decision-making and judgment" (p. 150).

Intelligence consists of a variety of different abilities that are necessary in order to sustain existence and progress within the environment within which a person exists (Anastasi, 1996). Sternberg and Detterman (1986) have provided a consensus definition of intelligence as "the capacity to learn from experience, using meta-cognitive processes to enhance learning, and the ability to adapt to the surrounding environment which may require different adaptations within different social and cultural contexts" (p. 469). Common examples of intelligence tests include the Wechsler Scales, the Kaufman Scales, and the Stanford-Binet.

The assessment of intellectual functioning has its roots in the early works of Binet and Wechsler and is one key area in which clinical psychologists continue to seek to document and understand individual differences in intellectual capacity. Over the course of its history, in reviewing a number of definitions of intelligence, Groth-Marnat (1997) has noted that intelligence, understood from psychometric, neurobiological, developmental, and information-processing perspectives, encompasses ability in five critical areas: thinking abstractly, learning from one's experience, problem-solving capacity, adjustment to novel circumstances, and using one's abilities to attain a desirable objective.

Undoubtedly, the Wechsler scales are the most frequently used tools for assessing intelligence in children, adolescents, and adults. This is in large part attributable to the history of clinical and empirical work associated with these scales (Benson, Hulac, & Kranzler, 2010), which has established them as the "gold standard" (Stanos, 2004). While intelligence comprises an overall global capacity affecting an individual's behavior on the whole, it is itself a product of qualitatively distinct abilities (Psychological Corporation, 1997). Intellectual assessment is yet another skill unique to the clinical psychologist.

Achievement measures the extent of knowledge an individual possesses within a specific content domain. Common individually administered achievement tests include the Wechsler Individual Achievement Test, the Woodcock Johnson, and the Wide Range Achievement Test. In general, achievement tests measure what a person has acquired in areas such as reading, arithmetic, spelling, and writing (Richard & Huprich, 2009). Aptitude tests measure homogeneous components of ability (Anastasi, 1996). There are also numerous measures of musical, clerical, and mechanical aptitudes. Assessing memory, a key ingredient for learning, encompasses an active and passive component, working memory and short-term memory, that reflect the information-processing capacity of a person (Psychological Corporation, 1997). One of the most well-known measures here is the Wechsler Memory Scales.

Clinical psychologists conduct cognitive assessments for any of a multitude of reasons, which invariably result from concerns that generate a referral question. Such assessments may be used to establish baseline functioning, track changes in functioning over time, explain failures to attain developmental milestones, document the adverse impact of an external insult (e.g., traumatic brain injury), or identify the effects of an internal malignant (e.g., brain tumor) or naturally occurring developmental process (e.g., aging process) (Freeman et al., 2008). The challenge for clinical psychologists is to make sense out of the vast array of information gleaned from a variety of different measures of cognitive ability, how these attributes characterize the uniqueness of the individual client, how they affect the functioning of the individual on a daily basis, and how they are likely to affect the future adaptation of the person. Of particular importance is explaining and predicting how specific factors and events within the social, psychological, medical/ biological, and environmental realms have coalesced to have an adverse impact on the client and how they may be expected to forecast his or her capacity to handle certain experiences in the future.

The work of the competent clinical psychologist is evidenced by a thorough, reliable, and valid interpretation that parsimoniously explains the problems confronting an individual at a given time within a given context of living. Of course, to do so successfully and precisely requires not only the ability to competently generate hypotheses but also to systematically test and rule out these potential explanations by considering the multitude of factors in context. Whatever the case, however, competent clinical cognitive assessment presupposes a thorough understanding of the unique processes being evaluated; a sound grasp of the empirical literature related to each process; advanced skill in selecting, administering, scoring, and interpreting such measures; experience with a population of interest; and, ultimately, skills in meaningfully synthesizing data.

In sum, clinical psychologists in clinical, educational, medical, and legal settings are frequently called upon to assess the cognitive capacities of clients and patients. To do so competently requires a thorough understanding of available scales, their psychometric properties, administration skills, scoring, and interpretation.

Personality Assessment   One of the mainstays of clinical psychology practice is the assessment of personality. Personality may be defined as stable and long-standing patterns of thinking, perceiving, and behaving that characterize an individual's transactions with the environment. More specifically, Millon, Grossman, Millon, Meragher, and Ramnath (2004) have described personality as deeply rooted traits that find their expression in all areas of functioning. The assessment of personality is a high-level skill that usually entails the selection, administration, scoring, and interpretation of a variety of different devices designed to tap one or more areas of personality functioning. Over the course of time, numerous measures of personality emerging from different schools of thought have been developed and studied; they generally fall into one of two domains, projective and objective measures.

The use of projective drawings and incomplete sentence blanks has a long and hallowed tradition in clinical psychology, not to mention controversy. Examples include the Rorschach, the Thematic Apperception Test, the House Tree Person Test, and Projective Drawings. On the whole, projectives are based on a number of implicit assumptions about personality and its measurement. Most assuredly, the Rorschach is the striking example of the projectives (Groth-Marnat, 1997; Richard & Huprich, 2009). It remains one of the most frequently used tests in clinical practice, in graduate training programs in clinical psychology, and in clinical psychology internships. While the central tenet underlying this methodology is surprisingly simple, the scoring and interpretation is anything but so. Questions about validity and reliability continue to this day, but as Groth-Marnat (1997) has indicated, while validity findings are more variable, in general reliability and validity are adequate.

The Thematic Apperception Test, a projective test originally developed by Murray, requires clients to observe a series of structured cards depicting ambiguous situations; the client is asked to explain what is occurring, the thoughts and feelings of the main character, what led up to the situation portrayed, and the outcome (Groth-Marnat, 1997). While the procedure can be very useful in providing information about clients, controversy over reliability and validity persist.

The objective measurement of personality entails the use of standardized objective self-report items that load on scales assessing various aspects of personality. These scales are derived by developing, calibrating, and testing a pool of items that make up various subscales; individuals respond with a "true" or "false" or some other Likert-type scaling procedure. Inherent within the design of these types of measures is that groups of items are clustered together statistically to provide reliable and valid measures of various attributes. One of the greatest strengths of these measures is that the scoring of the items requires no human judgment or inference on the part of the examiner (Nichols, 2001).

Included among these measures are the Minnesota Multiphasic Personality Inventory (MMPI), the California Psychological Inventory, and the Millon Clinical Multi-Axial Inventory III. Perhaps the best-known, most widely recognized, and most frequently utilized test of personality and emotional adjustment is the MMPI. It represents the standardized use of objectively presented items that load on one or more scales reflecting critical aspects of personality functioning and psychopathology. This instrument has a long and rich tradition of empirical and clinical history attesting to its usefulness in clinical psychology circles. In the hands of a competent clinician, the MMPI is a powerful tool for assessing and understanding personality and necessitates a thorough consideration of the impact of demographic factors on the meaning of the scores. Nichols (2001) has outlined several important parameters related to competent use of the MMPI.

Family Systems Assessment   The family systems approach has a number of distinct assessment tools associated with it that emphasize important factors related to family functioning. Given the complexity, volatility, and changeability of family systems, family assessment presents many challenges (Skinner, Steinhauer, & Sitarenios, 2000) to the clinical psychologist. As noted by Butler (2008), "Family diagrams visually record the facts of functioning across at least three generations of the multigenerational family...facts of functioning are factual information about such things as physical problems, emotional symptoms, and educational achievement placed on family diagrams...[and] are assumed to reflect the emotional processes within the family" (p. 171). Butler (2008) has thoroughly described the method for interpreting data obtained from these measures. Later, the widely used family genogram was introduced, serving a key function in the work of McGoldrick, Gerson, and Shellenberger (1999), who emphasized the context of the family. As pointed out by Butler (2008), assessment through the genogram includes a consideration of the following variables: the structure of the family, its constituents, the marriage, sibling birth, spacing of the offspring, the life-cycle stage, cross-generational patterns, and parts played and functions served by family members.

Family functioning and patterns of transaction are often targets of interest for clinical psychologists working within family systems. Systematic assessment of critical areas of family functioning and related constructs is important in identifying important targets. One of the best-known and most comprehensive models of family treatment is the McMaster Approach. The assessment model derived from this approach is based on several critical assumptions, as described by Miller, Ryan, Keitner, Bishop, and Epstein (2000).

Miller et al. (2000) describe and define six areas of family functioning: the ability to solve problems, patterns and quality of relaying information to each other, engagement in functional tasks, the amount and degree of appropriate responses to expressed feelings, the extent of involvement of members with each other, and the means and extent to which influence is exerted over the behavior of its members. In addition to these dimensions, this model proposes that how members interact with each other influences the extent to which a family is functional or dysfunctional, necessitating change in the latter instance. Examples of assessment tools derived from this model include the Family Assessment Device (Epstein, Baldwin, & Bishop, 1983), the McMaster Clinical Rating Scale (Miller, Bishop, Epstein, & Keitner, 1994), and the McMaster Structured Interview for Family Functioning (Bishop, Epstein, Keitner, Miller, & Zlotnick, 1980).

Based on the Process Model of Family Functioning, Skinner and colleagues (2000) provide an interesting framework for conducting family assessment focusing on the ability of the family to negotiate typical, expected, and unexpected tasks challenging families. The Family Assessment Measure (FAM) is an unusual measure that is used to compile data on an overall measure of general family functioning, relationships between dyads within the family, and the perception of family members about their own functioning within the family. Comparisons across these domains can yield a clinically rich picture of the family.

Two other interesting models of assessment include the Beaver Systems Model of Family Functioning (Beavers & Hampson, 2000) and the Circumplex Model of Marital and Family Systems (Olson, 2000). Briefly, the Beaver Model emphasizes two important factors—competence (flexibility and adaptation) and style of interacting—which are combined to yield nine possible descriptors, three of which are considered functional (optimal, adequate, and mid-range group 3 families) and six clearly dysfunctional (mid-range groups 4 and 5, groups 6 and 7 borderline families, and groups 8 and 9 severely dysfunctional families) in need of treatment. The Circumplex Model (Olson, 2000) emphasizes three important dimensions considered by many to be vital to family functioning: cohesion, flexibility, and communication.

Gottman and Notarius (2002) provided a thorough review of empirical data on marital research and recommended the need for more research in what they considered five key areas. Comparisons of what behaviors differentiate distressed and nondistressed couples in vivo has much to offer from an assessment perspective (Van Windenfelt, 1995). Detecting and attending to observable regular and repetitive patterns of communicating and interacting reveals predictable sequences of interaction that constitute dysfunction and lead to dissatisfaction. Avoiding the all-too-common focus on pathological factors and seeking evidence for strengths such as emotional support, positive feelings, and intimate behaviors is important. Gottman and colleagues (2002) have pointed toward the relative absence of positive affect as opposed to the presence of negative affect that ultimately predicted divorce. Assessment of personality characteristics of partners is also likely to yield important information that influences styles of thinking, emoting, behaving, communicating, and relating in partners. Assessing the impact of stressors outside of the relationship per se and how these stressors creep into the relationship must be considered. Finally, the important role of marital cognitions, in the form of perceptual biases and selective attention as tapped through the Oral History Interview, was supported by Carrère, Buehlman, Gottman, Coan, and Ruckstuhl (2000). Another important framework for assessment stems from Gottman's Sound Marital House (Gottman et al., 2002), containing components that represent the building blocks for constructing and maintaining an effective marital relationship.

Self-Monitoring   Self-monitoring is a behavioral assessment technique designed to yield self-observed information in which the client is actively and collaboratively employed as a data collector (DiTomasso & Colameco,

1982; DiTomasso & Gilman, 2005). The targets of this data-collection process usually include any number of a variety of facets of the client and his or her environment. Clinical psychologists, especially those from the cognitive-behavioral tradition, employ client self-monitoring as an important tool that yields clinically useful information. This information directly informs the clinical decision-making process and serves as a tool for treatment planning. The logic behind self-monitoring is that through a standardized procedure clients can provide valid and reliable information related to their behavior, broadly defined of course. Antecedent and consequential conditions serve respectively as occasions for the emission of target behaviors as well as contingent reinforcers that serve to strengthen and maintain problematic behaviors. As is true with behavioral assessment data in general, self-observations may be recorded in vivo, in vitro, or during analog tasks and can easily be incorporated into an assessment battery.

Commonly, self-monitored data may include information on day, time, situation, thoughts, images, feelings, symptoms, behaviors, and consequences. An inherent aspect of this process in the analysis of these data is the association between each of these facets and potential causal relationships in conducting a thorough functional analysis (DiTomasso & Gilman, 2005; Sturmey, 2007). There are a multitude of possible self-monitoring devices available for clinical use, the design of which depends in large part on what exactly is being measured. Self-monitoring tools include things such as a food intake diary (Brownell, 2000), headache chart, mood diary (Beck, 1995; Burns, 1980), smoking chart, and the like. Each device includes specific measures of relevance to the problem at hand.

As outlined by DiTomasso and Colameco (1982), there appear to be a number of practical considerations for clinical psychologists when planning to competently employ a self-monitoring approach to assessment. Clients must be educated about self-monitoring, its importance and clinical utility, the critical importance of producing valid and reliable data, and exactly how to use the technique. The clinician must also carefully and precisely specify the objective components of the behavior to be recorded, communicate this definition to the client, and guide the patient in practice using the procedure. The clinician must weigh the practical considerations in using the strategy against the amount of information to be yielded. Inordinately complicated procedures that require a great deal of time, cost, energy, and inconvenience for the client may undermine data gathering. Also, historical and related changes in the client or his or her environment must be considered lest they be confused with changes associated with treatment.

Clinicians need to emphasize the need to collect self-observations over a wide variety of situations that occur naturally in the client's environment, or when necessary, even arrange a situation in which the response should occur (e.g., arranging for a social phobic to initiate a social encounter with a stranger in a public place). The clinician must highlight the importance of obtaining valid and reliable self-observed data from the client and reinforce the client's efforts at doing so. Caution is urged in ensuring that the client is not rewarded for producing data that only suggest improvement.

The psychologist should educate the client about the impact of reactivity effects on the behavior being observed, stress the importance of accuracy, and capitalize whenever possible on the therapeutic, albeit transient, benefits of self-observation to enhance the client's motivation and efficacy for change (Shelton & Rosen, 1980). Whenever feasible, the assessor should consider invoking the assistance of someone in the client's environment as an unobtrusive, random reliability checker. As a means of improving the accuracy of self-recordings, early research in this area supported the practice of informing self-observers that reliability will be checked, but not disclosing when the checks would occur (Lipinski & Nelson, 1974; Reid, 1970). Awareness of the potentially biasing impact of expectancy on global evaluations of a problem must also be considered. Research in behavioral assessment has ruled out the impact of expectancy biases when specific, behavioral observations are self-monitored or observed by others (Kent, O'Leary, Diament, & Dietz, 1974; Lipinski & Nelson, 1974; Redfield & Paul, 1976). Finally, clinicians should plan on obtaining repeated measurements of self-observed data that ideally span the time from baseline, throughout treatment, and ultimately at several follow-up points.

In summary, clinical psychologists have a number and variety of assessment methods at their disposal. Competent clinical assessment entails using a multimodal approach in synthesizing information from a variety of reliable and valid sources. These assessment data provide a foundation for determining a diagnosis and developing a case formulation.

Relationship Between Assessment, Diagnosis, and Case Formulation

Assessment, diagnosis, and case conceptualization are interdependent in a stepwise fashion, with diagnosis and formulation built upon assessment. We would propose that diagnosis and conceptualization are as only as good as the assessment from which they are derived. As noted previously, the quality, value, and clinical utility of psychological assessment itself hinges on a variety of factors related to the characteristics of the assessor, the assessment process, the methods chosen, the tools selected, their psychometric properties, the problems being assessed, the setting in which assessment is conducted, the explicit purpose of the evaluation, as well as characteristics of the assessment. Potential biases, reliability issues, and validity concerns loom large and in turn can directly affect related processes. For these reasons the assessment process can have a dramatic impact on the diagnoses assigned as well as the conceptualization of a case. We would suggest that valid, reliable psychological assessment coupled with competent clinical judgment is a prerequisite to accurate diagnosis and case formulation.

Clinical judgment errors in terms of questions asked or not asked and the manner in which clinical information is synthesized can markedly affect the diagnostic process. There is reason to believe that the diagnostic process can be improved by standardizing the diagnostic process through a more structured format. However, blind allegiance to one form of assessment can certainly undermine and overlook other essential information that may serve to qualify the diagnoses assigned.

One important consideration in diagnosis is the concept of an essential criterion (Zimmerman, 1994) that must be met in order for a patient to qualify for a given diagnosis. For example, while depressed mood is an essential ingredient of a mood disorder, recurrent unexpected anxiety attacks accompanied by sympathetic arousal and fear of the symptoms themselves are important determinants of a panic disorder diagnosis. However, competent clinicians realize that differential diagnosis requires consideration of other factors that may serve to mimic a psychological disturbance—hypothyroidism in depression and pheochromocytoma in panic, for example. Among a host of factors, the overlap in diagnostic criteria of psychological disorders, comorbidity, level of clinical severity, ability to report symptoms, and cultural factors further serve to cloud the picture and provide challenges to clinicians.

Psychological assessment is also critical for case formulation. It is difficult to imagine a clinically useful case conceptualization that does not rely on psychological assessment of some sort. There are a variety of case conceptualization formats discussed in this book, and each relies on the use of psychological data. Improperly conducted assessments provide flawed data that may serve to fuel one conceptualization over another. As Needleman (2005) has noted, the conceptualization itself is actually a product of the synthesis of "empirically validated or theoretically-derived assessment methods; collaboration with clients; and clinical judgment" (p. 98). An inaccurate conceptualization may then be used to support a problematic treatment plan.

Models emerging from diverse theoretical orientations obviously include and emphasize and prefer some factors over others, evidenced by the observations made, hypotheses derived, and assessment strategies employed. To illustrate the relationship between assessment and case formulation we will use the example of cognitive-behavioral case conceptualization.

Needleman (2005), employing components of his own model (Needleman, 1999) as well as that of Persons (1989), has provided an exhaustive list of components of case conceptualization that mutually influence each other, including a comprehensive list of client problems; related precipitating stressors; diagnostic data; core underlying beliefs and conditional beliefs; information-processing strategies; coping strategies; maladaptive thoughts, feelings, and behavioral responses to current environmental triggers; client positive characteristics; and a variety of mechanisms that serve to sustain problems. Each of these critical components is clearly influenced by the technical characteristics of the data-gathering strategies, the openness and willingness of the assessor to consider competing hypotheses, as well as the integrity of the model from which the conceptualization is derived (Needleman, 2005).

While competent psychological assessment presupposes knowledge and skills in selecting, administering, scoring, integrating, and interpreting data gathered from psychological approaches, other factors warrant consideration as well. Careful consideration of the host of factors that essentially define assessment, the characteristics of the processes themselves that can undermine and bias it, and an attitude of scientific skepticism, scrutiny, and self-awareness are crucial.

Finally, the ethical practice of assessment entails a number of critical components. A foundational ethical competence in assessment dictates that clinical psychologists are responsible for possessing a sound basis for their interpretations; use assessment strategies appropriately; obtain informed consent; release test data prudently; demonstrate knowledge of the host of factors that may influence test performance; exhibit care in interpretation; prevent the use of assessments by those unqualified to do so; base all findings on current test data and tests; and exhibit caution in the use of test services, explain the results of assessment, and keep test materials secure (APA, 2002).

Benchmark Competencies for Assessment

In attaining and maintaining competence in assessment, there are a number of benchmark competencies to be achieved as one moves forward from entry into a graduate program to readiness for practicum experiences, to readiness for beginning internship, and to ultimate completion of the doctorate and being prepared to begin practice. The Competency Benchmarks Work Group (Fouad et al., 2009) proposed assessment as a functional competency comprising several components. The components of competency development in assessment include knowledge of principles of measurement and psychometrics, understanding of methods of evaluation, choosing appropriate measures that provide answers to questions, diagnostic skills, ability to formulate and recommend, and ability to communicate the results of the assessment process.

Assessing Competence in Assessment

Kaslow and colleagues (2009) recommend a host of relevant methods for psychologists to self-assess in the assessment domain. The recommended methods vary as a function of the component being assessed. We present some general recommendations based on their work. "Very useful" methods and "useful" methods include the following: annual reviews, consumer surveys, objective structured clinical examinations, performance ratings, portfolios, record reviews, simulations, standardized patients, oral exams, written exams, and 360-degree evaluations. Competent psychologists welcome information about their knowledge and skill in the assessment realm and seek to utilize a variety of methods to document, sustain, and expand their competence in the realm of practice.

Concluding Remarks

Assessment competence will remain a critical aspect of the role of the clinical psychologist and one that distinguishes clinical psychology practice from other specialists outside of psychology. Clinical psychologists who seek to provide assessment services must be prepared to meet the challenges confronting them in the daily practice of their craft. Effectiveness in assessment presupposes the possession of critical knowledge, skills, and attitudes. Achievement, maintenance, and expansion of competencies at various stages of professional development in this domain require focused self-assessment planning based on one or more evaluation tools and actions to consolidate competence.

THREE

Case Formulation Models

A 35-year-old healthy female patient is referred by her primary care physician to a clinical psychologist for problems related to panic and fear of having a heart attack. During the past year she has experienced a variety of interpersonal stressors, including witnessing the unexpected death of her father. Since that time the client reports several instances of panic attacks each day; they come on suddenly, appear out of the blue, and peak quickly. She has had over 30 visits to the emergency room of her local hospital as well as numerous visits to her physician. Three key components of her panic attacks are shortness of breath, accelerated heart rate, and chest pain. Despite repeated medical reassurance and a clean bill of health, she firmly believes that she will suddenly stop breathing and die from a heart attack. She has a deep sense of vulnerability encapsulated in the catastrophic belief that something terrible will happen to her at any moment. As a result she feels unsafe when home alone or outside of the house and has stopped all physical exercise and use of caffeine. Her clinical psychologist is challenged with conceptualizing the onset and maintenance of her problem and developing an effective treatment plan to resolve her concerns.

As implied by the foregoing case, an important distinguishing competency of the specialist in clinical psychology is the ability to conduct a comprehensive and intensive assessment of a client. The ability to gather, synthesize, and interpret information from a variety of reliable and valid sources is paramount to the effective process of assessment, diagnosis, and treatment. One critical area of competence in clinical psychology, then, lies in the process known as case formulation or conceptualization. Fouad and colleagues (2009) view the ability to conceptualize cases as one of six pivotal components of the Functional Competency of assessment. Eells (1997) has defined case formulation in this manner: "Case formulation is essentially a hypothesis about the causes, precipitants, and maintaining influences of a person's psychological, interpersonal, and behavioral problems... It should serve as a blue-print guiding treatment, as a marker for change, and as a structure enabling the therapist to understand the patient better" (pp. 1–2). The clinical psychologist must, then, be able to develop a clear and coherent model that accounts for the problems and symptoms of the individual presenting for care.

Case conceptualization is a higher-level activity that requires the integration and synthesis of collected information or data about an individual from a theoretical model that forms the basis for explaining and predicting the behavior of this individual. The ultimate product is a clinically useful and theoretically informed model that adequately captures and thoroughly accounts for the essence of an individual's complaints and forms some cogent, overarching explanation. Ideally, this model provides a foundation for understanding the client's presentation (Nezu, Nezu, & Lombardo, 2004).

Case conceptualization represents a process that is theoretically bound, meaning that different theoretical orientations posit specific constructs about which the clinician must be knowledgeable. In this sense, competence in formulating an individual case necessitates a firm grounding in a given model of psychopathology and treatment (see Hollon & Dimidjian, 2009). Each model has its own set of constructs that are theoretically tied in a formalized manner to explain the problems of a client. Each formulation model, then, places primary emphasis on one or more key constructs and may minimize, ignore, or downplay constructs that are central to other models. In any case, the clinical psychologist needs a guide for handling problems that emerge in practice, managing treatment decisions, and applying theoretical constructs in a practical context. Case formulation fulfills this need.

Currently, there exist a number of case formulation models, each associated with a given theoretical perspective. Eells (1997) has elucidated how specific models of case formulation are inherently tied to a clinician's assumptions about the causes of psychopathology, the adoption of either a categorical or continuum perspective of abnormality, and what essentially is seen as constituting mental health and dysfunction. Some common case conceptualization models include Psychodynamic (Luborsky, 1976), Functional Analytic (Sturmey, 2007), Behavioral (Wolpe & Turkat,

1985), and Cognitive-Behavioral (Beck, 1995; Kuyken, Padesky & Dudley, 2009; Needleman, 1999; Nezu et al., 2004; Persons, 1989). Before providing a brief description of each model, we present a more general review of the goals and functions of case formulation. These goals and functions provide important information about the development and application of a case formulation model in a competent manner. Most importantly, the competent clinical psychologist is keenly aware of the many advantages that case formulation provides in the clinical context.

Goals and Functions of Case Formulation

The goals and functions of case conceptualization underscore the need for the clinical psychologist to possess a number of important competencies. Generally, a sound formulation model provides a theoretical framework that allows the practitioner to explain and predict a client's behavior, overcomes the limitations of diagnostic systems, and enhances the therapeutic relationship. Moreover, among others, a formulation serves as a basis for psychoeducation, overcoming practical problems, and enhancing treatment effectiveness. The very process of formulation itself, then, highlights the need for requisite knowledge and skills in a number of areas.

In a sense case conceptualization may be construed as a theoretically based template that the competent clinical psychologist may fit over the details gathered about an individual client, organizing the information in a clinically relevant and meaningful manner. This template helps to guide the clinician in searching for and gathering critical information that facilitates a thorough understanding of the client, thereby guiding the clinical psychologist in this process. This ever-evolving process is responsive to the ongoing collection of assessment information that is self-correcting in a continuous manner. The conceptualization is tailor-fitted to the individual patient. Clinical psychologists must be careful to avoid forming conceptualizations that attend only to confirmatory data and ignore disconfirming information. Ultimately, through a model, the clinician must accurately and meaningfully synthesize and integrate the thoughts, feelings, behaviors, beliefs, and symptoms of the client.

A formulation model must also meet the goal of providing a thorough understanding of the patient's problems (Persons, 1989). In this sense, it must possess both an explanatory and predictive capacity. In employing a given model the competent clinical psychologist must ask how well the model explains or accounts for the current problems and symptoms of the client. Likewise, the model must also be able to predict the future behavior of the client. Explaining behavior, however, is far easier than predicting it. Some theoretical models may be more successful in attempting to understand behavior but less successful in reliably and validly predicting it. Whatever the case, the point is that the model chosen by the clinical psychologist in any given case may influence the successful treatment of the client (see Barber & Crits-Christoph, 1993).

In competently employing a conceptualization model, the psychologist seeks to understand the unique characteristics of the client. The competent psychologist realizes that no two clients who share the same diagnosis are truly alike (Kiesler, 1973). Case conceptualization helps to account for individual differences between clients and how similar problems may emerge from different causes (Needleman, 1999). Formulation, therefore, enables the psychologist to overcome the significant limitations associated with the available diagnostic system and to capture the unique idiosyncrasies of the client (Needleman, 1999). A critical challenge in treatment planning for any clinician is comprehensively capturing and understanding the unique essence of a client, over and above whether a client meets a minimum number of criteria necessary to warrant a given diagnosis. The DSM-IV diagnostic system, for example, has been criticized by some behaviorally oriented practitioners on these grounds. DiTomasso and Gosch (2002b) have noted that a problem with structural classification resides in the notion that behaviors defining the diagnostic criteria across patients may actually result from unique causes based on learning experiences that ultimately must be addressed to adequately design tailored interventions.

Nevertheless, the DSM system, while not perfect, is essentially evidence-based and is a standard tool used by all clinical psychologists, who must be competent in its use for case conceptualization. A conceptualization model of a client, therefore, underscores the need for bridging the gap between a diagnostic label, the distinct characteristics of the client, and effective treatment planning. It provides a mechanism for appreciating the individual client working with a given clinician in a unique therapeutic context and consequentially offers numerous benefits regarding the therapeutic relationship.

The competent clinical psychologist is capable of using the formulation model to inform the therapeutic relationship. The information gleaned from the conceptualization is likely to be useful in facilitating the collaboration between the client and therapist (Persons, 1989; Needleman, 1999) and may increase the quality of the therapeutic alliance. Considering that the working alliance comprises the agreement on the goals and tasks of therapy and the bond between client and psychologist (Horvath & Bedi, 2002), it is understandable how a formulation may be helpful in fostering a more effective alliance. The profound importance of the therapeutic alliance (Duncan, Miler, Wampold, & Hubble, 2010) is supported by an extensive body of research (see Chapter 11). Competent psychologists are able to build effective therapeutic relationships (Duncan, Miler, Wampold, & Hubble, 2010; Norcross, 2002), which are characterized by elements such as perceived warmth, empathy, understanding, respect, and congruence. These characteristics are more likely to be facilitated by a thorough understanding of the client embedded within a sound formulation model.

The formulation may also provide a number of other advantages. It may provide a list of factors that may not only potentially rupture a therapeutic alliance but repair one as well. Second, it may help to explain a client's reaction to the therapist or even a therapist's reactions to a client. Finally, it may assist the clinician by providing a means for explaining the repeated experiences of the client both inside and outside of the consulting room. In any given instance, these factors may profoundly influence the course and outcome of treatment. Competent clinicians are not only attuned to these factors but are skilled in gleaning relevant information from these experiences and using them in the service of the client.

Case conceptualizations may also serve an important function in assisting clinical psychologists to navigate their way through complex clinical situations. For example, by helping to prioritize a client's problem list, the model may allow the clinician to determine how and whether progress on some problems would have a theoretical basis for generalizing to other problems. As an important bridge between theory and practice, the formulation of a patient may also provide a more systematic approach to handling patient problems in the clinical context, including alliance ruptures, anger, and unexpected reactions or events. By helping to address unforeseen issues that typically develop in the therapeutic context (Persons, 1989) and issues that are largely ignored by theories (Persons, 1989), the competent clinical psychologist is in a better position to handle problems (e.g., transference and countertransference reactions, resistance). The conceptualization may mediate its effects by helping the clinician to generate hypotheses, handle practical problems, develop useful solutions, inform clinical decisions, tailor the treatment to the client, provide parsimonious explanations for problem behaviors, and improve clinical decision-making (Nezu et al., 2004).

In this age of evidence-based treatments, transporting effective treatments into the consulting room, while no easy task, is critical. A number of factors may impede generalization from the randomized clinical trial to the client in the office. An accurate formulation may enhance the impact of treatment and provide a basis for extrapolation from standardized treatment protocols (Needleman, 1999) by guiding the clinical psychologist in customizing the treatment to the patient. As Nezu et al. (2004) put it, "One size does not fit all" (p. 5). The implication here is that the empirical basis of treatments is not a "cookbook" approach, which is all too often an unjustified criticism of manualized treatment protocols. A competent psychologist understands that case conceptualization provides the vehicle for flexibility (Kendall, Chu, Gifford, Hayes, & Nauta, 1998) that is the key for clinical application and effectiveness. Indeed, some treatment manuals, such as interpersonal psychotherapy for binge eating disorder, dictate formulating a case conceptualization. A similar point may be made about treating major depression through cognitive therapy, problem-solving therapy, or interpersonal therapy.

Case conceptualizations are particularly useful in promoting a client's understanding of his or her problems (Needleman, 1999). In developing a formulation, the competent clinical psychologist engages the client, obtains feedback about goodness of fit, and alters the model to maximize the fit for the client. Clients who have an understanding of their problems may be better able to accept the need for treatment, develop enhanced motivation for treatment (Needleman, 1999), view the treatment as more credible, be more likely to assimilate treatment into their lives, and adhere to treatment recommendations. A thorough understanding of the client's problem may also help to identify treatment barriers and obstacles (Persons, 1989). Finally, helping the client to appreciate that a problem is treatable may help to instill a sense of hopefulness (Needleman, 1999). A competent psychologist harnesses the benefits of fostering the client's understanding of his or her problems and uses them to maximize outcome in the treatment of the client. Kuyken and colleagues (2009) report how case conceptualization offers a variety of additional benefits that are likely to have an impact on the therapeutic process and outcomes. They identified several functions of the case conceptualization, which we summarize below.

A case conceptualization provides a vehicle for synthesizing the client's experience with existing theoretical models and research data (Kuyken et al., 2009). In this sense the client's problem is tied and connected to an existing model of personality, psychopathology, and behavior change. In doing so, the psychologist has a frame of reference for systematically organizing his or her thinking about the client. This function makes therapy more targeted and goal-oriented, as opposed to ambiguous and misguided. It also provides a method for matching the client to a treatment.

A formulation model can normalize the problems of clients, provide a validation of their experiences (Kuyken et al., 2009), and explain the onset, exacerbation, and perpetuation of their problems. This psychoeducational function offers many potential benefits to clients, most importantly a clear and coherent explanation of their problems. A well-constructed and communicated formulation may represent the first time a client hears and begins to fully appreciate how the unique interplay of life events and ongoing patterns explain the onset and maintenance of his or her problems.

As a collaborative process, case formulation actively invites the participation of the client, valuing his or her input in this important process (Kuyken et al., 2009). In this manner, the client becomes an active participant in this collaborative endeavor, teaming up with the clinical psychologist to build and refine a model. This process also empowers the client and provides a means for him or her to more objectively view his or her problems. The client may then be more able to step back and obtain some distance in viewing and understanding problems. Competent clinical psychologists have expertise in methods of engaging clients in a collaborative process (Duncan et al., 2010) with an aim toward targeting core issues.

By elucidating the relationship between presenting problems and identifying key core issues to address, a model can make the treatment of intricate, complicated and multiple problems more achievable (Kuyken et al., 2009). It may also serve as a mechanism for operationalizing problems, goals, and treatment targets. Competent clinicians are capable of defining client problems, facilitating the determination of measurable goals, and pinpointing targets for intervention.

Based on a sound rationale and valid, reliable assessment information, a model may help the clinical psychologist not only to order the delivery of interventions but to select those strategies that have the greatest likelihood of impact (Kuyken et al., 2009). In this sense a formulation model may serve a treatment-maximizing function. Likewise, the identification of primary and secondary comorbid problems may assist the clinician in determining focal points of intervention that are most likely to yield the broadest level of impact and treatment efficiency. For example, in a patient with panic disorder and secondary depression, targeting the primary panic problem first may serve to alleviate the associated secondary depression. Likewise, a competent psychologist uses a conceptualization to choose among a myriad of possible interventions by capitalizing on specific skills or characteristics of the client. While a highly intelligent client may respond best to a cognitive therapy intervention, a person of borderline intellectual functioning may benefit more from behaviorally based strategies.

A formulation may also provide a basis for determining the positive characteristics, traits, and coping abilities that the client brings to therapy. Without a conceptualization, these factors may have otherwise gone unrecognized by the therapist. Moreover, many clients, especially those with serious, chronic problems, may not have ever fully appreciated how their hopeful persistence in helping themselves is a powerful personal resource. Instead of focusing only on pathology, then, a formulation model may assist the clinician in elucidating positive attributes that can be reinforced and lead to behavior change and its maintenance. Capitalizing on client assets may simply enhance treatment effectiveness. However, to use these assets requires competency on the psychologist's part to identify assets, harness them, and creatively incorporate them into the treatment process.

By distilling the client's problem into one or more common denominators, a formulation model may suggest the most potent and least costly treatment (Kuyken et al., 2009). A formulation may help to target the treatment of one or more core issues that provide the common thread across a number of seemingly disparate presenting problems. In this sense, treating one problem may be expected to generalize to other related and secondary problems. The competent clinician must be capable of identifying common elements and patterns across problem areas as well as foreseeing the development of problems during therapeutic encounters.

An accurate model may cue or prime the clinician to expect and more effectively address problems that are likely to emerge with a given client and undermine progress (Kuyken et al., 2009). A formulation model may place the clinician on high alert for early warning signs of problems that are emerging. More importantly, the working model may allow the clinician to proactively prepare to address these issues in a more systematic and organized fashion. For example, the triggers and activated schemas that drive maladaptive interpersonal responses in the client's social world are likely to manifest themselves in the psychologist's office. Armed with a well-grounded formulation, the competent clinical psychologist is in a better position to skillfully and collaboratively assist the client in attacking and restructuring these irrational beliefs.

A model may make it more likely for the clinician to effectively handle the client who is not progressing in treatment by highlighting factors that suggest the need for alternatives (Kuyken et al., 2009). In addition, a formulation may prove useful in handling patients who are worsening. Lack of progress and deterioration may highlight the need for additional data or a possible reformulation of the client's problem. A competent psychologist is able to recognize these failures and move forward in trying to resolve these issues. Ongoing monitoring of progress is, therefore, a prerequisite.

As a work in progress, then, case formulation is a fluid process, subject to ongoing data and evaluation that may signal the need for modification (Kuyken et al., 2009; Nezu & Nezu, 2010). Based on the client's progress or lack thereof, the original formulation is either confirmed or subject to modification through a process of successive approximations. This process necessitates that the psychologist engage in ongoing assessment and evaluation and be keenly aware of newly acquired information about the client that may require altering the original conceptualization. This reconceptualization should provide an opportunity for the psychologist to rethink the complex and difficult case and enhance the working model to account for new information. However, most of all, this reformulation should improve treatment process and outcome.

Finally, a formulation may assist the clinical psychologist in supervising a case or in seeking or offering a consultative opinion (Kuyken et al., 2009). In this sense, through supervision the model may provide a vehicle for communicating about the important elements of a case and thereby increase the likelihood of identifying some strategic interventions. Competent psychologists also recognize the critical value and the many associated benefits derived from consulting with trusted, expert colleagues about case formulation issues. Such consultations can often yield dramatic improvements not only in the conceptualization of a challenging client but also in fostering a more effective treatment process and facilitating better outcomes.

Available Conceptualization Models

In this section we provide a brief review of several available case conceptualization models. Each model provides a useful vehicle for formulating patient problems and facilitating treatment planning from a unique theoretical perspective. We then identify commonalities across these models and propose a transtheoretical model for the case formulation process.

PSYCHODYNAMIC MODEL

Not unlike other forms of therapeutic intervention, psychodynamically based approaches rely on a unique conceptualization—a dynamic formulation. A dynamic formulation is rooted in a systematic attempt to determine each patient's unique problem and to develop an intervention plan that resolves it. A number of dynamic case formulation models exist, such as Luborsky's Core Conflictual Relationship Theme (Luborsky, 1976, 1977; Luborsky & Crits-Christoph, 1997); the Idiographic Conflict Formulation Method (Perry, Augusto, & Cooper, 1989); the Plan Formulation Method (Weiss, Sampson, & the Mount Zion Psychotherapy Research Group, 1986); the Consensual Response Method (Horowitz, Rosenberg, Ureno, Kalehzan, & O'Halloran, 1989); the Role Relationship Model Formulation (Horowitz, 1989); the Cyclical Maladaptive Pattern (Strupp & Binder, 1984); and Frame Analysis (Dahl, Kächele, & Thomä, 1988). Barber and Crits-Christoph (1993) have discussed the inherent challenges in comparing the various methods due to differences in specific domains addressed; the volume of material to be considered; the diverse behaviors requiring explanation; the amount of information needed to conduct the formulation; and differences in foci (including the patient's historical information and transference).

We chose here to briefly describe one of the most popular methods, Core Conflictual Relationship Theme (CCRT), as elucidated in the work of Luborsky (1984) and Luborsky and Crits-Christoph (1997). This model employs descriptions from patients to identify and describe patterns evident in their interpersonal relationships. In describing the CCRT methods, Barber and Crits-Christoph (1993) discuss how CCRT employs patient narratives to elucidate relationship patterns and conflicts by considering the patient's wishes, anticipated or real responses obtained from others, and the patient's reactions to the responses obtained from others. Reliability and validity data for the CCRT method are positive. For example, based on the CCRT model, accurate interpretations have been associated not only with improved outcomes but also with sustaining a sound helping alliance and improving a poor alliance, while the degree to which patients understand their CCRT also positively correlated with outcome (Barber & Crits-Christoph, 1993).

Further, Crits-Christoph, Connolly, Azarian, Crits-Christoph, and Shappell (1996), in an uncontrolled trial with patients with generalized anxiety disorder, provided evidence for brief, supportive-expressive therapy on measures of anxiety, depression, worry, and interpersonal issues. Schwartz and Crits-Christoph (2002) provide a thorough CCRT formulation and treatment plan for the case of a young woman presenting with severe levels of anxiety and phobic avoidances. In describing this patient, Schwartz and Crits-Christoph (2002) noted, "A summarization of the elements of Sandra's CCRT is as follows: Wish: To be safe and protected, to trust and depend upon others, to be appreciated and valued...Response of Other (RO): Abuse, punishment, abandonment, disinterest...Response of Self (RS): Anxiety, anger, fear, loneliness and disconnection. Clearly, these relationship patterns have an integral role in generating and escalating Sandra's symptom patterns. Where once particular relationships provided her with responses to be feared, she has generalized this response to the world at large" (p. 250).

FUNCTIONAL ANALYTIC MODEL

The Functional Analytic Model of case conceptualization is based on the operant conditioning model, providing a key example of how theory relates to formulation. This operant model places primary emphasis on environmental factors that occur before, during, and contingent upon the emission of a target response. The most basic assumption of this model is, then, that a client's behavior is learned as a result of his or her unique history of consequences associated with behavior (Cooper, Heron, & Hewerd, 2007; O'Neill et al., 1997). The focus on observable behaviors and the profound impact of environmental influences on behavior are, therefore, critical in explaining and predicting the client's behavior. Clients acquire functional behaviors that promote their well-being as well as dysfunctional behaviors that serve to undermine them and motivate them to seek treatment.

Case conceptualization from this perspective requires the clinical psychologist to attend to three primary, interrelated components: antecedent events, conditions, and cues (A) that precede the occurrence of the behaviors, setting the stage for them to occur; the given, problem behaviors (B) that are targets for change; and the consequences (C) that contingently follow the target behavior (Spiegler & Guevremont, 2003). Functional assessment and ultimate analysis call for a thorough review of the antecedent and consequent events that serve to maintain the client's problem behaviors that are judged to be in need of change. The resultant analysis thereby points specifically to a plan for experimentally altering either or both of the antecedent stimulus situations or the consequences that follow the behaviors for effecting behavior change (Schloss & Smith, 1994).

In summarizing this model in the context of health behaviors, Gosch, DiTomasso, & Findiesen (2010) have noted: "Antecedents strongly influence the occurrence of behavior. Antecedents may be the focus of an intervention when they set the stage for a maladaptive behavior to occur (e.g., having potato chips in the kitchen of someone trying to maintain a low-salt diet), or when they are not present to influence the occurrence of a behavior (e.g., failing to provide a person with written postoperative care instructions)" (p. 251). There are basically three types of antecedents. First, setting events, so-called contextual factors, influence the likelihood that certain behaviors will be emitted (Spiegler & Guevremont, 2003). Second, internal states and events within the client, such as feeling angry and making negative attributions of intentions about another's behavior, also serve to influence behavior. Third, verbal, environmental, physical, and behavioral prompts, specific cues that guide and facilitate perfor- mance of a behavior (Kazdin, 2001), also affect the emission of behavior. Spiegler and Guevremont (2003) indicate that prerequisite knowledge, skills, and resources necessary to perform a behavior are also important considerations.

The clinical psychologist must also be competent in understanding the specific types of consequences that serve to strengthen or weaken the future likelihood of behavior. A formulation based on this model, then, focuses on the identification of the variety of possible sources influencing the behavior of the client that are functionally and empirically observed to influence the behavior of the client over time and situations (Kazdin & Weisz, 2003).

The conceptualization must also account for the manner in which the behavior of the client alters the environment so as to maintain the contin- gencies by eliciting given types of responses from important individuals in the client's environment who may come to serve as discriminative cues for the occurrence of the behavior. The identification of the functions served by the maladaptive behavior is critical, typically including (a) promoting avoidance or escape, (b) obtaining sensory stimulation, (c) seeking atten- tion, and (d) receiving positive tangible reinforcement (Kazdin, 2001). The identification of functional relationships between environmental events and responses is quite complex (Cooper et al., 2007), with changes in one behavior leading to changes in another (Gosch et al., 2010). The compe- tently developed conceptualization will inform the application of inter- ventions designed to replace maladaptive responses with more adaptive coping responses.

BEHAVIORAL MODEL

The earliest traditional behavioral model, called behavior analysis (Wolpe, 1990), required clinicians to meticulously examine stimulus–response relationships from a classical conditioning perspective. Wolpe (1990) con- sidered this process so important that he referred to it as the "Achilles heel" of behavior therapy. Failure to adequately depict stimulus–response relationships was believed to account for the failure of clients to improve, thereby necessitating a reanalysis of the problem. This reanalysis process necessitated a number of steps related to identifying stimulus–response connections.

As elucidated by Wolpe and Turkat (1985), perhaps the primary means of enhancing the effectiveness of psychological interventions is to develop a comprehensive analysis of those factors responsible for precipitating and maintaining psychological disorders. Wolpe and Turkat (1985) described the importance of obtaining a thorough idiosyncratic and operational understanding of the client's problems. To achieve this goal, behavior analysis necessitates a thorough and meticulous structure based on a behavioral interview focusing on the presenting complaint, the patient's problems, the onset and course of each problem, the identification of predisposing variables, and the ongoing development and validation of hypotheses. Ultimately, the clinician should have a comprehensive understanding of the patient that is shared with the patient and adjusted accordingly (Wolpe and Turkat, 1985).

Cognitive-Behavioral Models

Following the emergence of the cognitive revolution in psychotherapy, a number of cognitive-behavioral formulation models were developed. These approaches are briefly described below.

J. BECK'S MODEL

Judith Beck (1995) proposed a cognitive model for understanding the client. In using this approach clinicians must consider a number of factors in beginning the conceptualization and in ultimately hypothesizing what led to the development of the problems the client is experiencing. Beck (1995) emphasized that the clinician must use a variety of factors, including the client's present diagnosis; factors leading to the emergence and maintenance of current problems; maladaptive cognitions and their relationship to the client's feelings, behaviors, and physical symptoms; the impact of early learning events; underlying beliefs; coping mechanisms; the cognitive triad; and current stress factors. The competent psychologist creates a formulation by identifying and synthesizing the client's core beliefs, intermediate beliefs, automatic thoughts, situations and feelings, behaviors, and physical reactions.

PERSONS' MODEL

Another early cognitive-behavioral model was proposed by Persons (1989), who incorporated seven key elements into her paradigm. Persons (1989) emphasized the importance of delineating the problem list; the hypothesized core mechanism underlying the problems; how the hypothesized mechanism explains the problems on the client's list; the relationship between the mechanism and the problems; the precipitants of the client's presenting problems; origins of the mechanism; and predicted roadblocks to treatment. The problem list includes the most comprehensive list of problems the client is experiencing and includes the identified problem with which the client presents, cognitions, behaviors, and mood, each of which is interdependent. Persons (1989) describes how to choose and identify problems from those reported and not reported by the client, how this list may change over time, and the importance of using standardized measures and observational strategies.

The hypothesized mechanism is at the very core of the formulation and provides the key cognitive underlying belief that accounts for the problems on the list. This mechanism is stated in the form of an irrational core belief that drives the thoughts, feelings, and behaviors of the client, which affect each other and confirm the underlying mechanism. The clinical psychologist must also be capable of explaining clearly how the presenting problems of the client are explained by this mechanism and how the mechanism has led to the development of the problems. Persons (1989) believes that the degree to which the mechanism is able to account for the problems provides a test of its clinical utility. Identifying the origins of the core mechanism requires the clinician to identify key events in the life of the client that resulted in the client learning this core belief. Finally, delineating predicted barriers to treatment is necessary to anticipate and resolve issues that may arise during treatment.

A brief example of a case conceptualization using Persons' model involves the case of the female patient described at the beginning of this chapter. During a vigorous, medically approved workout, she experienced accelerated heart rate and some shortness of breath and became immediately concerned that she was experiencing a heart attack. Over the subsequent weeks she immediately rushed herself to the hospital on numerous occasions, only to find the emergency room physician repeatedly telling her she had an anxiety attack. Despite being told she was not experiencing a cardiac event, she subsequently became hypervigilant about her heart rate, to the extent that she continued to interpret an increase in heart rate as a sign of imminent danger. Other triggers included hearing others talking about a person who had a heart attack, news stories related to heart health, and the like. Her automatic thoughts included themes related to dying suddenly from a heart attack, which served to increase her panic, anxiety, worry, and related hyperventilation symptoms of panic, such as paresthesias and chest discomfort. In the face of these symptoms she frequently would call her primary care physician or go to the emergency room. Her automatic thoughts, feelings, and behaviors were traced to her underlying beliefs, attitudes, and assumptions related to vulnerability and threat that something horrible and catastrophic could happen to her at any moment

NEEDLEMAN'S MODEL

Needleman (1999) proposed a model that includes elements of Beck (1995) and Persons (1989). His model incorporates several key components: demographic information; a description of the client's presenting problem; circumstances that led to the emergence of the presenting problem; a comprehensive list of problems, concerns, and behaviors of relevance to treatment; DSM-IV diagnoses and personality traits; core beliefs; sources of core beliefs; vicious cycles and factors that maintain problems; treatment goals; factors expected to interfere with therapy; and a treatment plan. The competent clinical psychologist must be capable of gathering and synthesizing this information into a coherent, working model.

A brief clinical example of Needleman's model involves the case of a 45-year-old African American man who had a longstanding history of generalized anxiety problems and chronic hypochondriacal concerns. He was raised by an overly worrisome grandmother who was highly focused on his physical well-being following his hospitalization at age 10 for a serious infection from which it took months to recover. Current precipitants of his symptoms included a recent job loss, a new job out of his area of expertise, high self-demands for perfection, environmental demands for performance, and the recent diagnosis of a close friend with a life-threatening illness. Any experiences of physical symptoms, especially pain, discomfort, or weakness, reinforced hypervigilance of his symptoms, coupled with extreme catastrophic negative interpretations. His daily level of tension hovered around 75 to 80 subjective units of discomfort, and he worried around 70% to 80% of the day. Generally, any physical symptoms resulted in a pattern of interpreting the symptoms as indicators of a serious medical problem, seeking medical advice, obtaining unnecessary medical tests, and experiencing extreme fear of obtaining diagnostic tests resulting from the potential identification of a terminal diagnosis. His underlying belief was that he was suffering from a serious medical problem and this problem would ultimately lead to his death. He also believed that other things in his life could go wrong at any moment, which set into motion chronic worrying about events and situations in his life, with difficulty controlling the worry. The apparent origins of his problems stemmed from the development of a serious medical problem when younger, now long resolved, and an extreme level of perfectionism. His chronic level of arousal was fueled by overestimating the probability of negative events and catastrophizing.

NEZU AND NEZU'S MODEL

Perhaps the most detailed and comprehensive formulation model is found in the work of Nezu and colleagues (2004), emerging from a problem-solving perspective. Nezu et al. (2004) offer a useful model for guiding clinical decisions "to help the clinician more easily apply ideographically to clinical practice that set of relevant nomothetic information found in the research literature" (p. 3). In other words, these authors present a model that is designed to bridge the gap that often exists between the art and science of clinical practice in professional psychology. In effectively applying this model, the clinical psychologist must be competent in collecting and synthesizing a comprehensive picture of the client's presenting problems; conducting a functional analysis of specific variables causally related to the client's problems; determining treatment targets, goals, and objectives; and selecting, customizing, and implementing interventions designed to alter these targets.

Nezu et al. (2004) apply the problem-solving model to the process of case conceptualization in a unique manner. They apply a problem orientation that focuses on two areas. First, multiple pathways to the development of problem behavior, including biological, psychological, and social factors, as well as their interaction in precipitating and maintaining problem behavior must be considered. Second, adopting a systems perspective, they argue as follows: "In this manner, the reciprocal relationships among the various cognitive, affective, behavioral, environmental, and biological factors can comprise a constellation of causal chains within an overall network, unique to a given individual" (p. 16).

Nezu and Nezu (2010) have clearly elucidated a step-by-step process that the clinical psychologist must follow in conducting a case formulation. Initially, the clinical psychologist must determine ultimate outcomes from broadly defined areas of the client's life, specify instrumental outcomes within the patient (cognitive, affective, behavioral, biological, social, and cultural domain) and environment (physical and social), and thoroughly attend to all empirically identified factors that are relevant to the client. Next, the clinician must perform a functional analysis by integrating stimulus antecedents, organismic variables, response behaviors, and consequences to identify causal relationships between various instrumental outcomes and instrumental and ultimate outcomes. The clinician, then, creates a clinical pathogenesis map that graphically documents and illustrates relationships among distal (predisposing) variables, stimulus (precipitant) variables, organismic (mediating and moderating) variables, client responses, and consequences (reinforcing and maintaining factors). After completing the map the clinician chooses initial targets for treatment that are likely to enhance treatment outcome. Finally, the validity of the conceptualization is assessed through a process of obtaining social validation and testing of hypotheses based on the formulation.

The development of an effective treatment plan entails generating a list of potential treatment strategies for each of the instrumental outcomes with a keen eye toward the extent to which a given treatment can yield a desirable outcome, whether the therapist is skilled to deliver it, whether the client and significant others, when relevant, can likely utilize it, and the consequences associated with the treatment. Nezu and Nezu (2010) recommend the use of a goal attainment map that ties together the ultimate outcomes, barriers to treatment, and intervention strategies, followed by social validation and testing of the map.

KUYKEN, PADESKY, AND DUDLEY'S MODEL

Kuyken and colleagues (2009) present a model of collaborative-based case formulation. They describe critical elements that fuel the conceptualization process: collaborative empiricism, evolvement over time, and the incorporation of patient strengths. Using a metaphor of a crucible, Kuyken et al. (2009) emphasize how the integration of the patient's experience, relevant theory, and empirical research provide a descriptive and explanatory model of the client's problems through a process of collaboration. Positive attributes of the client are utilized to identify roads to change and to ensure the development of hardiness. The clinical psychologist must also carefully consider cultural factors and other experiences; physical factors (genetics, nutrition, substance use); cognitive, emotional, and behavioral factors; and automatic thoughts, underlying assumptions, and core beliefs.

HOLLON AND DIMIDJIAN'S MODEL

Hollon and Dimidjian (2009) have offered a cognitive-behavioral model for depression. According to these authors, an individual who is susceptible to depression is prone to making negative interpretations about himself or herself, the surrounding environment, and the future, coupled with a negatively biased distorted thinking process. Conditional and unconditional beliefs and underlying assumptions are characterized by negative cognitive content. The clinician must, then, be competent at gathering such information through a collaborative, empirical process with the client ultimately designed to uncover the client's dysfunctional beliefs, automatic thoughts, and distorted thinking processes. These data serve as a basis for actively teaching the client a process of considering the validity of these thoughts and beliefs. This is achieved through a series of cognitive interventions and behavioral experiments with the ultimate goal of restructuring these dysfunctional cognitions.

In sum, after reviewing all of the preceding case conceptualization models across theoretical perspectives, we offer a transtheoretical model of case formulation that captures the inherent competencies required to perform a case conceptualization. As shown in Table 3.1, a metaperspective on competency in this arena warrants the integration of critical knowledge, skills, and attitudes.

There is little doubt that clinical psychologists must be competent in developing case formulations to effectively explain patient problems and to serve as a sound, theoretical basis for treatment planning. Without a formulation, therapy is likely to be vague, unstructured, untargeted, and misguided. We have reviewed a variety of models stemming from several theoretical schools of thought and the associated competencies required in the use of each model. Each model emphasizes consideration of factors that constitute key elements of the given model. As a whole these models are driven by theories of personality and psychopathology, are internally consistent, and are comprehensive in nature. Yet no one theory is able to account for all of the variance in explaining patient behavior and treatment effectiveness. Competent clinical psychologists are aware of formulation models, are knowledgeable about and skilled in using one or more models, select a working model that fits with their theoretical perspective and orientation, and flexibly use a model or elements of models that work best for understanding a specific patient and problem and choosing targeted interventions. Finally, in the spirit of Eells' (1997) work, competent formulators are masters at addressing and resolving the opposing forces that exist between achieving one goal at the expense of another, including

TABLE 3.1 Transtheoretical Competence in Case Conceptualization

I. Choosing a model
  1. Select a model that is consistent with your theoretical orientation.
  2. Understand the theory and associated constructs on which the formulation model is built.
  3. Apply the model as a guide to the data-collection process, including the interview, measures administered, and observations made.
  4. Employ measures that provide reliable and valid means of assessing important constructs.
II. Building the relationship
  1. Foster a relationship that is based on respect, trust, understanding, and empathy.
  2. Facilitate a sound working alliance.
  3. Maintain a climate of safety in which client feels free to share problems and related information.
  4. Solicit ongoing formative feedback throughout the process.
III. Collecting information
  1. Systematically solicit and record information in a format that underlies the model.
  2. Employ multiple methods of data collection.
  3. Consider the validity and reliability of the information obtained.
  4. Clarify information regularly.
  5. Consider factors that may undermine the quality of the information obtained.
  6. Consider factors outside of the model itself that may be of relevance or importance.
  7. Address factors of individual and cultural diversity.
IV. Synthesizing information
  1. Integrate information using a hypothesis testing approach.
  2. Organize the information into a coherent working model of the client.
  3. Collaborate with the client in an ongoing fashion to adjust the fit of the model for the client.
  4. Test the model to determine its usefulness for explaining and predicting client behavior.
V. Designing and evaluating treatment
  1. Use the model to develop a treatment plan.
  2. Identify and address barriers to progress.
  3. Understand the client–therapist relationship.
  4. Select interventions that will maximize likelihood of change.
  5. Based on ongoing progress or lack thereof, readjust the model as needed.

expediency versus thoroughness, intricacy versus parsimony, biased information versus verifiable facts, empirical observation versus interpretation, and customized versus generalized conceptualizations.

Benchmark Competencies for Case Conceptualization

In attaining and sustaining competence in case formulation, Fouad et al. (2009) view this process from a developmental framework by identifying critical elements progressing through practicum readiness, internship readiness, and readiness to assume practice. The emergence of competence in conceptualizing cases proceeds from achieving basic knowledge in this area, to the use of a variety of approaches of collecting information, to ultimately being able to derive a valid formulation independently from the assessment material gathered.

Assessing Competence in Case Formulation

Kaslow and colleagues (2009) recommend a variety of "very useful" and "useful" tools in assessing competence in this area. Strategies include case reviews and consumer surveys, oral and written examinations, performance ratings, simulations, annual reviews, self-assessment, process/outcome information, rating forms, objective structured clinical examinations, standardized patients and standard oral examinations.

Concluding Remarks

Competence in case formulation is critical for practicing clinical psychologists. Clinical psychologists must immerse themselves in a model that is compatible with their theoretical orientation and must be able to facilitate a working relationship with the client that fosters the data-collection process. Competence in synthesizing, organizing, and integrating clinical information and using the information as a means for developing a sound treatment plan is crucial. The competent clinical psychologist is committed to attaining and maintaining competence in case formulation. To do so effectively requires a commitment to ongoing self-assessment, solicitation of feedback from a variety of sources, and use of these feedback mechanisms to assimilate this information into an ongoing professional quality assurance plan.

PART III

Functional Competency:
Intervention

FOUR

Interpersonal Psychotherapy

As previously discussed, the competency benchmarks (Fouad et al., 2009) include "intervention" as a Functional Competency. A professional psychologist may be competent practicing within one psychotherapy paradigm but not another. In this chapter we describe one empirically supported treatment, interpersonal therapy (IPT), and provide a brief overview of its development and usage. We then explain how various assessment methods are used to evaluate competence in IPT across four progressive levels. Finally, we close with a brief discussion of future directions of IPT as an evidence-based treatment.

What Is IPT?

IPT is an empirically supported, time-limited, present-focused psychotherapy, originally developed for depression, that conceptualizes patients' current problems within an interpersonal context. IPT does not directly address unconscious processes or explore transference or countertransference. Treatment places an emphasis on eliciting affect in sessions, and the clinician guides the patient to identify and express his or her emotions (we will subsequently use "her" for ease of reading). Clinicians validate these feelings and help the patient consider such emotions as "inner wisdom" that can inform her decisions and behavior (Bleiberg & Markowitz, 2008). Clearly, the "relationship" competency is also imperative here. While the impact of personality and cognitive factors is acknowledged by the IPT therapist, such factors are not the focus of change (Goldstein & Gruenberg, 2002). The premise of IPT is that while disorders such as major depression may be multidetermined, such dysfunction occurs and persists within a social and interpersonal context. For example, while a person may have a biological predisposition toward depression, the depressive episode may be triggered by a life stressor such as a divorce or job loss. Through IPT, patients gain insight into the connection between the ebb and flow of their depressive symptoms and the events and stressors within their daily lives. Patients also learn ways of coping with their interpersonal stressors and, consequently, their symptoms (Weissman, Markowitz, & Klerman, 2000). In this chapter, we focus primarily on IPT for depression and provide a brief overview of the development of IPT for depression and its successful adaptation across disorders and patient populations. We close with a brief overview of the training and certification process to authenticating competence in IPT. Such certification documents competency in the "intervention" of IPT, but such competence may not translate across other treatment paradigms.

Historical Context

IPT was developed by Klerman and colleagues (Klerman, Weissman, Rounsaville, & Chevron, 1984) at the Yale University Depression Research Unit as a theoretical psychotherapy placebo for a randomized controlled trial (RCT) of amitriptyline (a tricyclic) for depression (Bleiberg & Markowitz, 2008; Weissman, 2006). IPT was largely based on the interpersonal school founded by Adolf Meyer and Harry Stack Sullivan (Weissman et al., 2000). In contrast to the prevailing zeitgeist of psychoanalytic theory, Meyer's conceptualization of psychiatric disorders emphasized the psychosocial and interpersonal context within which the problems were occurring. This idea was consistent with the contemporary work of Bowlby and Harlow. John Bowlby (1973) had similarly theorized that dysfunctional attachments, or the disruption of secure ones, could be a risk factor for depression, and Harry Harlow had graphically demonstrated the horrifying effects that loss of attachment and social isolation had on monkeys (see Blum, 2002, for a riveting account of Harlow and his work). Interestingly, Sullivan's theory proposed that life events and loss in *adulthood* influenced later depression, in direct contrast to Freudian theory that held child events as causing adult psychopathology. Klerman and colleagues reviewed the contemporary research literature, which illustrated a link between depression and bereavement, dysfunctional relationships, role transitions, and poor social functioning (Bleiberg & Markowitz, 2008). In this perspective, the "unit of observation" is the individual's circle of intimacy rather than the individual herself. Sullivan's use of the term "interpersonal" is clearly distinguished from the prevailing "*intra*personal/*intra*psychic" approach (Weissman et al., 2000).

At the time that Klerman and colleagues had designed IPT for inclusion in the RCT for amitriptyline, there had been no studies of psychotherapy with sufficient sample size and power to draw any conclusions. Interestingly, when Klerman was developing the therapy for the purposes of this 8-month RCT, he was influenced by Aaron T. Beck's early work developing cognitive therapy, as Beck had sent Klerman a 100-page document (basically a manual) at the time, detailing the treatment procedures prescribed in cognitive therapy (Weissman, 2006).

Depression as medical illness. IPT characterizes depression as a "clinical disorder," adopting the medical model of characterizing depression as an illness; IPT quite deliberately places the individual in the "sick role." The implications of this conceptualization are that the patient is not "blamed" for being sick. The patient is faultless, in fact, as she has merely developed an illness. The therapist frames the depression as an illness, but a *treatable* illness. Again consistent with the medical model, the clinician prescribes a course of treatment for the illness: IPT. This frame of reference is designed to remoralize the depressed patient, particularly since depression is commonly associated with guilt, self-blame, and self-criticism. In theory, this conceptualization of depression as a medical illness makes IPT particularly compatible with pharmacotherapy for depression and combined pharmacotherapy and IPT for depression (Bleiberg & Markowitz, 2008).

Depression as related to recent life stressors. Life events can trigger depression, and depression makes it harder to manage life stressors. Thus, IPT focuses on resolving significant interpersonal problems in the patient's life. Resolving such interpersonal problems is believed to provide symptom relief for the depressed patient. Treatment begins with assessment using the interpersonal inventory: a comprehensive, semistructured interview about the patient's interpersonal functioning and current and past relationships. This instrument assesses the relation between current onset of symptoms and any changes in important relationships (e.g., the onset of a depression and the death of a parent). Four classes of interpersonal problems are assessed: (a) Grief (loss of relationships or loss of healthy self); (b) Interpersonal role disputes; (c) Interpersonal role transitions; and (d) Interpersonal skill deficits. These four categories of interpersonal problems are detailed below.

The Four Categories of Interpersonal Problems

Grief. This problem area concerns complicated or unresolved grief following the loss of a significant person or relationship. The clinician facilitates the grieving process, encouraging emotional expression, and explores the meaning of the relationship to the patient. Because complicated grief may reflect conflicting emotions about the relationship or loved one, the IPT clinician validates and normalizes negative emotions, encouraging the patient to accept any such negative feelings and ultimately let go of the associated guilt (Bleiberg & Markowitz, 2008). Ultimately, the clinician guides the patient to pursue new relationships or activities to help fill the void left by the lost relationship and move forward.

Role disputes. A role dispute is a conflict with a significant other: coworker, spouse, friend, relative, and so forth. The IPT clinician and patient examine the relationship, the nature of the conflict, and possible solutions to the conflict (Bleiberg & Markowitz, 2008). For patients with depression, the tendency to be self-sacrificing and put others' needs before their own is common, as is conflict avoidance and self-blame. The IPT therapist, again, conveys that the conflict is not the patient's fault and validates and normalizes her negative emotions. Together, the patient and clinician explore ways that the patient can better express herself through in-session role-plays. In this way, the clinician can help the patient practice and implement attempts to resolve, or ultimately dissolve, the problematic relationship.

Role transitions. A role transition issue involves a significant life change, such as relocating, having a newborn, divorcing, and retiring. Even for positive or anticipated life changes, IPT views such life events as stressors. For the depressed patient, it may be important to mourn the loss of the old role or self and explore the pros and cons of the new role. The clinician can also guide the patient to examine ways in which she can retain any positive aspects of the old role, while conceptualizing this loss of role as a new beginning with new opportunities.

Interpersonal deficits. "Interpersonal skill deficits" is used as the default problem of focus when the individual reports no significant life events or relationship problems coinciding with the depression. In this case, the client does not meet criteria for the other three problem categories. Patients falling under this category are typically socially isolated and have either a pattern of unrewarding relationships or chronic difficulty establishing and maintaining significant social bonds (Bleiberg & Markowitz, 2008). In contrast to the prior three problem areas, IPT for interpersonal deficits explicitly focuses on the therapeutic alliance within session (Bleiberg & Markowitz, 2008). The clinician encourages the patient to voice her feelings as difficulties arise in the patient–therapist relationship. In this way, the therapeutic relationship can serve as a model, and springboard, for the patient forming future relationships.

Phases of IPT

IPT for depression comprises three distinct phases—initial, middle, and termination—as detailed below (Bleiberg & Markowitz, 2008).

Initial phase (sessions 1–3). The overarching goals of this phase are to (a) ascertain the diagnosis, (b) establish the interpersonal context for the depression, (c) remoralize the patient and inspire hope, (d) forge a therapeutic alliance, and (e) orient to treatment. During this phase the clinician conveys that the patient's symptoms are the result of an illness (depression) and things will get better. The clinician provides psychoeducation on depression, particularly depression's effects on social functioning. The clinician places the patient in the "sick role," conducts the interpersonal inventory interview, and identifies the relevant problem areas for this patient (Bleiberg & Markowitz, 2008).

Middle phase (sessions 4–9). The bulk of IPT for depression is the middle phase. At this point, the diagnosis has been made, the relevant information from the interpersonal inventory has been gleaned, and the problems are determined. During this phase, each session begins with the clinician's question: "How have you been feeling since we last met?" (Bleiberg & Markowitz, 2008). The patient reports on her recent mood and events, and the clinician looks to explicitly connect the two in order to reinforce the interpersonal nature and reactivity of the symptoms (e.g., "Well, it makes sense that you felt depressed given that interaction you had with your daughter"). Many patients with depression (and other disorders, of course) commonly neglect their own needs and wants and feel powerless and hopeless. Consequently, in reviewing the patient's report of recent mood and events, the IPT clinician deliberately inquires as to what the patient wanted in each interpersonal interaction and explores with the patient what she could have done differently to get what she wanted in that interaction (Bleiberg & Markowitz, 2008). The clinician never blames the patient because the patient is viewed as blameless. Rather, the depression is blamed for her difficulties, and the clinician's stance is open, nonjudgmental, and nondirective. Role-plays are an important intervention in IPT, used to give the patient practice acting on behalf of her own needs. The IPT clinician encourages the patient to take interpersonal risks, with the expectation that although it may be anxiety-provoking and uncomfortable at first, taking such risks will become easier over time. Such new behavior is believed to provide a buffer against depressive symptoms and perhaps improve her quality of life. The clinician explicitly praises and encourages the patient for assertive and adaptive actions and empathizes with the difficulty of change.

Termination phase (sessions 10–12). During the termination phase, the clinician assesses the extent to which the problem area has improved and attributes any observed progress to the patient's own actions. The therapist conveys optimism for continued progress and the expectation that, over time, such observed improvements will likely generalize across other areas of her life. The clinician and patient also discuss relapse prevention, as applicable. To the extent to which the patient has not observed improvement, the clinician explicitly reinforces the attribution that the *treatment* has failed in this regard, not the patient. In this case, the clinician may recommend either extending IPT or referring the patient for another treatment modality.

CASE EXAMPLE

Daphne was a 41-year-old, married woman who worked for the postal service. She described herself as depressed and stated that she would secretly binge at night to cope with her low mood and stress. Daphne described her marriage as a happy one; however, she felt too ashamed to tell her husband about her frequent binging, though she believed he would be supportive. Daphne's primary complaint was her supervisor at work. She described him as domineering and openly critical, often in front of coworkers. In the past 5 years of reporting to this supervisor, Daphne states she has gained 50 pounds.

Daphne's case was conceptualized primarily as a "role dispute." Treatment included validating Daphne's feelings, normalizing her response, and ultimately addressing her relationships with both her boss and husband. This included encouraging Daphne to express herself more and asking for her needs to be met. Treatment included in-session rehearsals of Daphne asserting herself and role-plays but did not include food logs, other diaries, or any nutritional counseling.

Efficacy of IPT

IPT is the second-most-researched psychotherapy in the world (after cognitive-behavioral therapy [CBT]), with more than 150 empirical studies substantiating its efficacy (Stuart & Robertson, 2003; Stuart, Robertson, & O'Hara, 2006). While this body of evidence is too extensive to review in detail, a few important studies bear mention here. Arguably, the crown jewel among the empirical studies supporting IPT is the National Institute of Mental Health's (NIMH) Treatment of Depression Collaborative Research Program (NIMH-TDCRP; Elkin et al., 1989). This controversial, oft-cited study compared IPT, CBT, pill placebo, and imipramine for major depression, and, at the time, was the largest randomized, controlled, multisite, clinical trial in history. Experienced therapists, manuals, supervision, and adherence tests were all utilized to ensure treatment fidelity. Initial analyses found evidence to support the efficacy of IPT for the most depressed study participants (Elkin et al., 1989); however, controversy and debate about the study's methodology and conclusions ensued for years after publication.

Like CBT (see following chapter), IPT has been associated with observable changes in brain metabolism commensurate with symptom relief from major depression (e.g., Brody et al., 2001). Interestingly, these brain changes, observable through neuroimaging, were qualitatively different from those observed in the corresponding study participants who evidenced improvement on paroxetine (Brody et al., 2001).

While the efficacy of IPT for depression has been well established, there have been more recent developments in two areas: (a) applying IPT across disorders, age groups, and treatment formats and (b) establishing the effectiveness of IPT outside the confines of clinical trials.

Adaptations of IPT

Eating disorders. The first eating disorder to which IPT was applied in the research literature was bulimia nervosa (BN). The original IPT for depression has been adapted for BN, but the modified treatment notably does not address food or binging as a focus of treatment. Interestingly, in a large multisite RCT comparing CBT and IPT for BN, CBT was found to be superior at posttreatment (20 weeks), but at 1-year follow-up, participants receiving IPT and CBT were virtually indistinguishable (Agras, Walsh, Fairburn, Wilson, & Kraemer, 2000). These intriguing results suggest that not only does IPT engender lasting improvements for BN, but that the effects of IPT continue to operate and generalize posttreatment.

In addition to bulimia nervosa, IPT has also been successfully adapted for binge eating disorder (BED), a new eating disorder diagnosis slated for inclusion in DSM-5. One recent and provocative study supporting IPT was a multisite, longitudinal RCT comparing IPT, CBT-guided self-help (CBTgsh), and behavioral weight loss (BWL) for BED (Wilson, Wilfley, Agras, & Bryson, 2010). Consistent with the previously discussed study of IPT for BN, what is remarkable about the study by Wilson and colleagues (2010) is not that IPT and CBT were both superior to BWL at 2-year follow-up per se; rather, it is that IPT engendered significant outcomes without ever directly intervening on the disordered eating (disclosure: S. Cahn was one of five IPT therapists on this trial). How can 60% of patients treated with IPT for BED, which has a chronic and unremitting course when left untreated, be in remission at 2-year follow-up (Wilson et al., 2010) when food and binging is not even a focus of treatment? Perhaps even more provocative is that CBTgsh demonstrated comparable outcomes *with* food and binging being the direct area of intervention (Wilson et al., 2010). Such results are intriguing as they suggest a mechanism of action for IPT distinct from other treatments.

Within the diagnostic category of eating disorders, IPT has also been extended to treat anorexia nervosa. In a somewhat anomalous finding, McIntosh and colleagues (2005) found that in an RCT of IPT, CBT, and a "supportive psychotherapy" for inpatient females, nonspecific supportive psychotherapy was superior to IPT, with CBT faring the worst of the three. These findings remain unreplicated.

Non-Western culture. In addition to being applied across disorders, IPT has also been successfully applied cross-culturally. For example, in one laudable study (Bolton et al., 2003), researchers adapted individual IPT for depression to treat depressed adults in rural, southwest Uganda using a 16-week, group treatment format. This African area has a 21% prevalence of depressive symptoms among adults and one of the highest rates of HIV infection in the world (see Bolton et al., 2003; Clougherty, Verdeli, Mufson, & Young, 2006). At posttreatment, only 6.5% of the IPT group met criteria for depression versus the control group's 54.7% (Bolton et al., 2003). This RCT demonstrated that IPT (a) is effective, not just efficacious; (b) can be successfully disseminated and applied cross-culturally; and (c) can be effective outside of Western culture in a group format.

Formats and age groups. This therapy has been successful across a wide range of disorders and age groups and in both individual and group formats. In addition to the Ugandan study discussed above, the format and timeframe of IPT have been modified across many studies and patient populations. For example, one research group adapted IPT to a monthly basis for maintenance in the treatment of recurrent depression (Frank, Kupfer, Wagner, McEachran, & Cornes, 1991). IPT has also been modified to treat depression in cancer (e.g., Donnelly et al., 2000), depression in coronary artery disease (Lespérance et al., 2007), postpartum depression (O'Hara, Stuart, Gorman, & Wenzel, 2000), and perinatal depression in women with sexual abuse histories (Grote et al., 2012). Interestingly, O'Hara and colleagues found that IPT is associated with enduring change, longitudinally, even for women whose depression had not resolved at posttreatment (Nylen, O'Hara, Brock, Moel, Gorman, & Stuart, 2010). Individual IPT has also been successfully adapted to be administered by phone (Donnelly et al., 2000). Finally, IPT for depression has also been successfully adapted across the lifespan, from adolescents (e.g., Mufson & Fairbanks, 1996) to the elderly (e.g., Carreira et al., 2008).

Competence in IPT: Challenges in the United States

In the United States, there is a major obstacle to the wide certification of competence in IPT, and that obstacle is lack of dissemination. The International Society for Interpersonal Psychotherapy (ISIPT) is the dominant organization associated with IPT, founded in Chicago in 2000 (Stuart et al., 2006). With good reason, therefore, the ISIPT's primary goal is dissemination. Despite a wealth of evidence supporting its efficacy, IPT has not "caught on" in the United States in the way that CBT has grown in popularity and name recognition. Advocates of IPT have argued that the reason for this incongruity is that there has been (a) a lack of a "model" training program and certification and similarly (b) a historical lack of certification guidelines for therapists (Stuart et al., 2006). Interestingly, in the United Kingdom, Netherlands, and Australia, certification in empirically supported treatments is required for professional practice (Stuart et al., 2006). These countries have witnessed a burgeoning in IPT supervision and training programs, whereas in the United States dissemination has lagged behind research by more than 30 years (Stuart et al., 2006). In 2003, the ISIPT did adopt a set of training guidelines for therapist certification, but obviously such certification is more in demand in those countries such as the United Kingdom that require such credentialing. Perhaps unsurprisingly, the ISIPT borrowed heavily from the curriculum previously established in the United Kingdom when establishing its certification guidelines. The ISIPT's guidelines for its four progressive levels of IPT accreditation are detailed below (Stuart et al., 2006):

1. Level A: (IPT interest)

   - Completion of a day-long IPT training seminar

2. Level B: (Basic training as an IPT therapist)

   - Completion of a recognized clinical training program with training in psychiatric disorders and psychotherapy

   - Completion of a 2- to 4-day IPT training course recognized by the ISIPT

   - Clinical supervision in IPT for at least two cases across at least two patient populations (e.g., adolescents and adults), with at least 4 hours of supervision per case

   - Video or audio recording of all sessions, with at least three sessions from each case reviewed by the clinical supervisor at random

   - All cases and sessions must be deemed to demonstrate both adherence and competence.

3. Level C: (Continuing education/development as an IPT therapist)

   - Achievement of Level B

   - Treat at least two IPT cases annually

   - Ongoing IPT supervision

   - Remain active in IPT through participating in IPT research and/or conference

4. Level D: (IPT supervisor/trainer)

   - Achievement of Level B and ongoing work at Level C

   - Completion of at least ten supervised IPT cases

   - Supervision of at least two training cases annually

   - Completion of ISIPT-approved supervisors' workshop

   - Membership in ISIPT supervisors' network

Concluding Remarks

Clearly the process of obtaining ISIPT certification in IPT represents a sustained time and financial commitment, not the least of which is the labor-intensive nature of ongoing clinical supervision. While the efficacy of IPT is well established for a number of conditions, "dismantling" research is needed to establish the mechanisms of action for IPT and the optimal frequency and duration of treatment, both of which are yet unknown. Perhaps as clinical psychology in the United States continues to progress toward greater accountability and emphasis on empirically supported treatments, IPT will benefit from greater dissemination outside of research studies. If IPT becomes more widely disseminated, more psychologists would achieve competency in this intervention, which would certainly be a step toward alleviating the problem of IPT's underutilization.

FIVE

Cognitive and Behavioral Therapies

Cognitive-behavioral therapy (CBT) is quite literally the most researched psychotherapy in history, with the most empirical evidence to support its efficacy. A comprehensive review of CBT's staggering number of applications, and their respective efficacies, is outside the scope of this chapter; for that, we refer the interested reader to the separate volume in this series on CBT. Rather, here we (a) provide background on the interesting historical development of CBT, from the advent of both behavioral and cognitive therapies to their ultimate merging; (b) introduce empirical neurological evidence substantiating CBT's effects; and (c) present developments in the definition and evaluation of competency in CBT.

What Is CBT?

CBT is a problem-focused, psychoeducational, time-limited, present-oriented treatment. Its popularity has burgeoned in recent years. In this collaborative treatment, clinicians may assign homework, which may involve behavioral exercises, self-monitoring, and identifying thoughts and feelings. Unlike other more psychodynamic approaches, insight is seen as insufficient for change. Maladaptive behaviors are considered learned and therefore can be "unlearned." Therapists guide clients to identify and label their thoughts and feelings and implement interventions, such as cognitive restructuring and self-monitoring, that target both cognitive and behavioral domains.

Development of CBT

The development and emergence of CBT occurred in three distinct phases. The first phase, the evolution of behavior therapy, occurred in the period between 1950 and 1970 in a concurrent but independent series of events in the United States and the United Kingdom (see Rachman, 1997). The second phase, the development of cognitive therapy, occurred in the United States beginning in the 1960s and emerged in the late 1980s (see Rachman, 1997). Behavioral and cognitive therapies by and large merged as they were compatible and complementary on many levels. Most recently, the field has witnessed what has been termed the "third wave," which integrates the principles of acceptance and mindfulness into CBT.

THE FIRST WAVE—BEHAVIOR THERAPY

Historical Background on Learning-Based Approaches   The very early seeds of behavior therapy were contained in the animal research conducted in the early 1900s. Two important principles emerged from this period that have proven fundamental to behavior therapy. The first was that of *classical conditioning* (famously discovered by the Russian Ivan Pavlov in his work with dogs). American Edward Thorndike developed *the Law of Effect* (Thorndike, 1905) which postulated that responses producing a "satisfying" effect will increase in frequency, while responses producing a "discomforting" effect will decrease. This scientific advance paved the way for the second fundamental principle established from the animal learning research, *operant conditioning*, developed by B. F. Skinner. American B. F. Skinner expanded upon *the Law of Effect* to include negative reinforcement, the removal of an existing aversive state (e.g., avoidance as negatively reinforcing)

South Africa and the United Kingdom   In the United Kingdom and South Africa in the 1950s, behavior therapy was evolving from the ideas of Hull, Pavlov, and Watson and focused on the treatment of "neurotic adults." In South Africa, Wolpe was reportedly influenced by his experience in the South African army during World War II treating what is now referred to as posttraumatic stress disorder. Following prevailing wisdom at the time, he had used psychodynamic talk therapy and found it ineffective for this affliction (Rachman, 2000). Notably, Wolpe insisted on the systematic evaluation of all ideas, including his own, an early harbinger of empirically supported treatments.

Interestingly, Wolpe's research on fear induction in cats was performed in relative geographical and academic isolation in South Africa. While such geographical isolation (among other factors) might make South Africa an unlikely locale for the birthplace of behavior therapy, some have speculated that the culture at the time (including revolt against apartheid) fostered a hereticism among academics. In his research, Wolpe found that, contrary to what psychoanalytic theory would predict, he could experimentally produce fear without conflict.

Wolpe expanded upon Pavlov's earlier work developing the idea of reciprocal inhibition, positing that inducing a relaxed state would inhibit the experience of fear, as relaxation and fear states were believed to be mutually exclusive. Wolpe experimentally tested this theory, feeding hungry cats to inhibit their experience of fear. Wolpe stated that relaxation as an emotional state was successful, but any other emotional state incompatible with fear would also suffice (Rachman, 1997). Wolpe's (1958) *Psychotherapy by Reciprocal Inhibition* proved very influential, and he was the first to create and apply both *subjective units of distress* (SUDS) ratings and a hierarchy of feared situations (Hawton, Salkovskis, & Clark, 1989; Rachman, 2000). Patients were expected to perform extensive in vivo homework sessions in between treatment sessions, a stark contrast to the prevailing psychoanalysis of the time. Wolpe's work was arguably even better received, coming in the wake of the publication of Eysenck's (1952) controversial review article depicting the success rates of existing psychotherapy being no better than the rates of spontaneous remission. While the theoretical underpinnings of Wolpe's *Reciprocal Determinism* have been largely abandoned, the procedures have endured. In vivo situations have since been shown to be the most effective method to reduce conditioned anxiety, and the grading of exposure and the reciprocal inhibitory states such as relaxation have been shown to be unnecessary (see Hawton et al., 1989). Wolpe had basically developed the "right" treatment, based on the "wrong" theory.

Like Wolpe, the British had embraced the work of Pavlov. Hans Eysenck in particular was influenced by Hull's learning theory (see Rachman, 1997). Eysenck, the chair of psychiatry at the Institute of Psychiatry at the University of London, used his position to promote research and teaching in behavior therapy. Stanley Rachman, a student of Wolpe's before coming to Maudsley, did early work on developing aversion therapy, an application of operant conditioning (Hawton et al., 1989). Patient samples were typically "neurotic" adult outpatients, owing in part to samples of convenience (Rachman, 1997).

United States   Simultaneously, in the United States, some psychologists were applying Skinner's ideas (and associated animal research), such as the Skinner box, to hospitalized psychiatric patients (Rachman, 1997). In the prevailing paradigm of the time, clinically relevant problems were viewed as learned, maladaptive behaviors rather than any intrinsic disorder. In contrast to the movement in the United Kingdom, these classical and operant conditioning principles were applied to the most severely ill and long-term institutionalized patients, including those with schizophrenia and, later, self-injurious behavior and autism (Rachman, 1997). Ayllon and Azrin's (1968) work on token economies marked the first time a nonmedical treatment approach had been successfully applied to these populations (e.g., patients with schizophrenia). Azrin later extended this approach to nonpsychiatric populations, including the toilet training of children (Azrin & Foxx, 1977), demonstrating that behavioral principles could be successfully applied to produce behavior change (often within one day!) for challenges inherent in normal child development. In fact, this approach to toilet training has endured decades later and remains popular to this day.

As opposed to the development in the United Kingdom, Skinnerian *psychologists* championed the movement rather than psychiatrists. In contrast to the British, the American behaviorists disavowed any genetic contribution to psychiatric disorders. Thus, the paradigm shifted from conceptualizing neurosis as caused by conflict to neurosis as caused by learning. Following this theory to its logical conclusion, the treatment focus should then be unlearning rather than conflict resolution. In fact, the advent of behavior therapy played a significant role in the advancement of the profession of clinical psychology, which was formerly confined to the domain of assessment (see Chapter 1).

While the two parallel camps of behavior therapists disagreed on whether psychiatric problems were purely "environmental" or had any biological basis, both groups agreed on the necessity of empiricism. During this time, behavior therapy exhibited significant gains in the treatment of anxiety disorders and avoidance in particular, as well as oppositional behavior, but showed disappointing results when applied to the "appetitive" disorders such as eating disorders, alcoholism, and depression (see Rachman, 1997). Indeed, the early exuberance for behavior therapy began to wane as treatment failures in behavior therapy mounted (see Foa & Emmelkamp, 1983). The absence of success in the area of depression, combined with the obvious cognitive element in major depression (e.g., patients negatively evaluating themselves while engaging in ostensibly pleasurable activities), paved the way for the development of cognitive therapy.

THE SECOND WAVE—COGNITIVE THERAPY

CBT focuses on identifying and addressing maladaptive patterns of cognition and behavior that interfere with functioning (Beck, 1995). CBT is predicated upon the *cognitive model*, which posits that individuals' feelings and behaviors are guided by their perceptions and interpretations of events (Beck, 1995). A self-described frustrated psychiatrist trained in psychoanalysis, Aaron T. Beck developed a cognitive theory of depression, and associated treatment, based on his personal experience that showed a disappointing success rate for psychoanalysis in depression. He first proposed that individuals develop *schemata* (or *core beliefs*), enduring patterns of evaluating and interpreting their world, which are global and inflexible (Beck, 1964). He proposed that these schemata develop from early childhood (and sometimes later) experiences as people naturally form implicit rules and assumptions in attempt to understand the world (Beck, Rush, Shaw, & Emery, 1979). Hollon and Beck (1986) define cognitive therapies as "those approaches that attempt to modify existing or anticipated disorders by virtue of altering cognitions or cognitive processes" (p. 443).

A. T. Beck first applied cognitive theory to depression and proposed that significant early negative experiences, such as rejection or abandonment by a parent, for example, may lead a child to develop a maladaptive early schema such as "I am unlovable." Having a rigid core belief such as "I am unlovable" may render an individual vulnerable to depression and is considered maladaptive even if the individual is currently functioning well. This is because given that once the individual is faced with a precipitating life stressor (e.g., the demise of a romantic relationship), this hitherto dormant schema may be reactivated. Furthermore, individuals may selectively attend to events that offer confirmatory evidence for the schema and discount or ignore disconfirming evidence.

Once an underlying schema is reactivated it then, in turn, activates underlying "rules and assumptions" or *intermediate beliefs* such as "If someone does not approve of me, it means I am inadequate." Such rules and assumptions are, in turn, believed to generate negative *automatic thoughts:* immediate, reactionary, and situationally specific perceptions, such as "I'll never get this job."

Based on this theoretical framework, the cognitive-behavioral therapist attempts to interrupt this cycle by guiding clients to (a) identify negative automatic thoughts (which are often unconscious), (b) question these individual cognitions, (c) challenge or test the underlying maladaptive assumptions or rules, and (d) replace maladaptive beliefs with more rational beliefs. As automatic thoughts are generally the most accessible to the patient's conscious awareness, cognitive work in therapy first addresses cognitions at the automatic thought level. As themes in automatic thoughts emerge across situations, the emphasis in therapy then progresses to examining intermediate beliefs and schemata (Beck, 1995). A fundamental tenet of the cognitive model is that maladaptive or inaccurate beliefs can be unlearned and rejected and replaced with new, more accurate and rational beliefs in therapy.

Another fundamental component of CBT is the identification and modification of dysfunctional behaviors. Psychotherapy involves exploring the antecedents and consequences of the maladaptive behavioral patterns and may include structured in vivo behavioral assignments to assist individuals in modifying both their distorted cognitions and maladaptive behaviors. Cognitive interventions have been roughly categorized as falling into three general types: cognitive restructuring, problem-solving, and focused on coping skills (Mahoney & Arnkoff, 1978).

THE "THIRD WAVE"

If considering behavior and cognitive therapies respectively as first and second "waves," over the past 20 years a "third wave" of CBT has evolved. These more recent therapies include *Dialectical Behavior Therapy* (DBT), *Acceptance and Commitment Therapy* (ACT), *Mindfulness-Based Cognitive Therapy* (MBCT), *Functional Analytic Psychotherapy* (FAP), *Cognitive Behavioral Analysis System of Psychotherapy* (CBSAP), and *Integrative Behavioral Couple Therapy* (IBCT; Öst, 2008). Steven Hayes (2004), founder of ACT, has explained the "third wave" as such:

> *Grounded in an empirical, principle-focused approach, the third wave of behavioral and cognitive therapy is particularly sensitive to the context and functions of psychological phenomena, not just their form, and thus tends to emphasize contextual and experiential change strategies in addition to more direct and didactic ones. These treatments tend to seek the construction of broad, flexible, and effective repertoires over an eliminative approach to narrowly defined problems, and to emphasize the relevance of the issues they examine for clinicians as well as clients. The third wave reformulates and synthesizes previous generations of behavioral and cognitive therapy and carries them forward into questions, issues, and domains previously addressed primarily by other traditions, in hope of improving both understanding and outcomes.* (Hayes, 2004, p. 658; italics in original)

The "third wave" therapies have similarities and differences. They all include emphasis on mindfulness, the client's personal values, cognitive defusion, relationships, the importance of the therapeutic relationship, and treatment rationale (Hayes, 2004; Öst, 2008). These respective treatments vary, however, in the degree to which they are consistent with a Skinnerian radical behavioral perspective. Interestingly, whereas traditional cognitive therapy has focused on altering maladaptive cognitions, mindfulness-based CBT approaches often advocate for identifying the thought and accepting it without resistance so as to minimize its emotional import. One may be instructed to watch thoughts go by one's mind like clouds, for instance, observing them without judging or being sucked into the storyline. In this way, psychological change is achieved without combating the problematic thoughts, but rather by *transcending* them. Such approaches have been successfully applied to obsessive-compulsive disorder, chronic depression, and borderline personality disorder, for example (Öst, 2008).

NEUROLOGICAL EVIDENCE FOR EFFICACY OF CBT

CBT has been the subject of a myriad of clinical trials and remains the type of therapy with the most clinical evidence supporting it. CBT has been established as the gold standard treatment for many psychiatric disorders, including bulimia nervosa (see Wilson, Grilo, & Vitousek, 2007), panic disorder (Clark et al., 1994), and obsessive-compulsive disorder in children and adolescents (O'Kearney, Anstey, & von Sanden, 2006), and adults (Hoffman & Smits, 2008). In fact, exciting recent research has used neuroimaging to examine whether observable behavioral, cognitive, and emotional changes following CBT are reflected in and concordant with neurological changes. In fact, positron emission tomography (PET) technology has been used to demonstrate that those with obsessive-compulsive disorder who responded to behavior therapy showed decreased glucose metabolism in the caudate nucleus compared to nonresponders (Schwartz, Stoessel, Baxter, Martin, & Phelps, 1996). Further research has found that brain activity has been able to predict treatment response: patients with higher metabolic activity in the left orbitofrontal cortex demonstrated positive response to behavior therapy, and those with lower activity in this area responded better to fluoxetine (Brody et al., 1998). Schwartz (1998) found that those who were successfully treated with CBT for obsessive-compulsive disorder differed significantly from those treated with CBT whose symptoms had not remitted posttreatment.

Additionally, adults suffering from depression who are successfully treated with CBT show different neurological changes than those with depression successfully treated with paroxetine (Goldapple et al., 2004). Specifically, those successfully treated with CBT showed significantly increased metabolic activity in the hippocampus and dorsal cingulate and decreased metabolic activity in the dorsal, ventral, and medial frontal cortex. Those who were successfully treated with paroxetine, however, demonstrated increased metabolic activity in the prefrontal cortex and decreased metabolic activity in the hippocampus and subgenual cingulate (Goldapple et al., 2004). Such findings suggest that competently applied CBT not only elicits neurological changes but does so through a different pathway than pharmacological treatment.

Additionally, functional magnetic resonance imaging (fMRI) has been found to *predict* those who will respond to CBT for depression based on the location of their abnormal brain activity (Siegle,Cameron, & Thase, 2006). Those suffering from depression who demonstrated low reactivity in the subgenual cingulate cortex but high reactivity in the amygdala showed the greatest benefit from CBT, suggesting that CBT is particularly effective for those suffering from depression who are highly emotional reactive (Siegle et al., 2006). Notably, study participants were required to be unmedicated for their depression, so no conclusions can be drawn for those who suffer from depression with only partial remission from medication.

Competency in CBT

Psychotherapy is difficult to standardize and disseminate, particularly compared to psychopharmacology. Treatment manuals and standardized treatment plans have helped with treatment fidelity both inside and outside of clinical trials, but that does not inherently address the therapist's competence in delivering the treatment. Momentum had been building to define and assess both treatment fidelity (adherence) and therapist competence, as well as how to train clinicians to competence in CBT.

DEFINING COMPETENCE IN CBT

Due in part to major efforts in the United Kingdom to disseminate CBT and train existing providers in this treatment modality, the United Kingdom has commissioned work to outline the fundamental competencies of CBT. Through expert consensus, a framework was developed that outlined five core competency domains: (a) generic clinical competence,

(b) basic CBT competencies, (c) specific behavioral and cognitive therapy techniques, (d) problem-specific competencies, and (e) meta-competencies (which guide the application of all interventions; Rakovshik & McManus, 2010; Roth & Pilling, 2008). Within the five domains of core competence are more than 50 specific competencies (Rakovshik & McManus, 2010; Roth & Pilling, 2008). The UK's increasing emphasis on operationalizing competence in psychotherapy over the past 20 years can be witnessed by the advent of the UK's Centre for Outcomes, Research and Effectiveness (CORE) and later, their Improving Access to Psychological Therapies (IAPT) program. The American Psychological Association Task Force and the National Council of Schools and Programs of Professional Psychology have similarly made significant efforts in defining and assessing competence, as discussed throughout this volume.

COMPETENCE: ASSESSING KNOWLEDGE IN CBT

Recent research, however, does reflect a growing emphasis on the definition and assessment of competence in CBT. Methods of assessment have included direct measure of knowledge base in CBT, typically focusing on the treatment's specific interventions and procedures (see Fairburn & Cooper, 2011; Herschell, Kolko, Baumann, & Davis, 2010; Rakovshik & McManus, 2010). This knowledge base is akin to a Foundational Competency. Empirically, the relation between foundational knowledge and actual skill is tenuous. For example, increased knowledge in CBT has failed to result in a corresponding increase in skill, at least in the treatment of substance abuse (Walters, Matson, Baer, & Ziedonis, 2005). Perhaps one is reminded of the cynical cliché, "Those who can't do, teach."

COMPETENCE: ASSESSING SKILL IN CBT

Therapist competence is a construct that has not been defined or applied consistently in the literature. As Rakovshik and McManus (2010) observe, "In the existing literature, the term 'therapist competence' has been variably employed, denoting constructs as disparate as therapists' self-reported increases in confidence or knowledge or skills following training, or assessor ratings of structured interviews or demonstrations of clinical skills" (p. 497). And there is no evidence of a reliable, significant correlation among these disparate definitions; increases in confidence may not correspond to any improvements in assessor-rated demonstrations. Patient outcomes have also been used as one marker of therapist competence in CBT, but this method carries obvious limitations, the most obvious being the confounds of patient illness severity and duration. To appreciate the significance of this confound, consider the method of evaluating reproductive endocrinologists treating infertility by their outcomes (resulting rates of successful pregnancies). Such physicians would appear more competent by turning away the patients with the lowest probabilities of success (older patients with multiple in vitro failures, etc.), while accepting only the patients most likely to be successful. Patient sample may be a better predictor of outcome than physician expertise. Yet, at least in research settings, there is modest support for CBT competence predicting outcome. For example, greater competence in CBT has been empirically associated with superior outcomes in depression for patients with greater comorbidity (Strunk, Brotman, DeRubeis, & Hollon, 2010).

Methods to assess competence in delivering CBT vary. Fairburn and Cooper (2011) have recommended holding therapist competence assessments to the same standards as randomized controlled trials. For example, the assessor of competence is usually a supervisor, unblinded to patient outcomes, and may be biased by a personal relationship with the therapist—not to mention, if a supervisor is responsible for a junior colleague or student's training, there may be a potential vested interest in deeming him or her competent. Standardized measures have been developed to assess both competence in general CBT, such as the Cognitive Therapy Scale—Revised (CTS-R; Blackburn, James, Milne, & Reichelt, 2001), and CBT for specific disorders, such as the Cognitive Therapy Competence Scale for Social Phobia (CTCS-SP; Clark et al., 2006). Yet there is little empirical evidence to support either a specific cutoff or "threshold" of competence on such rating scales or their overall validity (see Fairburn & Cooper, 2011).

LICENSURE AND BOARD CERTIFICATION

Regulating bodies also certify competence in order to protect the public. Licensing is required for all psychologists throughout the United States. The national licensing examination, the Examination for Professional Practice of Psychology, notably assesses broad knowledge, but certainly not competence. Some states have historically required an oral examination as an attempt to certify competence. Applicants may be asked to identify their theoretical orientation, such as CBT, for example, and defend their course of treatment of a client applying this treatment approach. While such a system has its limitations (e.g., "How does it differ from treatment fidelity or adherence?" "Who will evaluate the 'experts'?" "What constitutes competence when every client is different?" "How does such a system keep pace with the evolving science and treatment development?"), the advent of such competence-based education and evaluation may suggest a sea change and a new bar for clinical psychologists in credentialing, accountability, and consumer protection. Yet, New Jersey's oral examination for licensure in psychology has recently been slated for elimination. Such a change may reflect, at least in part, the expense, resource-intensive nature, and often problematic validity and interrater reliability that can plague some in vivo examinations (c.f., Biggerstaff, 1994).

While the American Medical Association recognizes board certification in a specialty as evidence of competence, until recently clinical psychology had no corresponding system. Today, the American Board of Professional Psychology (ABPP) is the predominant body overseeing competency-based credentialing in 13 specialty areas of clinical psychology (the Academy of Cognitive Therapy also credentials cognitive therapists). Psychologists are credentialed by submitting their requisite qualifications and successfully completing a clinical oral examination judged by experts in the subspecialty. The fundamental mission of ABPP is to enhance consumer protection by certifying competent clinical psychologists (see www.ABPP.org).

COMPETENCE: TRAINING THERAPISTS TO BE COMPETENT IN CBT

While CBT is an empirically supported treatment, *training* in CBT is not evidence-based (Rakovshik & McManus, 2010). Yet there is a tremendous need to disseminate empirically supported treatments such as CBT, in part due to federal and state initiatives, both nationally and abroad (see Clark et al., 2009; McHugh & Barlow, 2010). Efforts to operationalize and assess such competence have been growing. One method suitable for training clinicians to be competent in CBT, and/or assessing such competence, is the standardized role-play, or "standardized patient," whereby a trained actor represents a mock patient. The mock case is developed to reflect desired symptoms or features, and the clinician is evaluated based on his or her selection and skill in applying the relevant (CBT) clinical interventions. These standardized cases can also be developed to represent varying patient severity, and such competence assessments can be completed before and after training and can be correlated to patient outcomes (see Fairburn & Cooper, 2011). Standardized role-plays can be recorded, with multiple raters evaluating the recording to establish interrater reliability. The Internet has also offered significant possibilities in supporting the dissemination of CBT on a larger scale. Role-plays, in addition to training workshops, supervision, and so forth, can potentially be conducted online, greatly reducing, if not eliminating, the need for travel.

Concluding Remarks

In sum, CBT reflects the integration of two empirically-supported treatment models: behavioral and cognitive therapies. CBT is a well-researched, theory-based treatment model that has been effectively applied across multiple modalities and conditions. Advances in the field point to neurological changes that correspond to improvements following CBT. More recently, there has been an international movement within the field to determine how best to (a) define competence in CBT, (b) effectively train clinicians to be competent in CBT, and (c) evaluate and credential such competence, either in general or problem-specific CBT.

SIX

Family Systems Approaches

A clinical psychologist, practicing within any given theoretical framework, must possess special competencies that are dictated by the assumptions of the model. Therapies falling under the rubric of systems approaches are based on explicit assumptions that guide clinical practice. A comprehensive review of systems theory is outside of the scope of this chapter; instead, we refer the reader to a separate volume in this series on couples and family psychology. The following chapter will briefly review basic foundations of systems theory, highlighting universal issues systems therapists consider, and current avenues of research in the area of systems treatments. Furthermore, competent practice will be described as dictated by several governing boards of psychology. Finally, behavioral benchmarks for differing levels of training and assessment tools for measuring competency will be discussed as related to establishing and maintaining professional competence in systems therapies.

Family systems approaches in psychology focus not on the individual itself, although the individual certainly has an important influence (Nichols, 1987), but rather on the system of which the individual is a part. Bronfenbrenner (1979) describes the person as living within a set of systems that all play a role in a person's development. The inner layer of the system, the microsystem, consists of family, school/work, neighborhood, religious affiliations, and all that is in the immediate surroundings of the individual. The mesosystem, the middle layer, is created by the relationships that exist between members of the microsystem. The outer layer, the exosystem, encompasses aspects of the individual's life that are not direct influences or a part of his or her everyday life but nevertheless play a role in influencing the person's environment and development (Bronfenbrenner, 1979). Given this perspective, being competent in a systems approach entails considering not just the individual but rather the entire context of the individual's life, the many different influences encountered, the effects of these influences on other aspects of the individual's life, and how these factors are all connected and interrelated. It is these influences and life contexts that play a role in the development and growth of the individual as well as the overall functioning of the family system (Robbins, Mayorga, & Szapocznik, 2003).

Similar to other areas of psychology, there are various theories within a systems approach. However, these different schools of thought have now become less pronounced (Goldenberg & Goldenberg, 2009) and are unified by the basic premise that a person does not live in a vacuum but is part of a larger environment. Current practice often involves an integration of aspects of different interventions and theories to best serve and accommodate the needs of the patient (Goldenberg & Goldenberg, 2009). A competent psychologist considering a systems-oriented approach should become familiar with the array of therapies and techniques within systems theories to determine the most effective path to achieve the therapeutic goals set in treatment.

A competent psychologist not only is familiar with different treatment approaches but is cognizant of the importance of empirical validation. When family therapy first evolved, there was little evidence to support its use. Family systems theories were developed and welcomed by psychologists in clinical practice, but there were not many researchers investigating the possible empirical support for these theories. However, over time there have been great advances in regard to research and family therapy, and there are now many treatments founded in systems theory whose efficacy and effectiveness are supported empirically. For example, treatments such as Multidimensional Family Therapy (Liddle, 2002) and Multisystemic Therapy (Henggeler, Schoenwald, Borduin, Rowland, & Cunningham, 2009) have demonstrated empirical support for their use in decreasing a variety of symptoms and having a positive impact on family functioning (Henggeler et al., 2009; Liddle et al., 2001).

Basic Foundations

Although each theory within a systems approach has its own vision, way of understanding psychopathology, and techniques employed to improve overall functioning, some basic philosophies and themes are universal. For example, a therapist must possess good social skills and have the capacity to take charge of and direct the therapy sessions, which can get quite overwhelming if many family members are present. Doherty and McDaniel (2010) provide an overview of some of the other universal issues that systems therapists consider and encounter during therapy.

INTERACTION PATTERNS

A basic tenet of family therapy is to recognize and modify the problematic interaction patterns, roles, and responsibilities within the family to improve the overall functioning of the system. Family functioning is of primary importance, and levels of cohesion and individuation are often used to describe different types of family functioning. A family system requires a balance between family connectedness and reliance on each other emotionally (cohesion) and their differentiation from each other as individuals (individuation). In terms that Salvador Minuchin would use, problematic relationships may involve *enmeshment*, not allowing a person to think differently or to individuate from the family system, or *disengagement*, where there seems to be little connection between family members (Minuchin, 1974). Family therapists evaluate where the difficulties in family functioning lie and address them as needed. For example, a family that lacks cohesion and is disengaged may be asked to participate in an exercise promoting togetherness.

Boundaries is a concept often discussed in family therapy. Disengagement and enmeshment fall within the realm of boundary issues; however, in addition, there are other areas associated with relationship boundaries that are observed and assessed within the family system. *Triangulation* is a concept that refers to a specific type of interaction occurring between family members. In essence, triangulation occurs when two people's interaction patterns are problematic, and a third person becomes involved in an attempt to stabilize the relationship. The third person then becomes part of a triangle, which may in fact be a contributor to the problem itself (Bowen, 1978). A similar idea in family therapy is referred to as a *coalition*. Coalitions form when some family members develop a bond and contradict another family member. Both Salvador Minuchin (1974) and Jay Haley (1976) discuss the formation of coalitions and agree that they can be dysfunctional and not in the best interest of the family. Family therapists are cognizant of the potential detrimental effects that triangulation and coalitions can have on family functioning and use therapy to modify these modes of interaction.

ADAPTABILITY

Adaptability is another important facet of family functioning. It is essential for families to be flexible and adaptable as family constellations, situations, and contexts change and family members mature and develop. With each change, the family system needs to accept, adjust, and adapt. When a family finds itself having trouble adapting to these changes, family members will often seek assistance in making the transition easier. As therapists are often called upon during this time of adjustment, they should be aware of recent modifications the family has made as well the family members' ability to adapt to these changes.

FAMILY HISTORY

Family systems theory identifies that behaviors and interaction patterns repeat themselves across generations. Likewise, there are belief systems unique to each family that are carried over from each generation, although culture also plays a role in the creation of these beliefs. Hence, the way the world is viewed and the way that the members of the family system interact with each other and with the rest of the world depend on the family's set of beliefs, which may or may not be functional and adaptable. Related to family life and family history, life-cycle events can play an important role within the family system and often serve as the antagonist for the family coming to therapy. As family members lose their old roles and/or gain new roles, they can struggle with the challenge of understanding and discovering who they are and what they need to do within the family. Family therapists recognize the importance of family history and beliefs and how these beliefs can continue to be passed down through the generations, possibly causing problematic interaction patterns among family members and with the outside world.

REFRAMING

In addition to universal themes in systems theory, some techniques are implemented consistently across family systems approaches. *Reframing* is one of those therapeutic techniques. In reframing, the therapist presents the family with an alternate way of viewing the situation, problem, or behavior. Typically reframing addresses an issue perceived to be a problem with a specific individual and reconstructs it to be viewed as a more systemic problem.

The preceding themes provide a glimpse of the large array of theories and strategies that make up the scope of family systems approaches. Each specific theory has its own unique understanding of how dysfunctional interactions are created and maintained within the family and how to most effectively intervene to have a positive impact on the family system. A competent clinical psychologist engaged in the world of family systems work considers the needs of the family being treated and is aware of the theoretical underpinnings of the techniques employed. Working within a systems framework requires the therapist to juggle the many personalities involved in the system, the connections and interactions between family members, the members' roles within the family context, and the role the therapist must play in helping the system work together in a functional, adaptable way.

Research Highlights

A competent clinical psychologist in family therapy should stay abreast of the most current research and cutting-edge techniques that have been supported in the literature. Carr (2009) reviewed research published in popular family therapy journals over the previous year. He reported many new developments in the world of family therapy, including some studies highlighting family therapy's effectiveness with specific populations. For example, Rowe and Liddle (2008) investigated the effectiveness of MDFT with an alcohol-abusing adolescent population, while Kendall, Hudson, Gosch, Flannery-Schroeder, and Suveg (2008) evaluated a family treatment modality in treating anxiety-disordered youth. The review by Carr (2009) demonstrates the many areas under investigation in family therapy research, such as issues of diversity (Cole, 2008), cost-effectiveness of treatment (Crane, 2008), and issues in training (Gouze & Wendel, 2008), as well as the efficacy of treatment for specific disorders (Lock, Le Grange, & Crosby, 2008). Given the many empirically validated treatments lending support for the use of family therapy (Sexton & Alexander, 2002), being informed of the latest research can lead to better service delivery and, as endorsed by Kaslow and colleagues (2009), further enhance the competency of psychologists practicing family psychology. Furthermore, in terms of practicality, insurance companies are interested in empirically supported treatments that are based on a definitive number of sessions (i.e., short term); hence, they are more apt to pay therapists for their services if the treatment is of shorter duration with proven effectiveness (Griffin, 1993).

Sexton, Alexander, and Mease (2004) recognize that although there is now existing research supporting family treatments, there is no comprehensive way of organizing and understanding the information available. They suggest considering a "level of evidence" approach in classifying studies. In a "level of evidence" approach, studies are categorized by level of empirical support based on specific criteria. The American Psychological Association's (APA) Task Force for Evidence-Based Treatment in Couples and Family Psychology was created to develop the structure and criteria for categorizing treatments based on varying levels of empirical support. The task force recommended three levels of categorization, with a further delineation of levels of efficacy within categories. This categorization provides professional psychologists with a standardized method of assessing the effectiveness and level of empirical support for specific treatment modalities and techniques. For further information on these guidelines, please see the task force's detailed report (Sexton et al., 2007).

Core Competencies in Professional Psychology

The field of psychology has been moving toward a competency-based approach. Kaslow, Celano, and Stanton (2004) provide an overview of their perspective on a competency-based approach to family systems work. Basing their recommendations on the core competencies in education and training highlighted for professional psychology programs (Kaslow et al., 2004), they discuss eight competencies as they relate to family psychology. They first discuss the application of scientific knowledge to practice and how a competent family psychologist should have a basic understanding of systems paradigms. This requires a shift in thinking from the psychologist's typical focus on the individual to the consideration of the interconnectedness of other factors, such as the individual's life context, interactions with others, and environment (Liddle, Santisteban, Levant, & Bray, 2002). The competent psychologist is knowledgeable in the area of evidence-based practice, including assessment, intervention, and consultation, and is familiar with the implementation of a systems-based approach in working with larger systems such as schools and healthcare providers.

Kaslow et al. (2004) then discuss competencies as related to assessment and intervention. They highlight the need for psychologists to be competent in administering and interpreting standardized assessment measures, including those best able to reflect systems functioning and outcomes. Furthermore, they underscore the necessity of recognizing the dynamics occurring within and between members of a system and the importance of a knowledge base in empirically supported interventions and assessment. They emphasize the importance of clinical judgment and the ability to integrate clinical skill with experience and the data available to support hypotheses and create interventions to best meet the family's needs. Consultation and collaboration, a competency extremely relevant to the family psychologist working with multiple systems, is further elucidated by Kaslow and colleagues (2004), with specific reference to healthcare and school settings as areas in which a family psychologist should be competent.

Supervision is a competency described similarly across disciplines (Kaslow et al., 2004). Case presentations, audio and videotapes, live supervision, and co-therapy are all effective ways of providing competent supervision to trainees. However, supervisors should be familiar with and integrate a variety of systems models in guiding students and providing supervision, while emphasizing empirically supported assessments and interventions (Kaslow et al., 2004). Relatedly, professional development as an area of competency focuses on the need for self-awareness and self-assessment in maintaining competency. Kaslow and colleagues (2004) advise those in the position of training students to model self-assessment and to help trainees become more adept and accurate in self-appraisal.

Kaslow and colleagues (2004) continue to discuss other areas of competency, such as ethical behavior, which should encompass all activities of a competent psychologist. Formal training in ethics should be taught through courses, supervision, other educational programming, and modeling. Furthermore, trainees should be versed in models of ethical decision-making and should have opportunities to practice decision-making both in and out of the classroom so they can fully understand and apply ethical standards. Just as ethics is an integral part of a competent psychologist's activities, so should individual and cultural diversity be considered an essential element of professional competency (Kaslow et al., 2009). Educators and supervisors should incorporate cultural awareness and sensitivity in all areas of professional training, including coursework as well as supervision, where it is incumbent upon therapists to consider the cultural influences of the family with whom they are working. Kaslow and colleagues (2009) conclude that by integrating the core competencies in training programs with regard to family psychology, the specialization of family systems will then be held to a standard that will instill a global confidence and competence in professionals involved in family work.

Certification in Professional Competency

The American Board of Professional Psychologists (ABPP) offers a board certification indicating competency in a specialty area based on education and training requirements as well as a competency examination. Among the 13 specialty areas to date, there is a board certification tailored to competency in couple and family psychology created by the American Board of Couple and Family Psychology, a specialty member board of ABPP. As declared in the mission statement of ABPP, becoming board certified provides the public with an assurance of high-quality care delivered by competent psychologists.

Competency as Determined by the American Association of Marriage and Family Therapy

The American Association of Marriage and Family Therapy (AAMFT) recognized the movement toward a competency-based approach, particularly in regard to training and evaluation, and created its own task force to consider standards of competent practice. Nelson and colleagues (2007) detail their experience as part of the task force responsible for developing core competencies essential to the practice of marital and family therapy. It is this task force that is now considered in reviewing the current state of competency-based training and evaluation for marital and family therapy.

One of the primary areas of task force discussion included the possible move from an educational focus (e.g., coursework, hours of direct clinical experience and supervision) to an outcome-based focus (e.g., knowledge and skills demonstrated) for therapists in training. A potential challenge in assessing competency based on outcome is the issue of measurement. Many of the skills required in marital and family therapy are not easily quantifiable or measurable. Furthermore, the task force raised concern that training based on outcome will encourage trainees and trainers to focus on the final outcome assessment rather than on the skills and techniques used in the therapy process itself. In addition, when assessing for outcome-oriented competency, sometimes the actual behavioral and outcome goals may be more abstract in conceptualization and may also be influenced by those making the outcome decisions. In other words, what someone views as a successful outcome may vary dramatically from what someone else views as a successful outcome. Moreover, evaluating outcome itself does not allow for the consideration or evaluation of the actual skills involved in reaching a particular outcome. When based on outcome alone, different supervisors may have different perceptions of what they view to be a demonstration of competency (i.e., a successful treatment outcome).

Despite these caveats and considerations, the task force worked diligently to create six domains considered to be required areas of core competency in marital and family therapy:

1. Admission to Treatment—interpersonal interactions prior to the start of treatment
2. Clinical Assessment and Diagnosis—evaluation and assessment of concerns to be attended to in treatment
3. Treatment Planning and Case Management—the therapist's ability to create appropriate treatment goals and activities within and outside the confines of the therapy session
4. Therapeutic Interventions—effectiveness of the therapist in improving patient functioning with various techniques
5. Legal Issues, Ethics and Standards—a competency that is essential in addressing the many ethical principles and values that can arise as part of the treatment process
6. Research and Program Evaluation—the effectiveness of providing therapeutic services

In addition to these six domains of competency, five subdomains were created to help organize each of the competencies:

1. Conceptual Skills—basic knowledge
2. Perceptual Skills—what the therapist perceives and interprets
3. Executive Skills—the actual interventions the therapist administers
4. Evaluative Skills—how the therapist evaluates the effectiveness of the intervention
5. Professional Skills—the professional life of the therapist, including how therapy is provided as well as professional identity

Once these domains and subdomains were established, the task force then set out to create and develop concrete items that could be part of each domain. For further information on the development of these competencies, please refer to Nelson and colleagues (2007).

IMPORTANCE OF THE ESTABLISHMENT OF CORE COMPETENCIES

Miller, Todahl, and Platt (2010) discuss some of the issues involved in developing core competencies in the area of marriage and family therapy, consider other disciplines' approaches in creating areas of competency, and reflect on how these approaches may or may not be applied in considering family systems. They discuss several reasons for moving ahead with a competency focus in marital and family therapy. They report that there are many practicing marital and family therapists, most being master's-level clinicians, raising the question of how the public can identify those competent in the field. Furthermore, managed-care administrators often decide on their own who is qualified to deliver clinical services and pay only those they deem to be competent. Creating a set of competencies can better ensure payment from insurance companies by providing them with the information they need to comfortably reimburse therapists, knowing the therapists have a high level of expertise. In essence, marital and family therapists must have standards of competencies to survive. Furthermore, as related to legislative concerns and health service committees, it has been stated that there is much variability among marital and family therapists, so applying competence-based standards to all therapists helps to alleviate this criticism.

One of the challenges posited by Miller and colleagues (2010) is the difficulty in creating behavioral benchmarks of competencies in regard to the specific course of therapy. Clinicians approach situations differently, and although final outcomes may be positive, the process of getting to that outcome may vary by family as well as by clinician. Therefore, they suggest that competency standards be based on outcomes rather than the process of reaching an outcome, an idea congruent with the discussions of the competency task force of the AAMFT. In considering other areas of specialization within psychology, there is a trend toward better understanding and delineating of competency. The sequence of developing competency across disciplines typically follows a specific format. First, the trainee is educated in the knowledge base related to the developing competency. Once educated, there is an evaluation of his or her level of understanding of the material and the application of the information in professional practice. This is followed by supervision and mentorship to help further develop skills, with the provision of evaluation and feedback. Finally, there is a final demonstration of overall ability, perhaps in the form of a competency-based test.

Competency Benchmarks

As described in previous chapters of this book, APA created a task force to consider and develop core competencies in professional psychology. Since the original Competencies Conference in 2002 (Kaslow et al., 2004), the task force has published recommendations for defining core competencies, benchmarks for measuring competencies, and an assessment toolkit useful in evaluating competencies in professional psychology (Kaslow et al., 2004, 2007, 2009; Fouad et al., 2009). Fouad and colleagues (2009) focus their efforts on 15 core competencies in professional psychology, delineating benchmarks as a standard for evaluating competency in given areas and at specific levels of training. They clearly define essential components of competency and accompanying behavioral indicators of demonstrated competence. These components and behavioral anchors were created to assess trainees' readiness to treat patients at different training levels, including practicum, internship, and entry into practice. Family systems theory falls within the realm of Foundational Competencies; however, it also encompasses Functional Competencies when viewed through a systems theory lens. Each of the 15 competencies is in and of itself an essential component of professional competency in systems theory and clinical psychology in general.

Competency Assessment Toolkit

In addition to competency benchmarks, Kaslow and colleagues (2009) provide training programs with a toolkit for assessing competency domains in professional psychology. Various methods of evaluation described include but are not limited to case presentations, patient outcome data, and structured oral examinations. Each of these methods of assessment can be useful tools in assessing trainees' competencies in a family systems approach.

Although the competencies, benchmarks, and assessment toolkit were created for professional psychology in general, training in family psychology would benefit from considering these guidelines and recommendations as well. It is not within the scope of this chapter to review these guidelines in detail as they pertain to family psychology; in fact, there is an entire book dedicated to specialty competencies in the area of couple and family psychology (Stanton, 2010). Please refer to the original articles (Kaslow et al., 2004, 2009; Fouad et al., 2009) and the specialty competencies book for further information.

Concluding Remarks

There is no doubt that a competence-based model in systems therapy is helpful to the profession in many ways. It provides assurance to the public, patients, managed-care companies, and members of the field that there is a way to hold therapists accountable, and it provides a standard method of evaluating therapists' professional capabilities and competencies. Furthermore, it provides training programs with a standardized way of assessing the progress and competency development of their psychologists in training. Given the diversity of approaches to systems work, at first glance this may seem quite challenging. Nevertheless, the AAMFT and APA task forces provided a strong foundation for the areas that warrant attention in regard to competencies and have created items broad enough to allow for different therapies to be evaluated fairly. Competency-based training seems to be the direction of the field of psychology; hence, work groups across the discipline have been discussing the effective integration of a competency-based model. Couple and family psychology appears to be following the current professional trend by considering and pursuing a competency-based model of training and practice.

SEVEN

Contemporary Psychodynamic

The evolution of psychodynamic theory reflects a maturation process evolving from traditional psychoanalytic theory. Modern applications consider attachment theories and relational perspectives in emphasizing interpersonal, family, social, biological, and cultural conditions influencing personality development, resilience and vulnerability, and health and illness (Borden, 2009; Huprich, 2009). Contemporary theorists draw attention to the complexity of psychological functioning and the respect for the dynamic and influential nature of the therapeutic relationship. The goal of this chapter is to outline core principles and key features reflecting the competent delivery of contemporary psychodynamic therapy, establishing a foundation for further exploration of contemporary approaches extending beyond traditional psychoanalytic theory.

Conceptual Foundations of Contemporary Psychodynamic Theory

FREUDIAN PSYCHOANALYTIC ROOTS

Although psychodynamic treatment differs from psychoanalysis, many Freudian ideas provide the foundation of current psychodynamic approaches. Sigmund Freud's "drive theory" (Freud, 1940) proposes that the most fundamental human motives are rooted in biology, and ongoing efforts to regulate sexual and aggressive impulses are paramount in human development, shaping adult personality. His psychosexual model of development identified a course of maturation from infancy and early childhood as critical in later adult personality formation. Resolution of conflicts arising in developmental stages and rational control of drive forces are considered necessary for optimal health (Borden, 2009). From this perspective, psychopathology arises from unresolved conflicts in key developmental periods. Contemporary models devalue the role of sexual and aggressive impulses in understanding human suffering but continue to emphasize present functioning as connected to unconscious motives arising from developmental conflicts.

Freud's development of psychic structures and the role of unconscious processes in understanding human behavior distinguish psychoanalysis from other theoretical models. Freud identified three domains of mental processes: the *unconscious,* containing instinctual urges, impulses, and desires containing unacceptable feelings and thoughts; the *preconscious,* containing acceptable feelings and thoughts accessible to awareness through focus and attention; and the *conscious,* containing awareness at the moment. Freud's structural model of the mind (1923) was developed to explain his observation of patients' use of various strategies to avoid experiencing upsetting unconscious material. He believed these strategies, coined "defenses," were unknown to patients and were designed to protect the individual from experiencing painful unconscious material.

In approach to treatment, modern psychodynamic therapy tends to operate on an interpretive-supportive continuum (Summers & Barber 2010), judiciously relying upon the use of traditional psychoanalytic techniques to facilitate emotional experience and insight into previously unconscious motives of behavior. Westen (1998) identified five major postulates defining contemporary psychodynamic theory based on traditional psychoanalytic principles. These five principles best distinguish psychodynamic therapy from other established forms of therapy that focus on conscious cognitions, behavior change, and symptom reduction (Huprich, 2009).

1. Much of mental life, including thoughts, feelings, and motives, is unconscious, which means people can behave in ways or can develop symptoms that are inexplicable to themselves.

2. Mental processes, including affective and motivational processes, operate in parallel so that, toward the same person or situation, individuals can have conflicting feelings that motivate them in opposing ways and often lead to compromise solutions.

3. Stable personality patterns begin to form in childhood, and childhood experiences play an important role in personality development, particularly in shaping the ways people form later social relationships.

4. Mental representations of the self, others, and relationships guide people's interactions with others and influence the way they become psychologically symptomatic.

5. Personality development involves not only learning to regulate sexual and aggressive feelings but also moving from an immature, socially dependent state to a mature, interdependent state.

ATTACHMENT THEORY

Attachment theory, originally formulated by child psychiatrist and psychoanalyst John Bowlby (1969), and further developed through the seminal research conducted by developmental psychologist Mary Ainsworth and her colleagues (1978), has provided psychodynamic theorists with an empirical base adhering to the basic postulates defining psychodynamic approaches. Bowlby (1969) theorized that human beings are born with an innate psychobiological system (the attachment behavioral system) necessary for survival, instinctually driving them to seek proximity toward significant others (attachment figures). To attain actual or perceived security, the system is automatically activated when a threat to one's security is appraised. In Bowlby's view, infant bonds with caregivers extended beyond traditional "drive theory" and represented an innate need for connection, safety, and security. He described attachment theory as a way of understanding human beings' propensity to make strong bonds with others and account for the many forms of emotional distress arising from unwilling separation and loss (Bowlby, 1979). Attachment theory suggests that (1) infants are born with a predisposition to form attachments with primary caregivers; (2) children organize thinking and behavior to preserve attachment relationships crucial to survival and optimal health; (3) children will maintain such relationships even at great cost to their functioning and well-being; and (4) disturbances in attachment originate in parents' inability to address the child's need for comfort, reassurance, and security (Slade, 1998). Bowlby assumed that all people, regardless of age, rely upon others, and the attachment system remains active over the entire lifespan (Shaver & Mikulincer, 2005).

Attachment theory has been viewed as a bridge connecting contemporary psychodynamic theories with common supported postulates (Shaver & Mikulincer, 2005). First and foremost, the basic principle of attachment theory emphasizes childhood experiences in the formation of adult personality. Attachment figures failing to attend to the needs of a developing child influence the child's cognitive and social development (Fraley

& Shaver, 2000; Shaver & Mikulincer, 2005). When a sense of security is not attained, self-efficacy is compromised and one's environment appears threatening and unpredictable. Such interactions have been theorized to have enduring, long-term effects on personality development mediated by mental representations termed "attachment working models" (Bowlby, 1973). According to Bowlby (1969), relationships with attachment figures inform working models of both self and others, creating a cognitive template that allows a person to predict future interactions and create a sense of safety necessary for the development of intimate connections. Contemporary dynamic theorists emphasize relationships with early attachment figures and working models of self and others as critical in understanding resilience, adjustment, and mental health (Dozier, Stovall, & Albus, 1999).

Additionally, attachment research suggests that many components of the attachment behavioral system operate beyond an individual's conscious awareness (Mikulincer & Shaver, 2003). Psychodynamic theory suggests people can behave in ways or develop symptoms inexplicable to themselves (Westen, 1998), and attachment research provides an empirical base to support unconscious motives of behavior. For example, autonomic activation of the attachment system by appraisals of threat and danger can operate at the unconscious level, as avoidant/anxious individuals have been shown to suppress/deny needs for protection and safety associated with painful attachment-related memories and thoughts (Cassidy & Kobak, 1988; Mikulincer & Shaver, 2003). Contemporary theory suggests that working models can be identified and examined but are often automatic and are held out of awareness by defensive maneuvers (Bowlby, 1988). Psychodynamic approaches seek to identify unconscious strategies (defenses) people utilize to minimize the experience of stress and distress (Shaver & Mikulincer, 2005), such as cognitive maneuvers employed to suppress thoughts related to rejection, separation, and loss (Mikulincer & Shaver, 2003). Treatment approaches emphasize the development of insight into previously unconscious motives, or "wishes," influencing current functioning, seeking resolution of past conflicts and developing more adaptive means of relating to others.

RELATIONAL THEORY AND INTEGRATIVE PERSPECTIVES

The emergence of relational treatment models best distinguishes contemporary psychodynamic therapy from traditional psychoanalysis. Relational models synthesize interpersonal and object relations theories, attachment theory and research, concepts and principles from cognitive science, and observations from object relational infant research to inform treatment (Messer & Warren, 1995). Many relational theorists orient their approach in opposition to psychoanalytic drive theory and formulate psychological distress in the context of interpersonal relationships. Contemporary theorists emphasize the need for relationships, not the urges originating in bodily sensations, as the chief driving force of human behavior (Masling, 2003). The therapeutic relationship establishes a process of learning essential to reinstating arrested developmental processes, modifying internalized representations of self and others, developing interpersonal skills, and improving social functioning (Borden, 2009). Transference reactions are conceptualized as patterns of expectations established throughout development and offer keen insight into cognitive representations of self and others, constructions of meaning, and maladaptive behaviors within interpersonal situations (Borden, 2009). Clinicians seek opportunities to recognize, clarify, and revise maladaptive perceptions and patterns of relating (Borden, 2009). The underlying assumption of modern relational approaches suggests that improved interpersonal functioning reduces difficulties associated with all forms of psychopathology (Roth & Fonagy, 2005; Wampold, 2007).

Distinctive Features in Clinical Practice

Empirical studies comparing the process and technique of manualized psychodynamic therapy with other forms of psychotherapy have identified seven distinguishable features based on the examination of session recordings and transcripts (Blagys & Hilsenroth, 2002): (1) Focus on affect and expression of emotion; (2) Exploration of attempts to avoid distressing thoughts and emotions; (3) Identification of recurring themes and patterns; (4) A developmental focus through the discussion of past experiences; (5) A focus on interpersonal relations; (6) Focus on the therapy relationship; and (7) Exploration of fantasy life.

THE ANALYTIC ATTITUDE AND UNCONSCIOUS MATERIAL

Experts in psychodynamic treatment emphasize an analytic attitude that reflects attentiveness to the client's unconscious communications and to the unfolding of the transference (Lemma, Roth, & Pilling, 2008). Striving for "neutrality," the therapist empathizes with the client's subjective experience while at the same time being curious about its unconscious meaning. This is in stark contrast to the position of the more directive cognitive-behavioral therapist, who emphasizes an active style in session. The therapist can facilitate unconscious communication by knowing when to allow silence, listening for recurring affective and interpersonal themes (Lemma et al., 2008). Active listening emphasizes a detailed focus on and tracking of the often-subtle changes in a client's state of mind; this reflects the central importance of the therapist's receptivity to the client's unconscious communications.

Competencies in Assessment

PSYCHODYNAMIC DIAGNOSTIC MANUAL

The Psychodynamic Diagnostic Manual (PDM Task Force, 2006) was developed in response to concerns with the DSM system of classification and diagnosis of psychiatric disorders. Collaboratively developed with contributions from the American Psychoanalytic Association, the International Psychoanalytic Association, Division 39 (Psychoanalysis) of the American Psychological Association, the American Academy of Psychoanalysis, and the National Membership Committee on Psychoanalysis, the PDM articulates a common terminology among psychoanalytic and psychodynamic clinicians. The PDM aims at providing a more extensive description of the patient's internal life and provides a deeper understanding of naturally occurring patterns (PDM Task Force, 2006). The PDM evaluates functioning on three dimensions:

1. Personality patterns and disorders (P Axis)

2. Mental functioning (M Axis)

3. Manifest symptoms and concerns (S Axis)

According to the PDM, all assessment must begin by understanding symptoms or problems through a complete evaluation of the individual's experience. Thus, evaluating personality organization is a critical element of the assessment process. The P Axis is designed to assess the patient's personality structure—specifically, patterns of relating to others, an ability to form a therapeutic alliance, and coping strategies used to defend against upsetting material. Personality organization is viewed on a continuum ranging from the healthy personality, to the neurotic personality, to the borderline personality.

The M Axis was designed to provide a more extensive and accurate description of overall level of psychological functioning when compared to the DSM-IV-TR Global Assessment of Functioning Scale. These capacities are scaled from *healthy* to *impaired,* assessing *optimal age-appropriate mental capacities* ranging from mild and moderate to major defects. This section provides an opportunity for the clinician to integrate data obtained from psychodiagnostic batteries as well as observations into a broader perspective on the overall functioning of the patient.

The S Axis provides assessment of symptom patterns associated with many of the Axis I disorders in the DSM. In accordance with the general underlying principles of the PDM, the S axis attempts to provide a greater description of the patient's subjective experience. This diagnostic approach encourages the clinician to conceptualize symptom presentation relative to presenting problems (such as the patient's medical issues or life events).

CURRENT STRESSORS

In assessing a new client, it is necessary to evaluate "why now?"—in other words, what is occurring in this individual's life motivating him or her to enter treatment at this time? Knowledge of current stressors is critical in evaluating how patients cope with and defend against stressful or upsetting life events (Huprich, 2009). Individuals enter treatment with various challenges affecting daily functioning. It is vital not to make assumptions about which challenges are currently most critical. For example, an individual may have a history of significant trauma but is entering treatment with goals of coping with a challenging coworker. Respecting the individual's current life situation and goals for treatment is essential in building a therapeutic relationship and addressing current problems.

BIOLOGICAL AND TEMPERAMENT FACTORS

In accordance with current perspectives in clinical psychology, the mind and body are invariably united, and genetic predispositions to psychological well-being are critical factors in assessment. Advancements in understanding biological factors contributing to mental illness have provided a multitude of psychopharmacological interventions that may be essential to ethical treatment. In addition, medical conditions, injuries, and chronic illnesses affect quality of life and psychological well-being. Ethical practice includes educating patients about treatment options, providing appropriate referrals when necessary, and collaborating with other disciplines (i.e., primary care, psychiatry).

SOCIOCULTURAL FACTORS

In an attempt to understand the inner world of the patient, attention to the individual's social and cultural environment are essential to a thorough evaluation. Interventions must be culturally relevant, as patterns of thinking, feeling, and behaving are connected to one's social and cultural environment. Age, gender, gender identity, race, ethnicity, culture, religion, spirituality, physical presentation, and political affiliation, to name a few, must be investigated to truly understand the patient's subjective experience.

EGO FUNCTIONING

Ego functioning is a broad domain reflecting various psychological abilities. For example, *reality testing* reflects an individual's ability to accurately perceive and understand his or her environment. Impairment of reality testing ranges from mild distortions to severe psychosis. *Affect regulation* refers to the individual's ability to modulate distressing emotions. *Impulse control* is considered an ability to manage aggressive or libidinal desires. Common problems with impulse control could include anger outbursts, sexual promiscuity, substance abuse, and binge eating. *Judgment* reflects one's decision-making skills, particularly an ability to anticipate and evaluate consequences in order to make effective decisions. *Thought processes* are assessed as the ability to have logical, coherent, and abstract thoughts. In stressful situations, thought processes can become disorganized. The presence of chronic or severe problems in conceptual thinking is frequently associated with schizophrenia and manic episodes. In addition, *defensive functioning* and *object relations* fall under the category of ego functioning.

DEFENSES

When assessing defense mechanisms employed by the patient, two components should be considered: maturity and habitual use (Huprich, 2009). Vaillant's (1977) categorization of defenses on a continuum from pathological to mature is widely referenced. Table 7.1 presents commonly identified defense mechanism across levels of functioning.

OBJECT RELATIONS

When assessing the patient's capacities for meaningful and intimate relationships, the clinician carefully attends to how each individual perceives himself or herself and others. This is critical to understanding the patient's inner world, as well as predicting future transferential patterns. Careful investigation of object relations serves the dual function of gathering critical information for future interventions and providing empathic understanding essential for the development of a therapeutic alliance.

TABLE 7.1 **Vaillant's (1977) Categorization of Defense Mechanisms**

LEVEL 1, PATHOLOGICAL	LEVEL 2, IMMATURE	LEVEL 3, NEUROTIC	LEVEL 4, MATURE
Delusional projection	Acting out	Displacement	Altruism
Denial	Fantasy	Dissociation	Humor
Distortion	Idealization	Hypochondriasis	Identification
Splitting	Passive aggression	Intellectualization	Introjection
Extreme projection	Projection	Isolation	Sublimation
	Projective identification	Rationalization	Thought suppression
	Somatization	Reaction formation	
		Regression	
		Repression	

Object relations at the most poorly developed level reveals an inability to separate one from others, representing a fusion of experiences impairing reality testing and interpersonal functioning (Huprich, 2009). At a more advanced level, psychological maturity and sophistication become evident. A greater flexibility in viewing self and others suggests the individual has the capacity to realistically evaluate the positive and negative aspects of self and others. Impulse control and affect regulation appear strongly associated with object relations.

Mechanisms of Change and Therapeutic Goals

THE THERAPEUTIC RELATIONSHIP

The development of a strong therapeutic alliance through a genuine, authentic, and trusting relationship is most consistently associated with positive outcomes (Martin, Garske, & Davis, 2000). Contemporary psychodynamic therapy places a great emphasis on specific therapist variables essential to relationship building (Wampold, 2001). It is only within this relationship that change can occur. The client can explore painful affect and develop subsequent insight into unconscious motives of behavior, essential for lasting change, only when he or she can allow himself or herself to become emotionally vulnerable. The therapeutic relationship establishes a process of learning essential to reinstating arrested developmental processes, modifying internalized representations of self and others, developing interpersonal skills, and improving social functioning (Borden, 2009). Regardless of the theoretical orientation of the therapist, what appears to be most important in psychotherapy outcome research are (a) the practitioner's qualities as a human being (warmth, empathy, respect, flexibility) and (b) the extent of attention given to establishing and maintaining a therapeutic alliance (Norcross, 2002).

INSIGHT AND THE CORRECTIVE EMOTIONAL EXPERIENCE

Psychodynamic therapy identifies pursuit of insight as critical in effecting therapeutic change (Messer & McWilliams, 2007). In fact, psychodynamic approaches to treatment are often referred to as *insight-oriented* therapy (Frank, 1993; Messer & McWilliams, 2007). As behavior theorists suggest "change the behavior and insight will follow," modern relational theorists believe insight occurs when a patient feels emotionally safe relating to the therapist in ways differing from past behavior with significant objects (Messer & McWilliams, 2007). Essentially, psychodynamic formulation suggests that insight is developed within the therapeutic dyad and generalized into behavior change outside therapy. However, intellectual insight alone is not believed to be sufficient in creating lasting emotional and behavioral change.

The *corrective emotional experience* is considered a fundamental therapeutic principle encompassing insight through exposure to previously distressing thoughts and emotions, unconsciously guiding present thinking and relating. The goal is "to re-expose the patient, under more favorable circumstances, to emotional situations which he or she could not handle in the past. The patient, in order to be helped, must undergo a corrective emotional experience suitable to repair the traumatic influence of previous experiences" (Alexander & French, 1946, p. 66).

RESOLUTION OF CONFLICT

Contemporary theorists emphasize the ability to tolerate painful affect as central in behavior change. Insight into defense mechanisms protecting the individual from emotional pain provides opportunities to explore developmental traumas that influence present functioning. Using a developmental model to help explain current distress, psychodynamic therapy attempts to understand current perceptions, feelings, and behaviors as arising from critical experiences within development. To develop more adaptive and healthy ways of thinking and behaving, it is necessary to resolve past conflicts influencing maladaptive thoughts and behaviors. Experiencing painful affect previously defended against is conceptualized as a vital change process and influential in developing more adaptive ways of relating to others.

Intervention Strategies

EMOTIONAL EXPLORATION

Classical psychodynamic approaches attempted to facilitate the experience of affects previously unexpressed, or amplify affects suppressed, denied, or ignored (Summers & Barber, 2010). Psychodynamic theorists suggest that the experience of intense affect associated with painful memories facilitates cognitive insight. *Catharsis* refers to the expression, or release, of painful emotions. *Catharsis* is believed to provide clients with a sense of relief and is believed to be associated with a cognitive shift, creating distance between past and present. Intense negative affect decreases as the patient generates adaptive and realistic perceptions detached from historical baggage that have a negative impact on functioning (Summers & Barber, 2010). *Guided exploration* and *open-ended interviewing* provide a context for empathic understanding, clarification of emotion/behaviors, and interpretation of identified thoughts, feelings, and behaviors.

INTERPRETATION OF TRANSFERENCE

Transference is considered a core concept in psychodynamic psychotherapy. Originally regarded by Freud (1905/1953) as a living reconstruction of the patient's repressed historical past "transferred" into the therapeutic relationship, contemporary theorists recognize that the distinct reactions occurring within a unique therapeutic relationship are more complex and may reflect the therapeutic alliance or the real relationship between the patient and therapist (Hoglend, 2004). Transference interpretations are central to facilitating patient insight into previously unconscious motives of behavior. Interpretations of transference in psychodynamic therapy seek to establish connections between internal conflicts, past or present objects, and the relationship to the therapist (Hoglend 2004). The fundamental theory suggests that ongoing interactions between patient and therapist are influenced by the patient's past or current relationships, and focusing on the themes and conflicts arising within the therapeutic relationship will illuminate the true nature of problems experienced outside of therapy (Kernberg, Diamond, Yeomans, Clarkin, & Levy, 2008). Experiencing insight through transference analysis is theorized to create strong and lasting impressions on patients, while a focus exclusively on relationships outside of therapy may invite more intellectual speculation (Kernberg et al., 2008; Messer & McWilliams, 2007). This *corrective emotional experience,* described earlier, is believed to facilitate lasting change.

INTERPRETATION OF COUNTERTRANSFERENCE

Traditionally, experiences of countertransference have been viewed as an impediment to therapeutic progress. Requiring careful scrutiny by the therapist, strong feelings toward a particular client were assessed as irrational and prevented the therapist from remaining objective (Huprich, 2009). Contemporary perspectives characterize experiences of countertransference as providing invaluable information about the patient. The clinician's experience with the client may offer important information regarding others' experience with the individual. When the relationship is secure and the therapist is skilled in delivering potentially hurtful feedback, thoughts and feelings about the client can facilitate insight into previously unconscious ways of relating to others. From a relational perspective, providing the client with this type of feedback is an important aspect of a genuine and authentic relationship and necessary in creating cognitive shifts.

INTERPRETATION OF RESISTANCE

Despite a conscious desire to be alleviated from pain, clients inevitably resist change. Psychodynamic therapy interprets resistance as a defense serving some protective function for the individual (Huprich, 2009). Resistance is complicated and occurs at many levels for many types of reasons. It is beyond the scope of this chapter to identify all the potential causes of resistance, but it is a necessary component of psychodynamic treatment to identify, assess, and process resistance as it occurs. Understanding the function of resistance is necessary to determining maintaining factors supporting maladaptive patterns of relating. A competent psychodynamic clinician must respect the complexity of a client's behavior and take the necessary steps to understand both unconscious and conscious motives of resistance.

TRANSFORMING INSIGHT INTO BEHAVIORAL CHANGE

Traditional psychoanalytic drive/structural theory believed that the process of making conflicted unconscious mental material conscious was sufficient in motivating behavioral change. Most contemporary approaches conclude that insight is the driving force behind behavioral change but emphasize the therapist as a coach and mentor around life issues, particularly interpersonal issues. In the case of brief dynamic therapy, interpersonal skills are emphasized as a simultaneous process resulting from insight into interpersonal patterns of relating. Interpersonal pattern recognition reflects a developmental model of therapy emphasizing identification and recognition of meanings/themes embedded within past and present interpersonal interactions (Binder, 2004). Skills related to self-reflection, self-monitoring, and cognitive flexibility fosters the capacity to improvise in initiating and responding to interpersonal behavior. Emphasis is placed on new learning, as insight into past maladaptive patterns of relating with others informs future interventions.

Competency Benchmarks

To this point, the most extensive competencies required for the effective delivery of psychodynamic therapy have been developed in the United Kingdom. The British Psychological Society's Centre for Outcomes Research and Effectiveness (CORE) developed competence frameworks that constitute "statements of evidence" for the development of the National Occupational Standards for the psychological therapies. At present the evidence base for the effectiveness of psychodynamic therapy is not as extensive as that for the effectiveness of other therapeutic modalities (such as cognitive-behavioral therapy), and the benchmarks represent expert consensus based on the available research. CORE has outlined five core competencies domains for the delivery of effective psychodynamic therapy: (a) generic clinical competence, (b) basic psychoanalytic/psychodynamic competencies, (c) specific psychoanalytic/psychodynamic techniques, (d) problem-specific competencies/adaptations, and (e) meta-competencies (which guide the application of psychodynamic interventions; Lemma et al., 2008). This document provides an extensive list of basic psychodynamic competencies and four specific analytic/dynamic techniques. The four specific techniques unique to psychodynamic treatment are the ability to make dynamic interpretations; the ability to work in the transference; the ability to work in the countertransference; and the ability to recognize and work with defenses.

The field continues to evolve in defining core competencies, benchmarks for measuring competencies, and tools useful in evaluating competencies (Kaslow et al., 2004, 2007, 2009; Fouad et al., 2009). As referred to throughout this volume, the reader is encouraged to explore the Competency Benchmarks Work Group's (Fouad et al., 2009) list of Foundational Competencies for the broad range of skills required in the field of professional psychology, including those needed for the effective delivery of psychotherapy across theoretical models. In addition, Kaslow and colleagues (2009) provide training programs with a useful toolkit to establish methods of assessment and to provide behavioral anchors to determine trainees' readiness for the various levels of training, including practicum, internship, and entry into practice. Since psychodynamic therapy is complex, fluid, and dynamic, assessing for competence can be challenging. The use of performance reviews, case presentations, client/patient process and outcome data, consumer surveys, live or recorded performance ratings, objective structured clinical examinations, portfolios, record reviews, self-assessment, simulations/role-plays, standardized client interviews, structured oral examinations, and written examinations are recommended to assess for and develop core competencies (Kaslow et al., 2009).

Concluding Remarks

Modern psychodynamic theory has evolved from its traditional psychoanalytic roots to consider attachment theories and relational perspectives in developing a rich understanding of personality development and symptom presentation. Contemporary theorists draw attention to the complexity of psychological functioning and the respect for the dynamic and influential nature of the therapeutic relationship in effecting change. Considering the fluid nature of dynamic treatment and its attention to abstract concepts and ideas, assessing core competencies is challenging. The establishment of guidelines and behavioral anchors to evaluate the development of psychodynamic clinicians is critical to the further development of contemporary approaches in modern practice.

PART IV

Other Functional Competencies

EIGHT

Consultation

Clinical psychologists, not too infrequently, find themselves in the role of providing expert consultative services to individual colleagues, groups, programs, or organizations. In this role, the consultant attempts to improve the ability of the consultee to solve real-life professional problems by enhancing and solidifying problem-solving abilities and/or effectively addressing factors that undermine effective problem resolution. An implicit assumption of consultation is that by participating in this process, the service recipient will learn to more effectively handle similar problems in the future and, ultimately, rely less, if not at all, on the consultant. This competency refers to a specific professional interaction that occurs between the clinical psychologist and a peer or client focusing on the resolution of a given problem (Arredondo, Shealy, Neale, & Winfrey, 2004; McHolland, 1992). Consultation is a collaborative endeavor in which the clinical psychologist intervenes in an indirect manner without assuming responsibility for the direct delivery of the service. Today, consultation is quickly emerging as one of the most important competencies in clinical psychology (e.g., James & Folen, 2005). As a competency area, there are specific knowledge, skills, and attitudes that are critical to being able to conduct effective consultation. In this chapter, we review the consultation competency, its unique and distinguishing characteristics, the critical components of consultation, the process of consultation, specific types of consultation, competency benchmarks, and methods of competency assessment in this domain.

Over 40 years ago, Caplan (1970) defined consultation as a "process of interaction between two professionals, the consultant who is a specialist, and the consultee, who invokes the consultant's help in regard to a current work problem with which he(she) is having some difficulty and which he(she) has decided is within the other's area of specialized competence" (p.19). Over the ensuing years consultation has become a competency domain that can be distinguished from other domains on a number of parameters. Effective consultation requires a specific skill mix, although traditionally it is one area of education and training that has been limited, if not given less priority, in the training of clinical psychologists.

In light of recent changes in healthcare delivery with the strong emphasis on integrated healthcare, consultation has assumed a role of central importance for the clinical psychologist. According to Stanton (2010), the expected knowledge, skills, and attitudes for consultation are encompassed within five critical facets of this competency, as espoused by the National Council of Schools and Programs of Professional Psychology: knowledge of empirically based theories, models, and interventions; research and evaluation methods; problem-solving strategies; engagement in the consultation process and establishing consultative relationships; and ethical and professional issues. To appreciate competency development in this area, it is important to consider those things that differentiate consultation from other competencies.

Distinguishing Features of Consultation

Consultation differs in many important ways from other roles assumed by the clinical psychologist. Caplan (1970) delineated several distinctive features of the consultation process. Understanding these characteristics has important implications for clinical psychologists seeking to serve as competent consultants. Consultants are experts within a given field in a given specialty who offer assistance related to specific problems experienced by others called consultees. A consultant, by definition, possesses special knowledge, skills, attitudes, and competencies that are essential in solving problems being experienced within the professional realm by the consultee. The consultee may or may not be within the same profession of the consultant but often lacks the knowledge, experience, skills, values, or objectivity that are deemed critical to addressing the questions or problems being confronted by the consultee.

The problems typically addressed by consultants may be found in a patient of the consultee, in a program within a service delivery unit, in an organization, or even within the consultee himself or herself. Whatever the case, the clinical psychologist must have expertise in handling such problems to be capable of assisting the consultee in resolving the issue at hand. The consultant must possess expertise in the specified area of the consultation problem and realm. A consideration of some of the typical kinds of problems confronting consultants within each realm will help to clarify this competency. As we describe these problems, the prerequisite competencies will be clear.

In the patient realm, consultants may be asked to offer guidance on issues related to diagnosis, assessment, conceptualization, management, treatment, and evaluation. Embedded within this realm may be specific professional, clinical, ethical, or legal matters. For example, a consultee may seek expert opinion on the assessment and management of a challenging violence-prone patient on an inpatient psychiatric unit. The presumption is that, as a direct result of the consultation, the consultee will be better able to manage this patient on the unit.

In the programmatic realm, a consultant may be contracted to provide expertise in creating, developing, revising, refining, or evaluating a specialized program offered in a service delivery unit. Here, for example, an expert in substance abuse may be asked to reengineer an outpatient program to include the latest in stages of change and motivational interviewing protocols. In an organization, a consultant may be charged with the task of conducting surveys, focus groups, and interviews of minorities to evaluate the organization's openness to diversity and sensitivities of the administration and staff and to recommend changes at an organizational level. Finally, a community mental health therapist engaging in boundary crossings with a personality-disordered patient may seek out consultation to address the distorted beliefs and assumptions fueling this countertransference. An implicit assumption in this instance is simply that the therapist will be able to more effectively provide services to this patient.

There are several unique characteristics about the consultative process (Caplan, 1970; Cos, DiTomasso, Cirilli, & Finkelstein, 2010). First, the consultant offers services to some other professional (or group of professionals) who, while directly responsible for the outcome, need expert input. The role of the consultant is indirect in this sense. Even if the consultant sees a patient of another professional, the focus is on providing information to the consultee to improve the services ultimately being offered to the patient. Second, consultants do not, by definition, assume professional responsibility for the case; the consultee, be it an individual or an organization, maintains full professional responsibility for the outcome. Third, the consultant conducts an assessment of the problem to determine how best to assist the consultee. The consultant must obtain information, analyze and synthesize it, formulate and test hypotheses, and develop a solution. Fourth, on the basis of assessment, the consultant provides a formal set of suggestions or recommendations that in his or her professional opinion will improve, if not resolve, the matter. These recommendations, if accepted, are implemented by the consultee. The consultee may choose to accept or reject the recommendations of the consultant and proceed accordingly. There is, then, no guarantee that the consultee will adopt the recommendations of the consultant. Fifth, the evaluation of the outcome of the recommendations rests squarely upon the consultee, who may or may not be required to demonstrate that change has resulted. Finally, an inherent assumption is that as a function of the consultation, the consultee will be better prepared to handle similar professional challenges in the future and, as a result, rely less upon the consultant. Implied here is a process of change in the consultee that supports improvement.

SUPERVISION

Consultation clearly differs from competence in supervision. The process of supervision has several distinctive characteristics. Clinical supervision implicitly and explicitly involves the critical function of a more senior psychologist carefully overseeing the work of a supervisee who is most often within the same profession. For example, a licensed psychologist may be charged with the role of supervising a practicum student or intern in clinical psychology. Unlike consultants, however, supervisors decide on the number and type of patients seen by a supervisee; take professional responsibility for regularly reviewing the clinical work of the supervise; evaluate the quality of the performance of the supervisee; examine and provide feedback on work products (e.g., reports or taped sessions); and work toward improving the competency level of the supervisee in a variety of domains relevant to effective professional practice in foundational and functional areas.

The supervisor assumes the primary responsibility for the clinical work of the supervisee, ensures that the client is aware of the supervisory status of the supervisee, and signs off on all professional documentation. The supervisor is also responsible for selecting the clients of the supervisee, determining their appropriateness for the level of the supervisee, and interceding and seeing the client when it is deemed to be professionally necessary. Supervisors also perform an evaluative function by engaging in a standardized and formal reporting process that attests to the competence or incompetence of the supervisee. In the latter instance, supervision serves a gatekeeping function by identifying those who may not be fit for the role of the clinical psychologist.

PSYCHOTHERAPY

Consultation is also clearly distinguished from psychotherapy. Psycho-therapists, of course, directly assist clients who are suffering from psychological distress, perform a psychological assessment, assign a diagnosis, develop a case formulation, create a treatment plan, directly intervene with a set of psychological procedures, and assume professional responsibility for what happens to the client. Consultants simply do not perform psychotherapy-focused activities with the consultee. The roles and activities of the consultant and therapist differ. This is not to say, however, that the skill mixes necessary for success in each role are mutually exclusive. Rather, the consultant often uses his or her expertise in the psychotherapeutic realm to assist the consultee with tasks such as assessment, diagnosis, case conceptualization, and treatment planning and implementation.

Elements of Consultation

There are a number of critical components to the process of psychological consultation, and to fully function as a competent consultant, the clinical psychologist must be able to address each one. The ability to do so lays the foundation for the establishment of an effective process and outcome. These components appear interdependent, sequential, and necessary to achieve an effective process and outcome. We describe each of these areas in more detail below.

ACHIEVING EXPERTISE

One prerequisite for consultation is the attainment of a specified area of expertise. As a competency issue, this underscores the fact that no clinical psychologist could conceivably serve as a consultant for all problems, let alone in all areas, topics, or specialties; few, if any, psychologists could be so skilled or gifted. Preparation as a clinical psychologist in no way guarantees that one would be able to consult in any given area. Rather, one must have a recognized set of advanced educational, training, supervised, and professional experiences and accomplishments that uniquely qualify one to offer services as a consultant in a specified area. Recognition of these skills by other professionals provides a sense of credibility, which is indeed why one is sought out as an expert.

The label "consultant," then, bestows a distinction upon a clinical psychologist that implies a special level of expertise and experience and signifies that one possesses the special competence to provide assistance to other professionals. Psychological consultation in a specific area by definition requires knowledge, experience, and skills related to handling specific problems, populations, strategies, methodologies, services, techniques, research strategies, and the like. A consultant must have the requisite background to offer the service.

Identifying oneself as and agreeing to serve as a consultant implies a professional and ethical responsibility that one is indeed competent to perform the requisite roles and functions. For example, it would be difficult to justify a situation in which a radical behaviorist offers consultation services to a consultee seeking assistance in developing a psychodynamic formulation of a challenging client. On the other hand, a consultee requesting a functional analytic formulation would be well served by seeking the expertise of a behaviorist as opposed to a psychoanalyst.

DEVELOPING A CONSULTATIVE RELATIONSHIP

To conduct consultation, one must possess foundational skills in establishing and maintaining a sound professional relationship. This competency rests on the consultant possessing solid general interpersonal skills (rapport building, active listening, conveying understanding) and skills in forming a working alliance. Expertise in and of itself alone provides no guarantee that one would be sought out or contracted to consult or that one could even perform the role. Good social skills, a strong desire to help, and skill in handling difficult situations, each coupled with problem-solving skills and a good knowledge base, are prerequisites. Above all, the consultant must be capable of creating and nurturing a safe and comfortable atmosphere in which the consultee is free to share concerns and expose relevant deficits.

SETTING AN AGENDA

Good consultation begins with a clear-cut agenda. The competent consultant allows for the development of a mutually agreed-upon agenda for consultative sessions. Mutually developing an agenda emphasizes the important contribution of the consultee and communicates a collaborative focus. The agenda also provides a roadmap that guides the process of consultative sessions and the overall process itself. Moreover, it allows for the consultative dyad to remain focused and to agree about the course of the process. Without a clear agenda, there is the risk that the consultative process may stray from the course required to address the problem. Also, an agenda may help to maximize the use of the time available and assist in achieving the desired goals.

DEVELOPING MEASURABLE GOALS

The aim of any consultation is squarely rooted in the goals of the consultation itself. However, consultees differ in their ability to specify target goals and objectives that should serve as the focal point for the consultation. Consultees may not be specific in describing objective, measurable, behavioral, and attainable goals. Ambiguous goals run the risk of leading to a process that is vague and undirected and likely to fail.

A consultant must, then, be capable of taking what the consultee reports as the presenting problem and helping ferret out a clearly definable set of outcome goals. Both consultee and consultant must understand what the ultimate goals of the process are expected to achieve. These goals will serve to direct and guide the consultation, document a baseline, establish evidence that the process is helpful or unhelpful, and, ultimately, substantiate the outcome. Ambiguous, undefined goals lead to vague and undefined consultation services with no discernible means to guide the process.

GATHERING USEFUL INFORMATION

Consultants must be skilled at extracting the information needed to solve the problem. This means they must know what questions to ask, how much to ask, how to ask questions most effectively, and how to use this information to attain the consultee's goals. Because consultation is a time-limited process, the consultant must know critical questions to ask and must be capable of reviewing information already obtained by the consultee. As a result, consultants must develop and test out hypotheses that account for the problem situation and, in turn, influence the line of questioning followed by the consultant.

The consultant must be able to organize the information obtained from a consultee into a coherent and meaningful whole. For example, a consultant may discover that a consultee lacks knowledge and skills in evaluating diagnostic criteria and considering differential diagnostic issues in a given case. This information may prove to be critically useful in developing a plan to assist the consultee in developing a diagnostic formulation. Ultimately, however, the success of the consultation may hinge on motivating the consultee to seek educational experiences to rectify this knowledge deficiency and, most importantly, teaching the consultee how to frame diagnostic questions to yield more reliable and valid information from the consultee's client.

ORIENTING TO THE MODEL

Consultants must have a framework for conceptualizing the process, usually rooted in a theoretical orientation that, in turn, leads to consistency in building a model of the problem confronting the consultee. Explaining the model to the consultee educates him or her about what deserves most attention in working with the client. This didactic component provides a framework or guide in helping both the consultant and the consultee to mutually process the problem situation, formulate a conceptualization, provide insight into the problem, offer a means for solving it, and facilitate goal attainment.

Clinical psychologists may practice consultation from different theoretical orientations. This orientation may dictate what the consultant considers most important in solving the problem. Take the case of a challenging client whose behavior in sessions poses concern for the consultee. A behaviorally oriented consultant will be most likely to lead the consultee through a process of identifying discriminative stimuli, ongoing reinforcers, and maintaining factors in explaining the client's behavior toward the consultee during a therapeutic session. A psychodynamically trained consultant is more likely to focus the consultee on the quality of the therapeutic alliance and suggest addressing transference and countertransference issues. Whatever the case, a model provides theoretical consistency to the process and is likely to be useful.

DIDACTIC TRAINING, IMPLEMENTING EMPIRICALLY BASED INTERVENTIONS, AND FOSTERING PROBLEM RESOLUTION

The consultant must also be capable of teaching the consultee to become more skilled at addressing the problem that defines the need for the consultation itself. An implicit goal of any consultation is for the consultee to be more skilled as a result of the process. This essentially requires the consultant to assess the level of the consultee's knowledge and skill at the initiation of the consultation, identifying areas of strength, noting deficits and areas in need of improvement, and providing education to enhance the knowledge, skills, and attitudes of the consultee.

For instance, a consultee who seeks consultation in the interpretation of a Rorschach may require some education about how to interpret specific markers on a protocol. In another case, a consultee may require instruction about how to create an exposure hierarchy and deliver exposure therapy for a panic patient. In another instance, a consultant may need to assist a consultee in maintaining appropriate boundaries with a borderline patient.

In any case, as a result of the consultation the consultee must derive some benefit from the experience that will improve his or her practice.

As noted by Stanton (2010), the consultant must be armed with knowledge of empirically based theories, models, and interventions. Theories, models, and interventions that are based on empirical evidence will enhance the likelihood of a successful consultation. Theories and models are most helpful in guiding the consultative process by providing a schema for understanding problems and a vehicle for guiding decision-making about the most important and salient elements to address. An empirical basis for interventions provides a solid foundation for ensuring that the recommended strategies will yield a positive outcome. The consultant, of course, must be skilled at transporting empirically tested strategies into the context within which the consultee and patient are operating.

Also, Stanton (2010) has emphasized the importance of problem-solving. The consultant must be an expert problem-solver who is proficient in guiding the consultee through this process. As opposed to simply and directly telling the consultee what to do, it seems prudent in most instances to stimulate a problem-solving process by building on the strengths of the consultee and employing a discovery method, such as Socratic questioning. In this manner, the consultant is actively teaching the consultee how to think about problems and providing guidance in achieving problem solution. Of course, this process entails identifying the problem, considering causes of the problem through hypothesis development, brainstorming possible solutions, evaluating the pros and cons of each solution, choosing the best possible solution, addressing potential barriers, facilitating implementation of the solution, evaluating the outcome, and reassessing the problem when the result is less than successful.

SOLICITING ONGOING FEEDBACK

Consultants must be committed to eliciting feedback from the consultee about the process itself. This feedback serves a number of important functions. First, feedback provides general and specific means for judging the extent to which the consultee is finding the experience to be helpful and whether it is meeting expectations. Second, it provides a method for facilitating successive approximations leading to the adjustment of the process to maximize the likelihood of a positive outcome for the consultee. Third, it provides a direct line of communication between the consultant and the consultee through which the consultant can evaluate his or her effectiveness, make necessary accommodations, and facilitate an ideal outcome.

EVALUATING THE OUTCOME OF CONSULTATION

As with any other competency, offering oneself as a consultant promotes the reasonable expectation that the consultee and indirectly the consultee's client will be better off from having invoked the services of the consultant. The consultant must be creative in designing and/or selecting means by which outcomes can be validly and reliably assessed. Knowledge of research and evaluation methods is extremely valuable. Multimodal assessment from multiple sources (if available) across multiple occasions may be most useful here (DiTomasso & Gilman, 2005). Otherwise, pretest–posttest measures may serve the function. In any case, consultants must seek baseline, ongoing, and follow-up measurements to substantiate that stable, meaningful, and practically significant change has occurred as a result of the consultative process.

Patient-Centered Case Consultation and Consultee-Centered Case Consultation

In this section we will describe two types of mental health consultation, with an eye focused on required skills.

The focus of patient-centered case consultation (PCCC) is on a patient who is being seen by a mental health professional and about whom the consultee has important questions. PCCC refers to a professional interaction in which the consultee seeks answers to one or more questions of significance posed by the consultee. These questions typically are relevant to the patient's welfare and guide the manner in which the patient is handled. The reasons a consultee might desire assistance are many and varied. Common situations generally include issues related to assessment, diagnosis, formulation, treatment, and disposition. Each of these may directly influence the quality of care offered to the client as well as his or her ultimate outcome.

By seeking help from the consultant, the consultee is acknowledging that he or she lacks the knowledge, skill, and experience to solve the problem. Practicing within the limits of one's own competence is an ethical responsibility of all professionals, including clinical psychologists, and is grounded in the principle of beneficence (do no harm). In these instances the consultee is invoking these ethical guidelines in obtaining assistance from a credible expert to solve a problem that is beyond his or her expertise. The implicit assumption is that without the assistance of the consultant, the client's problem may never be resolved by the consultee alone.

The promotion of a collaborative relationship is therefore necessary to initiate and complete the process. The consultant must be capable of creating a working climate of trust, respect, understanding, and collaboration. The consultee must, in turn, feel safe enough to expose his or her lack of knowledge, skill, or experience to the consultant, all the while trusting that the consultant will not be judgmental and that help will occur. Once rapport is firmly established, the work may proceed.

The problem for which the consultee seeks help becomes a focal point for the goals of the consultation. Competent PCCC necessitates a clear focus and the determination of specific answerable questions (e.g., What are the diagnoses of this patient?). Rarely is there simply one question; more often, there are a series of more complex interrelated questions that themselves challenge the consultee and what he or she is trying to achieve. Delineating these questions is a first step toward creating goals and objectives. This task can usually be easily accomplished by reframing the consultee's questions as declarative statements in the form of goals. For example, if a consultee is puzzled about how to treat a complex case of obsessive-compulsive disorder (OCD), the goal would obviously be to identify and develop an effective treatment plan for OCD. Whatever they turn out to be, the goals of PCCC drive the process.

The quality of the PCCC is a direct function of the information solicited by the consultant. For example, the questions posed by the consultee about a treatment issue may be based on an inaccurate diagnosis or formulation. The consultant must, therefore, be capable of independently confirming clinical information based on what the consultee reports, prior information gathered by the consultee, a review of standardized measures already available, or even conducting a session with the patient. Whatever the case, the consultant who offers advice based on inadequate or invalid information may do more harm than good. The consultant should be thoroughly familiar with what clinical information is necessary to establish a sound basis for consultation. In essence, the consultant must be clear about what needs to be known about the client, the assessment, the treatment process, and whatever else is deemed necessary to accurately answer the consultee's questions.

The consultation process must yield an outcome that fully addresses the reason for the consultation, answers the critical questions posed by the consultee, and provides one or more specific recommendations for a solution. In the end, the true measure of consultation is whether the consultee finds the process to have been productive and worthwhile. This outcome issue has several components. The consultant must obtain baseline information about where the consultee lies at the beginning of the consultation. A clear sense of what the consultee knows and does not know, what the consultee is and is not capable of doing, and any other factors that undermine the effectiveness of the consultee must be determined. The solicitation of ongoing formative observations will assist the consultant in learning whether the process is progressing in a positive direction. The value of the experience is determined by the extent to which the information is usable. Also, the outcome based on implementation of the recommendations of the consultant must prove effective in improving the situation by achieving the goals. Finally, the consultee must be capable at some point in relying less upon the consultant and solving future, similar problems independently.

Another form of consultation focuses on the consultee: consultee-centered case consultation (CCCC). As described by Cos and colleagues (2010), a cognitive model proposed by DiTomasso (2009) details the process in working in situations when the focus of the consultation is the consultee. While there are other available models, we chose to highlight that with which we are most familiar. In these circumstances the *raison d'être* for the consultation is embedded within the reaction of the consultee to a patient or group of patients. By definition, the consultant is experiencing a reaction that creates a problem in managing the patient. In other words, while the consultee may have a correct formulation or treatment plan, his or her reactions to the patient interfere with the handling of the case and undermine efforts to address the patient's problem. Simply put, the focus of CCCC is the consultee's problematic reaction or response to the patient, which essentially characterizes a countertransference reaction. The patient in this context becomes a stimulus or trigger for an attitude, belief, or assumption that causes and fuels the consultee's behavior in relation to the patient.

These reactions may be manifested in a variety of potentially countertherapeutic responses, boundary crossings (and even violations), avoidance, overinvolvement, oversights, and the like that affect the judgment of the practitioner. Herein lies the danger: the consultee may find himself or herself either overreacting to or ignoring important aspects of the case.

The core problem in CCCC is often embedded within the thoughts, attitudes, beliefs, and assumptions the consultee makes about the patient, which are not typically apparent to or characteristic of the consultee. The astute consultant will focus upon the intensity of the reaction and the emotional responses of the consultee in the clinical context as well as the unusual nature of the reaction, which is often more muted, if not absent, in his or her handling of other cases. The question of importance here is specifically what it is about this patient, at this given time, in this given context, that elicits the observed reaction of the consultee. The answer is often rooted in the unrealistic beliefs of the consultee. These beliefs are contained in cognitive schema activated by characteristics of the patient that serve to drive the consultee's thoughts and feelings about the patient and that influence his or her behavior toward the patient, each of which reciprocally influences the other. The overarching goal is to identify unrealistic thoughts, assumptions, and beliefs that the consultee holds about the patient; to determine the relationship between these factors and the consultee's reaction to the patient; and to target and alter these unrealistic cognitive elements as a means of resolving the problem.

This model of consultation (DiTomasso, 2009) rests upon several assumptions: (a) Consultees actively process their professional encounters with patients before, during, and after they occur; (b) The thoughts, beliefs, and assumptions a consultee has about a given patient directly affect his or her feelings about and behaviors toward the patient; (c) Cognitive processing errors may distort the perspective of the consultee; (d) Distorted thinking is associated with the consultee's emotional reactions and behaviors that may have an adverse impact on the clinical process and interfere with assessment and treatment by undermining his or her ability to address the patient and the patient's presenting problems; (e) Making the consultee aware of his or her thoughts, assumptions, beliefs, and behaviors is a critical step in solving the consultee's problems with the patient; (f) Actively teaching the consultee how to conceptualize his or her experiences with the patient and strategies for altering dysfunctional cognitive material is critical in achieving the consultation goals; and (g) Learning how to modify and restructure negative cognitions will assist the consultee in handling the patient in question as well as other patients in the future.

The CCCC model requires that the consultant structure the consultation process in a manner that maximizes the likelihood of success. These steps (Cos et al., 2010) entail building rapport; delineating the goals and setting the agenda; soliciting important information about the patient; educating the consultee about the cognitive model itself; developing a conceptualization; proposing it to the consultee; tailoring it based on consultee feedback; restructuring unrealistic cognitions and replacing them with realistic ones; deriving effective strategies for managing the patient; obtaining ongoing and summative feedback about the process; and obtaining outcome data.

Program Development and Related Forms of Consultation

While up to this point we have focused on consultation with individuals, a consultant may also focus on the development of programs that serve clients. Clinical psychologists are often sought out by mental health agencies and related organizations to create a program to meet the needs of a special population or to lend their expertise on a special project. Whatever the case, once again, a psychologist with specific competencies within a given area of the specialty may be contracted to share wisdom regarding the development and implementation of a specific program. Normally, consultants will be contacted by top administrators who have a vision for a project that may or may not be shared by others in the organization.

Examples are varied and many. Agencies or hospitals may need the advanced knowledge and skills of a clinical psychologist to develop any number of possible specialized services, such as an inpatient eating disorders unit, an intensive outpatient program for the seriously mentally ill, a motivational interviewing program for an outpatient substance abuse program for teenagers, a childhood anxiety service of a larger clinic, disseminating empirically based protocols into community agencies, and the like. Other related requests for consulting may capitalize on non–service-related activities such as consulting with a doctoral-level training program on curriculum development in clinical psychology, training issues, or even an accreditation process. Whatever the purpose for which a consultant has been contracted, several considerations must be addressed.

An organization in need of consultative service that desires to develop a special project will identify and contact a potential consultant to hire. This process is fraught with potential issues of which the consultant must be astutely aware. The idea of seeking someone outside the organization may engender problems in and of itself. The consultant must be knowledgeable about how the system operates, who wields the power, issues from within and outside that are affecting the system, and other related issues. These issues may make the difference between whether the program succeeds or not.

Careful planning is often required to ensure successful program development. A consultant may guide an organization through a process designed to help decide the prudence of such a decision. One such approach from the business world is a SWOT analysis (Dyson, 2004). SWOT stands for four major areas of consideration: the strengths of an organization, its weaknesses, and opportunities and threats in the environment. For example, in considering the implementation of a new program, a clinical psychologist consultant might guide members of an organization through an analysis that considers each facet. Strengths may focus on a variety of factors related to the organization, including unique advantages of a proposed program, the ability and potential of the organization to deliver a high-quality program, current available resources, knowledge, and experience of professionals on staff, expertise among staff, availability of start-up funds, and the like.

Weaknesses may help to focus on factors that may undermine success, such as lack of licensed therapists, reimbursement limitations, lack of accreditation, and the like. Opportunities reflect things such as new markets opening up, lack of competitors, and new avenues for income streams. Threats are defined as factors that present obstacles, including lack of trained staff, a hiring freeze, staffing problems, and pending adverse legislation. Guiding an organization through this process may help the consultant to identify the prudence of a decision by thoroughly considering the available strengths, prospects, vulnerabilities, and obstacles to be overcome. This is just one example among many in which clinical psychologists can provide effective consultation.

In the subsequent sections we address competency benchmarks and tools for assessing competency in this domain. This information is intended to assist clinical psychologists in examining their own competency development in the area of consultation and in considering relevant tools for assessing competency in this domain.

Benchmark Competencies for Consultation

In attaining and maintaining competence in consultation, a number of benchmark competencies must be achieved as the budding clinical psychologist proceeds from entry into a doctoral program, to readiness for practicum experiences, to readiness for beginning internship, and to ultimate completion of the doctorate and being prepared to begin practice. The Competency Benchmarks Work Group (Fouad et al., 2009) proposed that consultation as a Functional Competency comprises several components: understanding the consultation role, handling referral questions, conducting assessments, communicating the findings gathered from assessments, applying effective interventions, using the theoretical and empirical knowledge base in psychology to fuel the consultative process, and assessing the outcomes of one's consultative services.

Assessing Competence in Consultation

Kaslow and colleagues (2009) recommend a menu of relevant tools to help psychologists to self-assess in the consultation domain. The recommended methods vary as a function of the component being assessed. We present some general recommendations based on their work. "Very useful" methods include the following: case reviews, consumer surveys, collection of both process and outcome data, and performance ratings. "Useful" methods include the use of rating forms and 360-degree evaluations. In developing and sustaining competency, clinical psychologists must systematically engage in a process of self-assessment by using self-evaluation to identify goals and means for improving their skills.

Concluding Remarks

Consultation is likely to continue to increase in importance over the next decade. Clinical psychologists who seek to provide consultative services must be prepared to meet the unique challenges presented in consulting about problems of consultees related to patients, the consultee himself or herself, or organizations. Effective consultation necessitates an array of skills embedded in empirically based knowledge, theories, models, and strategies. Achievement of benchmark competencies in this area and focused assessment planning based on one or more evaluation tools are necessary.

NINE

Supervision, Management, Administration, and Teaching

Clinical psychologists are most often associated with the delivery of assessment and therapy services; however, many engage in a variety of other professional activities, such as supervision, teaching, management, and administration. There is considerable responsibility involved with each of these roles, as these endeavors position the psychologist to be an influential force in guiding and training students, administering organizational tasks in a leadership role, managing other professionals, and teaching in areas of personal expertise. Furthermore, psychologists are often asked to make decisions that may have a direct impact on students, trainees, clients, colleagues, and employees. Psychologists may be asked to supervise a case with which they have great expertise, or to speak on a topic about which they have little knowledge. How these situations are handled is often a reflection of the competence level of the psychologist.

The American Psychological Association (APA)'s Ethical Principles and Code of Conduct (APA, 2002) states that psychologists are obligated to be competent in any area in which they practice. Teaching, supervision, management, and administration may all be in the realm of a clinical psychologist's responsibilities and in fact are viewed as among the core competencies essential for competent practice as a clinical psychologist (Fouad et al., 2009; Rodolfa et al., 2005). Nevertheless, psychologists are not necessarily properly prepared to provide these services. Many graduate training programs now offer courses in supervision, often including a management and/or consultation component, most likely due to the delineation of supervision and consultation as competencies essential to the training of clinical psychologists (APA Committee on Accreditation,

2002). However, programs vary tremendously in the amount and quality of training provided.

Given that clinical psychologists widely participate in supervision, teaching, management, and administration, it is critical to consider factors that may determine levels of competency. This chapter provides the reader with an overview of the qualities necessary for professional competence in these areas and further describes behavioral benchmarks and assessment tools for measuring competency in psychologists and psychologists in training. A common element across these activities is the dissemination of information and refinement of skills of others who are conceivably less knowledgeable and proficient in a particular area. Furthermore, all of these activities entail the management and evaluation of others who are under the psychologist's direction and guidance. The clinical psychologist has the unique opportunity to support, encourage, and inspire others while at the same time oversee and guide them in professional practice.

Supervision

Just as competency is an essential ingredient in other areas of psychology, it is incumbent upon a clinical psychologist to be competent in the area of supervision. Maintaining a high level of competency in supervision requires a continual process of educating oneself in the most current literature available in treatment and assessment, preserving ethical standards, upholding sensitivity to and awareness of issues of diversity, employing social skills, and providing feedback in a supportive way (Kaslow, 2004). For example, the important role of the supervisor and related competencies is supported by legislation enacted in Pennsylvania mandating that by December 1, 2015, primary supervisors of psychology trainees must have completed either a supervision course in a doctoral program or three continuing education hours in the area of supervision. Furthermore, in the current culture of competence-based training, psychologists are now beginning to consider how leaders can facilitate an atmosphere of competency-based supervision in their training programs (Kaslow, Falender, & Grus, 2012). Competent supervision encompasses many different skill sets, best provided in an environment amenable to a competency-based approach (Kaslow et al., 2012).

KNOWLEDGE

A competent supervisor is fluent in basic theories and therapeutic techniques in the areas in which supervision is being provided. Supervisors must, by definition, as well as in theory, have more knowledge, training, and experience than a supervisee to effectively guide him or her through the process of working with clients (Malloy, Dobbins, Ducheny, & Winfrey, 2010). Obviously, a supervisor should also be competent in the actual provision of psychotherapy. If a supervisor is less familiar with treating a particular disorder, the supervisor may find it most appropriate to refer the case to another supervisor. Alternately, if the supervisor has some familiarity with the disorder, the supervisor may choose to research the area in more depth to achieve a better understanding of the problem and how it is best treated. Regardless of the decision made, a competent psychologist will consider all the options and choose the one that best serves the needs of the client, while still considering the needs of the supervisee. Competent supervision necessitates self-reflection and self-evaluation as to the legitimacy of serving in the role of supervisor.

ROLE MODELING AND MENTORING

Clinical supervisors serve as both role models and mentors for students, helping them to become more skilled in their craft (Malloy et al., 2010). As a mentor, the supervisor educates, monitors, and coaches the supervisee in how to best treat clients and how to deal with challenges as they occur. Supervisees use their time with their supervisor to hone their skills as a therapist. Supervisees typically value, listen to, and follow the advice of a supervisor to advance their skill set; hence, supervisory experiences can have a significant impact on psychologists' development and are often remembered years after training is complete.

Many psychologists can easily recall their training supervisors, specific instances when the supervisors were helpful, and what was said that was deemed to be beneficial. Furthermore, many continue to follow the advice and mentoring they received years before in supervision. Supervisees' experiences in supervision will serve as the foundation for their own first encounters as a supervisor (Falender & Shafranske, 2004). A competent psychologist is cognizant of the influence he or she has as a role model and reflects that responsibility in the decisions that are made during the supervisory process.

SELF-CARE

Supervisors are responsible for talking with supervisees about their mental state and level of self-care. Supervisors not only provide guidance regarding the care of clients, but also impart advice as to how to be a successful professional. Ensuring that supervisees are aware of their own thoughts and feelings that may be roused by a client is an important aspect of supervision. Learning to maintain one's personal level of functioning to ensure optimal services is a key task for supervisees. Furthermore, ensuring that the supervisees' personal reactions do not affect treatment is essential. Supervisors must, then, be capable of recognizing how the personal issues and reactions of the novice may undermine the therapeutic process. Being cognizant of the reactions of the supervisees, providing feedback, and advocating for the implementation of a self-care plan are all helpful ways to develop their repertoire of skills. Modeling self-care practices is an important aspect of competency, as it demonstrates to the supervisees that to best serve clients, one must also be sure to care for oneself.

PROTECTING THE PUBLIC

Supervisors are obligated to protect the public and ensure that supervisees are providing services competently (Knapp & Vandecreek, 2006). Supervisors are ultimately responsible for the clients and the quality of care provided by the supervisee from an ethical, legal, and professional standpoint. Although the student may be the one treating the client, the supervisor has an ethical obligation to ensure quality care. Furthermore, the client is legally considered to be in the care of the supervisor, so the supervisor holds legal responsibility for the client's course of treatment. In the supervisor's role of protecting the public, he or she is held responsible for making decisions that will best serve the client's welfare and ensure quality of care. If the supervisee is not performing at a standard of excellence, the supervisor is responsible for teaching and demonstrating for the supervisee how to become more skilled in practice. Supervisors perform an evaluative function and must be capable of assessing the performance of the supervisee, providing corrective feedback, establishing goals, developing remedial plans, monitoring performance, and coaching.

INTERPERSONAL SKILLS

Clinical psychologists should have competency not only in theory, therapeutic techniques, and delivery of mental health services, but also in human relationships. The basis of therapy and supervision is in fact a series of interpersonal interactions. Supervisors must establish positive relationships with their supervisees. Supervisees need to feel supported and safe to speak about their treatment sessions, yet also be able to accept constructive feedback on how to improve. Supervisees must feel that they are being listened to and that their needs are being addressed. The supervisee wants to be viewed as competent in the supervisor's eyes, which underscores the importance of building a relationship of trust. In an atmosphere of trust, the trainee will more likely feel comfortable sharing the difficulties encountered in providing services to clients.

In addition, supervisors should work to develop supervisees' sense of competency while at the same time providing guidance that will enable them to be better clinicians. One of the authors can clearly remember her first meeting with a supervisor on internship: it was very powerful and continues to be a source of inspiration. The supervisor was able to provide supervision in a way that capitalized on her strengths and provided support and encouragement so that she felt comfortable, capable, and competent to make diagnostic and treatment decisions on her own. These types of interactions are crucial to a training psychologist's development and help define the essence of a competent and effective supervisor. Supervision is an interpersonal process, and supervisors should always be aware of the power differential that exists between the supervisor and supervisee (Malloy et al., 2010).

QUALITIES OF THE SUPERVISOR

There are many different types of supervisors providing supervision in a variety of ways; however, there are also universal traits viewed to be essential to high-quality supervision. These characteristics include good clinical skills, a proficient knowledge base in the area being supervised, strong interpersonal skills, and a demonstrated interest in the supervisory role. Furthermore, a competent supervisor can identify the problems faced by clients, help the supervisee generate options to deal with these problems, and consider and encourage the clinician's strengths in implementing a treatment plan (Knapp & Vandecreek, 2006). In addition, an important but often overlooked aspect of good supervision is allowing the supervisee the opportunity to provide feedback about the supervisory experience. As is typical in structured academic courses, supervisees complete evaluations to ensure appropriate feedback to supervisors regarding their strengths and weaknesses. A competent supervisor is open to evaluation and possible change in style and practice as suggested by supervisees based on their supervisory experiences.

QUALITIES OF THE SUPERVISEE

There are many qualities that can describe a good supervisor—but what about a supervisee? Are there qualities that are important for the supervisee to have to facilitate a positive supervisory relationship? Falender and Shafranske (2004) reviewed the literature on this topic and reported that supervisors enjoy supervisees who actively participate during supervision, ask for help when appropriate but at the same time are self-sufficient, and are willing to learn and grow. They further summarize their assessment of what constitutes quality supervision based on the current literature, citing quality supervision as competency-based, individualized to the supervisees, promoting professionalism, and infusing the most current knowledge of treatment into the supervision. Furthermore, the climate of supervision should be nurturing and positive (Falender & Shafranske, 2004). From the outset, competent supervisors set the parameters of supervision, clearly specify mutual expectations, and carefully delineate the responsibilities and functions of each individual.

PERSPECTIVES ON COMPETENT SUPERVISION

Newman (2010) shares his ideas of what is required to be a competent supervisor in cognitive-behavioral therapy (CBT). Although specifically referencing a knowledge base in CBT, some of the descriptors of a competent supervisor are applicable to supervisors of any theoretical orientation. Newman describes supervisor competency as having foundational knowledge of CBT (or other theoretical orientation of practice), an awareness of cultural diversity and competency, and the opportunity for the supervisee to grow and develop his or her skills. The supervisor should protect clients by recognizing if a supervisee is handling something unprofessionally and should be the gatekeeper to ensure that the services being provided are appropriate and imparted effectively. In addition, Newman (2010) describes the functional responsibilities of a competent supervisor as listening to recorded sessions and providing feedback, helping supervisees conceptualize cases in a CBT perspective (or other theoretical orientation preference), and conveying the skills and techniques necessary to treat the client. Moreover, a supervisor should be mindful of the difference between supervision and therapy and ensure that the boundary between the two is kept clear.

Clinical supervision is one of the duties often assumed by psychologists, and many graduate programs now include it as part of their curriculum. Falender and colleagues (2004) report several considerations in regard to supervision. They describe supervision as a lifelong process requiring consideration of diversity, legal and ethical issues, the influence of personal and professional factors, and the recognition of assessment by oneself and one's peers (Falender et al., 2004). They further discuss areas of competency that supervisors must demonstrate. Knowledge in the area of which they are supervising is of utmost importance, as is more general knowledge about ethics and diversity. A supervisor must behave in an ethical manner and must be conversant in ethical and professional codes of conduct, standards, and guidelines. Knowledge of and compliance with ethical codes enables the supervisor to model appropriate behavior as well as train others in recognizing ethical dilemmas and in an ethical decision-making process. Social skills are another essential part of supervision. A supervisor must have the skills to be able to provide feedback in a supportive way so that the supervisee can process the information and learn from it. Supervisors need to be able to think flexibly, adapt their supervision to the individual, and acknowledge when it may be fruitful to go to someone else for supervision with more expertise regarding a particular issue. Values are another area of noted importance. A supervisor is responsible for the supervisee as well as the client and must treat both with respect, valuing both but keeping in mind the importance and obligation toward sustaining the client's well-being. Supervisors must be able to effectively assess both the supervisee and their own competence in handling a variety of personal and professional issues.

Management and Administration

Management and administrative responsibilities are important activities frequently performed by clinical psychologists in many types of settings, but not often acknowledged (Malloy et al., 2010). Psychologists may find themselves managing others as part of a community-centered agency, being administratively accountable for the implementation of policies and procedures of an outpatient clinic, being responsible for aspects of a graduate training program such as a clinical training director, or overseeing data collection and entry as part of a research study. Moreover, being responsible for a private practice requires managerial skills such as preparing documents (e.g., informed consent) with care to ensure that both legal and ethical guidelines are upheld, collecting fees, and scheduling clients. Supervision itself can be considered a form of one-on-one management. A supervisor is responsible for managing someone who is less knowledgeable than the psychologist in a specific area and providing the structure, guidance, feedback, and evaluation necessary for the supervisee to further develop a skill set and perform his or her job effectively.

Psychologists may also find themselves in administrative roles requiring competencies in other areas to facilitate effective management. Fluency in managed care and all of its nuances is a must for those in an administrative position in a clinical setting. Furthermore, electronic recordkeeping is a developing area requiring understanding and consideration of a broad range of issues, such as the ethical challenges involved in deciding who has access to the information. A competent administrator and manager must be familiar with the most recent trends in the profession and seeks out continuing education to become more familiar with these areas.

Clinical psychologists are in an ideal position to assume managerial roles, as a large part of doctoral training involves understanding and learning how to work with people of diverse backgrounds. Psychologists must be skilled in social interactions and relationship formation and maintenance, and these are also indispensable ingredients in being a successful manager. Furthermore, many of the activities graduate students find themselves participating in have a managerial component, such as working with clients, helping out on a research study, and managing one's own time with the multiple responsibilities psychologists hold.

Management and administration is viewed as a joint competency in the benchmarks as delineated by Fouad et al. (2009). Competency in management requires an understanding of the specific role played in a particular organization and the ability to respond appropriately within that role. As a manager, the individual should be able to evaluate the delivery of services, identify possible areas of improvement, and recognize roles that others may play to maintain quality and efficiency. Competency in management and administration includes developing and complying with policies and procedures, completing necessary reports, understanding quality-improvement procedures, and being aware of and managing financial issues (Fouad et al., 2009). These qualities are essential to both managers and administrators, allowing them to recognize strengths and weaknesses within their own organization as well to identify the steps needed to lead the organization effectively.

Case Example Dr. Acumen is in a management position at Yourtown Community Psychological Services. He is viewed as a successful manager, demonstrated by very low staff turnover and consistent patient referrals in the clinic. Staff will attest that Dr. Acumen values each one of his employees. He recognizes the importance of therapists and clerical staff and is invested in meeting their needs so they can work most effectively. Furthermore, patients find him to be extremely receptive and responsive to feedback and evaluation.

Effective managers develop positive relationships with their staff and colleagues. They demonstrate integrity in making decisions while continuing to be both empathic and just (Malloy et al., 2010). They are cognizant and appreciative of the efforts demonstrated by staff and work toward enhancing the professional growth and development of both the agency and the individuals within it. Awareness of individual and cultural differences helps managers to create an atmosphere of collegiality and acceptance.

National Council of Schools and Professional Psychology's Defined Core Curriculum Competency in Supervision and Management

The National Council of Schools and Programs in Professional Psychology (NCSPP) advocates for graduate programs to offer comprehensive training in areas in which psychologists are expected to be competent. In addition to the competencies identified by an APA-created task force on the assessment of competence of professional psychology (Fouad et al., 2009; Kaslow et al., 2007, 2009), NCSPP delineates the skills necessary for competent practice that should be included in the core curriculum of education and training programs. Supervision and management is considered to be a combined curriculum area essential for development of competency and is described as consisting of five domains (NCSPP, 2007). As explained by Bent, Schindler, and Dobbins (1991), supervision and management are merged in the core curriculum standards as they share similar skills imperative for trainees' competency in professional psychology. Both involve directing, organizing, and facilitating psychological services to the public; management focuses more on an organization, while supervision focuses on the management of the individual.

According to NCSPP, the first domain of the supervision and management competency to be included in the curriculum of training programs is ensuring the well-being of the client or organization. The committee that created the defining criteria for the supervision and management competency proposed this as the first domain to emphasize the importance of securing client well-being. In the management of an organization and the management of a client (i.e., supervision), the deliverer of services must consider protecting and best serving clients as a priority.

The second domain involves "training and mentoring of supervisees and those being managed." This component refers to the role that managers and supervisors play in educating the people they supervise and manage, being good role models, and ensuring that supervisees are receiving the training they need to facilitate success in their jobs. The third domain involves evaluation and gatekeeping, referring to the role the supervisor and manager play in providing feedback to supervisees on their performance and in ensuring that only those qualified to pursue psychology do so. As a gatekeeper, the clinical psychologist is obligated to protect the public so that only competent people can move forward as psychologists.

The fourth domain of competency in supervision and management relates to ethics. Ethics is a theme that runs throughout all competencies of clinical psychology; in the area of supervision and management it includes being knowledgeable in the ethics code, acting within the ethical standards of professional practice, and ensuring that those being managed and/or supervised are also acting in accordance with professional ethical codes of practice. The fifth and last domain, "healthcare leadership and advocacy," refers to the roles and functions associated with managing programs or organizations as well as influencing organizational, governmental, and societal values and policies in the healthcare arena (NCSPP, 2007).

Many clinical psychologists participate in activities related to supervision and management. Given that supervision and management can be a significant component of a psychologist's professional life, it is evident that they should be essential components of the core curriculum of training programs for professional psychologists. Psychologists in training may find themselves in classes geared toward instruction in these competencies or may encounter opportunities allowing them to practice these competencies in real-life situations. Supervision and management are areas in which all psychologists could benefit from continued training and development.

Teaching

Many clinical psychologists teach. Some assume the role of professor and devote their careers to teaching students at the undergraduate or graduate level. Others choose to fulfill this role by teaching as an adjunct faculty member at a college or university. In addition to formal teaching positions, psychologists perform teaching roles as supervisors and as presenters in various formats such as workshops, in-service programs, continuing education sessions, and case conferences. Furthermore, psychologists can take on a teaching role in news clips and in the papers they publish. The clinical psychologist who chooses to teach as part of his or her professional role must be capable of meeting several important criteria. Unfortunately, like most professors in other disciplines, there is little, if any, training offered in this skill. In fact, it would be safe to say that most clinical psychology professors have never taken a course in education, let alone the art of teaching!

PRINCIPLES OF TEACHING

Psychologists must be competent in the subject area in which they are teaching. If the subject matter is not an area of expertise, they must take the necessary steps to become knowledgeable in that area, as is dictated by the APA's Ethical Principles and Code of Conduct (APA, 2002). *Ethical Dimensions of College and University Teaching: Understanding and Honoring the Special Relationship between Students and Teachers* (Fisch, 1996) delineates several important principles that underlie and pervade the teaching process: honesty, promise-keeping, respect, and fairness.

Honesty   The clinical psychologist in the role of a teacher must be committed to being honest in the disposition of his or her duties by being careful to present all perspectives and to avoid having his or her own preconceptions and biases influence what is taught, how it is taught, and what is conveyed to students. As learners, students have the right to hear the facts presented in a balanced manner, with the pros and cons, assets and limitations, presented openly and honestly. Teachers employ honesty by making their students aware of their own opinions and how these may affect what they learn. Without honesty, a sense of trust may never develop between teacher and learner.

Promise-Keeping   The competent teacher is one who fulfills his or her teaching obligations by agreeing to the contract (i.e., a syllabus) into which students enter. Following the contract includes adhering to the goals, objectives, readings, assignments, and tests as outlined for the course. The syllabus represents a contract with students, clearly delineating the responsibilities and expectations of the participants. This process begins well before a class is initiated, as a great deal of forethought must be exercised about how the content and assignments fit within the overall goals and objectives of the course and, in turn, how these ultimately fit within the mission, goals, and objectives of an educational program. In addition to meeting the students' expectations regarding the syllabus, clinical psychologists are expected to follow through on their commitment to students and the teaching process by returning graded assignments to students in a timely fashion. And when a teacher tells students that he or she will get back to them with specific information, it is incumbent upon the teacher to deliver.

Respect   The educational process is based on a foundation of mutual respect for and between the participants. As a teacher, the clinical psychologist must be acutely aware of the differential power that exists between teacher and student, be cognizant of how that power may manifest itself both inside and outside of the classroom, and respect the boundaries between roles. Competency in teaching includes demonstrated interest in teaching by being approachable and available to students and supportive, respectful, and accepting of student ideas. Moreover, teachers must insist upon respect on the students' part in regard to classroom behavior and consideration of others in the class.

Fairness   Teaching must occur within a context of intention to be fair in all that involves the students. This includes maintaining a sense of fairness and objectivity in judging the performance of students and being aware of factors that may influence the grading of students on subjective assignments. Fairness may manifest itself in a decision to use an electronic device to score an objective exam, to develop and apply a scoring rubric, and to blindly grade papers and essays. Likewise, teachers must ensure that all forms of assessment are tied to the course objectives, promote the acquisition and/or demonstration of competencies, and provide an accurate assessment of the student.

ETHICAL DIMENSIONS OF TEACHING

Understanding and Honoring the Special Relationship between Students and Teachers (Fisch, 1996) also dictates that faculty members abide by a number of critical principles. First, teachers must maintain a high level of competence in the subject matter of the courses they teach; otherwise, the learning of students may be severely undermined. Students rely upon faculty to present courses that are updated and adequately represent the content domain of the subject. Failure to do so may lead to the presentation of outdated material and a biased view of the subject matter. Most importantly, by failing to acquire the most recent information available, students may be shortchanged.

Second, teachers must develop and maintain a level of competence in teaching, including the effective delivery of the material. Psychologists may need to seek out coursework, training programs, readings, and supervision in the pedagogical process. Mentoring in the teaching skill is critical, and graduate departments should provide training and supervision in teaching. Like any other role, a solid grounding in the theory and application of teaching is essential (Svinicki & McKeachie, 2011). Likewise, given the role of technology today, teachers must be familiar with many types of vehicles for delivering course content (e.g., online classrooms, videoconferencing) and proficient in those they choose to use to disseminate information. In addition, knowledge and skill in using audiovisual devices to enhance student learning are necessary. Finally, careful consideration of learning objectives and methods of delivering content and other experiences that maximize learning is essential. For example, attempting to teach the administration of the WISC-IV could not be accomplished without supervised practice regardless of how much knowledge an individual learns about the scales.

Third, as professional teachers, clinical psychologists are committed to foster the professional development of their students. This means providing the requisite knowledge base and written, verbal, and experiential opportunities to develop competencies. Fostering students' development also includes sincerity in teaching on the part of the teacher. Students are aware of the teacher's motivation, passion, and interest in their learning. By providing an environment of enthusiasm for learning, passion for the topic area, and genuine interest and concern for students' well-being and ability to grasp the material, teachers make their commitment evident, and this enhances the students' motivation.

Fourth, collaborating with colleagues is crucial. When faculty members do not get along, students suffer. When there is camaraderie between faculty members, students are provided with an excellent model of collegiality.

Competency Benchmarks

As highlighted throughout this book, there has been a strong move toward a competency-based approach in professional psychology (Falender & Shafranske, 2004). Supervision/teaching and management/administration are areas determined to be Functional Competency domains in psychology (Rodolfa et al., 2005); nevertheless, the field needs clearly defined standards for psychologists to be trained in and to exhibit mastery of to be considered competent (Malloy et al., 2010). In response to this need, Fouad and colleagues (2009) recommend benchmarks that psychologists in training should reach to demonstrate competency in a particular area.

They describe the components necessary for competency at three developmental points in training as well as the behavioral indicators of the competency, providing educators and supervisors with a framework to assess competency in areas fundamental to competent practice. Although the benchmarks created focus on 15 core competencies crucial to psychology, for the purposes of this chapter, the benchmarks related to supervision, management/administration, and teaching will be summarized.

SUPERVISION

Supervision benchmarks, as defined by Fouad and colleagues (2009), encompass many areas. Psychologists in training are expected to be knowledgeable in the process of supervision as well as the roles and responsibilities of both the supervisor and supervisee. They should be able to define professional goals as related to therapy and assessment and evaluate progress toward these goals in the supervisory relationship. As they ready for independent practice, psychologists should have the additional ability to identify, describe, and apply a personal model of supervision. Competent clinical psychologists are aware of issues of competency in supervision and are able to articulate a plan for dealing with these issues when they arise.

Skill development and participation in the supervisory process are defined as additional benchmarks essential to competent practice. For the training psychologist beginning practicum experiences, skill development and participation include the ability to communicate effectively and accept feedback from supervisors. Trainees ready for internship should have completed coursework on supervision and be knowledgeable in the area of clinical skill development based on the supervision literature. Furthermore, readiness for internship includes the ability to initiate and seek supervision, integrate feedback into practice, and reflect upon the supervisory process itself. Those ready for independent practice are additionally expected to be able to articulate and provide supervision to develop the skills of other clinicians and to facilitate excellent care to clients.

Psychologists in training should demonstrate knowledge and sensitivity regarding individual and cultural differences and recognize how these differences may play a role in the supervisory process. Psychologists in training ready for internship are able to integrate issues of diversity in the supervisory context and demonstrate sensitivity to differences in the provision of supervision. Basic knowledge of ethical and legal issues surrounding the practice of supervision is a necessary component of competency, and as clinical psychologists begin independent practice, understanding and demonstrating ethical, legal, and professional standards related to supervision is essential.

MANAGEMENT

The competency of management as defined by Fouad and colleagues (2009) encompasses several components. The first element of competent practice involves management itself, including managing the delivery of professional services and responding appropriately to the process and hierarchy of management. Administration, considered to be another component of the management competency, includes awareness of and compliance with policies and procedures such as timeliness, appropriate recordkeeping, and quality assurance. Furthermore, as psychologists in training progress, involvement in the development of these policies is appropriate. Leadership is the third benchmark related to the management competency. As psychologists advance in graduate programs, they begin to demonstrate leadership skills by participating in system change, implementation of ideas, and accomplishment of set objectives. Lastly, evaluating management and leadership abilities is the final competency benchmark. This is highlighted by the ability to identify the strengths and weaknesses of an organization and/or leadership and to describe how to be an effective manager and leader.

TEACHING

Regarding the competency of teaching, Fouad and colleagues (2009) propose two basic benchmarks: knowledge and teaching skills. Psychologists in training should acquire knowledge about different teaching and learning styles, outcome-assessment tools, and how to assess teaching effectiveness and should be able to communicate effectively. They should be able to present coherently on a specific topic, and as they ready for internship, they should be able to describe different teaching methods, flexibly apply any learning accommodations needed, and demonstrate creativity in the teaching process. As psychologists ready for independent practice, they should be able to effectively teach on a variety of topics, assess the success of the learning, and integrate feedback on the teaching process for future endeavors.

Competency Assessment

As professional psychology turned toward a competency-based focus in education and training (Kaslow et al, 2004), the need for a systematic way to assess Foundational and Functional Competencies became evident. In response to this need, APA appointed a work group to develop an assessment toolkit that would provide training programs with a mechanism for methodical assessment of competencies (Kaslow et al., 2009). In addition to outlining various assessment tools, Kaslow and colleagues (2009) rate the usefulness of these measures for evaluating specific areas of competency.

SUPERVISION

Supervision itself can be effectively evaluated in a myriad of ways. Kaslow and colleagues (2009) report many of these methods as being "very useful" for assessment. Annual reviews, rating forms, and 360-degree evaluations are considered to be useful methods of assessing the supervision competency. Descriptions of these assessment tools and their utility are provided in the following management and teaching sections. In addition, role-plays and case and record reviews are deemed to be helpful assessment techniques.

Role-plays are artificial interactions or skits where people play different roles to learn or practice a skill. For supervisory purposes, the most common form of role-play would include the enactment of therapist and client interactions. The benefit of this type of assessment is that it provides an opportunity for psychologists in training to practice new skills and to demonstrate competency in specific areas, albeit within simulated circumstances. The artificial nature of the reproduction of interactions can also present a challenge: the imitation of real life is just that, imitation, and may not fully represent the intricacies and seriousness of the reality of situations. In addition, people may act differently when they know the situation is not real as compared to when they are facing a real-life crisis. Nevertheless, role-plays can be used as a tool to evaluate supervisees' abilities to apply particular therapeutic skills.

Case and record reviews are methods of evaluating competency via summaries of client history, treatment intervention, and treatment progress and outcome. Record reviews require the review of the client's chart to determine quality of care, accuracy of the diagnosis and treatment plan, implementation of therapeutic interventions, course of treatment, and competency of the treating therapist. Benefits of this type of assessment include its low cost and the fact that cases can be reviewed retroactively and over time. However, reading a record does not provide a full picture of the nuances of treatment implementation, process, and outcome. Furthermore, case reviews rely on the therapist to provide a summary of the case, which in itself holds potential bias. Nevertheless, case reviews are often performed in a presentation style, allowing the evaluators to ask questions and discuss the case with the treating psychologist. Having the ability to discuss the case creates an environment more conducive to accurately evaluating competency.

MANAGEMENT

When assessing for managerial competencies, Kaslow and colleagues (2009) suggest two different methods as being "very useful" tools of assessment. The 360-degree evaluation is a broad-based evaluation of competency based on ratings from raters knowledgeable in different aspects of the psychologist's life. Raters can be recruited from a myriad of personal associations, such as supervisors, peers, supervisees, as well as the individual himself or herself. This is an excellent method of evaluating a broad range of behaviors, as it fosters the gathering and combining of information from multiple reporters in multiple settings and allows the person being evaluated the opportunity to see how he or she is viewed by others as well as help to identify areas of strength and areas in need of improvement. The challenges of this type of assessment include the difficulty in creating questions general enough to be applicable to all those who may be involved in the evaluation. In addition, it may be difficult to collate and understand the information when it is coming from many raters; some raters may be questionable in terms of accuracy of report. Furthermore, this type of assessment is time-intensive and can be a costly approach to evaluation.

Another type of assessment touted as being "very useful" for assessing competency in management is the consumer survey (Kaslow et al., 2009). Consumer surveys evaluate consumer satisfaction with services provided—not necessarily the outcome or progress, but rather the consumer's perception of satisfaction and fulfilled expectations. Consumer surveys are easily administered and scored and cost-effective to implement. Concerns related to consumer surveys focus on the data itself: how the measures are solicited, language barriers, motives of completion, and honesty in reporting. Nevertheless, these concerns can be relevant to any measure, so although limitations should be recognized and considered, there may be more benefits than limitations for using this type of evaluation to assess managerial competency.

TEACHING

Kaslow and colleagues (2009) recommend several methods deemed to be "very useful" in assessing teaching competence. One of these methods, annual performance reviews, can be performed by supervisors, faculty, and sometimes peers to evaluate specific competences delineated in the review. Annual performance reviews are easy and inexpensive to administer and allow for multiple competencies to be evaluated by multiple raters. Similarly, rating forms in which behaviors are rated on a Likert scale are also useful evaluation tools of teaching competency. They provide an easy, cost-effective method for assessing competency and pinpoint areas of strength and areas in need of improvement.

Finally, self-assessments provide a means of evaluation allowing the psychologist in training to become increasingly aware of successes and disappointments in teaching and whether predetermined goals are being achieved. Self-assessments allow for self-reflection and the recognition of competency levels in different areas of teaching; however, self-assessments can be biased because the self-observer must be particularly astute to accurately appraise his or her own performance.

SELF-ASSESSMENT ACROSS COMPETENCIES

Self-assessment can be an effective method of assessing many types of competencies. In self-assessment, the person being assessed is responsible for determining his or her areas of strength and areas in need of improvement, creating a plan to address the areas in need of improvement, and monitoring his or her performance and development in these areas. Self-assessment provides the person with an opportunity to be more cognizant of his or her behavior and to be proactive in making changes as appropriate. Benefits to this type of assessment are that the person being evaluated becomes more aware of his or her competencies and the assessment method facilitates self-reflection. The main challenge of self-assessment is that it requires accurate evaluations and perceptions, something that is difficult to do: people tend to overestimate their abilities. Self-assessment is best used in combination with other assessment methods, such as the 360-degree evaluation model, which can include self-assessment as part of the complete evaluation. Self-assessment has been deemed to be a "very useful" evaluation tool for all types of competencies, including the areas discussed in this chapter: supervision, management, administration, and teaching.

Conclusions

Supervision, management, administration, and teaching are activities clinical psychologists may be involved in on a daily basis. Establishing competency as a clinical psychologist, therefore, includes demonstrating competency in these skills. More recently, advances such as the development of (1) core competencies in professional psychology (Donovan & Ponce, 2009), (2) benchmarks for measuring competency across training levels (Fouad et al., 2009), and (3) assessment tools for evaluating competency (Kaslow et al., 2009) have made it easier for graduate programs to tailor training to highlight the areas necessary for competent professional practice in clinical psychology.

Instructing and guiding students to become competent therapists requires many steps. Psychologists in training must become fluent in the therapies and techniques they are implementing with clients and exhibit strong interpersonal skills. Supervisors must have the knowledge base and competency to direct and guide students in the therapist role. Furthermore, supervisors must possess their own strengths in both interpersonal skills and the provision of therapy to serve as skilled role models. Moreover, it is important for supervisors to form positive relationships with their supervisees to create a comfortable environment for sharing successes and challenges and accepting and receiving feedback openly.

Given that supervision can be considered a type of management, the areas reflecting competency in supervision are similar to those for management and administration. To be a competent manager and administrator, a psychologist must have a solid knowledge base in the area that requires management. Managers are quite often interacting with others, so clinical psychologists in the role of managers must possess strong interpersonal skills fostering the resolution of conflicts, problem-solving, and the effective management of people and situations. Administrators must have similar expertise, in addition to proficiency in organizational issues such as creating and adhering to policies and procedures and budget planning. The training of clinical psychologists encourages a smooth transition to a managerial or administrative role, as many activities carried out by psychologists involve the facilitation of positive interpersonal relationships and are in the realm of management and administration.

There is an art and science to teaching that encompasses important competencies. These competencies fall within the realm of content domains, instruction, relationships with students, and evaluation of student performance. Clinical psychologists have a responsibility toward students to be proficient in teaching methods and evaluation and to be knowledgeable in the areas they are teaching. In addition to expertise in the areas being taught and skillful manner of presenting the information, clinical psychologists in the teaching role should be adept at establishing positive, respectful relationships with their students. Teaching itself should parallel working with clients in the sense that the clinical psychologist demonstrates competencies related to the area of practice—in this case, teaching.

The clinical psychologist must be competent in the areas in which he or she chooses to participate in professional practice. This chapter touched upon several activities psychologists may find themselves involved in and issues to consider in maintaining competency. Whether the clinical psychologist is in a supervision session, teaching a course, or managing a private practice, he or she must perform at optimal levels to ensure high-quality care to clients, exceptional guidance and support to students, and excellence in leadership.

TEN

Science Base and Research Competency

Role of Science in Clinical Psychology

Scientific training is an important element in the preparation of clinical psychologists, regardless of whether they are ultimately active in research as a professional. Scientific methods and critical examination should be integrated into training and practice itself (Belar & Perry, 1992). Of course, whether doctoral training in clinical psychology has actually realized this goal today is grounds for debate. Nonetheless, the critical importance of empirically based decision-making in clinical psychology is clear.

The role of an empirical basis for clinical practice is fundamental to clinical psychology as a discipline. This scientifically minded approach is rooted in the training of clinical psychologists as demonstrated through established theories, research, and principles and constructs in the science of psychology, and the scientific basis of professional practice itself. Clinical psychologists must be thoroughly grounded in areas such as the biological, social, cognitive, affective, and developmental foundations of behavior, abnormality, and individual differences as well as the means and methods of scientific inquiry, research design and methodology, evaluation strategies, and methods of data analysis (see Belar & Perry, 1992). Moreover, clinical psychologists must be trained in the scientific underpinnings of professional practice specifically related to the roles they fulfill in practicing their craft, including assessment, diagnosis, and intervention, including skills in relationship formation and sensitivity to individual and cultural diversity and ethical considerations. Clinical psychologists must become critical consumers of the professional literature, experts in the knowledge base relevant to their practice, and skilled in applying this evolving knowledge, all in the interest of providing services that will engender clinically significant change in those who seek services.

Given the significance of the scientific competence, there is consensus that training in "scientific-mindedness" should actually begin at the undergraduate level (see Bieschke, Fouad, Collins, & Halonen, 2004). Halonen and colleagues have proposed a rubric for training undergraduates in the skill of scientific inquiry that incorporates eight categories of scientific-mindedness: (a) descriptive skills, (b) conceptualization, (c) problem-solving, (d) ethical reasoning, (e) scientific values and attitudes, (f) communication skills, (g) collaboration skills, and (h) self-assessment (Halonen, Bosack, Clay, & McCarthy, 2003). This recommendation is similar to the consensus statement advanced by the American Psychological Association (APA)'s Scientific Foundations and Research Competencies Work Group (Bieschke et al., 2004; Sexton, Hanes, & Kinser, 2010). This work group proposed five fundamental subcomponents of the scientifically minded competency (Bieschke et al., 2004):

1. Identify and apply current scientific knowledge consistently and appropriately
2. Contribute to body of knowledge
3. Critically review interventions and associated outcomes
4. Remain vigilant about sociocultural variables' impact on scientific practice
5. Routinely present one's work to the scrutiny of colleagues, stakeholders, and the public

While there is consensus that scientific-mindedness is central to the identity of clinical psychology, there is pluralism when it comes to the training models favored to impart these skills. We review the two dominant doctoral training models here, the scientist-practitioner model and the practitioner-scholar model.

Training Models in Clinical Psychology

SCIENTIST-PRACTITIONER MODEL

The primary principles of the scientist-practitioner model are critical thinking and bridging the gap between science and practice (Belar & Perry, 1992). Jones and Mehr (2007) further articulated three vital assumptions at the core of the scientist-practitioner model: (1) Psychologists are expected to develop the requisite knowledge and skills to both produce and consume scientific knowledge generated by clinical research in order to facilitate effective psychological practice; (2) Research is necessary to develop a knowledge base of successful practice; and (3) Direct involvement in clinical practice and research activities interacts in a manner that contributes to the study of important social issues. In short, the ideal realization of the scientist-practitioner model is a professional who uses systematic scientific methods to develop, guide, and enhance his or her practice, with the client's best interest of paramount importance (Jones & Mehr, 2007).

However, the scientist-practitioner model has been criticized on several grounds. Proponents of the Vail model (the "practitioner-scholar" model of graduate training in clinical psychology) have posed the questions: *If you are looking to produce expert clinicians, how would you "backwards plan" graduate training? Would you ground the training in research, or would you emphasize clinical foundations?* Proponents of the Vail model argue the latter. While the Boulder model (the scientist-practitioner model of graduate training in clinical psychology) has long been the dominant training model, graduate schools following the alternative practitioner-scholar model graduate a greater (and increasing) number of clinical psychologists (see Peterson, 2003).

PRACTITIONER-SCHOLAR MODEL

The Vail model of training focuses primarily on training clinicians who are practitioner-scholars. These are professional psychologists who are trained to be master clinicians and who use the professional literature as a basis for solving questions relevant to their clinical practice. Training in the Vail model emphasizes the use of the research literature to inform one's practice. However, many graduate programs in clinical psychology following the Vail model require an empirical dissertation, giving students training in formulating and testing hypotheses, data collection, data interpretation, and drawing conclusions.

Clinical Psychologists as Producers of Research and Science

Regardless of their training, clinical psychologists contribute to knowledge in a variety of ways. Some clinical psychologists, especially those in research-oriented academic settings, develop programs of research in clearly defined areas that systematically seek to answer questions over a series of investigations. These investigations, funded or unfunded, provide opportunities for clinical psychology faculty to mentor students in the art and science of conducting research. Others, especially practitioners from some theoretical orientations, systematically evaluate patient progress in treatment through the repeated administration of valid and reliable assessment tools. In applied settings, clinical psychologists might also seek to evaluate the impact of a program being delivered to patients in a particular setting. And of course, scientist-practitioner clinical psychologists developing new treatments and novel applications are the predominant force behind psychotherapy treatment outcome studies.

Gap Between Science and Practice

There is little question that the much-discussed gap between science and practice has persisted for many years in the field of clinical psychology. While trained in the same specialty, researchers and practitioners in clinical psychology have traditionally had very different, if not opposing, perspectives. Clinicians often believed that randomized controlled trials (RCTs) bore little resemblance to what they did in the consulting room with a given patient with a given problem. And clinicians, like most of us, place a value on autonomy. As Kazdin (2008) conciliatorily points out, however: "Research and practice are united in their commitment to providing the best of psychological knowledge and methods to improve the quality of patient care" (p. 146).

Problems of Dissemination and Translation

Nonetheless, problems remain regarding the dissemination of research findings into clinical and community settings. Also of note is the time lag between research discoveries and implementation. For example, proponents of interpersonal therapy (IPT) bemoan the three-decade lag between research findings supporting IPT and implementation in routine clinical practice in the United States (see Chapter 4; Stuart, Roberston, & O'Hara, 2006).

Sexton and colleagues (2010) have offered the following four attitudes as prerequisites to bridging science into practice: (1) a scientific-mindedness to both research and practice; (2) an essential curiosity about how things work and what works, as well as an openness to new explanations and theories; (3) an acceptance of the inherent ambiguity and evolutionary nature of what we know about practice and research; and (4) a willingness to embrace the dialectical nature of science and practice.

The fact that clinical psychologists are trained within different models certainly contributes to this gap, but another, more systemic factor bears consideration here: contingencies and incentives.

In countries such as the United Kingdom where there is nationalized medicine and the bill for psychological services is ultimately footed by the government, guidelines enforcing evidence-based practice can easily be implemented at the federal level. For example, in the United Kingdom, the government has allocated more than a half-billion U.S. dollars toward training clinicians in empirically supported treatments such as cognitive-behavioral therapy. Without training in evidence-based psychological treatments, clinicians may struggle to make a living. While the United States is certainly moving in the direction of evidence-based practice and greater accountability, the contrast is clear.

Clinical Psychologists as Consumers

Do clinical psychologists who practice as full-time clinicians read the research literature? Do they need to?

EFFECTIVENESS (BENCHMARKING STUDIES)

First, ultimately, clinical psychologists are consumers of the scientific literature. Witness the proliferation of manualized treatments and popular professional volumes such as Peter Nathan's *What Works for Whom?*, in its second edition at the time of this writing. While some critics have dismissed the research literature (e.g., clinical trials) as irrelevant to clinical practice (see Westen, Novotny, & Thompson-Brenner, 2004), a movement toward investigating efficacy has overcome many of those criticisms. A growing body of research (benchmarking studies) has demonstrated that, in fact, when manualized treatments previously supported by RCTs are applied to real-life clinical settings, these treatments show effectiveness comparable to the RCT. These benchmarking studies have, in part, assuaged the concern for some that the participants in RCTs are so dissimilar to real-life, everyday patients that the treatment's effects would not generalize to the general outpatient population. In fact, researchers have documented that clinical trial participants are, indeed, typically a more chronic, comorbid, and refractory patient population and tougher to treat (Crits-Cristoph, Wilson, & Hollon, 2005; Wilson, 1997). When benchmarking studies are conducted, inclusion and exclusion criteria are relaxed and fewer prospective participants are excluded. Studies applying an empirically supported manualized treatment for social anxiety disorder, for example, have shown comparable effectiveness in a real-life outpatient population (e.g., Wade, Treat, & Stuart, 1998).

Despite this proliferation of evidence, the impact of clinical research on clinical practice has long been modest—hence the aforementioned gap (Barlow, 1981; Nathan, 2000). With many notable exceptions, practicing clinical psychologists, on the whole, are only minimally aware of recent clinical research findings and mistakenly believe that the research evidence for evidence-based psychotherapy is weaker than it actually is. Indeed, even leading clinical research "experts" endorse beliefs about psychotherapy that are unsupported by research (Boisvert & Faust, 2003, 2006).

While the technology of psychological treatments has advanced, barriers to dissemination remain. First, there is simply not an existing business model for psychological treatments comparable to that of the pharmaceutical industry, where significant monies are budgeted toward clinician education and marketing (see DiTomasso, Cahn, Cirilli, & Mochan, 2010). Consider that from January to September 2007 alone, Sepracor spent a staggering $264.4 million in the direct-to-consumer marketing of one single drug for insomnia (Lunesta), and this even represents a decline from the same period the prior year (DiTomasso et al., 2010; "Spending Review," 2008). As an important aside, the evidence base supporting pharmacological psychiatric treatments may give one pause when both published and unpublished studies are examined in totality. In a provocative study made possible by the Freedom of Information Act, 94% of studies favorable to antidepressants went on to be published in the medical literature, whereas only half of studies with negative findings did so (Turner, Matthews, Linardatos, Tell, & Rosenthal, 2008). The advertising-fueled popularity of antidepressants, contrasted with their arguably misrepresented, if not unimpressive, empirical support, provides an elegant counterpoint to empirically supported psychological treatments: psychological treatments have a negligible, if existing, marketing budget—a clear barrier to dissemination. This phenomenon certainly contributes to the significant time lag between the advent and empirical support of a treatment and when (and if) it becomes widely adopted. Clearly, training in, and understanding of, psychological treatments and their associated empirical support is a significant component of the science competence in clinical psychology. The absence of an analogous system of dissemination and incentives clearly presents an obstacle for clinical psychologists to attaining scientific competence.

In an effort to address this disparity between the state of science and practice, the APA established a Presidential Task Force on Evidence-Based Practice (APA Presidential Task Force, 2006). This task force notably proclaimed that "psychology—as a science and as a profession—is distinctive in combining scientific commitment with an emphasis on human relationships and individual differences" (p. 6). Division 12 (Clinical Psychology) of APA also maintains a website with free access that lists and periodically updates empirically supported psychological treatments for various psychological (and medical) disorders (www.psychologicaltreatments.org).

CONTINUED COMPETENCE

Despite professional psychologists' unfamiliarity with the latest outcome research, the requirement for continuing education is standard practice for licensure. At the time of this writing, every state and the District of Columbia require continuing education for psychologists' licensure, with the exception of seven states: Colorado, Connecticut, Hawaii, Illinois, Michigan, New Jersey, and New York (APA, 2006). The APA defines continuing education in psychology as "an ongoing process consisting of formal learning activities that: (1) are relevant to psychological practice, education, and science; (2) enable psychologists to keep pace with emerging issues and technologies; and (3) allow psychologists to maintain, develop, and increase competencies in order to improve services to the public and enhance contributions to the profession" (APA, 2005a, p. 2). While the APA does not require that continuing education programs document their efficacy or empirical basis, psychologists must have some competency in science and research or critical thinking to discern the ultimate effectiveness, or at least scientific basis, of the presented approach.

ACCOUNTABILITY

There is a strong movement toward accountability in the field. Practically speaking, clinical psychologists are under increasing scrutiny to justify their treatment plans and interventions. There are documented instances of health insurance companies such as Oxford Health Plans retroactively denying psychotherapy insurance claims in New York, New Jersey, and Connecticut. After auditing patient records, the health insurance company demanded that psychiatrists repay between $10,000 and $150,000 because the psychotherapy was insufficiently documented; Oxford even deemed the associated psychotherapy notes as insufficient documentation that patients received the services billed (Perez-Peña, 2003). In the

United Kingdom, the government will not pay for treatment that is not empirically supported if there is an alternate treatment available with greater documented efficacy (see National Institute of Clinical Excellence; http://www.nice.org.uk/).

What Is the Risk of *Not* Having Competence in Science and Research?

There is increasing awareness that applying a treatment lacking empirical support may come at considerable risk to the patient. The most common risk to the patient is the waste of time and money and the absence of improvement. Increasingly, however, data are suggesting that, in addition to not improving, some clients are actually demonstrably harmed by psychological treatments. This is not a theoretical concern founded on fear and speculation: 10% of patients have been found to get worse as a result of psychotherapy (Boisvert & Faust, 2003).

Unfortunately, potentially harmful psychological treatments have been documented (e.g., Lilienfeld, 2007). A notable example is "critical stress debriefing," traditionally used during times of natural disaster, mass violence, and terrorism, including after September 11, 2001 (see Lilienfeld, 2007). This brief treatment was designed to be implemented with large groups of survivors at the time of the incident to prevent later onset of posttraumatic stress disorder (PTSD). Despite having a reasonable theoretical rationale, recent research indicates a lack of scientific support that individuals will benefit from this treatment; in fact, it is associated with an increased risk that survivors will develop PTSD (see Lilienfeld, 2007).

Clearly, clients may get worse from psychotherapy despite psychologists' best efforts. Indeed, interventions with perhaps the best of intentions, including "boot camps" for troubled children and "scared straight" crime-prevention programs, have been associated with exacerbation rather than amelioration of the problem in a notable proportion of participants (see Lilienfeld, 2007). Such findings may remind us of the medical adage *Primum non nocere—first do no harm*. Indeed, the principle of nonmaleficence is an explicit part of the APA's ethical code (2002). In fact, in an extreme example, a "rebirthing" intervention (an intervention devoid of empirical support) ended in the death of a 12-year-old girl, Candace Newmaker, and jail time for the "clinicians" (Lowe, 2001). Clearly, if clinical psychologists are to (a) abide by their ethical code and do no harm and (b) be secure in their accountability, we must be knowledgeable in what works for whom and practice only within our scope of competence.

By obtaining and utilizing this competency, clinical psychologists can potentially make better-informed clinical decisions, even if that decision is to refer out.

Relying on clinical intuition and general clinical skills can thus be woefully inadequate, particularly when facing presenting problems outside one's competence. This reinforces the need for clinical psychologists to be competent in accessing and critically evaluating the available treatment research (e.g., RCTs) for a given disorder (e.g., social anxiety disorder).

Clinical Psychologists as Local Clinical Scientists

While clinical psychologists have long been known to be both producers and consumers of the research literature, some have advocated for greater recognition of the scientific method as applied in clinical practice on a patient-by-patient basis (Peterson, Peterson, Abrams, & Stricker, 1997). The "local clinical scientist" model emphasizes the importance of "specific space-time, local factors" (Trierweiler, Stricker, & Peterson, 2010) and the clinician as applied scientist, constantly developing and testing theories about the client, including diagnosis, case formulation, and appropriate interventions. The local clinical scientist model is closely aligned with the Vail practitioner-scholar model of training discussed earlier.

At this time, the local clinical scientist model is fundamentally an aspirational model of clinical practice. It prescribes a scientific approach to conducting psychotherapy and regards clinical practice as a form of data collection. The model explains how clinicians should analyze new information, synthesize it with existing information, and/or alter the prevailing conceptualization of the client's problems and behaviors, and ultimately respond in the moment with a client and continuously throughout the course of treatment. In this way, Trierweiler and colleagues (2010) draw a parallel with the scientific method, equating the clinician with the scientist. Similarly, Rodolfa and colleagues (2005) have advocated a cube model to establish competencies in these areas, but to our knowledge there are no data yet establishing the feasibility of such an assessment system. At this time, it is unclear how such skills would be operationalized and practically taught and naturalistically evaluated. In fact, whether, and to what degree, clinicians can, and do, simultaneously consider multiple factors and continuously integrate them into their clinical decision-making in an ongoing, scientific, and unbiased manner is debatable and yet unproven (Dawes, 1996; Wilson, 1997).

While it is appealing to view the clinical psychologist as functioning as a local clinical scientist, there is ample evidence to suggest that even if clinicians choose to work in such a fashion, our biases and heuristics as human beings can limit our ability to do so (see Dawes, 1996). In fact, empirical data suggest that, in reality, once clinicians establish a diagnosis, they rarely change it. Clinicians' case formulations are also notoriously resistant to change, and it's in our nature to discount disconfirming evidence rather than abandon our original formulation (see Dawes 1996; Wilson, 1997). Of critical importance, and perhaps ironically, there is yet no body of scientific research establishing that adopting a "local clinical scientist" approach yields outcomes superior to those associated with empirically supported treatment manuals. This remains a testable hypothesis, however.

In conclusion, there is a strong and growing science base within the field of clinical psychology. Future directions for optimizing science-based competence may include (a) the expansion of clinical practice networks so that the accumulated knowledge and experience of clinicians in practice is not lost (Kazdin, 2008); (b) the proliferation of clinician-friendly, transdiagnostic, empirically supported manuals, such as a unified protocol for emotional disorders (Barlow, 2010a); and (c) progressive efforts to define, operationalize, train, and assess clinical psychologist trainees in the research and evaluation competency (e.g., Kenkel & Peterson, 2010; Rodolfa et al., 2005). Ultimately, in today's climate of accountability and outcomes assessment, the competent clinical psychologist must be trained to provide and evaluate appropriate clinical services that maximize the likelihood of generating clinically meaningful outcomes.

Benchmarks for Competency in Scientific Knowledge and Methods

The important role of scientific knowledge and methods as a foundation for competent clinical practice is undoubtedly a given today. Fouad and colleagues (2009) have made a solid case for this viewpoint by clearly defining and delineating critical competency benchmarks in this domain, specifically regarding understanding of research in psychology, its methods of scientific inquiry, and the role of the biological, cognitive, social, and affective bases in explaining behavior. Competent clinicians must respect, understand, and apply all that psychological science offers in their daily professional work. Thus, competent clinical psychologists approach their professional work with a scientific mindset that drives the application of scientific methodology in the service of clinical practice.

Assessing Competency in Scientific Knowledge and Methods

As delineated by Kaslow and colleagues (2009), there are a variety of "useful" and "very useful" strategies for assessing competency in this domain. These tools include annual reviews, written examinations, and standardized oral exams for assessing scientific attitudes and foundations of psychology. For assessment of the scientific basis of professional practice, they recommend case reviews, consumer surveys, objective structured clinical examinations, portfolio reviews, performance ratings, and the use of standardized cases. Competent practitioners in clinical psychology seek a variety of methods of formative and summative feedback as a means for evaluating, sustaining, and enhancing their competencies in this important domain.

Concluding Remarks

The importance of scientific training in clinical psychology is paramount. In contemporary professional practice, consumers (and insurers) expect that professional services have some basis in evidence. Competent clinical psychologists embrace scientific skepticism and use the core knowledge base in clinical psychology as the foundation for professional practice. Clinical psychologists have a responsibility to keep abreast of the evolving body of knowledge in the field, especially as it relates to the delivery of services.

PART V

Foundational Competencies

ELEVEN

Relationship Competency

Undoubtedly, one of the most important competencies of the clinical psychologist is the relationship competency. This competency was initially defined by McHolland (1992) as "the capacity to develop and maintain a constructive working alliance with clients…including but not limited to (a) intellectual curiosity and flexibility, (b) open-mindedness, (c) belief in the capacity for change in human attitudes and behavior, (d) appreciation of individual and cultural diversity, (e) personal integrity and honesty, and (f) a value of self-awareness" (p. 162). The important contributions of the therapy relationship across a variety of psychotherapeutic models have been highlighted for many years by many different authors (Norcross, 2002; Duncan, Miller, Wampold, & Hubble, 2010; Wampold, 2005). Recently, however, Peterson et al. (1997) expanded the definition to include the capability of the psychologist to collaboratively interface with numerous others, such as peers, coworkers, learners, supervisors, professionals outside of psychology, and even organizations. This competency, foundational in nature, is so important that it permeates every professional interaction of the clinical psychologist. It reflects the ability of the psychologist to use himself or herself as a tool to accomplish professional tasks both within and outside of the consulting room. It is virtually inconceivable, then, to consider the roles and functions of a clinical psychologist without considering the impact of the professional relationship.

In this chapter, we review the following: how the relationship competency fuels the effectiveness of the various roles clinical psychologists assume; what specifically constitutes effective relating in clinical psychology; the working alliance and its relationship to clinical outcome; positive and negative therapist characteristics; relationship skills and interprofessional collaboration; fostering the development of relationship skills; relationship competency benchmarks; and assessment of competence in this domain.

Professional Roles

Considering the typical roles assumed by the clinical psychologist allows for a fuller appreciation of the crucial importance of the relationship competency. In their daily work, clinical psychologists may engage in one or more of a variety of professional roles. These roles include clinician, teacher, mentor, consultant, supervisor, administrator, and researcher (DiTomasso, Knapp, Golden, Morris, & Veit, 2010). A careful examination of the interpersonal substrate of each of these roles reveals that deficiencies in the competency realm may undermine the potential for achieving success as a clinical psychologist in each area. We posit that the relationship competency is the common underlying thread that binds together each role the clinical psychologist assumes in his or her professional work.

CLINICIAN

Much of the available research in this area has focused on the critical role of the relationship competency in face-to-face clinical work (Duncan et al., 2010; Norcross, 2002; Wampold, 2005). Clinical psychologists often provide direct services related to psychological interventions with their clients. As we review later, there is a substantial amount of sound evidence today to support the critical importance of the relationship in psychotherapy. The relationship may thus be considered a critical factor in fostering client change. There is also much reason to believe that relationship factors may be just as important in other realms of professional practice, such as teaching and mentoring students.

TEACHER AND MENTOR

The art of teaching and mentoring requires the ability to establish a relationship with learners in ways that serve as a basis for motivating and fostering role modeling (Svinicki & McKeachie, 2011) as well as the acquisition of important attitudes, knowledge, and skills. The relationship medium provides a mechanism through which students and mentees come to identify with professors, emulate them, and imitate them. Learners are more likely to be positively influenced by teachers with whom they share a positive relationship.

CONSULTANT

As a consultant, the clinical psychologist must be adept at establishing a trusting relationship that allows the consultee to join forces with the consultant in seeking a solution to a professional problem in which the consultant has expertise. The relationship competency undoubtedly plays an important role in this regard. The consultation relationship is embedded in an atmosphere of trust and safety in which the consultee must be free to share his or her questions and problems related to a challenging professional dilemma. In effect, consultees must be comfortable enough to risk demonstrating their knowledge and skill deficits and blind spots, accept the feedback, and take away from the consultative relationship useful problem-solving strategies.

LEADER

The charisma of many successful leaders and administrators finds its expression in their abilities to form functional relationships with their staff. Effective leaders can bond with their staff members, motivate them, and provide direction, feedback, evaluation, and coaching. Effective leaders use their relationship skills as a means to encourage staff members in the pursuit of mutual goals that are critical to the success of an organization.

SUPERVISOR

Valuing the strengths and attributes of supervisees and recognizing areas in need of improvement are more easily achieved in the context of a sound supervisory relationship. Effective supervision fosters the supervisee's participation in activities such as self-reflection, problem identification, goal setting, treatment planning, and implementation and evaluation of solutions. Effective supervisors create a safe atmosphere in which supervisees are free to risk sharing what they do not yet know and acquiring critical knowledge about themselves and their craft.

RESEARCHER

Finally, as a researcher, the importance of collaborating with other scholars, securing settings in which to gather data, and handling the sensitive nature of data collection with participants is clear. In the pursuit of knowledge, collaborating with fellow scientists is also essential and proceeds through numerous stages in which relationship skills and negotiation play an important role.

In summary, the relationship capacity of the professional psychologist is crucial because it cuts across several domains related to critical roles and functions. On the other hand, of course, the relational competency does not necessarily guarantee competency in other functional domains: it is not difficult to imagine a person with good relational skills who lacks the technical knowledge and skills to perform his or her role competently. On the other hand, there are some excellent technicians who leave much to be desired in their social skills with clients. The point is that relationship factors appear to provide a solid foundation for promoting effective performance in a variety of key areas. What factors, then, promote competence in the establishment of effective professional relationships?

Components of Effective Relating

Embedded within the relationship competency are a number of characteristics that form the basis for effective relating. There is some controversy as to whether individuals naturally possess relationship characteristics or whether individuals can learn them. Truth is likely to be found in both views (Mangione & Nadkarni, 2010). These characteristics include, but are not limited to, the ability of the psychologist to do a number of things: engender, establish, and nurture trust; form collaborative working relationships; convey respect, warmth, understanding, and empathy for others; maintain appropriate professional boundaries; foster a sense of teamwork; facilitate a sense of professional togetherness; convey openness to alternative ways of viewing things; express openness to differences; possess the capability for self-reflection and assessment; maintain an objective stance; demonstrate flexibility in relating; express the ability to negotiate differences; assimilate and abide by the norms of the profession; identify as a clinical psychologist; offer constructive feedback; and receive and benefit from feedback (Mangione & Nadkarni, 2010). These characteristics are essential to the daily professional functioning of the clinical psychologist; it is difficult to imagine that one would be able to do any of the things we expect the clinical psychologist to competently perform without these foundational relationship characteristics and skills.

A clinical psychologist's work includes interfacing with clients or patients, peers, and professionals outside of clinical psychology. Considering the multitude of possible interactions within and across each group, we contend that the relationship competency forms the core ingredient in the clinical psychologist's ability to navigate through the often complex, difficult, and challenging encounters and situations he or she confronts. Competency in this domain is therefore critical. Before discussing competency in working with different groups of individuals in more depth, it is important to consider the advantages of establishing and maintaining sound professional relationship skills.

ADVANTAGES OF RELATIONSHIP COMPETENCY

The relationship competency has been described as special, foundational, undergirding, central, developmental, complex, and cross-cutting (Mangione & Nadkarni, 2010). An examination of the common elements across each domain underscores the absolute importance of this competency, which, in essence, encompasses a sort of relational fitness to carry out the duties, roles, functions, and responsibilities of the clinical psychologist. We consider *relational fitness* as the inherent capacity to engage in those facilitative behaviors that are requisite to the daily functioning of the clinical psychologist. Individual differences in this construct may be used to form the basis for decisions regarding selection for entry into graduate clinical psychology programs, necessity for remediation, continuation in graduate programs, and, ultimately, graduation, licensure, and specialty certification as a professional.

On any given day a clinical psychologist may find himself or herself in any one or more of a variety of professional situations, such as assessing and treating a client, providing clinical supervision to an intern, or perhaps even collaborating with a primary care physician in treating a chronically ill patient. While success in each of these areas may require different, albeit somewhat related, functional skill sets, the common overarching outcome, in part, relies on the interpersonal skills of the clinical psychologist. The extent to which the clinical psychologist possesses and conveys relationship skills may in a real sense turn out to be as important, if not even more important at times, than what he or she knows. One might even argue that relationship skills are a prerequisite to effective work in each of these areas. Without such competency the psychologist may never get the opportunity to show what he or she knows or perform the expected tasks. There appear to be decisive advantages to possessing the relationship competency.

The relationship competency provides a solid relational substrate upon which the professional relationship is constructed (Mangione & Nadkarni, 2010). Given the number of potential issues that arise in professional relationships and that may rupture the working relationship, the skills to prevent unnecessary ruptures and repair unavoidable ones are essential. Given the type of work in which a clinical psychologist engages, problems can arise, problems that may not only threaten the process but also undermine the ultimate outcome. Moreover, by its very nature, the relationship competency comprises knowledge, skills, and attitudes that appear both necessary and sufficient, if not facilitative, to address common pitfalls. Knowledge of what factors constitute a sound professional relationship in any arena does not necessarily, however, translate into sound professional practice. One may cognitively appreciate facilitative factors but be unable to implement or create them. There is likely a continuum along which relationship skills vary. For example, one might expect a seasoned clinical psychologist to have more expertise than a first-year doctoral student, who is likely to be a novice at best. The pathway to attaining competence is marked by several milestones that are developmentally based. To fully appreciate the development of competence in this domain requires a careful consideration of what competent clinical psychologists ultimately need to know, do, and value. The identification of these criteria has been carefully accomplished by expert agreement in the field, based on an evaluation of the factors constituting the relationship competency at differing levels of professional development.

The Developmental Achievement Levels elucidated by the National Council of Schools and Programs of Professional Psychology provide comprehensive and carefully considered lists of knowledge, skills, and attitudes in relevant domains along a continuum from Novice, Intermediate, Advanced, Proficient, to Expert (Mangione & Nadkarni, 2010). Supervised and professional experiences appear to provide innumerable opportunities for exposure to situations that, in and of themselves, create educational processes for consolidating relationship skills, including trial and error, successive approximations, direct experience, vicarious experience, and opportunities for processing, mentoring, and assimilation of and accommodation to feedback. Relationship factors weigh heavily along the path to role attainment as a clinical psychologist, and ultimate development of skills in this arena is paramount.

In fostering the development of the relationship competency, Mangione and Nadkarni (2010) emphasized that clinical psychology training programs must be committed to both developing curricular experiences and activities that nurture this competency and assessing this competency in a variety of ways throughout training. Knowing what to do and how to handle problematic interactions ultimately is the result of a compilation of experiences assimilated over the course of time during and after graduate training. Finally, these same experiences and mentoring opportunities also provide for the development of critical attitudes in this area.

We posit that individuals, be they clients, colleagues, students, or other professionals, are more likely to be influenced by a clinical psychologist with whom they enjoy a positive working relationship. Relationship factors appear to play a key role in allowing for psychological influence and persuasion. People are more likely to be influenced by those whom they perceive as being warm, understanding, respectful, and empathic. Relationship factors are also more likely to exert their influence by creating a sense of satisfaction with the experience. It follows, then, that relationship factors may in many instances mediate the relationship between the application of a strategy and a positive outcome. Relationship factors are also likely to play a key role in fostering change, a goal of most if not all professional encounters. The relationship competency might be construed as a social medium that sets the stage for effective functioning as a clinical psychologist. The professional relationship thus provides significant and profound opportunities for carrying out the roles and functions of the clinical psychologist. There are several reasons for believing so.

In the clinical realm, for example, the professional relationship is an important vehicle for soliciting and gathering information, developing hypotheses to account for observations, developing formulations, testing and validating hypotheses, and forming a plan for intervening. Almost any professional activity in which the clinical psychologist engages necessitates the collection of information and a resulting professional course of action. In fact, the relationship with a client itself may provide important data about the interpersonal style of the client outside of the consulting room. While under any given circumstances the clinical psychologist asks key critical questions, the quality of the relationship created by the psychologist may affect whether, how much, how little, how reliable, and how valid the clinical information obtained ultimately is. For example, failure to engage the client in the process itself may seriously undermine the opportunity to obtain accurate information.

Clinical psychologists are trained to make careful observations and to pay close attention on a moment-by-moment basis so they can develop hypotheses that may be critical in understanding the problem at hand. For example, the client who complains that others in her work and social life avoid and dislike her may have no clue as to the subtle repetitive patterns of behavior that make interacting with her such an aversive experience. These patterns are likely to emerge and play themselves out in the therapeutic relationship. The keen observer who is actively processing his or her experiences with a client may discover critical information that goes well beyond what the client reports or even intends to convey. Failure to attend to such relational data may result in missing clinically useful information.

In the following sections we describe areas through which the relationship competency exerts its most influence: the working alliance, therapist characteristics, intraprofessional relationships and collaboration, and interprofessional relationships and collaboration. Clinical psychologists must be competent in each domain. Each of these domains and their specific criteria have important implications for each of the areas discussed in more depth below.

The Working Alliance

One of the best-researched constructs in the field of psychotherapy today is the working alliance. This construct occupies a central place in the tradecraft of the clinical psychologist, so much so that some authors suggest that ignoring it in daily practice constitutes unethical behavior (Castonguay, Constantino, & Holtforth, 2006). Despite its profound significance, and even though it can be traced back to the early works of Sigmund Freud, there is still no distinct or commonly agreed upon definition of this concept, evidenced in part by the other terms used to describe it.

The working alliance is sometimes also described as the therapeutic or helping alliance (Horvath & Bedi, 2002). While some approaches proclaim the primacy of the therapeutic alliance and relationship, others see it as necessary but not sufficient (Beck, 2005) for therapeutic change. Luborsky (1976) emphasized the crucial role of the alliance during the initial phase of therapy, which serves as the basis for the initiation of therapy, and later as essentially providing the foundation for the continuation of therapy. Simply put, without a sound alliance, therapy may not begin or be sustained. Edward Bordin (1994) is credited with elucidating the critically potent components of the therapeutic alliance. As noted by Horvath and Bedi (2002): "For Bordin, the alliance is fundamentally a collaborative entity and has three components: agreement on the therapeutic goals, consensus with respect to the tasks that make up therapy, and a bond between the client and therapist" (p. 39).

As this definition implies, the key components of the working alliance emphasize the need to establish and maintain consensual agreement, a positive bond between the participants, and the fostering of a collaborative enterprise to achieve the desired goals. Without these elements, it would be difficult to imagine that therapy could actually proceed. Proponents of this view argue that the alliance is a common thread across all therapies whose impact has been validated across different approaches, including even cognitive-behavioral therapy (e.g., Burns & Nolen-Hoeksama, 1992; Raue, Goldfried, & Barkham, 1997). The working alliance may, in part, be seen as accounting for the similar outcomes demonstrated across therapies (Wampold, 2005). Competent clinical psychologists are skilled at forming and sustaining a sound alliance when working with patients.

Based on an extensive review of the literature in this area, Horvath and Bedi (2002) elucidated several important elements of the alliance process between therapist and client: mutual collaborative partnering, positive affective bonding, and congruence on both the goals of therapy and the means by which to achieve them.

Their definition emphasizes the specific elements of the alliance and inherently has important implications from a competency perspective. For example, a poorly established bond and the existence of therapist and client collaborative problems are likely to undermine outcome (Martin, Garske, & Davis, 2000).

To establish a successful working alliance, the clinical psychologist must be capable of initiating, establishing, and maintaining a high-quality, strong, and collaborative relationship with clients from diverse backgrounds who are experiencing any one or more of a variety of psychological disorders. To accomplish this end is no small feat. The effective clinician must, therefore, be able to foster an affective link or connection in which clients can experience several key elements emanating from and directed toward the therapist, including a strong sense of trust and faith, likability, esteem for the other, and concern (Horvath & Bedi, 2002). These factors underlie the affective component of the alliance. The working alliance also requires the therapist to be skillful at assisting the client in identifying achievable goals, obtaining a sense of agreement about what the goals are, securing commitment to these goals, and facilitating agreement and assurance about the strategies for attaining the goals (Horvath & Bedi, 2002). The therapist must also be able to convey a genuine sense of responsibility and dedication to his or her role and create a process that allows the client to do the same, all the while both having trust and faith in each other's commitment to the process and a desirable outcome (Horvath & Bedi, 2002).

Castonguay and colleagues (2006) eloquently summarized the findings on the alliance by examining its relationship to the therapeutic outcome, its positive and negative relationships to specific client characteristics, its direct and inverse relationships with specific therapist behaviors and traits, and temporal factors related to the alliance and its predictability of outcome. They concluded the following: (1) The quality of the alliance is positively correlated with outcome over a number of treatment approaches and clinical disorders; (2) Client characteristics and behaviors may either enhance the quality of the alliance (e.g., degree of psychological-mindedness, change expectancies) or impede it (e.g., avoidance behavior, relational issues); (3) Therapist traits and actions may either enhance (e.g., warmth, flexible style) or undermine (e.g., inflexibility, poor boundaries, a critical stance) the quality of the alliance; and (4) Failure to establish an alliance early on in treatment fosters attrition. These findings have clear and significant implications for competent practice in clinical psychology.

Horvath and Bedi (2002) proposed three broad domains that encompass the specific strategies contributed by the therapist: the therapist's interpersonal skills, factors within the therapist, and what occurs between the client and therapist. They also identified and defined specific factors within each domain, all of which have important implications from a competency standpoint. These specific factors represent what the clinical psychologist must be able to do to create an effective alliance.

The *interpersonal skills* realm includes the ability to understand the client and his or her needs, creating a sound basis for responding to the client at a deeper level and fostering a sense of hopefulness that change is possible. These skills provide a solid basis for addressing and overcoming difficulties stemming from problematic beliefs, attitudes, assumptions, and expectations that may serve to threaten the strength of the alliance. Included within this interpersonal domain are communication skills, empathy, openness and exploration, experience and training, and destructive characteristics. In summarizing the findings in this area, Horvath and Bedi (2002) offered a sound basis for considering the impact of these variables. They appear directly related to the requisite competencies of the clinical psychologist in establishing a therapeutic alliance.

The *communication skills* of the clinical psychologist serve as a medium through which he or she can see the world through their clients' eyes, convey this understanding to clients, and allow clients to perceive the therapist's appreciation of their view of themselves, the world, and their future. Clinicians who are deficient in this most basic capacity are unlikely to be able to facilitate an effective partnership.

Competence in a number of other relevant areas also appears to be important. Empathy (Bohart, Elliott, Greenberg, & Watson, 2002) refers to the capacity of the clinician to fully understand and appreciate the manner in which the client perceives the world. It involves the ability of the therapist to place himself or herself in the shoes of the client and see the world through the perspective of the client, just as if he or she were the client (but of course never losing the "as if" component), and expressing or reflecting this feeling to the client (Rogers, 1951, 1957; Williams, 2002). To form and maintain an alliance and create the affective bond required to do so, the clinical psychologist must be competent in developing and conveying empathic responses that are geared to the individual client. In other words, the clinician must be capable of tracking the content and feelings of the client on a moment-by-moment basis and of reflecting this information back to the client, who must perceive this deep level of understanding. Factors that impede empathic understanding are likely to undermine the development of a sound helping partnership.

Clinicians who are *open to their own experiencing* have the capacity to explore their own experience without restraint, and those who are able to follow the lead of the client without assuming a controlling stance are more capable of forming effective alliances (Horvath & Bedi, 2002). This characteristic sounds very similar to what Rogers (1951) referred to as "genuineness," by which he meant that the therapist was a real person, open moment by moment to his or her own experience and never putting on a façade with the client.

The role of *therapist experience and training* is also of interest. One might assume that more training and experience would be positively related to the ability to form a helping relationship, but the research findings are mixed. Most notably, as reviewed by Horvath and Bedi (2002), it appears that experience level interacts with how skilled the client is in forming relationships. Clients who possess more serious relational deficiencies form better alliances with more versus less experienced psychologists, while experience level does not differentiate itself with less relationally impaired clients. It may very well be that more seasoned clinicians are better able to detect signs of low-quality alliances or those that are worsening and take the necessary therapeutic maneuvers to fix them (Horvath & Bedi, 2002). Of course, the behavior of the therapist that is probably related to certain traits may set the stage for behaviors that may make or break the alliance (Castonguay et al., 2006). The role of supervision and mentoring in assisting less experienced clinicians to learn and benefit from the wisdom of more experienced therapists is clear. This area appears to be one in which experience in practicing one's craft makes a difference.

Finally, an important consideration is what specific characteristics or *therapist behaviors* are associated with both low-quality alliances and with the possibility of alliance decay. Horvath and Bedi (2002) culled four factors from the literature in this area. Two of these factors have to do with the therapist's personal characteristics, two with the therapist's behaviors in session. These factors include therapists who are perceived as cold and irritable. These variables make perfect sense, in that these attitudes create a barrier to development and maintenance of an effective alliance. It is not difficult to imagine how these characteristics would be expected to erode the very basis upon which an alliance could be built or nurtured. They also note that a controlling therapist stance early in therapy and offering insights and interpretation too early in the process may be expected to produce similar effects. In these latter instances, it appears that it is not the strategy itself but rather the timing and flexibility in its application that is of importance, placing emphasis on the art of therapy.

These findings have important implications for sensitizing therapists to the need to reflect on their impact in the therapeutic session. Coupled with this is the importance of strategic timing of interventions. Horvath and Bedi (2002) warn therapists about the problems associated with forging ahead with a strategy and losing sight of where the client is in terms of acceptance of the technique. Persisting with a therapeutic strategy and failing to attend to the client's concerns may set into motion a process of damaging the alliance.

The next area of relevance in the intrapersonal domain is based on what is occurring within the therapist and its impact on the alliance. Simply put, awareness of one's own issues and problems and how these may invade the therapeutic process is important. Strupp and Binder (1984) considered certain characteristics within the therapist to be potentially destructive as far as the alliance is concerned, and this, of course, has important implications for outcome. Therapists with self-directed anger, affiliation difficulties, and hostile reactions to clients had poorer alliances—no surprise here! Once again, the implication from a competency standpoint centers upon the importance of self-reflection and awareness as well as the value of addressing unresolved issues. Competent clinical psychologists never underestimate the impact of their own characteristics on the alliance.

The final realm, the interactional, focuses on the interplay between the therapist and client and how this relates to the alliance. Simply put, it is important to examine the specific types of interactions that occur in therapy and how they are associated with the alliance. When therapist–client interplay is characterized by anger, competition, and control, the alliance suffers (Horvath & Bedi, 2002). Once again, these findings, while important, are not surprising. Certain therapist behaviors have the potential for eroding an alliance.

In sum, what do these findings (Castonguay et al., 2006; Horvath & Bedi, 2002) imply about the working alliance and competence of clinical psychologists in the relationship domain? The message is clear: what the therapist does during the therapeutic encounter, the client's characteristics, what the therapist brings to the table, how these factors affect the therapist's behaviors, and what happens between the therapist and the client during the course of a session and across sessions appear to play an important role in the therapeutic process and affect the quality of the alliance. Focusing on these areas in the training of clinical psychologists seems critical. Competent clinical psychologists maintain awareness of these issues and address them in an effective fashion. The relationship between the working alliance and outcome underscores the importance of this component of the relationship competency.

THE WORKING ALLIANCE AND CLINICAL OUTCOME

From the standpoint of competency development, the therapeutic alliance and its relationship to outcome warrant serious consideration from clinical psychologists. Attaining and maintaining competence in this realm requires not only a thorough understanding of the important factors affecting the alliance and outcome but also learning how to identify and resolve negative factors. Even more important, however, is a proactive approach designed to prevent the onset of events that are likely to preclude the development of an alliance or cause one to deteriorate. Clinical psychologists have a responsibility to keep abreast of important factors that potentially undermine the therapeutic alliance. They must be aware of these findings and utilize them in the interest of perfecting their craft and facilitating positive outcomes.

The research literature in general clearly supports that the quality of the working alliance is positively related to outcome in psychotherapy (Gelso & Carter, 1985; Horvath & Bedi, 2002; Horvath & Symonds, 1991; Orlinsky, Grawe, & Parks, 1994). Basing their conclusions on a meta-analysis of 79 studies over a very long time period (58 published and 21 unpublished), Martin and colleagues (2000) discovered that the conservative overall weighted r correlation estimate between the alliance and outcome was .22; they concluded that the effect of the alliance quality is moderate despite the multitude of variables that may affect the relationship. However, as Castonguay and colleagues (2006) pointed out, while the helping alliance is a critical key to client change, the cause-and-effect relationship between the alliance and the outcome has not been conclusively established.

Castonguay and colleagues (2006) also provided a comprehensive synopsis of what is known about the working alliance. We provide a brief overview of their important conclusions for consideration regarding their implications for competency development; for a thorough consideration of this topic, the reader is referred to the original source. First, the working alliance is positively associated with client outcome across a number of clinical disorders and treatment types, with effect sizes for this relationship correlation ranging from .22 to .26. Obviously, despite this association a great deal of outcome variance remains to be explained (Samstag et al., 2008). Second, the quality of a client's psychological-mindedness and change expectations are inversely related to outcome (e.g., avoidance and interpersonal problems). Third, specific therapist characteristics appear to be positively and negatively correlated with the quality of the alliance. For example, in a review Ackerman and Hilsenroth (2001) highlighted a number of therapist attributes that may not only impair the development of a sound helping alliance but may also undermine an already established one. These problems were evident in clinicians who were "rigid, uncertain, exploitative, critical, distant, tense, aloof, distracted" (Ackerman et al., 2001, p. 182). Later, Ackerman and Hilsenroth (2003) found that therapists whose personal characteristics contributed to the formation of a positive alliance displayed flexibility, honesty, and respectfulness. Considered in light of further evidence, the findings reveal that the early alliance forecasts outcome, that the variance accounted for by the alliance is not merely a function of symptom improvement, and, quite importantly, that a poor alliance early on in treatment is associated with premature dropout (Castonguay et al., 2006).

Other relevant work on poor outcome reveals evidence of hostile interactions in poor-outcome dyads in dynamic therapy (Henry, Schacht, & Strupp, 1986) and negative and hostile therapist behaviors associated with premature dropouts (Najavits & Strupp, 1994). In a study of dropout in time-limited psychotherapy, Piper and colleagues (1999) found that a number of factors distinguished dropouts from a matched group of completers. Of most relevance, premature terminators reported a weaker alliance early in treatment, while therapists did so at the last session of therapy. Most recently, Samstag and colleagues (2008) reported that mean alliance scores in patients who dropped out were significantly lower than in patients displaying good outcomes. Furthermore, dropouts' scores were significantly lower on both patient- and therapist-rated alliance than for patients showing poor outcomes. In addition, greater hostile complementary and interpersonal interactions were reported in the poor-outcome patients.

Castonguay and Beutler (2005) assembled a distinguished group of psychologists to evaluate the literature in four clinical areas—depression, anxiety, substance abuse, and personality disorders—and reviewed the literature on participant characteristics, relationship factors, and technique factors. The goal was to integrate findings and identify principles that were common across clinical domains and that were unique to a problem type. Their findings are directly relevant to competency development in the relationship domain. In the final integrative chapter, they reported a number of important principles related to the quality of the therapeutic relationship, therapist interpersonal skills, and therapist clinical skills. This well-designed and -implemented initiative yielded many important findings. Regarding the quality of the therapeutic relationship, two common principles emerged, attesting to the importance of the establishment and maintenance of a strong helping alliance and the need to foster a high level of therapeutic collaboration. The identified principles related to therapist interpersonal skills underscored the value and importance of empathic relating, caring, warmth, acceptance, and authenticity in facilitating change. Finally, common principles related to the amount and validity of relational interpretations and a flexible approach to resolving alliance ruptures were reported.

After reviewing the literature in this area, we agree with Castonguay and colleagues (2006) that "after many decades of process and outcome investigations, relationship variables have achieved a respected status in the field of psychotherapy. As noted by Castonguay et al. (2006), "Although the current empirical evidence cannot support Rogers' (1957) hypothesis that specific interpersonal conditions are sufficient for change, research, on alliance, in particular, has clearly demonstrated that the therapeutic relationship cannot be viewed as a nonspecific variable that is merely auxiliary to other active components of treatment" (pp. 276–277). The conclusion is clear: therapist characteristics and the therapeutic process are embedded in the relationship, with the potential for making the difference between benefit and deterioration.

Based on the conclusions and recommendations offered by Castonguay and colleagues (2006) and Horvath and Bedi (2002), we present several critical suggestions relevant to competency development in the relationship domain. For a more thorough consideration, the reader is urged to review the original sources. First, competent clinical psychologists realize that the alliance is crucial. Competency in developing an effective alliance early on in the treatment process is critical for establishing an effective therapeutic partnership and preventing premature dropout, especially with clients who have difficulties in the relationship realm. The earlier this is achieved the better, but research supports that the critical period is between the third and fifth sessions. The evidence also supports that the alliance should take precedence over other considerations early on, as without it there really is no therapy per se. Failure to establish a solid helping alliance, then, constitutes a red flag.

Second, the clinical psychologist must pay careful attention to the quality of the alliance during and throughout the therapeutic process over time. Failure to do so runs the risk of poor partnering with the client and the lack of a positive affective union.

Third, clinicians must be skilled at conveying and expressing empathy and instilling positive, realistic expectations for the future in clients in ways that the client can perceive. The efforts of any well-intentioned clinician are likely to fall short of the mark if these conditions are never perceived by the client. Prudence, then, would dictate that the therapist solicit and monitor the perceptions of the client in this regard and use these data to reinforce current efforts or to alter one's approach accordingly. The approach of the clinician must obviously be flexible enough to adapt to the client's needs, with an eye toward creating a safe therapeutic climate with an emphasis on collaboration. Failure to accommodate to the sensitivities and vulnerabilities of the client may otherwise undermine efforts to forge and sustain a helping alliance.

Fourth, therapists would be wise to attend to any differences that may exist between their perceptions of the alliance versus the client's perceptions. Discrepant perceptions are another red flag! A careful evaluation of the client's capacity for relationship development, potential limiting factors, preferential patterns of interacting, and the perceived value of the relationship is important. Clinical psychologists must be willing to use their interpersonal skills to create a safe climate in which collaborative efforts may be made. Recognizing clients who are at risk for poor alliance development and making concerted efforts to establish and maintain a healthy partnership are paramount.

Fifth, focusing too much on interventional strategies, especially during the early phase of treatment, as opposed to the quality of the alliance may undermine the therapy process. Therapist self-reflection and self-awareness are crucial, as well as sensitivity to what is happening in the relationship with the client. The clinical psychologist must be competent at seeking out instances of relationship ruptures and repairing them.

Finally, given the equivocal findings related to experience and training regarding alliance formation, except when working with more disturbed clients, clinicians must exert due caution when working with severely disturbed clients. Less experienced clinicians must know when to seek education, consultation, training, and supervision. Likewise, clinical psychologists must be self-aware and reflective about their own strengths, skill limitations, interpersonal sensitivities, reactivities, and reactions to clients (Castonguay & Beutler, 2005; Castonguay et al., 2006; Horvath & Bedi, 2002). Therapists should use their own emotional reactions to the client; recognize their feelings toward the client; examine their own thoughts, beliefs, and assumptions about the client; observe their own behaviors in relation to the client; and process any alliance ruptures.

Therapist Characteristics

While there is a substantial amount of evidence that psychological interventions have a positive impact on the lives of clients (Barlow, 2010a), recently there have been justified concerns about potential negative effects associated with psychological interventions (Barlow, 2010b). Interventions notwithstanding, therapist characteristics are also an important area of concern. The clinical psychologist must possess a number of important interpersonal characteristics, be capable of using himself or herself as a tool for facilitating change, and be proficient in the application of psychotherapeutic techniques to foster client change.

Some schools of thought emphasize the primacy of the therapeutic relationship itself (Martin et al., 2000; Wampold, 2005) and propose that it is more important than technique. Others, recognizing the importance of the relationship, focus on the primacy of treatment protocols (Barlow, 2010a; Beck, 2005; Rachman & Wilson, 2008). What is known today about the therapeutic relationship and its association with clinical outcome is in point of fact a critical consideration. The profound significance of the therapy relationship has its roots in the work of Carl Rogers (1951, 1957), perhaps the first empirically based clinical psychologist who tested his theoretical propositions about facilitative therapeutic conditions. While placing more or less emphasis on the relationship, all psychotherapies recognize its significance.

Today, the critical importance of the therapeutic relationship cannot be denied. Lambert and Barley (2002), for example, reported that the relationship factors, commonly referred to as common factors, account for 30% of the outcome in psychotherapy. While extratherapeutic factors (e.g., obtaining social support, chance events, problem remission over the passage of time) account for about 40% of the outcome, expectancy (e.g., placebo effects) and technique each accounts for only 15% of the outcome (Lambert & Barley, 2001). These findings substantiate that, on average, the therapeutic relationship, encompassing a variety of variables, forms a central ingredient associated with positive outcome. In describing these findings, Lambert and Barley (2002) called attention to the large number of treatment modalities, psychological disorders, measurements of client and therapist attributes, outcome measures, and research designs on which support for the therapeutic relationship is based, encompassing over 100 studies.

Notwithstanding limitations in measurement and methodology, there is enough confidence in the literature to assert that the therapeutic relationship is really very important (Castonguay et al., 2006), thereby underscoring the need for the clinical psychologist to attend to the relationship factors. While not an intervention in the classic sense of the word, one might consider the relationship as the "technique" in some forms of psychotherapy, with the therapist as the tool to facilitate change. While fully acknowledging the division according to theoretical orientations, in describing the importance of the therapeutic relationship Gelso and Carter (1985) stated: "Some believe that it is the sine qua non of good therapy, that client change flows naturally from the relationship itself; others maintain that a good relationship is important inasmuch it provides the counselor leverage in applying procedures and techniques that themselves are the central change agents" (p. 156). Whatever the case, practicing clinical psychologists today would attest to the importance of the therapeutic relationship in the consulting room.

Investigational efforts have been directed at examining the impact of the components of the therapeutic relationship per se—namely, therapist factors (e.g., characteristics and style), Rogers' (1957) facilitative conditions (e.g., empathy, positive regard and congruence), and the helping alliance, discussed earlier. In actuality, however, it is difficult to distinguish between them as they are intertwined, related, and dependent on each other (Lambert & Barley, 2001). We do so here to pinpoint essential components of the therapy experience that warrant therapist competence. Below, we examine the association between therapist factors and facilitative conditions and therapeutic outcome with an eye toward competency issues for clinical psychologists.

One of the most important factors is the therapeutic relationship. As Gelso and Carter (1985), defined it: "The relationship is the feelings and attitudes that therapist and client have toward one another, and the manner in which these are expressed" (p. 159).

THERAPIST CHARACTERISTICS AND OUTCOME IN PSYCHOTHERAPY

Decades of clinical process and outcome research support the conclusion that some therapists are more proficient at fostering beneficial outcomes in psychotherapy, others facilitate more negative results, and some produce better outcomes with certain types of clients than others (Lambert & Barley, 2001). While correlational in nature, the implications of these findings are nonetheless compelling and warrant attention from practitioners seeking to develop and sustain competence. If nothing else, these findings dictate consideration of the persona of the therapist as an active ingredient of the ultimate outcome. In response to the American Psychological Association (APA)'s Division 12 Task Force on Empirically Supported Treatments, Norcross (2002) spearheaded a project of the Task Force on Empirically Supported Therapy Relationships aimed at evaluating and identifying psychotherapy relationships that are "demonstrably effective, promising and probably effective, or insufficient research to judge" (p. 8).

Orlinsky and colleagues (1994) delineated a variety of therapist behaviors and factors that have been found to positively correlate with outcome, including the credibility and skill of the clinician, empathy, and affirmation of the patient. Some of these factors are similar to Rogers' conditions (1951, 1957) related to the therapist communicating an empathic appreciation of the client's experience, nonjudgmental caring, and congruence, although these conditions once described as "necessary and sufficient" do not appear to account for much variability in outcome; rather, they appear to exert their influence indirectly through the working alliance (Gelso & Carter, 1985). Tryon and Winograd (2002) also reviewed findings that show a great deal of support for the positive effects of goal consensus and collaborative involvement associated with positive outcome in psychotherapy. In advising psychologists on therapeutic practices in this regard, Tryon and Winograd (2002) urged clinicians to focus on topics of significance to the client and their attributed etiology as a means of fostering empathic understanding, building a partnership, and establishing goal congruence and engagement. They underscore the role of a mutual friendly, cooperative stance in facilitating positive outcomes.

In sum, what these findings imply is that inherent characteristics of therapists and the processes created in the therapeutic encounter appear to be associated with the outcome of therapy. We review findings about some of these important variables below and encourage the reader to consider what these findings imply about competent practice in clinical psychology.

Empathy   Bohart and colleagues (2002) reviewed the literature on the role of empathy in outcome. Empathy involves the ability of a therapist to assume the perspective of the client, see the world through the eyes of the client, and communicate that appreciation and understanding of meaning to the client. Bohart and colleagues (2002) proposed that empathy exerts its influence on outcome by positively influencing the relationship, providing opportunities for clients to learn, and helping to stimulate self-discovery and development of meaning out of experience.

Unconditional Positive Regard   Unconditional positive regard is a construct that captures the unconditional acceptance, respect, and prizing of the client by the therapist and is modestly associated with positive outcome by creating a platform for interventions or in and of itself (Farber & Lane, 2002). Whatever the case, clients who perceive positive regard from their therapists may be expected to fare better, and there appears to be good reason to incorporate it into the therapy endeavor. Farber and Lane (2002) emphasized two critical points: (1) providing positive regard for clients is strongly recommended and (2) therapists must make efforts to ensure that clients perceive this regard. Earlier, Didato (1971) reported that therapist liking for a patient was positively related to outcome

Congruence   Congruence captures the concept that the therapist presents himself or herself as a real and genuine person without a façade, is free and open to his or her own experience, and is himself or herself in the relationship (Rogers, 1957). While the relationship between congruence and outcome has yielded mixed results, Klein, Kolden, Michels, and Chisholm-Stockard (2002) argue that "there remains both empirical and theoretical support for it to continue to be considered as an important component of a more complex conception of the psychotherapy relationship" (p. 207). Clinical psychologists must take heed and use this information to maximize the likelihood of facilitating positive outcomes.

Feedback   Feedback entails a process of the therapist delivering information to the client about his or her thoughts, feelings, behaviors, attitudes, and assumptions with the intent of promoting personal growth in the context of a safe environment. Feedback in therapy is essentially designed to reinforce or strengthen a behavior, broadly defined, or to provide an impetus for promoting exploration, reflection, and behavior change (Claiborn, Goodyear, & Horner, 2002). It may also be used to draw attention to the discrepancy between what the patient is saying, how the patient is feeling, and how the patient is acting and to formulate specific, targeted feedback, all with an eye toward helping the client achieve his or her therapeutic goals. Crafting effective feedback should include consideration of factors that are likely to affect the outcome of the message, including an understanding of the client, the approach to therapy, and the goals of the client (Claiborn et al., 2002). Failure to carefully consider the implications of these factors may undermine the intended goal of feedback per se.

In sum, clinical psychologists should ask themselves whether they are capable of communicating empathically, experiencing and communicating unconditional positive regard for their clients, conveying genuineness in the therapy relationship, collaborating with clients on the goals of therapy, and obtaining consensus on the tasks of therapy. Despite the best of intentions, not all therapists are proficient at creating a relationship that yields benefits to clients.

There is also a plethora of research findings pointing to the association between certain factors and negative outcome. Barlow (2010b) suggested that to identify negative effects one might consider "slower response, less remission or recovery, higher rates of relapse or recurrence, or some combination of these" (p. 17). Given the association of the alliance with outcome, it makes sense that those factors undermining the alliance will ultimately undermine therapeutic outcome and possibly create psychological casualties.

Castonguay and colleagues (2006) pointed toward the negative effects of therapist inflexibility, boundary problems, and a critical stance toward clients. Therapist rigidity, an inability to draw and maintain appropriate boundary lines between client and therapist, and creating a climate in which clients feel criticized are hardly compatible with what is known to promote therapeutic improvement. Those characteristics in therapists that fuel a poor alliance or that erode an existing alliance may seriously limit the potential for benefit.

Horvath and Bedi (2002) emphasized how therapists who are perceived as cold, irritable, and controlling and who persist in implementing a strategy without considering the client's perspective may be expected to be less successful in their efforts. Strupp and Binder (1984) considered certain characteristics within the therapist to be potentially destructive as far as the alliance is concerned—which of course has important implications for outcome. Therapists who exhibited self-directed anger, affiliation difficulties, and hostile reactions to clients had poorer alliances. Henry and colleagues (1986) found more hostile interactions were evident in cases with poor outcome in dynamic therapy. Najavits and Strupp (1994) found an association between negative and hostile behaviors on the part of thera-pists and premature dropout from psychotherapy. In a study of dropout in individual psychotherapy, Piper and colleagues (1999) discovered that dropouts from therapy had weaker alliances and there was a persistent focus on transference by the therapist that fueled frustration and a strug-gle for power.

Based upon a review of 46 outcomes studies with adults, Mohr (1995) found that deficiencies in empathy, failure to accurately assess the level of severity of the client's problems, nonpositive therapist countertransference, high levels of interpretations of patient transference, and lack of agreement with patients about therapy were related to negative outcomes. Therapists' biased attitudes about patients (Didato, 1971) as well as technique errors have been found to contribute to negative outcome (Mohr, 1995). Finally, therapist–client transactions that are defined by anger, competition, and control have been demonstrated as problematic (Horvath & Bedi, 2002). For a comprehensive review of the influence of therapist factors on out-come, the reader is referred to Lambert (2010). The importance of compe-tence in handling transferential reactions is also evident.

Transference and Countertransference

The notions of transference and countertransference, while deeply rooted in psychoanalytic theory, are important concepts and common elements of the helping relationship that transcend theoretical orientation. Simply put, together they encompass the totality of the reactions that clients have toward therapists and vice versa. More technically, transference involves (a) a form of stimulus generalization of past experience (or conflicts) and displacements in the form of positive or negative attitudes, beliefs, assump-tions, feelings, and behaviors toward the therapist that is (b) triggered in response to the therapist's characteristics and that (c) involves a misper-ception or distortion on the part of the client (Gelso & Carter, 1985). The result is that the client may react to the therapist with a variety of different feelings, including love, attraction, resentment, dependence, and the like, that may hamper therapeutic progress.

Countertransference may be considered to comprise (a) the therapist's reaction to the client in the form of positive or negative attitudes, beliefs, assumptions, feelings, and behaviors that (b) is triggered by the client, the circumstances of the therapy, or events in the therapist's life that (c) are related to past relationships in the therapist's life and that (d) serve to meet the needs of the therapist as opposed to the client (Gelso & Carter, 1985).

Countertransference reactions, if left unattended, may drive the behavior of the therapist toward the client and result in therapeutic blunders, precipitate boundary crossings, and motivate other nontherapeutic maneuvers to the detriment of the client and the therapeutic endeavor.

The extent to which transference and countertransference are considered important and in need of attention varies across therapeutic models, as manifested in whether a model supports addressing, accepting, or simply disregarding these reactions. These reactions may more likely be precipitated with certain types of patients than others (e.g., Axis II patients) and have more emphasis in certain approaches to therapy. Regarding countertransference reactions, when working with highly disturbed patients, the experience of strong emotional responses is not uncommon; in this situation countertransference is unavoidable and can be useful if considered and analyzed (Gelso & Hayes, 2002). By using their emotional responses as a gauge and stimulus, therapists may be more likely to refrain from reacting with a countertransference reaction and can use the experience to explicate the transference–countertransference relationship and develop an effective therapeutic maneuver (Gelso & Hayes, 2002).

TRANSFERENCE AND OUTCOME

Gelso and Carter (1985) offered several general propositions about the role of transference and countertransference in psychotherapy. They assert that transference is more or less evident in all forms of psychotherapy, playing a significant role in the ensuing process and ultimate outcome. Furthermore, the path of transference can be differentiated by type of outcome (i.e., positive or negative) and is predictable based on the type of therapy. The manner in which the therapist handles transference reactions may affect both the process and outcome of therapy, particularly when the transference is negative and undermining the therapeutic process. Moreover, countertransference exists in all forms of psychotherapy, and addressing countertransference experiences can be a useful means of identifying important but less obvious client issues and working more effectively with clients.

Clinical psychologists who are astutely aware of patients' reactions to them as well as their own reactions to patients may find that they can understand and conceptualize their patients more effectively. Relatively speaking, more experienced and skillful therapists may not only be more aware of their countertransference reactions but also more adept at preventing these reactions from undermining therapy, whereas more anxious therapists have been found to engage in more avoidance of patient feelings, inaccurately describe information from a psychotherapy encounter, and fail to attend to patient feelings about them (Gelso & Hayes, 2002).

In sum, the working alliance, relationship factors, and transferential issues appear to play an important role in psychotherapy outcome. Competent clinical psychologists are astutely aware of these factors and make efforts to address them in ways that serve their clients. Relationship factors also appear to play an important role in working around and with other professionals.

Intraprofessional Relationships and Collaboration

The ability to establish and maintain effective working relationships with colleagues is another important area of competence. Clinical psychologists work side by side with colleagues in a variety of settings. It is difficult to imagine a successful organization in which the individuals making up the organization do not cooperate and collaborate with each other to some minimal extent. While each individual contributes to the attainment of a common mission, it is the manner in which these individuals work together that sets the stage for success. There are a variety of resources that address how to succeed in the role of administration (Hecht, Higgerson, Gmelch, & Tucker, 1999; Wheeler et al., 2008).

This competency, then, requires the ability to become a team member in forging the path toward a common goal. From an organizational perspective, the success of a program or operation appears to depend on how well the individuals in the group can work together. This in large part may be a function of the relationships individuals establish with each other. Likewise, the role each individual plays within the larger group is important. However, existing contingencies in any professional environment may foster a toxic climate that undermines collaboration.

There are likely to be a variety of factors that contribute to a positive climate. These factors may be considered to fall within one or more areas, including intra-individual, inter-individual, and systemic domains. It is likely that certain characteristics of an individual have the potential to either ensure or threaten success. Hypothetically, it is quite likely that a professional's ability to form relationships has a significant impact in this regard. We would expect that the manner in which one conducts oneself in relationships would matter here. In the relationship category, it is quite likely that a variety of factors are likely to have an impact on success. These factors within the individual and displayed in interactional skills include but are not limited to respect, assertiveness, flexibility, self-awareness, openness, collegiality, conflict resolution, role-taking, openness to differences, and ethical decision-making and behavior (Mangione & Nadkarni, 2010).

Of course, the behavior of the clinical psychologist does not occur in a vacuum. An appreciation of the contextual factors operating systemically within an organization requires awareness on the part of the professional. For example, some environments, especially high-pressure ones, may promote a climate that encourages unhealthy behaviors related to factors such as limited resources, poor leadership, burdensome work schedules, unhealthy competition, pressures to produce, and the like. Under these circumstances the psychologist must be capable of identifying these factors, engaging in self-awareness, self-reflection, and self-care, stepping back and obtaining distance, and appropriately asserting himself or herself while striving hard to maintain sound working relationships and ethical behavior. Next, we address the importance of effectively relating with professionals in other disciplines, a task that is fraught with challenges.

Interprofessional Relationships and Collaboration

The importance of being able to initiate, develop, form, foster, and utilize professional relationships with those in other specialties outside of clinical psychology cannot be emphasized enough. Much of what clinical psychologists do on a daily basis necessitates effective interfacing with other professionals for the benefit of mutual clients. These groups include primary care physicians, psychiatrists, nurses, nurse practitioners, physician assistants, school administrators, teachers, guidance counselors, as well as others. The ultimate goal of any of these encounters is simply to maximize the potential benefit in the treatment of our clients. Since so many of the clients seen by clinical psychologists are concurrently being seen by professionals outside of psychology, the ability to work with other groups becomes paramount. Failure to do so may result in professionals working at cross-purposes, clients receiving mixed messages, and unintentional undermining of a treatment plan, each of which has potentially serious adverse consequences for a client.

The clinical psychologist today is in the middle of a revolution focused on integrating care. As a consequence, more clinical psychologists find themselves working closely with medical professionals in healthcare settings (Department of Health and Human Services, 2007). However, despite this initiative the average clinical psychologist may not collaborate very often with primary care physicians and professionals (Borresen & Ruddy, 2010;

DiTomasso et al., 2010). There is much reason to expect, however, that as the healthcare environment continues to evolve, clinical psychologists will find themselves in the position of having to effectively collaborate and integrate their services with medical professionals.

The clinical psychologist must be competent at collaboration, cooperation, and coordination, all within a spirit of mutual respect. As noted previously, collaboration is a complex process that has taken on even more significance in the current climate of integration of psychology and primary care medicine (Borresen & Ruddy, 2010; DiTomasso et al., 2010). However, the clinical psychologist faces numerous challenges in achieving effective and efficient collaboration due to roles and functions, professional language, existing and competing models of care, prejudices and biases, interprofessional conflicts at the national level, competition for patients, reimbursement issues, charting, time, ethical issues, and the like. One critical factor is the need to remember the common ground between professionals: the client. Remaining focused on this common ground paves the way for finding solutions to the problems confronting the clinical psychologist.

In considering these issues, Borresen and Ruddy (2010) defined collaboration as focusing on fostering a process of teamwork and cooperation with the ultimate intent of achieving shared goals. Implied within this viewpoint are some of the knowledge, skills, and attitudes the clinical psychologist must possess. DiTomasso and colleagues, (2010) elucidated three main areas of focus related to collaboration: clinical and professional issues, practical and logistical issues, and ethical/legal issues. Embedded within each of these domains are a host of factors that the clinical psychologist must be able to address and resolve.

Practical and logistical issues are those that are relevant to day-to-day operations and are related to the role of the clinical psychologist and other factors affecting implementation of these roles and functions (DiTomasso et al., 2010). DiTomasso and colleagues (2010) elucidated several critical factors worthy of consideration by the clinical psychologist. To collaborate requires that one become thoroughly familiar with the audience with whom one wishes to work. Understanding the roles and functions and other relevant factors seems critical. For example, in working with primary care physicians, the clinical psychologist must appreciate that these professionals perceive themselves in the role of coordinators of patient care, one that places significant time pressures on them, not to mention the burden of balancing multiple priorities simultaneously across a large number of patients competing for their time. Failure to be sensitive to these issues may significantly undermine attempts at collaboration. Time is undoubtedly one of the most valuable commodities in medical settings. Therefore, anything that takes the time of the physician must be perceived by the physician as equally, if not more, valuable and must be accomplished in the most effective manner with the least amount of time wasted. The most important issue is whether the time spent on collaboration is worth the time.

The clinical psychologist must become competent in capitalizing on what time is available, synthesizing the information and boiling it down to the most important and useful information, considering only what the physician absolutely needs to know and, more importantly, wants to know, and presenting the information in the most usable and transportable manner. When all is said and done, the criterion of interest is whether the physician can use the obtained information to benefit the patient.

Much of what we have argued here is also applicable to other professionals. Psychiatrists specializing in medication consultation often see about four patients an hour and may only be able to respond late in the evening or perhaps even a few to several days later. Others, such as high school teachers, may have back-to-back classes throughout the day, which significantly limits their availability. The point is clear: understanding the unique characteristics of settings, professional roles, common constraints, and the associated pressures on other professionals can go a long way to overcoming practical and logistical barriers.

Relevant clinical and professional issues also provide opportunities for collaboration with other professionals. DiTomasso and colleagues (2010) elaborated on how issues of differential diagnosis and opposing models of patient care can become sources of tension between psychologists and physicians. Such situations require a delicate balance of mutual respect and careful negotiation.

Despite the necessary commitment to collaboration, as Borresen and Ruddy (2010) suggested, the clinical psychologist must be able to reflect and examine his or her own beliefs and biases that may inhibit collaboration, expand models of formulating patient problems, and fully appreciate the competencies and roles of other professionals.

In conclusion, competence in the relationship domain requires that the clinical psychologist remain aware of and sensitive to the basic knowledge about successful alliances with clients, peers, and other professionals, keeping updated on the professional literature, updating skills, and engaging in self-reflection about his or her interactions.

Strategies for Fostering Competence

Whether a scientist-practitioner or a practitioner-scholar, clinical psychologists have a responsibility to be cognizant of the literature related to effective practice and to utilize this information in the service of their clients. This viewpoint has important implications about what psychologists should do in developing, refining, and maintaining their competence in the relationship domain. We describe and discuss a number of strategies below.

Self-Assessment and Self-Awareness

The process of refining and maintaining competency in the relationship domain begins with the commitment of the psychologist to engage in reflective practice and self-assessment (Rodolfa et al., 2005). This process entails examining one's own attitudes, beliefs, assumptions, feelings and behaviors in the role of the professional psychologist as a participant-observer. Being aware of one's strengths, limitations, blind spots, outcomes, and areas in need of improvement is a critical starting point. Awareness of what is transpiring on a moment-by-moment basis during the therapeutic encounter is critical (Castonguay et al., 2006; Lambert & Barley, 2001). Without self-observation and processing of patterns coupled with solicited feedback from trusted professional peers and supervisors, the clinician is practicing within a vacuum, is unlikely to identify important areas of concern, and, as a result, is even less likely to be able to address them. Flowing naturally from this process is the need for ongoing education and supervision.

Continuing Education

As a lifelong learner, the clinician must keep abreast of the latest findings and strategies for enhancing effectiveness in the relationship realm (Lambert & Barley, 2001). The literature on the therapeutic relationship, therapist interpersonal skills, therapist traits, and the working alliance is replete with critical information that relates directly to practice. As empirically based practitioners ourselves, we fully support and are invested in the development, application, and evaluation of psychological treatments that work (DiTomasso et al., 2010). Exclusively focusing on therapeutic techniques, however, is associated with the danger of diverting attention away from the "person" of the therapist who is delivering the technique. The clinical psychologist must embrace the entire situation and recognize that effective practice requires the synthesis and integration of technique (Barlow, 2010a), client and therapist factors (Ackerman & Hilsenroth, 2001, 2003; Norcross, 2002), therapeutic principles (Castonguay & Beutler, 2005), and, of course, the relationship (Norcross, 2002). Appreciating the multitude of factors in this situation will enhance the effectiveness of our clinical work.

Continuing education (Lambert & Barley, 2001) in the relationship realm as it relates to intervention is critical. Awareness of the relationship between specific characteristics and outcome is hardly enough. Coupling continuing education with clinical supervision can be quite beneficial for identifying, refining, and practicing skills that are likely to enhance competency. Given the potential impact of the therapist on outcome, it is likely that the psychological state of the practitioner himself or herself is important.

Consultation, Supervision, and Referral

In the everyday world of practice, psychologists confront clinical situations and clients who are quite challenging. These clients are most likely individuals who are at high risk for attrition and negative outcome. Clinical psychologists must recognize these situations early on and seek consultation from peers and/or clinical supervision to overcome such difficulties. These activities may be helpful in offsetting the likelihood of negative effects (Barlow, 2010b; Lillenfield, 2007).

In other circumstances a clinical psychologist may simply find it most prudent to refer patients to other more experienced practitioners or those with a relevant specialization. For example, a highly challenging and complex borderline patient may warrant a therapist with specialized training in a dialectical behavioral approach (Linehan & Korsland, 2003). Another patient may require a clinician with experience and skills in treating patients with eating disorders. Of course, while it is best never to take on clients who are beyond one's level of expertise and experience, this situation may not be obvious at the outset. Common situations warranting referral may include when patients are not improving, when they are worsening, when the working alliance is beyond repair, when the therapist judges that a case exceeds his or her competence level, or when the only ethical course of action is to transfer or refer the patient.

Self-Care

The APA Code of Ethics (APA, 2002) underscores the responsibility of the psychologist to maintain self-awareness of factors that are likely to interfere with the ability to fulfill his or her professional obligations to clients. The underlying principle of beneficence (Knapp & VandeCreek, 2006) necessitates that clinical psychologists do no harm. In a field where the delivery of service is based on the interaction between a provider and an individual who is typically vulnerable for one or more reasons, the psychological state of the provider is paramount.

Self-care (Lambert & Barley, 2001), then, becomes a critical factor that may influence the delivery of service. The psychologist's failure to address his or her own personal factors may affect the therapy relationship. Even the most technically competent clinical psychologist, when experiencing the effects of unaddressed, insurmountable stressors, may engage in behaviors or display attitudes that undermine the integrity of the therapeutic process. Self-care, then, may be crucial in protecting the welfare of clients. Self-care probably stems from a variety of sources, including self-awareness, self-monitoring, professional feedback, client feedback, outcome evaluation, and positive physical and mental health practices. Clinical psychologists must be able to step back, obtain distance, and gain perspective about how to maximize their professional effectiveness.

CREATE A FACILITATIVE THERAPEUTIC CLIMATE

Based on outcomes, the research on the therapeutic relationship supports the need for clinical psychologists to create and sustain a therapeutic environment that emphasizes the effective element of empathy and the probably efficacious elements of positive regard and therapist congruence (Norcross, 2002). In this sense competent clinical practice necessitates three important factors. First, clients must perceive that they are understood based on the words and responses of the therapist, which may communicate and promote understanding, validation, exploration, and meaning on a moment-by-moment basis (Bohart et al., 2002). These empathic responses are aimed at allowing the therapist to truly appreciate the client's experiences "as if" the therapist was the client observing the world through the eyes of the client but never really abandoning the "as if" quality of the experience (Rogers, 1951). Second, competent therapists make efforts to convey a positive, caring, and respectful regard for their clients that validates the client's worth as a human being, engage in ongoing monitoring of it, and adapt their responses to the specific needs of the client as well as the given clinical context (Bohart et al., 2002).

The competent therapist is also a genuine, congruent individual who presents himself or herself as such in the therapeutic context. In describing congruence Klein and colleagues (2002) noted that:

> ...congruent responses may involve self-disclosure by therapists of personal information and life experiences...articulation of thoughts and feelings, opinions, feedback on behavior, and pointed questions...require mindful attention and self-reflection...are honest...are not disrespectful, overly intellectualized or insincere...are authentic and consistent with the therapist as a real person with likes, dislikes, preferences, beliefs and opinions...are flexibly guided by normative therapist role behavior and yet they are not rigidly role bound...[and] are cast in the language of personal pronouns. (p. 210)

Finally, competent therapists provide feedback to their clients. Claiborn et al. (2002) define feedback as data given to a client from the therapist about the client's behavior or the impact of the client's behavior; it may be described as positive or negative, collaborative, mutual, and structured.

ATTEND TO THE HELPING ALLIANCE

Given the wealth of findings relating the quality of the working alliance with outcome, the clinical psychologist must pay primary attention to this construct. The importance of being capable of establishing, monitoring, evaluating, and maintaining a strong therapeutic alliance in the form of agreement on the goals and tasks of therapy, as well as a positive affective bond, goes without saying (Castonguay et al., 2006). Clinical psychologists must be astute about and adept at engaging in those behaviors that are likely to foster a strong positive partnership and avoid those behaviors that have been shown to undermine it. Attending to the alliance from the first moment of the therapeutic encounter (Castonguay et al., 2006) may make a difference as to whether the encounter constitutes a therapeutic experience for the client. Establishing a sound alliance early in treatment is crucial and predicts outcome (Gelso & Carter, 1985).

MONITOR THE ALLIANCE THROUGHOUT THERAPY

Competent psychologists are capable of recognizing and addressing alliance ruptures. They must develop a sense of the types of clients with whom they have difficulty establishing a working alliance and with whom fostering an alliance is likely to be a challenge. They must be prepared to address these problems and must be acutely focused on the ongoing interaction and process between the client and themselves, be attuned to the earliest signs of a possible alliance rupture, and engage in a process that is most likely to resolve the rupture (Castonguay et al., 2006).

Without maintaining ongoing awareness and monitoring, clinical psychologists risk losing valuable opportunities to repair a process that is going or has gone awry. They must never lose sight of the patient in the moment; must carefully observe the client's verbal and nonverbal reactions; must observe their own reactions; must identify their own thoughts, attitudes, beliefs, and assumptions; must readily admit their part in the rupture; must be motivated and capable of doing what needs to be done to accomplish resolution; and must observe the client's reactions, invite discussion, admit their contribution to the problem, and resolve it (Castonguay et al., 2006).

Burns's (1980) defusing technique may be particularly useful in these situations by recognizing and calling attention to the signs of a rupture, soliciting the client's perspective and reasons for the rupture, empathizing and understanding the reasons and how they relate to the rupture, displaying motivation to resolve it, admitting one's contribution to the problem, addressing any misconceptions the client may hold, and fostering a problem-solving approach. These so-called metacommunicative processes may offer much to the clinician in solving rupture problems (Safran, Muran, Samstag, & Stevens, 2002).

FORMAL MEASUREMENT OF THE ALLIANCE

The competent clinical psychologist must be prepared to consider employing one of the well-known measures of alliance in his or her clinical practice (Castonguay et al., 2006). Securing the perspective of the client, a more robust predictor of outcome than the clinician's viewpoint, seems prudent. It is also necessary for clinicians to be alert for common signs of rupture, such as client withdrawal and disengagement during the therapy process, evidence of hostile and angry reactions toward the therapist, and confrontation of the therapist (Muran, Safran, Samstag, & Winston, 2005).

In the area of dynamic psychotherapy process, negative and hostile behaviors on the part of the therapist (Najavits & Strupp, 1994) were associated with premature attrition, while hostile transactions characterized the dyadic process in poor outcomes (Henry et al., 1986). Piper and colleagues (1999) reported that dropouts from treatment relative to a group of matched group of completers displayed evidence of a weaker alliance. Samstag and colleagues (2008) found mean alliance scores in a group of dropouts to be significantly lower than patients with a good outcome, while dropouts also scored significantly lower than clients with a poor outcome on both client and therapist alliance measures. Finally, clients who experienced poor outcomes, relative to those with good outcomes, had the highest counts of hostile interpersonal behaviors, with more hostile complementary interactions in these patients relative to those with good outcomes. Failure to recognize these markers may, then, undermine the therapeutic partnership and threaten outcome.

Further, given that discrepancies in the evaluation of the alliance may occur, and coupled with the benefits likely to ensue from resolving discrepancies, particularly during the midpoint to latter stages of therapy (Castonguay et al., 2006), the measurement of the alliance may serve as a critical focal point for fostering a positive outcome. Alliance measurement is a yardstick for determining the ongoing nature of the process between participants.

RECOGNIZE THAT WHAT CLIENTS THINK IS MOST IMPORTANT

Clinical psychologists must heavily weigh the client's perspective on the therapeutic alliance for a number of reasons. Castonguay and colleagues (2006) emphasized three points in this regard. First, given that the client's perspective of the therapeutic alliance is what is most predictive of therapeutic outcome, it must be solicited, assessed, and addressed. Second, clinicians must be willing to question their own assessment of the quality of the alliance. Third, addressing perceived discrepancies and engaging in strategies to align perceptions, especially in the middle and latter stages of therapy, are also important.

ADDRESS TRANSFERENCE AND COUNTERTRANSFERENCE ISSUES APPROPRIATELY

There is reason to expect that understanding and addressing these phenomena may provide some benefit in steering the course of therapy. For example, in the literature on countertransference, the evidence, although tenuous, suggests that countertransference does exert an influence on treatment outcomes and that managing countertransference is beneficial (Gelso & Hayes, 2002). Countertransference management comprises five components: self-awareness, clear boundaries, ability to control one's own anxiety responses, ability to demonstrate empathic understanding and sustaining focus on the client, and ability to tap theoretical constructs to conceptualize the patient regarding the helping relationship (Gelso & Hayes, 2002; Gelso, Lattas, Gomez, & Fassinger, 2002). Clinical psychologists must be able to recognize that "if CT [countertransference] is part of avoiding the patient's feelings, recalling the content of sessions accurately, and becoming overinvolved in the patient's problems, then it is a good bet that its effects on the treatment outcome are negative... if CT behavior is negatively related to sound working alliances and to supervisors' evaluations of effectiveness, then it also seems safe to suggest that uncontrolled CT is harmful to treatment" (Gelso & Hayes, 2002, p. 279). These findings compel clinical psychologists to be proactive in addressing the impact of transferential phenomena affecting the process and outcome of treatment.

In conclusion, overall, relationship factors constitute a rich source of information for the practicing clinical psychologist. The literature finds that therapist personal characteristics; therapist behavior in sessions; the capacity to facilitate, monitor, sustain, and maintain a working alliance; and the reactions of therapists and clients to each other are vital. The impact of clinical research on therapist effects in psychotherapy compels clinical psychologists to commit to keeping abreast of the literature and to use these data to enhance their effectiveness. Otherwise, the gap between research and practice limits the potential for informing practitioners about means and mechanisms for facilitating positive outcomes, preventing deterioration effects, and preventing attrition.

This literature behooves clinical psychologists to assume a broad-based perspective by attending to the therapist and therapist attitudes and behaviors as an intervention package in and of itself in a sense. Moreover, in the hands of an interpersonally inept practitioner, even the most empirically based treatment protocols may prove less effective. Clinical psychologists must capitalize on all factors at their disposal to tailor their craft in ways that maximize positive outcomes and reduce the likelihood of negative outcomes. Relationship factors are one of the key ingredients.

Considering the long history of psychotherapy as a transaction between individuals, one who is vulnerable and in need of help and one who is an expert in the art and science of helping, what can be more central than the relationship itself, the social substrate through which positive influence exerts its impact? Psychotherapy is undoubtedly a social psychological process, and clinical psychologists are applied social-psychological practitioners whose characteristics and abilities to create a helping relationship are paramount. Finally, attending to factors that promote effective relationships and collaboration with fellow psychologists as well as experts in other disciplines appears self-evident. In the next section, we address identifying and measuring competency in the relationship domain.

BENCHMARK COMPETENCIES FOR RELATIONSHIPS

In attaining and sustaining competence in relationships, Fouad and colleagues (2009) defined it as the ability to "relate effectively and meaningfully with individuals, groups and/or communities" (p. S12). They view this process from a developmental framework by identifying critical elements progressing through practicum readiness, internship readiness, and readiness to assume practice in three essential areas: interpersonal relationships, affective proficiencies, and expressive proficiencies. In the component of interpersonal relationships, the emergence of competence is ultimately manifested by the ability of the clinical psychologist to handle challenging relationships and maintain acceptable relationships with various professional and nonprofessional groups. Requisite affective skills benchmarks include indicators that support competence in handling challenging and problematic communications, accepting different points of view, and assimilating feedback from others (Fouad et al., 2009). In the expressive skills component, competent psychologists display critical skills in the use of language and in communication. Awareness of the components of competence is hardly enough, however. Competent clinical psychologists are committed to ongoing assessment of their competence.

ASSESSING COMPETENCE IN RELATIONSHIPS

Kaslow and colleagues (2009) recommended a variety of "very useful" and "useful" tools in assessing competence in this area. Strategies include annual reviews, case reviews, process/outcome data, rating forms, consumer surveys, objective structured clinical examinations, performance ratings, self-assessments, simulations, standardized patients, and 360-degree evaluations. Competent psychologists have an investment in developing and sustaining competence in the relationship domain. Doing so entails not only a clear understanding of the benchmarks of competence in this domain but also a plan for harnessing information from a variety of sources designed to provide relevant information as a basis for a quality assurance plan in the relationship domain.

Concluding Remarks

The relationship competency is undoubtedly a core critical competency that provides a solid foundation upon which much of what clinical psychologists do on a daily basis firmly rests. For this reason alone, attention to developing, maintaining, and enhancing knowledge, skills, and attitudes related to fostering effective professional relationships is vital. Competent psychologists are conscious of those factors that fuel sound relationships and use their relationship competence to foster effectiveness in their work.

TWELVE

Ethical Considerations in Clinical Psychology

Competent practice in clinical psychology requires an in-depth under-standing of the ethical and legal standards incumbent upon all psycholo-gists and proficiency in applying these principles in daily practice. Clinical psychologists often encounter ethical dilemmas, ranging from reporting suspected child abuse, to warning potential victims of violence, to decid-ing whether to accept gifts from clients. In deciding how to address these ethical concerns, a clinical psychologist considers the most appropriate course of action given the specific circumstances. A clinical psychologist has an ethical responsibility to know the ethical and legal guidelines of the profession of psychology and to practice competently within an ethical framework. Furthermore, a competent psychologist is familiar with the code of ethical conduct and strives to integrate these principles into the decision-making process.

Given the importance of ethical conduct and professional integrity in clinical psychology, this chapter will be devoted to the topic of ethical com-petence. Competency in ethics will be described, the Ethical Principles of Psychologists and Code of Conduct (American Psychological Association [APA], 2002) will be underscored, and the importance of a decision-making model in determining the most ethical path of conduct when ethical guidelines are ambiguous will be discussed. Given the scope of ethical practice, it is difficult, if not impossible, to address in one chapter all the ethical issues psychologists might encounter. Hence, we have pared down these concerns to several issues identified as common dilemmas psycholo-gists contend with, including the broad categories of confidentiality, mul-tiple relationships, boundaries, professional impairment, and self-care.

Furthermore, current trends in competency-based approaches to training will be reviewed, including the delineation of specific behaviors demonstrating competency, assessment methods, and possible remediation plans for those displaying problems in professional ethical competency.

Ethical Principles and Code of Conduct

Barnett (2007, 2008) describes ethical competency as reflecting several components, the first being positive ethics. Positive ethics refers to a psychologist's responsibility and desire to uphold the General Principles as delineated by the APA's Ethical Principles of Psychologists and Code of Conduct (APA, 2002). The General Principles were created to encourage and guide psychologists to uphold professional ethical ideals. In addition to considering these principles in ethical practice, Barnett (2008) further asserts that risk management, focusing on best practices to benefit clients and minimize risk to psychologists, and defensive practice, focusing on protecting psychologists, are strategies that can be used to promote ethical practice. Although all three elements can encourage ethical conduct, positive ethics is usually emphasized, as it provides an overall encompassing ethical framework affording the psychologist the opportunity to aspire to high ethical ideals while considering the needs of the client and minimizing risk to the psychologist (Barnett, 2008).

The Ethical Principles of Psychologists and Code of Conduct (APA, 2002) is recognized universally as the ethical guidelines for psychologists to abide by in ethical decision-making. The General Principles are viewed as idealistic aspirations for psychologists, while the Code of Conduct maintains specific statutes to be upheld. The Ethical Principles and Code of Conduct was created to provide psychologists with a guide to resolve moral dilemmas while at the same time protecting the public who seek services from this professional group (Bersoff, 2008). The Ethics Code imparts more than a set of guidelines; rather, it furnishes a set of regulations created and enforced by the Ethical Committee within APA (Bersoff, 2008).

Although it provides structure, guidelines, and specific rules, the Code of Conduct inherently contains ambiguities often requiring psychologists to rely upon professional judgment in making ethical decisions. The Ethics Committee that created the original code acknowledged the ambiguity in wording but explained this vagueness as being related to the potency of the ethical issue. The Committee described some principles as having clear ethical relevancy and defined them as a "psychologist's obligation" or as "unethical." Other principles, defined with more ambiguous and vague terminology, were described as "good ethical practice and ethical etiquette guidelines" but did not necessarily hold to the same level of consensus regarding enforceable ethical standards. (APA, 1953). The most recent version of the code now states:

> ...the modifiers used in some of the standards of the ethics code (e.g., reasonably, appropriate, potentially) are included in the standards when they would (1) allow professional judgment on the part of the psychologists, (2) eliminate injustice or inequality that would occur without the modifier, (3) ensure applicability across the broad range of activities conducted by psychologists, or (4) guard against a set of rigid rules that might be quickly outdated. As used in this Ethics Code, the term reasonable means the prevailing professional judgment of psychologists engaged in similar activities in similar circumstances given the knowledge the psychologist had or should have had at the time. (APA, 2002)

APA's current explanation of the Ethics Code highlights the reasoning behind some of the ambiguity and vagueness in phrasing and emphasizes psychologists' reliance on professional judgment in making decisions. Professional judgment is described as being based on the reasoning of the majority of psychologists involved in similar activities and similar circumstances. Therefore, it is understandable that each standard may not necessarily be construed in the same way for every client, every situation, and every circumstance, hence leading to some flexibility in interpretation.

This flexibility in interpretation is highlighted in a survey conducted by Manheim and colleagues (2002) to evaluate psychologists' responses to different ethical dilemmas. Results indicated that psychologists treating children and adolescents differed markedly in their responses to several situations compared to the responses of psychologists working with adults. The authors suggest that psychologists may need to reconsider the ethical standards as related to children and perhaps create separate guidelines more applicable to working with this population (Mannheim et al., 2002). Although there is certainly merit in this idea, one could argue that the current guidelines do allow for this variability by stating that professional judgment is based on the prevailing opinions of those working in similar activities in similar circumstances (APA, 2002).

Aside from differences in ethical decision-making based on client populations, there is a general sense of uncertainty in some areas of ethical conduct. In a survey of psychologists' responses to a sampling of ethical dilemmas, Haas, Malouf, and Mayerson (1986) discovered many variations in responding, even though all respondents were psychologists bound to adhere to the same ethical guidelines created by APA. This difference in responding highlights the variability in interpretation within the Ethics Code and, as elucidated in the document itself, underscores the need to rely upon professional judgment. Nevertheless, given the ambiguities in the Ethics Code and the many questions that arise from this ambiguity, a competent psychologist manages this uncertainty by creating a methodical way of responding that guides the decision-making process.

Model of Ethical Decision-Making

Decisions can be difficult to make, particularly when they involve a possible ethical violation. By following a decision-making model, psychologists have a systematic way of evaluating the many facets of the problem. De las Fuentes, Willmuth, and Yarrow (2005) suggest that a core component of ethical competency in psychology is having an ethical decision-making model to follow. Knapp and VandeCreek (2004) recognized the ambiguity in the Ethics Code and the need for a paradigm to promote competent decision-making and proposed a five-step model for psychologists to employ in making competent ethical decisions.

Knapp and VandeCreek (2006) provide a detailed explanation of what they consider to be the essential components of the ethical decision-making process. The first step is identifying the problem and considering what aspects of it may pose an ethical issue. In identifying ethical dilemmas, psychologists must be conversant in the Ethics Code so they can recognize conflicts. In considering different aspects of the problem, psychologists must respect all of the parties to which they hold a moral obligation. Furthermore, they must consider how each person could be affected by the ethical dilemma and any decision made.

The second step involves generating ideas and alternatives to deal with the ethical dilemma that are consistent with ethical principles. Psychologists must be able to brainstorm ideas, generate options, and consider different solutions to a problem. Recognizing the options can be challenging; hence, outside consultation is an excellent method of facilitating the decision-making process in this phase. Consultants can be useful in generating alternative solutions and providing feedback to help psychologists make a decision in an informed manner.

The third step in the decision-making process entails reviewing these options and the possible benefits and consequences of each. In evaluating the advantages and disadvantages of each alternative, the psychologist should review the hierarchy of ethical standards considered to be most important in the specific situation. At times the psychologist may be forced to choose between two ethical standards. Minimizing harm to all those involved is the ultimate goal, and psychologists must consider this goal in choosing which standard to uphold.

The fourth step involves choosing and following through with one of the options, ideally the one that minimizes harm to those involved. The way in which the solution is carried out is also important: a psychologist may need to make use of his or her interpersonal skill set in carrying out the decision with sensitivity.

The last stage includes evaluating the success of the option chosen and assessing whether harm was minimized. After implementing the decision, the outcome must be evaluated. As in any decision-making process, Knapp and VandeCreek (2006) highlight that an ethical decision is a good one if (a) it is based on a moral principle that can be justified as being of primary importance, (b) it has a good likelihood of success, (c) there is no other morally preferable option, (d) it offers the least possible infraction of ethics and minimizes negative consequences, and (e) it is made without the undue influence of other considerations. After the fact, the psychologist may realize that another solution would have been a better choice. The outcome of the decision often triggers the need for a new decision to be made, requiring the initiation of the decision-making process again. Thus, the competent psychologist faced with an ethical dilemma is an active and informed problem-solver.

> *Case example:* Dr. Speedy is the supervisor of a mobile crisis team. Dr. Speedy was called to help with an elderly woman who was standing in the middle of a major intersection, agitated, confused, and scantily dressed. It was clear to Dr. Speedy that the woman was suffering from Alzheimer's disease; however, he needed to decide quickly how to handle the situation. The ethical dilemma he faced was whether to involuntarily commit her for hospitalization, knowing that psychiatric care would not be the most appropriate approach, or take her back to her house. He decided taking her back home would be best if she had adequate support. After many unsuccessful attempts to contact family members, Dr. Speedy reconsidered his decision and instead brought the elderly woman to

a hospital. Although he realized this was not the most appropriate placement for her, he feared that leaving her alone at her house would put her at imminent risk, and recognized that a client's safety must be of primary concern when making an ethical decision.

Sometimes psychologists have the time to follow through with the decision-making process in a methodical way, but other times they have to make quick decisions. A clinical psychologist should be familiar with the Ethics Code and this five-step decision-making model so that, when the situation arises, it is possible to respond promptly with the professional judgment and integrity expected from a skilled specialist.

Decisions Involving Ethical and Legal Contradictions

Ethical guidelines are often consistent with legal responsibilities, so psychologists are typically able to uphold both their legal obligations and their ethical responsibilities without conflict. Nevertheless, sometimes ethical obligations and legal requirements do not coincide. In these instances, psychologists may find themselves in the difficult position of having to choose between following ethical or legal guidelines. When making a decision, psychologists should consider all the options, the people involved and affected by any decision made, the risks and consequences of any action pursued, and the courses of action causing the least amount of harm and the most benefit to the client (Knapp, Gottlieb, Berman, & Handelsman, 2007).

> *Case Example:* Dr. Youngster has been ordered by the court to testify in a child custody case. It had taken quite a while for the therapist and child to establish a good working relationship, and Dr. Youngster strongly believed that breaking the child's confidentiality would cause more harm than benefit for his child client. The dilemma brought forth was that testifying would require some breach in the child's confidentiality—but he risked being charged with contempt of court if he did not oblige.

The Ethics Code acknowledges that sometimes there is a discrepancy between ethical responsibility and the law. The Ethics Code states that the psychologist's first priority and commitment should be toward the Ethics Code itself and that the psychologist should try to resolve the conflict. If it is not feasible to resolve the issue, then the Ethics Code states that the psychologist may follow the law.

Knapp and colleagues (2007) point out that although the Ethics Code provides some guidelines, often they are not specific enough or clear enough to offer the direction necessary to solve the ethical dilemmas encountered by psychologists. For example, further examination of the phrasing of the Ethics Code in regard to ethical and legal conflicts indicates that the psychologist may follow the ethical guidelines but at other times may need to follow the law. Hence, psychologists are still in the predicament of deciding for themselves which guidelines to follow. The Ethics Committee of APA recognized this ambiguity in certain situations where there may be a conflict with the law and in 2010 amended the wording of two standards, including the introduction and applicability section, to clarify that interpretation of these standards can never be used to "justify or defend violating human rights" (APA, Ethical Principles of Psychologists and Code of Conduct; Standards 1.02 & 1.03).

Given that it is ultimately the psychologist's responsibility to decide to follow ethical standards or the law when there is a discrepancy, it is then incumbent upon psychologists to consult with others and consider additional resources to help come to a decision. Ethical decision-making is not easy; what may be an initial response can often change as all of the related factors are considered and understood. Furthermore, after thoughtfully considering all the alternatives, the choices to which psychologists believe they are limited may then be expanded to include other options.

Knapp and colleagues (2007) further suggest that clinical psychologists often need to rely on personal values to resolve some of these conflicts. They detail a decision-making process to aid psychologists in resolving ethical dilemmas that appear to be in contradiction to the law. They suggest that a psychologist understand what is required by law to verify whether there may in fact be a conflict. Next, the psychologist should carefully review the Ethics Code and ensure understanding of professional responsibility as dictated by the Ethics Code. In addition, the psychologist should seek consultation to ensure a full understanding of what is required from an ethical as well as a legal standpoint. If after careful review there does appear to be a discrepancy between the ethical obligation as a psychologist and the law, the psychologist should consider options that will allow both ethical and legal responsibilities to be met. If a resolution is impossible, the psychologist should decide whether to abide by the law with the least infraction to ethical responsibility possible, or to respect the ethical commitment with as minimal violation of the law as possible. With either choice, the psychologist must be prepared to accept any repercussions of the decision. If a psychologist firmly believes there is no other option than to defy the law, he or she should do so with the least amount of violation necessary to reach the desired goal (Knapp et al., 2007).

A competent psychologist documents everything pertaining to the ethical dilemma, including the thought processes involved in making the final decision. If legal responsibility is ascertained to be the first priority, then again, as stated by Knapp and colleagues (2007), the psychologist should minimize the breach in ethics as much as possible, perhaps by involving the client in the process. In the best-case scenario, as presented by Knapp and colleagues (2007), the psychologist can try to foresee any possible conflicts ahead of time. Given that these situations will arise, the most competent way to handle the situation is to seek consultation and use a formal decision-making process to help steer through the ambiguity.

In summary, ethical guidelines can differ from legal standards. A competent clinical psychologist considers the many issues involved in an ethical dilemma, seeks consultation, and uses a decision-making model to evaluate the best course of action.

Common Ethical Concerns

There are a number of ethical dilemmas confronting clinical psychologists on a frequent basis. According to reports of the APA Ethics Committee, the most cited categories of ethical misconduct for 2009 and 2010 included issues of dual relationships (both sexual and nonsexual) followed by inappropriate professional practice in regard to child custody, practicing outside of competency, and issues of fees/insurance or other (APA, 2010, 2011). There were also some violations of failure to uphold standards of the profession. The following sections describe common areas of complaint to the ethical board as well as other issues central to ethical practice.

INFORMED CONSENT

According to the Ethics Code (APA, 2002), a psychologist is required to obtain informed consent from clients and research participants before beginning treatment and/or research protocols, respectively. Informed consent is the first step in establishing a relationship with the client. By virtue of the act itself, talking to clients about the therapy process will allow them to share in the decisions made about treatment as well as promote openness and trust in the therapeutic relationship (Barnett, 2007). Informed consent has been found to be beneficial in promoting client participation, aiding in a quicker recovery, and helping to decrease anxiety (Handler, 1990; Pope & Vasquez, 2007).

Informed consent refers to the process of providing the client with all the information he or she needs to decide whether or not to participate in research, assessment, and/or psychotherapy. Informed consent should include information about what the client can expect from participation, the costs, the limits of confidentiality, and any other information that is needed to allow the client to make an informed decision about participation (APA, 2002). Ethically, psychologists are obligated to initiate the process and to provide clients with the information they need to make an informed choice, rather than waiting for them to ask questions and only then providing the necessary information (Barnett, 2007). Three conditions must be met for consent to be valid: (a) clients must be able to fully understand the information presented, (b) they must agree to the terms of their own volition, and (c) they must be competent to make the decision on their own (Gross, 2001).

Pope and Vasquez (2007) present a myriad of issues that should be considered when planning informed consent procedures for psychotherapy. They assert that consent procedures should include verification of the client's knowledge of who will be providing treatment and his or her understanding of the treating therapist's qualifications, the client's understanding of the purpose of coming to therapy, and the client's understanding of the treatment plan, including its duration and possible consequences. Furthermore, clients should be notified of any limitations to therapy (e.g., the psychologist is pregnant and will be taking a maternity leave for 3 months), the fee structure, any policies on missed appointments and handling of emergencies, and the limits to confidentiality. To aid psychologists in creating ethically sound consent forms, APA created sample documents. A competent psychologist is familiar with the ethical requirements of informed consent and integrates these guidelines into practice.

Presentation of Consent Forms   The manner in which information is presented can in itself determine a person's decision to consent to participate in therapy, assessment, or research. Psychologists can easily find themselves in the predicament of wanting to do what is ethically appropriate and providing clients with the knowledge they need to make informed choices, but at the same time they are invested in the client's initiation or continuation of treatment. This issue is most poignant when treatment itself is part of a research study, where there is added pressure on the investigator to recruit people to participate in the treatment. Unintentionally, the psychologist may gloss over certain issues, emphasize the benefits of participation, and marginalize the risks so it is more appealing and more likely for people to consent to participate. Psychologists should ensure that clients are fully and objectively informed of the aspects of participation so they can make a truly informed decision.

> *Case example:* Dr. Data, a psychologist at a university-based hospital, was conducting a study evaluating the efficacy of a new treatment he had developed for depression. After a patient was diagnosed with depression, Dr. Data would present the patient with a consent form while explaining that he was able to offer a state-of-the-art treatment aimed at relieving depressive symptomatology. Dr. Data did not inform the patient that this was an experimental treatment; he did not provide the patient with the alternative and more common option of treatment as usual at the hospital; nor did he discuss any risks involved in participating. The manner in which Dr. Data presented the consent form led patients to believe that the best treatment option for their depression was this "state-of-the-art" treatment. Dr. Data was eager to recruit participants in his study, and although he did not intentionally leave out the other information, he presented the study in a way that did not allow the patients to be fully informed.

In addition to ensuring that all of the information necessary for an informed consent is presented to prospective participants, the information must be presented in layman's language so that clients understand and feel comfortable in their agreement to participate. After reviewing consent information, it's best to confirm that clients understand what they are agreeing to by participating in the treatment, assessment, or research. Many psychologists will ask clients if they have any questions, but this method is not always sufficient for assessing understanding. A better way to fulfill the obligation of informed consent is to ask the client to summarize to what he or she is giving consent (Barnett, 2007). This provides an opportunity to correct misconceptions and clarify issues that may have been unclear or misunderstood. Furthermore, although there are no specific regulations about informed consent being in written form, it is highly recommended to do so. It is common practice for psychologists to ask clients to sign a written consent in addition to providing a verbal explanation of the information. Regardless of whether it is written, verbal, or both, documentation of informed consent is a must for all psychologists (APA, 2002).

Barnett (2007) reports that although there are guidelines delineating what must be included in informed consent materials, the amount of information and the level of detail to be included remain ambiguous. He suggests the following considerations: (1) presenting the information so that it clearly represents the expectations of participation as well as issues of competence; (2) selecting the amount of information to be disclosed; (3) choosing the manner in which the information is presented; and (4) considering the impact that diversity may have in obtaining informed consent (Barnett, 2007). Psychologists must keep ethical principles in the forefront of decision-making in regard to informed consent "for protecting clients' rights, promoting autonomy, and working to achieve the best possible outcomes" (Barnett, 2007, p. 181).

Treatment Plans   Informed consent is not a one-time endorsement but rather a process that continues throughout therapy (Johnson-Greene, 2007). A competent psychologist facilitates a collaborative relationship in which the treatment plan is reviewed and revised periodically with the client throughout treatment. With the advent of a new treatment plan, the therapist documents the goals, objectives, and means of attaining and evaluating the realization of those objectives as determined in tandem with the client. The therapist reviews the revised plan with the client and makes any changes as deemed necessary in collaboration with the client, and both therapist and client sign the revised treatment plan, consenting to its implementation. This periodic renegotiation of the treatment plan promotes collaboration between therapist and client while at the same time being respectful of the client's autonomy. The client is given the opportunity to participate in the treatment-planning process and once again to give consent to the terms of the revised treatment contract. Collaborating, reviewing, and agreeing on a treatment plan allows the client to fully understand and give consent to a course of treatment in an informed manner.

Monetary Issues   Discussion of fees, mode of payment, and any financial concerns should take place at the outset of therapy and should be part of the informed consent process. If it appears that a possible client will not be able to meet the financial responsibilities required for treatment by a particular psychologist, the psychologist should make a reasonable and appropriate referral to another psychologist or agency that would be able to accommodate his or her financial situation (Koocher & Keith-Spiegel, 2008). Ethical practice dictates addressing these issues before therapy is to begin. Other issues related to fees can include charges for missed appointments. There is no ethical violation of doing so; however, competent practice ensures that this policy is discussed with and agreed upon by clients in advance, ideally as part of the informed consent procedure.

CONFIDENTIALITY

Confidentiality is a mainstay of competent psychological practice. One of the key points discussed by virtually all psychologists at an initial meeting with a new client is the issue of and limits to confidentiality. Most people entering into the therapeutic relationship enter with the idea that most, if not all, of what is discussed in therapy will remain confidential. In fact, clients not only prefer that information about themselves remains confidential but expect that to be the case (VandeCreek, Miars, & Herzog, 1987). Psychologists are ethically obligated to ensure and protect their clients' confidentiality to the highest degree possible, but at the same time, given clients' expectations, they must also be clear in discussing the limits of confidentiality. The basis for any relationship involves trust, and if trust is broken, the therapeutic relationship can easily be damaged (Smith-Bell & Winslade, 1994). In response to a perceived breach of trust, clients may feel betrayed by the therapist, may begin to be uncooperative in therapy, or may terminate therapy altogether (Smith-Bell & Winslade, 1994). The competent psychologist is cognizant of these issues and addresses confidentiality and its limits with those entering therapy.

Working with Minors   When discussing confidentiality as related to minors, deciding on the limits of confidentiality can be more challenging. Factors to consider in deciding the level of disclosure include the age of the client, the presenting problem, the needs and concerns of the parents and the child, the client's cognitive ability and maturity level, and state regulations regarding confidentiality and minors (Gustafson & McNamara, 1987).

> *Case example:* Joe, a 13-year-old client, told his therapist that he was "smoking weed" on a regular basis, unbeknownst to his parents. The therapist talked to Joe about sharing this information with his parents, but Joe was adamant that he was not ready to discuss it with them, as he knew they would not approve of his behavior. At the end of the session Joe's father asked to speak with the therapist privately and asked the therapist if Joe was using drugs. The therapist was placed in a difficult situation. If she disclosed to his father that Joe was "smoking weed," she would violate the trust

she had built up with Joe. But if she responded "no" or even "I didn't know," then she would be lying to his father, something she viewed as an ethical and moral violation. She asked the father if he had asked his son the same question. When Joe's father replied no, the therapist encouraged him to have an open dialog with his son when they got home that night.

Confidentiality with minors can be quite challenging, and the competent psychologist must be proactive in considering how issues of confidentiality will be handled. Gustafson and McNamara (1987) argue that an adolescent who is not provided with the security of confidentiality may decide to forgo treatment altogether or may not fully participate in therapy because of concerns that the information revealed will be shared with others. This situation can easily be avoided by clearly discussing the limits of confidentiality and ensuring that the client is aware of what will remain confidential and what may need to be shared. Koocher (2008) recommends openly discussing confidentiality and the limits of confidentiality with all parties involved. Specifically with adolescents, it is important to discuss that there may be issues the adolescent does not want his or her parents to know about, and for all concerned to come to an agreement on how these issues will be handled before treatment is to begin.

Duty to Warn   When considering confidentiality, one of the challenges faced by psychologists is the ethical obligation to warn an intended victim of violence if the psychologist is privy to this information, regardless of whether it was discovered in the context of therapy. The basic tenet is that the protection of life is of utmost importance and should be prioritized before confidentiality. The *Tarasoff* case (*Tarasoff vs. Board of Regents of the University of California*, 1976) was the catalyst for this matter, when the Supreme Court ruled that the protection of individual privacy must end when danger to the public begins. When discussing confidentiality, psychologists are obligated to inform clients of the limits of confidentiality, including the required disclosure of information when there is a threat to the client's life or someone else's life. The dilemma faced by psychologists is that clients need to feel comfortable disclosing private information; however, certain information disclosed by clients may not be able to be kept confidential. This inconsistency may present as a barrier to treatment for some who may then be fearful of disclosing information or may not pursue treatment at all. Furthermore, if these limits are not made clear and the client discloses information that the psychologist is obligated to make public, the client may then lose trust in the therapist and in the mental health system. The psychologist is essentially placed in the position of deciding if the client is dangerous and if someone specific is in danger of being harmed, or if the client is unlikely to follow through with any threat. Although the law is clear that psychologists must warn someone who is in imminent danger, the issue then becomes how certain anyone can be of a possible imminent threat. A psychologist must balance the therapeutic relationship and the trust that has been developed within that relationship with the determination of whether an imminent threat exists. The competent psychologist must rely on professional judgment and strong assessment skills in making this determination.

Breaches in Confidentiality   Confidentiality seems like an easy enough ethical guideline to uphold, but ethical dilemmas that fall into the realm of confidentiality arise quite often. When APA members were asked to report on any incidents they found to be challenging in the realm of ethics, issues related to confidentiality were one of the top three categories identified (dual relationships and payment for services were the other two; Pope & Vetter, 1992). Pope and Vasquez (2007) discuss how, unknowingly and unintentionally, psychologists can lose sight of the importance of confidentiality and the stringency with which ethics needs to be upheld. They pinpoint several common situations in which confidentiality can easily be broken, such as referral sources, public conversations, and medical records (Pope & Vasquez, 2007).

Referral sources. It is not unusual to obtain a referral from someone who is then curious as to whether the referred patient followed up with an appointment. It is also not unusual to be thankful for the referral and, as is common in everyday life, want to acknowledge and thank the referrer for making the referral.

> *Case example:* Dr. Benevolent referred his client's adult son, Marc, to Dr. Goodintentions. Dr. Benevolent ran into Dr. Goodintentions while jogging and asked if Marc had ever followed through with the referral. Dr. Benevolent was eager to help his client's son and was hoping that Marc had called Dr. Goodintentions, as he felt that Marc would really benefit from her care. Dr. Goodintentions thanked Dr. Benevolent for the referral and let him know Marc had started seeing her and was doing well. Unless given explicit permission to do so by the client, however, this is a violation of the

client's confidentiality. Although the client may have received the referral name from someone else, it is up to the client to decide if he or she wants the referrer to know if the referral was pursued. Furthermore, commenting on how he was doing in therapy was clearly a violation of confidentiality as well.

Privacy in conversation. Psychologists must be ever-vigilant about protecting the identity of clients (Pope & Vasquez, 2007).

Case example: Dr. Smith and Dr. Jones are in an office elevator, heading downstairs for lunch. They are discussing, Mary, a client Dr. Smith finds to be "difficult." Unbeknownst to them, Mary's sister, who works in a medical office two floors above, was riding in the elevator with them. She knew who Dr. Smith was, knew Mary was in treatment with him, and was able to discern that the conversation was about her sister, even though they did not use her name. Although Mary's name was never stated, this conversation was a violation of her confidentiality, as it was clear to a bystander whom they were discussing.

There may be occasions when a psychologist seeking consultation accidentally discloses information about the client specific enough for the consultant or others in the vicinity to know about whom they are speaking. A competent psychologist should be aware of the possibility of these indiscretions and monitor the details provided to the consultant. Furthermore, these conversations should be held in a private area, better protecting the client's confidentiality.

Privacy in records. Pope and Vasquez (2007) discuss the issue of written records and the importance of keeping those records, as well as any identifying information, out of public view. It is not uncommon to walk into a psychologist's office and notice files sitting on the desk, perhaps files from clients last seen that now need progress notes completed. This can be a violation of confidentiality if the names are printed on the outside of the file, or if the office is left unattended and unlocked. Most often these occurrences are unintentional, yet this clearly highlights the need for psychologists to be vigilant in protecting their clients' privacy and ensuring that records are secured from public eye.

Privacy of children and adolescents. One of the most common issues of confidentiality in regard to children is encountered when contacting schools. It is necessary to obtain consent from the family before contacting a school; obtaining a written consent specifying what information can be shared clarifies for the therapist and the school what information can and cannot be revealed. A clinical psychologist not only values the importance of the written consent but ensures that both family members and the therapist understand and feel comfortable with any collaboration taking place with the school.

> *Case example:* Dr. Booksmart, a child psychologist, felt it was imperative to obtain information from a school about Jon, but Jon's parents were adamant that the school should not know Jon was seeking therapeutic services. A compromise was reached whereby Dr. Booksmart was given permission to call the school and say that she was helping Jon learn better study skills, which was in fact part of the reason for the referral, and would find it helpful to have the school's input on a few issues. In this example, all parties were clear from the start about what could be shared, hence alleviating any misunderstandings or unwanted breaches in confidentiality.

Nevertheless, just as with adults, there are situations in which the psychologist may need to consider breaking the confidentiality of a child or adolescent by sharing information with parents. In a study assessing factors that play a role in psychologists' decisions to break confidentiality of adolescents, participants were presented with vignettes of ethical dilemmas and asked to rate the degree to which it was ethically acceptable to break confidentiality (Sullivan, Ramirez, Rae, Razo, & George, 2002). The two factors viewed to be most instrumental in the decision-making process were the negative nature of the adolescent's behavior and the therapist's interest in maintaining the therapeutic process. Deciding that a behavior is negative requires an assessment of the risks involved for the adolescent. As Sullivan and colleagues (2002) reiterated, this risk assessment should be based on empirical data of normal adolescent development and normative risk-taking behaviors. The intensity, frequency, and duration of the behavior must be considered as well. The higher the intensity, duration, and frequency of the behavior, the more likely it is that the psychologist would feel obligated to break confidentiality (Rae, Sullivan, Razo, George, & Ramirez, 2002). Furthermore, if the behavior itself was considered outside the norm for adolescents, it was likely that confidentiality would be breached, even if the duration was not excessive (Rae et al., 2002).

Sullivan and colleagues (2002) discussed how the second factor, the importance of maintaining the therapeutic relationship, affected the decision-making process and highlighted the need for psychologists to openly discuss confidentiality with the family from the start of treatment. They also discussed considering how to break confidentiality, if necessary, in a way that will maintain the relationship. In working with adolescents, it may be helpful to talk with the adolescent first about the concerning behavior and encourage the adolescent to disclose this information himself or herself to the parents. In this way, the psychologist is not forced to decide whether to break confidentiality. An alternative approach is to tell the parents about the behavior with the adolescent present. These methods help to maintain the relationship and may mitigate the potential ill will associated with the breach in confidentiality.

Finally, Sullivan and colleagues (2002) emphasize that even though the therapeutic relationship is important, psychologists must be wary of choosing the relationship over client safety, which is ultimately of primary concern. As with any ethical dilemma, all factors playing a role in the decision need to be considered and evaluated, but a competent psychologist regards the client's well-being and physical safety as the overriding concern.

Confidentiality as an ethical obligation. Psychologists are obligated to protect client privacy and are ethically bound to act in a way that promotes client welfare, avoids harm, and respects client autonomy (i.e., allow a client to decide when, where, and to whom information is to be released). Furthermore, when confidentiality is upheld, clients will ideally develop more confidence and trust in what can be discussed in therapy with the assurance that it will remain private information. A competent psychologist not only provides a safe environment for the client to discuss sensitive information but also is certain to explain the limits of confidentiality so that the client is fully cognizant of when confidentiality may need to be broken. For families, it is imperative to discuss how information obtained through private conversation with family members will be handled. For children and adolescents, it is important to discuss what information will and will not be shared with parents. There are variations of how psychologists handle issues of confidentiality, but regardless of the decision, the psychologist's ethical obligation to breach confidentiality for certain situations should be made clear to all parties involved. Clients should be made aware of the psychologist's ethical obligations at the start of treatment, and should confidentiality need to be breached, a competent psychologist again discusses the ethical obligation to break confidentiality before this breach is made.

ELECTRONIC MEDICAL RECORDS

A more current issue related to the ethics of confidentiality involves the use of electronic medical records. It is becoming more and more common for medical records to be stored electronically, especially in medical settings and places involving multidisciplinary teams (Richards, 2009). This presents a whole new scope of ethical issues warranting consideration. Questions related to who has access to these records and what information should be kept within them and notifying patients of the limits of confidentiality in regard to these records are all of utmost concern. APA (2007) created guidelines to help psychologists in traversing the world of electronic recordkeeping so that client confidentiality is upheld to the highest extent possible while still maintaining records in the way delineated by the Ethics Code and state mandates. APA (2007) asserts that although the state sets the guidelines for recordkeeping, the psychologist should consider the client's desires and the directives of the agency.

By using an electronic record, anyone on a client's medical team can access information identifying that the client is being seen by a psychologist, when he or she is being seen, and the client's diagnosis, regardless of the client's consent to allow other medical providers to have access to this information (Richards, 2009). Unless psychotherapy notes summarizing the content of the session are kept separate, they are considered part of the general medical record and can be viewed by others on the medical team and/or the insurance carrier if the information is needed to aid in diagnosis, treatment planning, billing, and healthcare administrative needs. Certain facilities allow psychological notes to be blocked so that only those with permission are allowed to access them.

In addition to who has access to records, the psychologist must be wary of other potential breaches of confidentiality. Psychologists need to institute measures to protect themselves from unauthorized and unintended disclosures (Baker & Bufka, 2011) caused by damage to computers via hackers, viruses, or stolen equipment (Drogin, Connell, Foote, & Sturm, 2010). Patient data should be secured through network security protocols, including strict password protection with complex passwords and encrypted database access. This will ensure that even if unauthorized users acquire access to the record, they will not be able to read it. Computers should have virus protection software that is updated regularly. Electronic records should be identified by case numbers rather than social security numbers to further protect client identifiers (APA, 2007).

An electronic recordkeeping system is very different from what many psychologists are accustomed to, and many do not realize the potential for breaches in confidentiality. Nevertheless, psychologists are ethically obligated to be aware of and inform clients of these potential limits to confidentiality. As electronic recordkeeping becomes the standard of practice, psychologists will need to balance the ethical responsibility of protecting their clients' confidentiality with following the regulations for documentation set by the state and federal government (Richards, 2009). Open dialog and disclosure of the possible breaches to confidentiality from the start of treatment are basic practices that should be part of a clinical psychologist's repertoire.

MULTIPLE RELATIONSHIPS

The issue of multiple relationships is an area that psychologists confront with some regularity, particularly those who live in a rural region, a small town, or an area with only a few therapists. In these instances, it might not be unusual for a child's teacher to approach the psychologist about working with his or her son or daughter or for a psychologist who volunteers at a community event to find a client in charge of the volunteers. Although the psychologist and client may find themselves in communal social situations, the psychologist's approach should be to continue to maintain the client's confidentiality.

Within the realm of multiple relationships, ethical practice includes avoiding the treatment of friends; however, treating family members or friends of current clients is less clear. A psychologist should consider and evaluate the risks associated with accepting these referrals before making a final decision (Koocher & Keith-Spiegel, 2008). In addition to carefully considering whom to treat, a psychologist must also be aware of personal vulnerabilities, such as sexual attraction to a client. Seeking consultation to ensure objectivity will aid the psychologist in upholding professional ethical standards. It is the responsibility of the psychologist to consider the many possibilities that could arise in the realm of multiple relationships and reflect on how these situations might be handled.

The Ethics Code defines multiple relationships as occurring:

> when a psychologist is in a professional role with a person and (1) at the same time is in another role with the same person, (2) at the same time is in a relationship with a person closely associated with or related to the person with whom they have the professional relationship, or (3) promises to enter into another relationship in

the future with the person or a person closely associated with or related to the person. A psychologist refrains from entering into multiple relationships if the relationship could reasonably be expected to impair the psychologist's objectivity, competence or effectiveness in performing his or her functions as a psychologist or otherwise risks exploitation or harm to the person with whom the professional relationship exists. Multiple relationships that would not reasonably be expected to cause impairment or risk exploitation or harm are not unethical. (Ethical Principles of Psychologists and Code of Conduct, Standard 3.05)

As clearly stated in the Ethics Code, not all multiple relationships pose an ethical violation. If the relationship may in some way affect the therapist's effectiveness, or if there is any risk of harm or exploitation to the client, then the relationship needs to be examined on the basis of ethical concerns. (Lamb, Catanzaro, & Moorman, 2004).

Although the Ethics Code addresses the issue of multiple relationships, there is room for interpretation and, as is consistent with the Ethics Code in general, there are many situations that do not neatly fit into the guidelines provided. Therefore, the psychologist must determine whether a relationship may be considered unethical. In a survey of mental health professionals, Borys and Pope (1989) presented a list of circumstances that could fall under the realm of possible multiple relationships and asked participants to rate the degree of ethical compliance. Interestingly, five categories were perceived to be unethical by the vast majority of respondents (i.e., having sex with a client; selling a product to a client; having sex with a client after treatment was complete; inviting a client to a social event; and providing therapy to an employee), but no situations were perceived to be unethical all the time by all respondents. This study clearly demonstrates the challenges psychologists encounter in determining the boundaries of ethical violations in regard to multiple relationships. Given the ambiguity that seems to exist, psychologists must employ a decision-making model that will foster the formulation of a well-thought-out resolution to an ethical dilemma. A competent psychologist reviews the Ethics Code regarding multiple relationships, considers the specifics of the situation including the possible dual relationship and potential consequences, considers other options that would preclude a dual relationship, and seeks consultation. Most importantly, a competent psychologist must consider the possible risk of harm to the client, keeping in mind that protecting a client from harm is the one of the ultimate goals of the Ethics Code. Furthermore, a psychologist should be self-aware and avoid any circumstances and/or relationships that could hinder his or her ability to work effectively.

BOUNDARIES

The Ethics Code discusses therapeutic boundaries regarding multiple relationships, but a variety of ethical concerns encompassed in the realm of appropriate boundaries are not clearly discussed. In these situations, the therapist's theoretical orientation can often shape his or her perspectives on what may or may not be considered unethical, as can other professionals with whom the psychologist works closely.

Self-Disclosure   Some psychologists consider self-disclosure to be a boundary violation (Gutheil & Gabbard, 1993). For instance, a psychodynamic-oriented therapist would most likely keep self-disclosure to a minimum because therapeutic neutrality is considered essential to the therapeutic process, although personal reactions to the client during the session are considered more acceptable (Goldfried, Burckell, & Eubanks-Carter, 2003). In contrast, a cognitive-behavioral therapist may consider self-disclosure as a modeling opportunity and an important component of treatment. Although appropriate boundaries should be maintained and the psychologist should reflect on the purpose and motivation for self-disclosure, self-disclosure has been found to enhance treatment by strengthening the therapeutic relationship, normalizing client concerns, increasing positive feelings and motivation, and providing a model of functional behavior for clients to emulate (Goldfried et al., 2003). A clinical psychologist is cognizant of any personal motivation for self-disclosure and makes the decision to do so only after thoughtful consideration of how it will aid in the ultimate goal of enhancing treatment effectiveness.

Gifts   Another ethical concern in the realm of boundaries is giving and receiving gifts or services. While it is generally considered that giving gifts breaches appropriate boundaries of therapy, there are no standards explicitly addressing this issue. The Ethics Code provides clarification in regard to bartering, indicating that it is acceptable under two conditions: "Psychologist may barter only if (1) it is not clinically contraindicated, and (2) the resulting arrangement is not exploitive" (Ethical Principles for Psychologists and Code of Conduct, Standard 6.05).

Knapp and Slattery (2004) distinguish between boundary crossings and boundary violations, clarifying that there are many instances where boundaries are crossed, but it is considered a violation only when it can become harmful to the patient. Giving and receiving gifts is an example of a potential boundary crossing but not necessarily a boundary violation.

> *Case example:* A student therapist was working with a woman who reached her 85th birthday. Consistent with socially acceptable behavior outside of the therapy room, the therapist gave the client flowers, knowing it was a milestone birthday and that the client would appreciate and enjoy the flowers on this special day. Did the therapist cross a boundary? Many would venture to say yes, as this was not something the therapist did on a regular basis, nor did she do it for any other client's birthday; this gesture was something unique for this client. However, was it a boundary violation? Many would say that this gesture was not a violation, as it did not place the client in harm's way and was in the realm of a natural social gesture of kindness at a moment that was special to the client.

A clinical psychologist must navigate through natural instincts as a human being and consider the ultimate goal of whether the behavior is helpful or harmful to the client.

Boundary Crossing   Boundary setting and the fluidness of those boundaries can be a contentious topic; many arguments have ensued over this issue (e.g., Brown, 1994; Gottlieb, 1994: Lazarus, 1994). Lazarus (1994) published a controversial article in which he reported his own experiences of breaking traditional therapeutic boundaries and the benefits that resulted in his relationships with his clients by doing so. This article was a catalyst for much debate on the topic and prompted many others to respond (e.g., Bennett, Bricklin, & VandeCreek, 1994; Borys, 1994). What became clear is that there are many different thoughts about the definition of appropriate and inappropriate behavior in terms of establishing boundaries with clients as well as what is considered to be a boundary crossing versus a boundary violation. As highlighted throughout this chapter, ethical codes of conduct can be ambiguous and vague and do not always provide psychologists with clear definitions and standards to follow. A psychologist must use professional judgment in determining what is considered an ethical violation. In making this determination, a psychologist must consider the ethical principles that exist, consult with others, and make informed thoughtful decisions based on this knowledge.

IMPAIRMENT

Part of being a competent psychologist involves recognizing any possible impairment in professional functioning. Impairment could result from a myriad of personal reasons (e.g., a sick child at home, anxiety over an impending move) and/or professional reasons (e.g., heavy workload, insensitive boss). Psychologists' responsibilities and obligations can be stressful—playing many roles in the same day, remaining helpful to clients when experiencing personal difficulties, dealing with emotionally charged issues and perhaps not having time to recover before being asked to handle the next issue (O'Connor, 2001). When not functioning at their best, psychologists may begin to act disrespectfully toward clients, perhaps viewing them in a more negative light or lacking the patience needed to treat them effectively. Psychologists may wish they did not have to help clients with their difficulties when the psychologists themselves are contending with their own problems. There may be noticeable signs of impairment in quality of work; perhaps the psychologist starts making mistakes. Psychologists may begin to lack energy in their efforts at work, lose interest in things that were once more appealing, or become anxious over their "to-do" lists (Pope & Vasquez, 2005). When distressed, psychologists report decreases in the quality of care provided to their clients (Guy, Poelstra, & Stark, 1989).

Impairment in professional activities is one of the basic defining characteristics of burnout (Freeman, Felgoise, & Davis, 2008). Stress and exhaustion are factors contributing to psychological burnout; however, it is the way the psychologist is affected by these factors in work performance, attitude, and ability to put forth effort that ultimately determines whether it is burnout. When experiencing burnout, a psychologist's judgment may be compromised and he or she may inadvertently make unethical decisions or behave unprofessionally (Freeman et al., 2008). As dictated by the Ethics Code, when personal issues prevent psychologists from working in a competent manner, they should choose not to involve themselves in those activities. Furthermore, they should seek consultation to help determine if they should stop working until these issues are no longer interfering with job performance (Ethics Code of Conduct, Standard 2.06). A clinical psychologist must have enough insight and self-awareness to recognize the possibility of impairment and desist from activities that will require working in an impaired state.

Given the complexity that already exists regarding ethics, it is understandable that when functioning is impaired and when psychologists are not as clear-headed in their thinking, it is easy to make ethical blunders.

Psychologists can help ensure their own level of competence by seeking consultation and by maintaining a social network of peers with whom to share ideas and receive support. Furthermore, they must take care of themselves to help prevent professional impairment.

SELF-CARE

Psychologists are in the business of taking care of others; whether it is clients, supervisees, or students, psychologists are often attending to others' needs. To do this successfully, psychologists must be cognizant of nurturing themselves as well. It is very important to balance life with both personal and professional activities. If psychologists are not engaging in things they enjoy on a personal level, then they are not experiencing the balance that is so important to self-care.

Everyone has an obligation to take care of himself or herself. If psychologists are not careful about their own self-care, then it is likely that they will not perform at an optimal level; in fact, they may behave in a way that could be harmful to clients. Pope and Vasquez (2005) describe factors that can lead to burnout vulnerability and discuss ways to reduce this possibility through self-care. They discuss issues such as isolation, particularly for the sole practitioner working with clients all day, and the importance of keeping a social network to help alleviate isolation. Participating in a weekly peer supervision group is a good solution to combat this vulnerability. The benefits of a peer supervision group are twofold: the group provides camaraderie and a social outlet to reduce isolation, and it provides an opportunity to think about cases and consult with peers to ensure the best treatment for clients.

Pope and Vasquez (2005) discuss monotony and the possible downfall of getting trapped in the same routine. For some people this can be desirable, but for others it can lead to negative feelings and impairment in functioning. Participating in a variety of activities allows a psychologist to divert from a routine, and for many, a good balance of activities may help in efforts toward self-care.

An issue that many people encounter across all disciplines is fatigue. How much time can truly be dedicated to something before feeling overwhelmed to the point where performance is adversely affected? Knowing one's limits and recognizing when fatigue may be setting in is helpful in preventing impairment and professional burnout. Competent practice includes being aware of personal tolerance levels before needing a break. Some psychologists can meet with five clients consecutively without a break; others prefer to have breaks after only a few sessions. Being cognizant of when fatigue sets in allows therapists to create an environment for themselves in which they can provide the best care possible for clients.

In addition to behaviors psychologists can engage in to create a positive working atmosphere, there are activities they can participate in outside of the office to facilitate performing to the best of their ability. Involvement in activities that keep psychologists physically healthy, active, and spiritually balanced can aid in preventing burnout (Pope & Vasquez, 2005). Many times when psychologists are stressed, self-care endeavors are the first activities dismissed. But because psychologists are in the service of providing mental health care, they must meet their own mental health needs before they can help others. If psychologists take care of themselves, then by definition they will be better psychologists and will be better able to respond to ethical decisions in a professional way.

Competency in Professional Practice

The Ethics Code specifically addresses the issue of competency: "Psychologists provide services, teach, and conduct research with populations and in areas only within the boundaries of their competence, based on their education, training, supervised experience, consultation, study, or professional experience" (Ethical Principles of Psychologists and Code of Conduct, Standard 2.01). Furthermore, the Ethics Code underscores the need to maintain competency by stating that "Psychologists undertake ongoing efforts to develop and maintain their competence" (Ethical Principles of Psychologists and Code of Conduct, Standard 2.03). Ethically, psychologists are bound to provide the best service possible to the public. In essence, this means being knowledgeable in the areas in which a psychologist may teach, supervise, conduct research, and/or treat clients. To be considered competent in a particular area, a psychologist should have formally studied the subject as well as have supervised experience related to the topic. Furthermore, psychologists should have familiarity with the population they are treating. Having experience with one population does not necessarily translate to competency with all populations: for example, treating children requires a different set of skills and specialization than treating adults.

Case example: Two psychologists in training were introduced to a child. The one who was accustomed to working with adults extended her hand toward the 7-year-old to shake his hand

and greeted him by saying it was nice to meet him. The second psychologist in training, who was comfortable working with children, bent down on her knees to physically be at the child's level, showed him a special trinket, knowing the child had a special interest in it, and was friendly yet casual in her demeanor. As may be evident, the second psychologist in training was the one who won accolades from the child; competency in a subject can best be learned from and demonstrated through experiences.

Although the Ethics Code does not specifically address the criteria defining competence, APA created a task force on the assessment of competence of professional psychology designed to "promote excellence in professional psychology, education and training through best practices in defining and measuring competency" (APA website). As highlighted throughout this book, there are now guiding principles, identifiable core competencies, benchmarks, and assessment tools recommended for assessing competence (Fouad et al, 2009; Kaslow et al., 2007, 2009) that were created by affiliates of this task force.

Part of being a competent psychologist is recognizing both personal areas of expertise and areas of less proficiency. When treating clients, it is the competent psychologist who refers a client out for a problem with which he or she possesses little experience, in contrast to working with the client without having the training or guidance to treat the client effectively. The competent psychologist not only practices within his or her realm of expertise but also acknowledges shortcomings and educates himself or herself in areas requiring more proficiency.

BENCHMARK COMPETENCIES

With the advent of a more competency-based approach in psychology, Fouad and colleagues (2009) created a document detailing benchmarks that psychologists in training should reach to demonstrate competency in a particular area. This document describes the components necessary for competency at three developmentally important points in training as well as the behavioral indicators of this competency, providing educators and supervisors with a framework to assess competency in areas essential for competent practice. Although the benchmarks created focus on 15 core competencies crucial to psychology, for purposes of this chapter, the benchmarks related to ethics will be summarized.

The first demonstration of ethical competency as discussed (Fouad et al., 2009) centers around knowledge of APA's Ethical Principles and

Code of Conduct. At each developmental juncture, familiarity with the Ethics Code increases such that as a practicum student, a psychologist in training should have basic knowledge of the Ethics Code and some idea of its application in the practicum setting. At internship level, psychologists in training are expected to have a more in-depth understanding of the Ethical Principles and Ethics Code as well as other laws, regulations, and professional standards that may apply in making ethical decisions. By the time a psychologist is ready for independent practice, competency should be demonstrated through a complete understanding of professional ethics in psychology, potential conflicts that can arise, and a decision-making process facilitating accurate assessment and solutions to ethical issues.

The second major area delineated by the benchmark document in regard to ethics includes the recognition and use of an ethical decision-making process. Practicum students should be able to articulate the importance of a decision-making model; interns should not only understand the importance but also identify and utilize an ethical decision-making model in making decisions. Finally, as described by Fouad and colleagues (2009), a psychologist competent to practice independently should demonstrate a true integration of ethics into his or her professional practice.

Fouad and colleagues (2009) describe one last area of ethical competency, which focuses on ethical conduct and behavior. Essential components of ethical conduct for practicum students include ethical attitudes and values exhibited through integrity, acceptance of others and new ideas, and the desire to help others. Interns should demonstrate similar behavior but also should be able to describe their own personal moral and ethical values. Psychologists ready for independent practice should competently integrate these values and ideals into their professional behavior and take responsibility for their own development and advancement in the area of ethical conduct.

Establishing competency benchmarks at different stages of a psychologist's development provides a means of assessing ethical competency as the psychologist advances toward independent practice. Clearly delineating expectations of what skills need to be demonstrated provides both psychologists and the public a means of understanding what skills are necessary for competency. Furthermore, having a reliable method of assessing for proficiency in a given area protects the public from harm and protects the psychologist by providing clear guidelines of what is required. Once the specific areas of ethical competency are established, the next step is determining the best methods of assessment.

COMPETENCY ASSESSMENT TOOLKIT

With the advent of a competency focus in psychology, the need for a systematic way to assess competency in the different foundational areas became apparent. Hence, Kaslow and colleagues (2009) developed an assessment toolkit to provide training programs with suggestions for the systematic assessment of competency. In addition to outlining various assessment tools, Kaslow and colleagues (2009) rate the usefulness of these different assessment measures for specific areas of competency. As this chapter focuses on ethics, the assessment measures deemed to be "very useful" by Kaslow and colleagues (2009) for the assessment of ethical competence will be considered. A more thorough review of the assessment tools and the usefulness of each measure for different components of competency can be found in the original article (Kaslow et al., 2009).

Annual reviews and case reviews are both considered to be "very useful" methods of assessing ethical competency by the competency assessment work group. In annual reviews, typically multiple assessors evaluate trainees' performance and trainees are then provided with feedback incorporating all of the evaluations. Annual reviews are an easy, cost-effective way of assessment and allow the evaluators to rate the psychologists in training on multiple competencies. A few caveats to this type of assessment are that annual reviews are time-consuming as well as susceptible to the biases of the evaluators and what the specific evaluators view to be important aspects for evaluation. Some of this bias can be alleviated by providing raters with specific questions and areas to focus their evaluation.

In a case review, the psychologist in training presents a case by summarizing the background information about the family and environment; the assessment, treatment plan, and intervention; the implementation of this plan; and the outcome. It is up to those listening to assess the student's skill. If the review is focused on ethical considerations, the student would perhaps be asked about an ethical dilemma encountered with the client, what the issues were, the decision-making process, and the ultimate decision and outcome. Case reviews allow a cost-effective, easily administered assessment of a student's competency. However, a caveat is that case reviews rely on the student's reports of the situation and his or her actions; these accounts may or may not be accurate, as there is most often no verification of its truth.

Kaslow and colleagues (2009) found standard oral and written examinations to be another "very useful" method of evaluating ethical competency. Written exams are extremely easy to administer, can assess many people at one time, and can be scored consistently. The challenge with written exams, particularly for ethics, is that although knowledge can be assessed, it is more difficult to assess true abilities and attitudes in real-life practice. The oral exam can better assess ethical competence by providing an opportunity to assess psychologists in training's knowledge, expertise, and approach in an in-depth manner, and it allows for discourse on ethical issues. However, this approach is costly and time-consuming and requires standardization in scoring and among administrators, which is very difficult to achieve, even with training.

Finally, Kaslow and colleagues (2009) pinpoint self-assessment as another "very useful" method of evaluating ethical competency. In self-assessment the individual is able to reflect upon his or her knowledge and behavior and evaluate personal progress in the particular competency. A benefit of self-assessment is that the student becomes aware of his or her personal competency and areas that can be improved upon. However, it requires the person to accurately assess his or her own personal competency, an attribute that tends to be overrated.

A competency assessment toolkit is essential in evaluating the competency levels of future psychologists. Kaslow and colleagues (2009) provide a broad summary of tools that may be helpful in assessing competency and detail which ones are best for specific areas. Although the measures described are the ones they perceive as being the most useful, the authors highlight other means of assessment that can also be useful in assessing ethical competency. Regardless of the method used, competency in professional ethics is something that should be formally assessed for the developing psychologist.

SELF-ASSESSMENT

Not only is self-assessment an effective tool to assess a trainee's competency, it is also something that all psychologists should practice on a regular basis. Self-assessment provides psychologists with an opportunity to reflect on their current knowledge of ethical issues and their behavior in regard to specific issues that may have arisen, as well as consider possible future situations in which they can be proactive to ensure the upkeep of ethical practice. Whether it is done on a yearly basis or after an incident occurs, a psychologist should be aware of personal competency and the implications of decisions made and evaluate the process of decision-making and the consequences of any action taken.

ADDRESSING PROBLEMS OF PROFESSIONAL COMPETENCE

Ethical standards have been established as a core competency in professional psychology (De las Fuentes et al., 2005; Fouad et al, 2009; Kaslow at al., 2004). Efforts have been made to delineate the essential components and behaviors that make up ethical competency (Fouad at al., 2009) and the manner in which ethical competency can be recognized and assessed (Kaslow et al., 2007, 2009). A question in the forefront of discussions on competence then becomes how to intervene when a psychologist or psychologist in training demonstrates problems with professional competence. The Council of Chairs of Training Councils, which is affiliated with the Education Directorate of APA, formed a work group to consider and address issues of professional competence. This group proposed eight initial recommendations of how to address problems in professional competence (Kaslow et al., 2007). Each proposal was written in broad terms so that it would be applicable to all areas of competence.

The first recommendation refers to the need for benchmarks to clearly define the essence of competence, including specific demonstrated behaviors and possible areas of weakness. Kaslow and colleagues (2007) stated that criteria must be established specifying competencies and the methods of assessing for them. They encourage supervisors to ensure trainees' awareness of the consequences of demonstrated problems in competence and of a structured remediation plan for those needing support to bolster their competence in a specific area. The work group promotes self-assessment as an effective tool to monitor professional competency. They suggest that psychologists reflect on their own behavior, seek peer review, and consult with others on a consistent and frequent basis so that self-assessment becomes part of the professional environment and a safeguard against problems in competence.

Kaslow and colleagues (2007) propose that when deciding how to assess and intervene with possible problematic behaviors, diversity and the impact of different beliefs should be considered. They recommend open communication across all levels of training so that problems in competency are transparent to all supervisors and that the individual is accurately and appropriately evaluated, monitored, and remediated. Should a psychologist in training require remediation, another formal assessment of competency should be given following the remediation. If it appears that the remediation has not been sufficient, it is then incumbent upon the psychologist to protect the public and do whatever is needed to ensure public safety, including the option of separating a trainee from a training program.

Elman and Forrest (2007) note that by thinking about issues as "professional competence problems," supervisors can specify the areas in need of help and the trainee is provided with a more specific set of issues to address. Rather than providing vague feedback, the supervisor can specify the exact areas requiring improvement. By specifying problematic areas, trainees will be better able to address problems in professional competence on their own.

Concluding Remarks

Proficiency in ethics and competency is a never-ending process for psychologists. Ethical issues will continue to challenge psychologists, and psychologists are encouraged to utilize their professional training and judgment in making decisions based on the APA's Ethical Principles and Code of Conduct. As was highlighted throughout this chapter, being familiar with the Ethics Code is not sufficient for ethical decision-making, as the ethical standards delineated by the Ethics Code are often ambiguous and multifaceted. The psychologist must interpret the code and decide what is ethical in a given situation. Given the complexity of the topic of ethics, it should be apparent why licensing boards may require a minimum number of continuing education hours specifically in the area of ethics. This forces psychologists to consider ethical topics on a semi-regular basis. Having experience in discussing ethical dilemmas and the decision-making process will likely enhance the psychologist's ability to manage future ethical issues. When faced with a possible ethical violation, competent psychologists are familiar with the Ethics Code and consider all the advantages and disadvantages of different responses for all those involved. Seeking consultation can provide new ideas and new perspectives, allowing the psychologist to recognize and consider all the issues that might exist. Regardless of the decision made, a competent psychologist takes responsibility for that decision. Training programs are positioned to educate trainees in ethical conduct and competent practice by providing the knowledge base as well as the assessment tools to ensure competency. Furthermore, psychologists in training programs have an ethical obligation to ensure that trainees are competent. Should trainees demonstrate problems in professional competence, a clear, standardized method of addressing these weaknesses should be in place.

Ethical practice is an essential part of clinical psychology because a mainstay of clinical practice involves trust. Lack of professional integrity and ethical conduct can ultimately lead to the demise of clinical psychology. Given that ethical dilemmas are common and that the Ethics Code does not often delineate a specific path to follow, psychologists must consider all the factors involved in a particular situation and make choices that can be supported as being most ethically sound.

THIRTEEN

Individual and Cultural Considerations

The rapid and ongoing diversification of the United States has highlighted the need to understand the individual and cultural differences that exist among the population. Currently, nonwhite racial and ethnic populations make up approximately 33.5% of all Americans, and it is estimated that by 2050 that number will rise to 51% (U.S. Census Bureau, 2010). In addition, the existing racial and ethnic disparities in access and utilization of behavioral health care (U.S. Department of Health and Human Services, 2001) have increased the urgency for culturally responsive practices and services.

By adapting a broad conceptualization of diversity, clinical psychologists identify the influence of cultural variables, along with other dimensions of identity (e.g., gender, age, sexual orientation, disability, religion/ spiritual orientation, education, and socioeconomic status), on individual and group behavior. The profession's ethical principles and code of conduct (American Psychological Association [APA] Ethics Code; APA, 2002) clearly state the obligation of all psychologists to provide competent services with individuals from diverse populations. Further, psychologists should not provide clinical services when doing so falls outside their boundaries of competence (Standard 2.01), and those in need of further training should take steps to ensure that they can provide competent professional services to individuals from diverse backgrounds.

The APA has compiled six prescriptive statements providing competency guidelines to meet the needs of individuals from diverse cultural backgrounds. The Guidelines on Multicultural Education, Training, Research, Practice, and Organizational Change for Psychologists (APA,

2003) not only describe the competent delivery of psychological services but also encourage psychologists to act as advocates and leaders in promoting social justice. These guidelines will provide a foundation for this chapter's exploration of individual and cultural considerations in the broad delivery of services conducted by clinical psychologists, including assessment, treatment, research, teaching, and organizational leadership. Readers are encouraged to become familiar with the APA guidelines and refer to the document for a more in-depth review of multicultural competencies.

Health and Mental Health Disparities

The term "health disparities" refers to the unequal distribution of disease and mortality across different groups (Carter-Pokras & Baquet, 2002). Well-documented evidence indicates that racial and ethnic disparities exist across a range of illnesses, and in the United States inequality exists in terms of access to quality healthcare (Asch et al., 2006). Behaviors such as tobacco use, lack of exercise, and an inadequate diet are responsible for an estimated 40% of premature mortality in the United States and are associated with lower socioeconomic conditions (McGinnis, Williams-Russo, & Knickman, 2002). The U.S. Surgeon General's Report *Mental Health: Culture, Race and Ethnicity* (2001) was based on the best available scientific evidence and concluded that the greatest burden of mental illness affects the largest racial and ethnic minority groups. There are clear differences in rates and patterns of mental health treatment for African Americans, Latinos, American Indians, and Asian Americans, such as (1) limited access to receptive and culturally compatible providers, (2) an underrepresentation in outpatient treatment, (3) an overrepresentation in inpatient and emergency treatment, and (4) a failure to receive critical early intervention during episodes of mental illness (Chun-Chung Chow, Jaffee, & Snowden, 2003). The APA established its guidelines on multicultural education, training, research, practice and organizational change for psychologists in response to the overwhelming data reflecting these mental health disparities.

Developing Multicultural Competence

The words "multiculturalism" and "diversity" have been used interchangeably in the literature and encompass all aspects of an individual's identity. When developing "multicultural" competence, psychologists are encouraged to recognize the broad dimensions of culture, such as race, ethnicity, language, sexual orientation, gender, age, disability, class status, education, and religious/spiritual orientation, amongst others (APA, 2003). Furthermore, each cultural dimension has unique issues and concerns. Broadly defined, multicultural competence involves (1) awareness of one's own attitudes and beliefs, (2) knowledge about cultural differences, and (3) skills in working with diverse groups (Sue, Arredondo, & McDavis, 1992). The following section explores multicultural competencies in the broad delivery of psychological services.

ASSESSMENT AND DIAGNOSIS

When performing a culturally sensitive assessment, the psychologist should remember that all behavior can be understood as being culturally bound. In the current managed care environment, empirically validated and culturally sensitive instruments have too often been replaced by symptom checklists and quickly formulated diagnoses designed to adapt to a medically derived model (Sanchez & Turner, 2003). With limited data from standardized tests and culturally sensitive assessment measures, a clinical psychologist is vulnerable to generating stereotypes and biased interpretations based on his or her own worldview and culturally derived assumptions of behaviors (Constantine & Sue, 2005). APA Multicultural Guideline #1 encourages psychologists to recognize that, as cultural beings, they may hold attitudes and beliefs that can detrimentally influence their perceptions of interactions with individuals who are ethnically and racially different from themselves. Competent psychologists understand the limitations of psychological instruments and are aware of how their own worldview influences both the interpretation of data and the conclusions they draw.

Several multicultural practice models offer guidelines and recommendations for conducting culturally sensitive assessments. One extensively utilized approach is the four-phase Multicultural Assessment Procedure (MAP) (Ridley, Li, & Hill, 1998). In Phase 1, questions about the client's cultural background are asked during the initial clinical interview. Phase I emphasizes awareness of transference, countertransference, ethical obligations, and the clinician's attention to his or her own cultural biases. In Phase 2, the clinician begins to examine evidence of cultural differences and develops working hypotheses about the effects of the client's culture on presenting problems. Clinicians are encouraged to explore which behaviors may be adaptive in the client's culture or representative of normative reactions. In Phase 3, psychological testing and medical evaluation are utilized to minimize cultural bias. Data are collected, interpreted, and compared to clinical impressions and DSM criteria. Phase 4 includes conclusions and recommendations, emphasizing the importance of a flexible conceptualization that incorporates the client's culture in treatment decisions.

Current approaches toward multicultural assessment stress the use of multiple methods of assessment beyond traditional standardized measures, including self-reports, measures of cultural identity, behavioral ratings, record reviews, interviews with family members, and consultation with professionals from the client's ethnic background. (Ponterotto, Gretchen, & Chauhan, 2001; Roysircar-Sodowsky & Kuo, 2001). Constantine and Sue (2005) suggest that training should emphasize the role of multicultural assessment by increasing the awareness of possible bias in trainees, teaching trainees strategies to reduce clinical bias, noting the psychometric limitations of tests, exposing students to standard and multicultural assessments simultaneously, and providing supervised practice.

CULTURALLY APPROPRIATE CLINICAL INTERVENTIONS

First and foremost, appropriate clinical interventions begin with an awareness of how all individuals are influenced by a variety of contexts, and psychologists are encouraged to view all behavior through a "cultural lens." APA's Guideline #5 states that psychologists should strive to apply culturally appropriate skills in clinical and other applied psychological practices. As Constantine and Sue (2005) point out, practicing in a culture-centered manner does not require an entirely new set of therapeutic skills; rather, a culturally competent psychologist is flexible in generating conceptualizations and adapting interventions to meet the diverse needs of clients. As we discussed in the section on assessment, certain behaviors that might initially appear problematic may actually be culturally adaptive or normative reactions. Since cultural and societal norms can vary greatly throughout regions, and common perceptions of normality are subject to change over time, a thorough understanding of cultural norms is necessary. To intervene through a cultural lens and reduce cultural bias, clinical psychologists must develop strong skills related to self-awareness and cultural sensitivity.

Self-Awareness and Assessment   Developing culturally appropriate clinical interventions requires psychologists not only to recognize and appreciate other cultural groups but also to develop a keen awareness of their own cultural heritage and social identity. Psychologists, like all people, are predisposed to biases and assumptions about themselves and others. For example, the United States has been founded upon principles encouraging independence, self-determination, self-reliance, and rational decision-making (Oyserman, Coon, & Kemmelmeier, 2002). These values are fully integrated in many facets of mainstream culture and unconsciously influence perceptions and beliefs. By contrast, other cultures may value collectivism, preferring an orientation toward harmony with others, conforming to a social hierarchy and social norms, and subordinating individual desires for the good of the group (Fiske, Kitayama, Markus, & Nisbett, 1998).

Clinical psychologists recognize the processes we use to organize the overwhelming amount of social information presented in our environment. *Social categorization theory* (Allport, 1954) explains how people make sense of their social world in an effort to strategize appropriate behaviors and predict potential harm (emotional or physical). In-groups and out-groups are then identified as a means of creating safety. Predominant stereotypes are developed and become the guiding set of beliefs influencing our emotional responses to and interactions with others. Social psychological research has identified an unconscious tendency for individuals to exaggerate differences between groups, favor our own in-group over the out-group, and develop strong prejudices toward the out-group (Tajfel & Turner, 1986). Clinical psychologists should develop an awareness of their own biases, accepting that their attitudes and beliefs are culturally limited. Once a psychologist adopts these principles, he or she can begin the process of self-evaluation necessary to treat those who are culturally different.

Multicultural Sensitivity and Knowledge   The APA encourages psychologists to recognize the importance of multicultural sensitivity/responsiveness, knowledge, and understanding about ethnically and racially different individuals. The term "clinical curiosity" reflects an attitude and desire to understand clients intimately through direct inquiry, with goals of understanding each client's individuality and distinct culture. Through direct inquiry, clinicians provide an open environment, suggesting a commitment to clarifying individual differences and learning more about the client's worldview. To understand an individual's culture is to assess the beliefs, customs, habits, and language shared by people living in a particular time and place (Kenrick, Neuberg, & Cialdini, 1999). Understanding an individual's culture is crucial for interpreting interpersonal relations, dimensions of adjustment, coping, learning, and behavior patterns and for identifying social support systems (Axelson, 1999).

Clinical psychologists should recognize cultural differences and express a desire to learn more about the client's culture. By taking into account the client's gender, culture, race, religion, age, sexual orientation, socioeconomic status, and other distinct aspects of individuality, the psychologist can communicate a commitment to developing a genuine and authentic therapeutic relationship. For example, attending to the client's experience of oppression brings attention to the historical experiences of various populations and how racism and oppression have influenced belief systems and values (Constantine & Sue, 2005).

It is unrealistic to believe any one clinician could attain the abundant knowledge of all cultures; rather, the competent clinical psychologist is aware of his or her limitations and commits to lifelong learning. Keeping abreast of the latest literature on best practices, seeking opportunities for personal and professional growth, developing a clinical curiosity toward understanding individual differences, and utilizing supervision when necessary are critical components for developing culturally appropriate clinical interventions.

CULTURALLY SENSITIVE RESEARCH

Psychological researchers are expected to be culturally sensitive by respecting the value of culture and ethics in conducting research with ethnically, linguistically, and racially diverse individuals (APA, 2003). The multicultural guidelines established by the APA represent a movement in the field to recognize cultural competence and thus encourage psychological research that increases the multicultural knowledge and skills of psychologists. The APA (2003) has identified several prominent concerns in evaluation of current research practices in the United States.

First, findings based on samples that are predominately white and middle-class have been inappropriately generalized to the greater population. Multicultural scholars have been critical of this practice and the field's failure to address external validity concerns (Fuertes, Bartolomeo, & Nicols, 2001; Sue, 1999). Most concerning would be using data from a predominately white sample to describe normal behavior or functioning, with behavior that deviates from those norms considered pathological or deviant (Hall, 2001; Rogler, 1999). Furthermore, large within-group differences have been ignored in the research, overlooking the great within-group heterogeneity of all major racial/ethnic groups in the United States and ignoring important variables such as geographical location, socioeconomic status, education, and national origin (APA, 2003; USDHHS, 2001).

Researchers are also vulnerable to their own cultural biases in both research design and the inferences they make about data. For example, viewing behavior as individualistically determined, in accordance with Western cultural ideals of individualism, minimizes the impact of cultural variables on behavior (APA, 2003; Perez, 1999). Culturally sensitive psychological researchers consider cultural hypotheses as possible explanations for their findings, examine moderator effects, and use statistical procedures to examine cultural variables (Quintana et al., 2001).

TEACHING MULTICULTURAL COMPETENCIES

As educators, psychologists are encouraged to employ the constructs of multiculturalism and diversity in psychological education. Psychologists employed in educational and training institutions are encouraged to make the multicultural focus thematic to the entire program. The APA (2003) recommends that psychologists move beyond single course offerings in multicultural practice and employ multicultural models in didactic courses across the curriculum. The APA encourages the review of philosophical models of multicultural training and specifically identifies race-based models (Carter, 1995; Helms, 1990); theories regarding oppression (Atkinson, Morten, & Sue, 1998); Multicultural Counseling and Therapy (MCT) (Sue, Ivey, & Pedersen, 1996); Multicultural Facets of Cultural Competence (Sue, 2001); common factors within psychotherapy and healing (Fischer, Jome, & Atkinson, 1998; Frank & Frank, 1991), and multicultural competency-based models (Arredondo & Arciniega, 2001). A range of emotional reactions is expected when an environment is created to openly discuss multicultural issues. The modeling and facilitation of respectful discussion is critical. Professors' amiability, nonjudgmental demeanor, enthusiasm, self-disclosure, and overall leadership in the class have been identified as sources of encouragement and positive modeling (Lenington-Lara, 1999).

MULTICULTURAL LEADERSHIP AND ORGANIZATIONAL CHANGE

As stated in the APA Multicultural Guidelines (2003), psychologists must (1) be prepared to facilitate culturally informed organizational development of policies and practices; (2) understand the dynamic nature of the profession and be prepared to assume various roles, such as change agent, advocate, and consultant; and (3) understand frameworks and models of multiculturalism to facilitate organizational change. An organization that evolves with a diverse culture and rapid societal change reviews its policies, practices, and organizational structures to remove barriers that may discriminate against or disadvantage people on the basis of race, gender, or sexual orientation (Robinson & Howard-Hamilton, 2000). Psychologists are encouraged to be active change agents and policy planners in different sectors of society and to serve as organizational leaders in the profession, the private sector, government agencies, and other work environments.

Gender and Diversity

In accordance with a multidimensional approach toward understanding human distress and disability, clinical psychologists consider the unique biological, psychological, and sociocultural influences related to gender, gender roles, gender expectations, and gender-specific susceptibility to mental illness. Approximately twice as many adult women are diagnosed with depression than men (Hyde, Mezulis, & Abramson, 2008), while boys are significantly more likely than girls to engage in both aggressive and nonaggressive antisocial behavior (National Institute of Mental Health, 2000). These statistics represent just a few of the differences in behavior and susceptibility to various forms of physical and mental illness. Since examination of the vast and complex variables associated with gender is beyond the scope of this chapter, general considerations are presented with the goal of future investigation into these specific topics at greater depth.

Gender socialization refers to the learning of behavior and attitudes considered appropriate for a given sex. Each family system is critical in reinforcing gender roles, but so are one's friends, school, work, and the mass media. Considering the examples above, the socialization of boys to conform to traditional masculine traits in the form of toughness, aggression, and dominance may increase the potential for boys to engage in violence (Feder, Levant, & Dean, 2007). Conversely, girls are encouraged to express a wide range of emotions, while for boys outward expressions of vulnerability are discouraged, punished, and suppressed (Froschl & Sprung, 2005).

Gender stereotypes provide working templates for how men and women *should* behave. Interpersonal and psychological conflicts can arise within gender role expectations. Gender roles are culturally dependent, so the individual's distinct ethnic and cultural background should be considered. Since gender roles, stereotypes, and expectations differ among countries, regions, and religions, clinical psychologists should conduct a thorough evaluation of all influencing factors, designing culturally competent interventions (Best & Thomas, 2004).

Behavioral sex differences among genders are not unique to humans, and biological bases of understanding individual behavior among genders should be considered. Distinct developmental periods create unique presentations in behavior, and the competent psychologist is abreast of the distinct developmental stages and their impact on mental health. For example, early puberty has been identified as a vulnerability factor for girls that, when combined with stressors, can lead to depression (Hyde et al., 2008). Our evolutionary history is expressed through genetic predispositions interacting with our social environment, so it is important to understand innate predispositions toward aggression, competition, sexual expression, and social power when assessing the client. For example, gender differences in temperament may predispose boys to externalizing disorders and girls toward internalizing disorders, and hormonal variations have been associated with depression, anxiety, and aggression (Else-Quest, Hyde, Goldsmith, & Van Hulle, 2006).

Sexual Orientation

In December 1973, as a result of emerging scientific evidence and social advocacy, the American Psychiatric Association's Board of Trustees and general membership voted to remove homosexuality from the DSM. Shortly after, the APA concluded that:

> Homosexuality per se implies no impairment in judgment, stability, reliability, or general social and vocational capabilities. Further, the American Psychological Association urges all mental health professionals to take the lead in removing the stigma of mental illness that has long been associated with homosexual orientations. (APA, 1975, p. 663)

The APA has since passed numerous resolutions supporting LGB civil rights and psychological well-being (see APA, 2005a). Continued movements promoting efforts to change clients' sexual orientation have been denounced by the APA and are considered a clear ethical violation (APA, 2009). The APA (2009) concluded that none of the recent research on sexual orientation change efforts (1999–2007) meets methodological standards permitting conclusions regarding efficacy or safety. In 2007, the

APA established the Task Force on Appropriate Therapeutic Responses to Sexual Orientation and in 2009 published a comprehensive report disseminating the growing body of evidence on psychotherapy and the psychology of sexual orientation. The APA (2009, p. 2) established a multi-culturally competent and affirmative approach grounded in the following scientific facts:

- Same-sex sexual attractions, behavior, and orientations per se are normal and positive variants of human sexuality—in other words, they do not indicate either mental or developmental disorders.
- Homosexuality and bisexuality are stigmatized, and this stigma can have a variety of negative consequences (e.g., minority stress) throughout the lifespan.
- Same-sex sexual attractions and behavior occur in the context of a variety of sexual orientations and sexual orientation identities, and, for some, sexual orientation identity (i.e., individual or group membership and affiliation, self-labeling) is fluid or has an indefinite outcome.
- Gay men, lesbians, and bisexual individuals are able to form stable, committed relationships and families that are equivalent to heterosexual relationships and families in essential respects.
- Some individuals chose to live their lives in accordance with personal or religious values (e.g., telic congruence).

RECOMMENDED THERAPEUTIC INTERVENTIONS WITH ADULTS

As is the case with other minorities, a treatment focus aimed at mitigating the negative consequences of minority stress appears to provide the best outcomes (APA, 2009). Experiences of felt stigma, isolation and rejection from relationships and communities, poor social support, and conflicts between multiple identities and values are major factors in creating psychological distress (e.g., Bartoli & Gillem, 2008). A framework for the appropriate application of affirmative therapeutic applications has been established by the APA Task Force on Appropriate Therapeutic Responses to Sexual Orientation (2009) and represents the competent delivery of psychological services to individuals seeking treatment for concerns related to sexual orientation.

Acceptance and Support   A client-centered approach emphasizing unconditional positive regard, communication of support and empathy with the client, openness to the client's perspective, and encouragement of the client's positive self-concept are critical components of effective psychotherapy (Norcross, 2002). Exploring issues without criticism and condemnation and with an empathic attunement to the struggles and stress experienced is designed to reduce the distress caused by isolation, stigma, and shame. Creating this environment is necessary for the individual to develop a more coherent sense of self (Bartoli & Gillem, 2008).

Comprehensive Assessment   The literature suggests that individuals presenting with more severe distress about their homosexual orientation may have conservative religious beliefs, and the first step to addressing these conflicts includes a thorough assessment of the client's spiritual and religious beliefs, religious identity and motivations, and spiritual functioning (Hathaway, Scott, & Garver, 2004). In addition, a comprehensive assessment examining present stressors, psychological distress and coping strategies associated with current stressors (e.g., anxiety, depression, substance abuse, sexual compulsivity, posttraumatic stress disorder), negative effects from developmental experiences and traumas, and the impact of cultural and family norms is essential for understanding the complexity of the client's distress (APA, 2009).

Active Coping   Strategies used to resolve, endure, or diminish stressful life experiences should be thoroughly assessed and addressed as a critical aspect of treatment. *Cognitive interventions* aimed at modifying shame-inducing beliefs, such as, "I am unworthy or bad because I am attracted to the same sex and only if you are heterosexual can you be worthy" can reduce all-or-nothing thinking and alter negative self-appraisals (Beckstead & Isreal, 2007). *Acceptance-based strategies* aimed at coping with sexual attraction toward the same sex, rather than negatively judging, denying, or fighting against these feelings, can assist in coping. *Emotion-focused strategies* with goals of facilitating the process of grief and loss of one's values, life situation, and life goals have also been positively reported (Beckstead & Isreal, 2007). Strategies addressing *positive religious coping* may present clients with alternatives to the negative messages about homosexuality (Ano & Vasconcelles, 2005). For example, connecting the client to core values such as charity, hope, forgiveness, gratitude, kindness, and compassion may facilitate self-acceptance in the face of religious rejection (McMinn, 2005). Increasing *social support* through psychotherapy, self-help groups, and welcoming communities may also help relieve distress and experiences of felt shame.

Identity Exploration and Development   The APA's Task Force on Appropriate Therapeutic Responses to Sexual Orientation (2009) found the ability to fully explore a coherent sense of one's identity development to be central to effective treatment. A competent and ethical approach is supportive of each client's identity development without judgment on how he or she chooses to live out his or her sexual orientation. The treatment does not differ for those who choose to accept or reject their same-sex attractions. Psychologists value *self-determination,* respecting each individual's right to control or determine the course of his or her own life. Competent psychologists are aware that expressions of sexual orientation tend to vary greatly depending on ethnicity, culture, age, generation, gender, nationality, acculturation, and religion (Yarhouse, 2008).

CONSIDERATIONS FOR CHILDREN, ADOLESCENTS,
AND THEIR FAMILIES

First and foremost, despite current theories and programs designed to "prevent" or "cure" homosexuality, no empirical evidence exists suggesting that therapeutic interventions can alter adult same-sex sexual orientation (APA, 2009). Advocates of such an approach view homosexuality as a mental disorder, a concept that has been rejected by mental health professionals for 35 years. Involuntary and coercive methods to change are viewed as damaging and unethical, and current scientific evidence should be clearly articulated to clients. The APA (2009) recommends a multiculturally competent and client-centered approach to children, adolescents, and their families rather than efforts to change sexual orientation. Specific interventions should include providing education and support regarding developmental processes and milestones, interventions aimed at reducing internalized stigma in children and sexual stigma in parents, and affirmative information and education on LGB identities and lives. Family interventions designed to increase support and reduce rejection are necessary components of treatment. School and community interventions are recommended to reduce societal stigma and increase social support.

Spirituality and Religion

Due to increasing evidence demonstrating positive relationships between religious beliefs and health (e.g., Smith, McCullough, & Poll, 2003), the field of clinical psychology has become more interested in how religion and spirituality affect mental health and quality of life. Religion is a potent psychological force: history testifies to its ability to unify social groups and provide a sense of order and meaning in the face of tragedy. On the other hand, strongly held religious beliefs have also instigated war, aggression, and discrimination. The powerful force of religion and spirituality on the human experience cannot be ignored when developing a culturally competent case conceptualization.

Spirituality refers to one's personal relationship with God (or higher power or universal spirit), a desire to find personal meaning and direction in life, and a promotion of classic virtues such as love, compassion, and forgiveness (Thoresen & Plante, 2005). On the other hand, religion is more associated with beliefs, rules, practices, symbols, and rituals with a relationship to God or a higher power as its centerpiece. Estimates suggest that 10% to 25% of the American public consider themselves "spiritual but not religious," and it is unclear whether the concept of spirituality differs from that of religion on specific psychological correlates related to health and well-being (Thoresen & Plante, 2005).

The APA (2002) has identified religious and spiritual values as a form of human diversity and is now publishing the *Psychology of Religion and Spirituality* in collaboration with Division 36 (Psychology of Religion). Worthington and Sandage's (2001) review of the literature on religion and spirituality identified several implications for clinicians in clinical practice: (1) Clinicians should include religion and spirituality as a standard dimension of clinical assessment; (2) specific religion-accommodative therapies (e.g., Christian and Muslim) are available and effective, primarily for the treatment of depression; and (3) there is no clear evidence suggesting that therapists and clients must be matched on religion for therapy to be effective. Prayer, meditation, personal search for meaning, and self-regulation are important concepts associated with religious and spiritual practice that can be integrated into treatment. Psychologists should also consider a self-appraisal of their own beliefs and values, carefully monitoring how their own values could affect treatment. A culturally competent clinical psychologist will remain *clinically curious* about each individual's relationship with spirituality and religion and will develop a commitment to further training and supervision when necessary.

People with Disabilities

People with disabilities (PWDs) constitute 15% of the U.S. population (Cornish et al., 2008) and are defined as those who have "long-term physical, mental, intellectual or sensory impairments which in interaction with various barriers may hinder their full and effective participation in society on an equal basis with others" (United Nations Enable, 2006, Defining Disability Section). Similar to other minority groups, PWDs have been exposed to subjugation, intolerance, and discrimination and have been underrepresented in positions of power (Artman & Daniels, 2010). Conceptualizing PWDs from a multicultural framework with personal goals of implementing skillful clinical curiosity, developing a keen self-awareness of personal biases, and obtaining the necessary knowledge and skills to treat disabled individuals remains best practice. However, experts within the field caution against common mistakes performed by even the most experienced clinicians—for example, assuming that the disability is central to the client's presenting concerns, allowing the disability to define the individual while disregarding other important factors, unknowingly lowering standards of personal achievement, misinterpreting affect (depression/anger) as a normal aspect of adjustment, and misinterpreting affect as maladjustment (anger toward lack of accommodations) (Olkin & Taliaferro, 2006). In addition, Artman and Daniels (2010) recommend that psychologists be mindful of modifying websites, flyers, consent forms, handouts, and publications; scheduling appointments to meet specific needs (i.e., transit schedules); providing individual testing accommodations; providing a handicap-accessible environment (ramps, doors, bathrooms); and advocating for the client's rights when necessary.

BENCHMARKS FOR COMPETENCY IN INDIVIDUAL AND CULTURAL DIVERSITY

Since the APA has outlined guidelines for multicultural competence, the field continues to evolve in terms of defining core competencies, benchmarks for measuring competencies, and tools useful in evaluating competencies (Kaslow et al., 2004, 2007, 2009; Fouad et al., 2009). As is referred to throughout this volume, the reader is encouraged to explore the Competency Benchmarks Work Group's (Fouad et al., 2009) findings about foundational competence for the broad range of skills required in the field of professional psychology, including those in individual and cultural diversity.

ASSESSING COMPETENCY FOR INDIVIDUAL AND CULTURAL DIVERSITY

In addition, Kaslow and colleagues (2009) provide training programs with a useful toolkit to establish methods of assessment and provide behavioral anchors to determine trainees' readiness for the various levels of training, including practicum, internship, and entry into practice. Given the integral importance of sensitivity to and awareness of diversity to effective clinical psychology practice, ongoing and periodic assessment of competency in this domain is warranted. As diversity evolves in this country, clinical psychologists have a responsibility to keep their skills crisp and updated in working with diverse clientele.

Concluding Remarks

Multicultural competence includes a broad conceptualization of diversity, incorporating the impact of cultural variables and other dimensions of identity (e.g., gender, age, sexual orientation, disability, religion/spiritual orientation, education, and socioeconomic status) on individual and group behavior. Multicultural competence includes a broad array of skills needed to accurately assess and intervene with a diverse population. However, no skill is more important than that of self-awareness. Fundamental to the development of multicultural competence is a keen awareness of one's own cultural background and biases. Regardless of one's adherence to the diverse theoretical orientations or psychological interventions that exist in the field, the competent clinical psychologist assesses cultural variables and understands behavior to be culturally and contextually driven. The competency movement in professional psychology highlights the need to develop foundational skills and provides benchmarks for effective teaching and evaluation of those skills. As the field continues to evolve, greater attention to individual and cultural differences among the population will be necessary to advance our understanding of cultural variations in behavior, and thus guide effective intervention.

FOURTEEN

Professional Identification

In this chapter we examine the important role of professional identification in shaping the professional development and identity of the clinical psychologist. We begin by considering what we believe to be a variety of factors that define the clinical psychologist of today, with an emphasis on competency development in relevant areas. Emphasis is given to the following topics: mentoring, supervision, administration, accountability, training models, evidence-based practice, credentialing, continuing education, and lifelong learning. We conclude by examining important benchmark competencies and assessment of competencies regarding professional identification, with a consideration of current and future factors affecting the role of the clinical psychologist.

The acquisition of the professional identity of a clinical psychologist is undoubtedly a key factor in professional development. Professional identity comprises the acquisition of key attitudes relevant to one's role as a clinical psychologist, coupled with a deep sense of responsibility and duty to the specialty, respect for its mores and value system, and a sense of honor and fulfillment in performing its roles and functions in society (Bruss & Kopala, 1993; Elman, Illfelder-Kaye, & Robiner, 2005; Van Zandt, 1990). This critical process is developmental, sequential, and progressive in nature (Kaslow, McCarthy, Rogers, & Summerville, 1992), evolving over time as an individual assimilates the attitudes, values, assumptions, mores, and norms of the specialty. As a developmental process (Elman et al., 2005; Kaslow et al., 1992), professional identity unfolds as an individual progresses through a series of educational, training, mentoring, supervisory, clinical, and credentialing experiences marking the achievement of critical milestones and capstones that immerse the individual within the identity as he or she progresses within the specialty.

Many factors, both within and outside the specialty, as well as experiences inherent throughout the education, training, and credentialing of clinical psychologists, appear to play an important role in professional identity development. Along with the development of a strong professional identity comes the need to attain competence in those domains that define, distinguish, and determine the roles and functions of the clinical psychologist. Professional identification and professional competency as a clinical psychologist are intricately intertwined. One's identification as a professional psychologist influences the competencies one needs to acquire and sustain; one's competencies, in turn, define the identity. The establishment of a professional identity involves an integration of what one needs to be capable of knowing, doing, and valuing as a clinical psychologist.

Since clinical psychology's inception as a core specialty area in professional psychology, the specialty has progressed substantially. Over 45 years ago, in his Presidential Address to Division 12 of the American Psychological Association (APA), Garfield (1965) commented on the important effects of role definition, social factors fueling the need for psychological services, the ever-changing influence of societal factors, and existing disagreements between scientists and practitioners as they relate to professional identity. Today, despite substantial progress in the specialty of clinical psychology in most respects, perhaps little has changed about the variables affecting professional identity.

A number of factors have converged to help shape not only the definition of clinical psychology as a specialty, but what it truly means to be a clinical psychologist. The identity of the clinical psychologist has evolved over the past century, in part by the specification of core competencies and training conferences (Fouad et al., 2009; Kenkel & Peterson, 2010). Factors within the field of psychology and society have also shaped the roles and functions related to clinical psychology and have distinguished it from other specialty areas and professions.

The development of a professional identity is essential in creating well-rounded and competent professionals in the clinical psychology community. While developing a clear professional identity may unintentionally create and foster some potential negative interspecialty- and interdiscipline-related consequences, such as an in-group/out-group mentality, stereotypes, biases, professional exclusion, and even conflict, the advantages far outweigh the disadvantages. Developing and maintaining a clear and consistent professional identity allows a professional to become part of a professional group and to gain and maintain membership in a group that shares a common worldview; holds certain values, beliefs. and assumptions to be true; and, most importantly, provides a vehicle for expressing one's professional potential. Having a professional identity is also essential to lobbying efforts aimed at attaining parity and equivalent reimbursement for mental health services. Fouad and colleagues (2009) view professional identity as one of the five essential components of the foundational competency of professionalism.

Based, then, on a substrate of shared knowledge (information, theories, principles), skills (capabilities), and values (attitudes, norms, and mores), professional identification provides a means for capturing, delineating, and guiding one's professional, clinical, and scholarly endeavors (Tryon, 2010). Moreover, embracing a clear professional identity encompasses the need for achieving competence in critical domains of professional activities, a unique mix that in essence captures and communicates to society an ideal representation of the clinical psychologist. Many factors influence the professional identity of the clinical psychologist.

The professional identity of the clinical psychologist is in large part affected by factors related to the emergence and refinement of education and training standards (Fouad et al., 2009), clinical experiences and interests, mentoring, supervision, attainment of licensure, and achievement of specialty certification, all of which are critical elements in delineating expected competencies. Developing these competencies entails going through a series of sequential, developmentally graded, and increasingly complex educational and training experiences focused on the acquisition of clearly delineated knowledge, skills, and attitudes under conditions of high-quality mentorship and supervision. These cultivating factors help to shape and explain the very essence of who the professional portrays himself or herself to be, both privately and publicly. Identifying as a clinical psychologist requires knowing what a clinical psychologist needs to know, being able to do what a clinical psychologist does, and prizing what a clinical psychologist does and values.

The adoption of a theoretical orientation within the realm of professional identity further shapes professional development. Tryon (2010) has identified five components of professional identity: "(a) psychologists are classified by their theoretical orientation by themselves and by other people; (b) psychologists derive their professional identity from this classification; (c) this identification influences the professional organizations they join, the journals they read, the manuscripts and grants they review, the meetings they attend, and what they teach through workshops and/or classes; (d) allegiance to the in-group, by similarly classified individuals, is expected; and (e) defense of the in-group is valued and merits/motivates opposition to alternative approaches" (p. 9). Clinical psychologists must embrace the challenge of sustaining their own professional identity and promoting the professional identity of those students and trainees with whom they interact.

In the following sections, we examine a number of important factors that together help to define the identity of the clinical psychologist in the 21st century and that underlie the need for competency development in several areas. Assuming that more experienced clinical psychologists are charged with the task of promoting identity and development of protégés, we consider several areas of relevance in this regard: mentoring, supervision, administration, accountability, training models, evidence-based practice, credentialing, continuing education, and lifelong learning.

Clinical Psychologist as Mentor. During the education and training of clinical psychologists, the development, nurturing, and ultimate attainment of professional identity appears to be facilitated, if not highly influenced, by the availability of one or more high-quality mentoring relationships. A mentor may be defined as a trusted, experienced professional who guides the development of a less experienced individual in his or her quest to acquire the requisite knowledge, skills, and attitudes in critical competency domains that define the specialty. Relative to mentors, mentees possess less professional identity, experience, and accomplishments (Jacobi, 1991) and, by definition, competence. The goal of mentoring is to enhance the professional development of the mentee. Academic and practicing clinical psychologists often serve in the role of mentor, underscoring the need for competence attainment in this domain.

The mentoring process in clinical psychology is delivered through a variety of mentor–mentee interactions that help to shape how the mentee perceives himself or herself as a professional. In this regard, DiTomasso (2009) has noted:

> In the education and training of clinical psychologists, the process of mentoring, socializing and professionalizing students is a critical task. Perhaps no other task is as important in guiding students along the process of transformation into clinical psychologists. That our students acquire the requisite knowledge, skills and attitudes in their quest toward developing the identity of the clinical psychologist is paramount...Students who identify with faculty and supervisors are more likely to be positively influenced by those

professionals. By publicly investing ourselves in student development, professing our goal of fostering student professional development, demonstrating our commitment through our words and actions, and assuming a proactive and engaging stance, we increase the likelihood that students will be influenced by us. (p. 2)

Using a cognitive-behavioral framework as a model, DiTomasso (2009) proposed a mentoring plan for incorporation into doctoral programs that delineates 75 behaviors that constitute mentoring and help to promote the professional identity development of a mentee in clinical psychology. Examples of these behaviors include role-modeling, seizing teachable moments, shaping and reinforcing professional attitudes, stimulating and challenging students, appropriate use of self-disclosure, sharing professional experiences, and demonstrating active professional involvement, each of which is used to promote the development of the mentee.

The presumption is, then, that through the mentoring process the mentee will acquire critical attitudes, beliefs, and assumptions about what it means to be a clinical psychologist. Mentoring may influence the mentee by fueling the development of professional identification schema that contain the beliefs, attitudes, and assumptions that guide the thinking, behaviors, values, and feelings of the clinical psychologist (DiTomasso, 2009).

Based on interviews with managers and supervisees, Kram (1988) identified two major functions of mentoring: career and psychosocial. While career functions refer to those facets of the relationship designed to promote a mentee's learning about the day-to-day operations of the professional role, psychosocial functions facilitate the mentee's development of professional identity and competence (Kram, 1988). Considering what factors define effective mentors in the eyes of mentees emphasizes the requisite knowledge, skills, and attitudes of those seeking to serve as mentors. Competent clinical psychologists have a responsibility to promote professional identity development in those whom they teach, train, and supervise. In a national survey of 787 recent graduates of doctoral programs in clinical psychology, Clark, Harden, and Johnson (2000) reported on characteristics of mentors that graduates perceived in their most important mentor. In descending order of frequency, they were "supportive, intelligent, knowledgeable, ethical, caring, humorous, encouraging, honest, empathic, approachable, accepting, warm, available, genuine, [and] dedicated" (p. 264). Clinical psychologists seeking to promote identification in their mentees should take heed of these findings and aspire to attain these characteristics.

Clinical Psychologist as Supervisor. Whether in research or clinical settings, clinical psychologists often find themselves in the role of supervising less experienced individuals. In the clinical context, the quality of supervision is a key ingredient with far-reaching implications for the development of professional identity and competence (Barnett, Erickson Cornish, Goodyear, & Lichtenberg, 2007). Along the way toward professional identity development, the burgeoning professional is likely to have encountered several supervisors in a variety of contexts (Barnett et al., 2007).

Effective clinical supervision is now considered so important that skill in clinical supervision constitutes a core competency domain in the education and training of clinical psychologists, with a movement underfoot to require clinical supervisors to maintain continuing education in this area. The point here is that clinical competence does not ensure supervisory competence (Barnett et al., 2007), and those seeking to serve as supervisors have a responsibility to acquire the knowledge base, skill mix, training, and attitudes essential to providing effective supervision (Barnett et al.,, 2007). Barnett, Erickson Cornish, Goodyear, & Lichtenberg (2007) commented on the important role of apprenticeship training as a means of fostering skill acquisition and the refinement of professional attitudes. Farber and Kaslow (2010) stressed the importance of attitudes such as professionalism in providing the undergirding for the tasks in which clinical psychologists engage. Identification as a clinical psychologist is likely to be in part fueled by supervisory experiences that provide opportunities for attitude and value formation.

Clinical Psychologist as Administrator. Clinical psychologists frequently find themselves in the role of administrator, or at least responsible for overseeing administrative tasks in one or more specific settings. While relatively little emphasis is placed on training psychologists in this area, the fact is that clinical psychologists often assume administrative leadership roles in clinical or educational organizations. Also, of all of the roles with which a psychologist may be identified, administration is probably the most foreign, with the majority of psychologists learning on the job with little to no formal training. Effective assumption of the identity of an administrator requires an understanding of how organizations function as well as competencies in areas such as strategic planning, outcome evaluation, prioritizing tasks, setting goals, communication, feedback skills, management skills, group dynamics, teamwork facilitation, time management, balancing multiple priorities, and coaching. Even if they are not primarily in the role of administrator, clinical psychologists must be prepared to assume some ancillary administration functions in their daily work life.

Clinical Psychologist as Scientist-Practitioner, Practitioner-Scholar, or Clinical Scientist. The models under which clinical psychologists have received their education and training directly influence their professional identity by ensuring their attainment of specific competencies consistent with the given training model. We will provide some highlights of these models as they relate to professional identity. Traditionally, most clinical psychologists were trained in a model that emerged from the famous Boulder Conference, the scientist-practitioner model. This model, embraced by the field for many years, emphasized the integration of science and practice and aimed to train psychologists as both clinicians and scientists (Benjamin & Baker, 2000). According to the model, psychologists integrate the science of psychology and practice with the interplay between them such that activities in each domain mutually and reciprocally influence each other. Psychologists trained and practicing from this model are expected to be proficient in both conducting research and clinical practice and receive a PhD degree, which directly influences how they identify.

Dissatisfaction with the clinicians produced by this model and increasing demands for service resulted in the creation of a newer model that emerged during the Vail Conference, called the practitioner-scholar. According to this model, designed to prepare PsyD practitioners, the application of clinical service delivery must be informed by the scholarly literature. Clinical psychologists, then, must see themselves as local clinical scientists and critical consumers of the professional body of knowledge and seek to apply this information in the local environment of clinical service delivery, asking and answering questions directly relevant to daily clinical practice (Peterson, 1997). The Vail model places primary importance on training and function in the delivery of psychological services as well as its evaluation and improvement (Peterson, 1997). Psychological science is viewed as a human practice enterprise and psychological practice as a human science enterprise, mutually affecting each other (APA, 2002).

The newest model to emerge is that of the clinical scientist. As summarized by Rubin et al. (2007) and in line with McFall (1991), the clinical scientist model professes to train students "in psychological science that is directed at (a) the promotion of adaptive functioning; (b) the assessment, understanding, amelioration, and prevention of human problems in behavior, affect, cognition or health; and (c) the application of knowledge in ways consistent with scientific evidence)" (p. 454). The overarching point is simple: the model in which a clinical psychologist is trained appears to directly influence his or her professional identity and how that identity is manifested in professional activities, including roles, functions, and settings. In clinical psychology, for both PsyD and PhD programs accredited by the APA, the Commission on Accreditation (COA) accredits programs on the extent to which they meet the standards of the guidelines and principles of accreditation (APA, 2002). The difference in the models is basically, therefore, one of emphasis: practitioner-scientists are trained to produce research and apply it, while practitioner-scholars are trained to consume and apply it. Graduates of these programs not only identify with the model but also demonstrate competencies consistent with the training model and seek professional roles and contexts that allow them to express their identity.

Cook and Coyne (2005) have argued that irrespective of the type of training model, psychologists must be "scientifically literate" (p. 1191). Based on a study of students in scientific-practitioner programs, Luebbe, Radcliffe, Callands, Green, and Thorne (2007) compared students aspiring to clinical practice careers versus research futures on their views of Evidence-Based Practice in Psychology (EBPP). They reported that those seeking research careers displayed more positive attitudes about EBPP, believed that EBPP would have more of an impact on their careers, and were more likely to base treatment decisions on research as opposed to patient choices. The identification of attitudinal differences such as these are important to recognize and may ultimately be used as a basis for aligning training models on critical dimensions in the future.

On the other hand, unwarranted and malicious stereotypes about training models can hurt the identity of fellow psychologists, create division among the ranks, promote infighting, and marginalize colleagues. Social psychological theory and principles are useful in understanding the conflict between proponents of a model and students within each training model, including in-group versus out-group phenomena, stereotypes, biases, misattributions, and competition for limited resources (e.g., the current internship imbalance). We might add that this state of affairs is perplexing in a field that espouses sensitivity to diversity and awareness and openness to differences. Competent clinical psychologists have an obligation to respect their peers who have been trained in alternative models. Training models aside, the evidence in which clinical practice is embedded is another important factor influencing professional identity.

Clinical Psychologist as an Accountable Professional. Today, more so than at perhaps any other time in the history of professional psychology, clinical psychologists are challenged to demonstrate and substantiate that the professional services they offer truly make a difference in the lives of clients (Sanderson, 2003). A number of changes have contributed to the expectation of accountability. Accountability issues are evident in a number of arenas related to the interests and needs of stakeholders. These stakeholders include clinical psychologists themselves, clients, insurers, the government, and society in general. Accountability itself necessitates competence in the identification, assessment, analysis, interpretation, and dissemination of relevant outcomes to specific audiences. Clinical psychologists have a professional obligation to couch what they do within a value system characterized by scientific skepticism and an ongoing curiosity to seek answers to questions relevant to clinical practice.

Over the past 50 years or so, clinical psychologists have begun to raise issues of efficacy and effectiveness. Since Eysenck's (1952) article concluding that the efficacy of psychotherapy was no greater than the rate of spontaneous remission, the evidence base for psychotherapy remains a critical issue at the forefront of the specialty. Today, critical questions of whether what is being done to help others truly matters remain of great significance. Clinical psychology researchers have, thus, systematically focused on conducting investigations to identify relationship factors as well as processes and outcomes that are likely to be associated with or causally related to benefits that exceed the chance of spontaneous improvement in functioning and are mediated by potent factors over and above attention, placebo, and expectation effects. The questions of whether what clinical psychologists offer clients is better than receiving no service at all, or receiving a placebo or inactive treatment, and how treatments compare to each other are significant to professional identity.

Decisions about how to practice as a clinical psychologist are intricately tied to one's identity as a clinician and one's effectiveness as a practitioner as viewed by the public at large. Yet, more than three decades following the "Dodo Bird" verdict (Luborsky, Singer, & Luborsky, 1975) on the one hand, and despite what Barlow (2010c) recently described as thousands of clinical trials supporting the superior performance of some psychological treatments for specific problems on the other hand, controversy still abounds about the presumed equivalence of psychological therapies (Wampold, 2005). Years ago, Gordon Paul (1967) astutely called attention to the need to identify what type of treatment for what type of problem treated by what type of therapist produces what type of outcome.

The clinical psychologist, then, needs to know whether the services he or she chooses to offer in clinical practice actually produce stable and long-term benefits of a clinically significant nature. These issues have direct relevance to one's professional identity and underlie specific competencies necessary to critically evaluate, consume, and apply the professional literature in the service of clients. Failing to internalize accountability as a core value and simply ignoring empirical evidence engender problems that strike at the very heart of how a psychologist perceives himself or herself. Garfield's (1965) perspective, voiced years earlier, is just as compelling today in that some clinical psychologists risk being "a doctor who is not really a doctor, and a scientist who is not really scientific" (p. 358).

Documenting Outcomes. The documentation of clinical outcomes is yet another factor that fuels professional identity. The development, refinement, and use of psychological, cognitive, behavioral, biological, and social/interpersonal assessments has provided sensitive, valid, and reliable measures of change. Such measures have served to provide clinically relevant yardsticks with which to document one's accountability by reflecting levels of change on dimensions critical to effective functioning in clients. From an identity standpoint, clinical psychologists have a professional obligation to value the importance of and to seek ways to test the effectiveness of what they do. Documented beneficial outcomes are also likely to validate one's identity as a competent practitioner.

Emergence of Theory. Coupled with advances in measurement, the extension, refinement, and development of theories underlying behavior change have been helpful in fueling the accountability movement. In terms of professional identity, clinical psychologists have a professional obligation to keep abreast of advances in their specialty. For example, the melding of previously separate but related approaches, such as cognitive and behavioral, the development of short-term methods of treatment (e.g., short-term dynamic psychotherapy), and the emergence of "third wave" treatment approaches—including Dialectical Behavior Therapy (Linehan & Korsland, 2003), Acceptance and Commitment Therapy (Hayes, Pankey & Gregg, 2002), Functional Analytic Psychotherapy (Sturmey, 2007), and Mindfulness-Based Cognitive Therapy (Kabat-Zinn, 2005; Teasdale, 1988)—have expanded and enhanced the science of psychotherapy. Clinical psychologists have been at the forefront of the movement to revolutionize the science and art of psychosocial treatments, all in the interest of contributing to the welfare of humankind while creating a database of information supporting the efficacies of the treatment process. By the same token, the delineation of treatments that cause harm or that are ineffective is just as valuable (Barlow, 2010b; Lillenfield, 2007). Identification with treatments that foster improvement and disassociation from treatments that harm have a significant impact on professional identity. While practicing treatments that work will likely enhance one's professional credibility, practicing harmful or ineffective treatments may deservedly undermine one's professional credibility, let alone professional self-worth. The implications for professional identity and satisfaction with one's role are self-evident.

Societal Demands. Public demand for treatments that work and the solicitation of input from consumers have also solidified the role of accountability. Clinical psychologists have risen to the challenge of educating the public and professional community about the identification of best practices, empirically supported treatments (Barlow, 2010a; Chambless, et al., 1998), psychotherapy relationships that work (Norcross, 2002), and principles of behavior change across clinical disorders (Castonguay & Beutler, 2005). While rejected by some practitioners, the development of treatment manuals for therapists (Craske & Barlow, 2008) and client workbooks has also become popular. Finally, insurance carriers have entered into this arena by tracking outcomes, requiring documented ongoing reports of progress, and monitoring the efficacy of therapists.

This situation has led some psychologists to expand or alter their identity by seeking advanced training in new areas, changing their theoretical orientation, or even incorporating new tools into their therapeutic approach. Other clinical psychologists may inaccurately represent themselves as practitioners of a certain brand of therapy even when they basically practice from another orientation, a clear ethical violation.

In sum, over the past 20 years or so there has been an ever-increasing focus upon customizing the service delivery system from forces both within and outside of psychology. This process has manifested itself in areas directly relevant to competence of the clinical psychologist related to treatment models, length of treatments, costs of treatments, reimbursement, accessibility, and outcomes assessment. These interrelated areas have directly influenced the identity, roles, and functions of the clinical psychologist. For instance, the emergence and refinement of briefer models of treatment and their preference over long-term models are clearly evident. While this trend has been promoted, nurtured, and welcomed by psychologists of some theoretical persuasions, it has been rejected by others, who may view it both as an evil that undermines and erodes the very core upon which psychotherapy is based and as a serious threat to their basic identity as practitioners. Whatever the case, this issue is not without controversy and has created significant conflict within the specialty of clinical psychology itself. The plain truth is that current exigencies favor shorter rather than lengthier treatment models. Competent clinical psychologists respond to evidence about their work and alter their practice in ways that maximize outcomes. They also stay up to date by reading the literature, keeping abreast of findings, and expanding and broadening their toolkits.

Recent changes in the reimbursement system have created a number of problems for well-trained, experienced practitioners who identified as clinical psychologists. While patients lost the right to choose, many clinical psychologists lost the right to be chosen. In numerous situations, longstanding therapeutic relationships between clinical psychologists and clients were interrupted and eliminated. Likewise, physicians who had been accustomed to collaborating with specific individual clinical psychologist providers were forced into referring their patients to unknown providers. The emergence of Preferred Provider Organizations required psychologists to join panels, with the requirement that they agreed to charge less for service. Later, even quality point-of-service (QPOS) plans, which offer patients the option to seek providers out of network require patients to incur more costs by default by reducing the percentage of allowable reimbursement. Today, while some psychologists choose to participate in Health Maintenance Organization panels as providers at reduced reimbursable rates, many others have chosen not to do so and sought alternative means of securing their income by creating exclusively fee-for-service practices. Still others have expanded their scopes of practice by securing their income through coaching and mediation-type services, completely bypassing the insurance issues. In this sense, one's identity as a clinical psychologist may become diluted by assuming roles (e.g., coaching) that are not inherently part of the definition of the specialty.

Regardless of one's opinion about all of these changes, clinical psychologists have had to develop and assume a great deal of flexibility to survive in the marketplace. They must also be thoroughly knowledgeable about the variety of issues that exist in the marketplace. Clinical psychologists must rise to the challenges presented, in part, either directly or indirectly from accountability and seek creative and effective solutions, all the while striving to attain and maintain the highest level of commitment and adherence to professional, legal, and ethical standards. Accountability will likely continue to manifest itself in a number of ways that affect the identity of the clinical psychologist of the future. Addressing such challenges will require clear and consistent, carefully devised professionally and ethically based solutions. Sustaining a strong professional identity will likely guide clinical psychologists in making sound decisions designed to resolve these compelling matters. Assuming the identity of an effective practitioner appears critical in the professional marketplace of today and the future. The rise in popularity of evidence-based medicine, for example, provides further testimony to the public's demand for treatments that work. Moreover, one's credibility as a clinician by those outside of the field, such as physicians and patients, is likely to be affected by the psychologist's identity and commitment to empiricism.

Clinical Psychologist as an Evidence-Based Practitioner. The accountability issue is closely tied to the emergence of evidence-based psychology and the clinical psychologist's identity as an empirically based clinician. One of the issues confronting clinical psychologists today is the pressure to practice from an evidence-based framework. This situation has resulted in psychologists splitting into camps: those who identify as empirically based clinicians and those who view clinical practice as much more than simply the application of experimentally established treatment protocols. This controversy is captured nicely in the following quote from Rachman and Wilson (2008):

> A conversation between a psychologist and a senior engineer: The psychologist was explaining the steady adoption of demands for evidence-based psychological treatments, and the engineer listened with interest but was puzzled, and asked this question: "What was it based on before?" (p. 294)

This story underscores questions that have been raised about the efficacy and effectiveness of the process of psychotherapeutic treatment. Over the past couple of decades, the validation and support of psychological approaches and techniques have become some of the most important phenomena in the history of psychology (DiTomasso, Cahn, Cirilli, & Mochan, 2010). Competence in empirically based approaches is becoming increasingly important for clinical psychologists today and the professional identity they assume.

The impact of science upon practice and vice versa in the treatment of mental health and medical problems has increased the importance of carefully evaluating the potential benefits associated with assessments and interventions. Clinical psychologists are at a crossroads today. As the clinical research enterprise has evolved, there now exists a substantial scientific foundation of evidence based on demonstrable outcomes, replications, and generalizations that serves as a resource for selecting and applying psychological procedures (Barlow, 2010a). Based on a criterion of clinically significant improvement, some approaches for specific problems that have been considered therapeutic may not deserve this branding based on the evidence (DiTomasso et al., 2010).

The APA Presidential Task Force on Evidence-Based Practice (2005) professed psychology's allegiance to evidence-based psychological practice by emphasizing the application of empirically based principles of psychological assessment, case formulation, therapeutic relationships, and intervention. The task force defined "psychology—as a science and as a profession—[that] is distinctive in combining scientific commitment with an emphasis on human relationships and individual differences" (p. 6). Both empirically supported treatments and relationship factors support this initiative. To ignore empirical evidence or even deny its clinical utility has serious and significant professional, ethical, and legal implications relating to standards of practice. Failure to adopt an empirical focus may seriously undermine one's professional identity and development, if not success.

In this age of accountability, empiricism, and competency, clinical psychologists must be thoroughly knowledgeable about the evidence base for the approaches they practice, adjust their interventions to maximize outcomes, and examine, monitor, and enhance the outcomes produced by their own practice. Otherwise, the impact of the interventions may be undermined. The clinical psychologist must be open to all of the evidence, including findings that support his or her approach and even outcomes that refute it under certain conditions. Some critics, such as Wampold (2005), have criticized this literature by arguing that some treatments originally used in establishing another treatment as empirically supported were later themselves designated as empirically supported by subsequent research. Psychology is a continually evolving science that is open to new and emerging evidence and adjusts accordingly. The implication here is that clinical psychologists must maintain an attitude of openness to clinical data, a commitment to reading the literature, a devotion to integrating clinical information into clinical practice, and an obligation to seek training and supervision when deemed necessary. As a continually evolving applied science, the specialty of clinical psychology warrants that its practitioners appreciate the value of new knowledge and be willing to adopt information as a means of modifying existing practice to become more congruent with new evidence.

Ollendick and King (2004) reinforced how through continued and ongoing empirical efforts, the originally identified 25 empirically supported treatments had more than quadrupled by 2001. They concluded that there is evidence today supporting (a) the superiority of empirically supported treatments over treatments that are not empirically supported, (b) that there are identifiable specific therapies for given disorders, (c) that outcomes are similar in research settings and applied settings, and (d) that empirically supported treatments are better than treatment as usual and other bona fide therapies for true clinical problems. Those identifying as clinical psychologists must not only be cognizant of these findings but also prepared to act on them in the service of their clients. Competent clinicians seek and use knowledge in ways that enhance the effectiveness of their craft by offering services that have a documented track record of maximizing outcomes. Those identifying as clinical psychologists engage in those activities designed to enhance their effectiveness.

Clinician versus Technician: Efficacy versus Effectiveness. The development of an ever-growing list of evidence-based psychological treatments has been a significant accomplishment in the field of clinical psychology. The Division 12 Task Force on the Promotion and Dissemination of Psychological Procedures (Chamblesset al., 1998) has done much to promote the importance of empiricism in the psychological marketplace. This work group has also brought attention to issues such as the efficacy of treatments in clinical trials conducted in research settings versus the importance and challenges of extending these findings to clinical offices in the community and demonstrating effectiveness in these applied settings. As we discuss this trend, however, we are cautious to avoid suggesting in any way that practicing clinical psychologists who do not embrace this movement are any less effective in their work.

Differences between the research and clinical contexts related to patients, therapists, treatment delivery, settings, resources, barriers, and the like have presented challenges to clinical psychologists. It is not simply a matter of whether efficacious treatments are or are not effective in applied contexts. Rather, it is a matter of systematically identifying what unique challenges are present in applied settings and addressing them to yield a better fit. Likewise, the application and testing of manualized treatments have clearly underscored the need for flexibility within the context of fidelity (Kendall, Chu, Gifford, Hayes, & Nauta, 1998), meaning that overly strict and rigid adherence to a manual may undermine the effectiveness of treatment. Likewise, the failure of manuals to attend to the therapeutic alliance and to incorporate clinical judgment have also raised concerns among clinical psychologists (Borntrager, Chorpita, Higa-McMillan, & Weisz, 2009). Nonetheless, the challenge here is for clinical psychologists to maintain adherence to the critical components of treatment efficacy and the science of therapy and expand their toolkits, all the while tailoring the treatment to the patient—the art of therapy.

Earlier, we described how the evidence-based issue has affected the identity of the clinical psychologist. The application of manualized treatments, or lack thereof, is central to this identity. While historically many clinicians have objected to this approach (see Wilson, 1997), we maintain that this opposition is due in part to misconceptions about the manualization of treatments. Perhaps the most frequent arguments relate to the fear that such approaches are too mechanistic, miss the true essence of therapy, and make psychotherapy a "cookbook," with the clinical psychologist relegated to the role and identity of a mere technician (see Wilson, 1997). We certainly would not argue for an approach that promotes less autonomy or freedom to make professional determinations.

Clinical psychologists who are experienced with manualized approaches, however, recognize that the application of such strategies involves much more than simply blind adherence to a strict set of procedures. In point of fact, it is somewhat difficult to imagine a competent clinical psychologist following a protocol so closely as to miss clinically important and relevant information. Messer (2004), a proponent of empirically based short-term dynamic therapy, noted that the treatment of complex cases often involves more than simply the application of a treatment manual, which may, in and of itself, overlook important facets of a case. Clinical psychologists who maintain an identity as empirically based practitioners with a strong commitment to applying psychological knowledge in the service of their clientele are likely to view themselves and be considered by others to be more than simply technicians. The dissemination of empirically supported approaches into practice, however, presents some unique challenges to the practicing clinician who identifies as an empiricist. Competence in transporting empirical treatments into practice is critical.

Transporting Research into Practice. A major initiative in the field of clinical psychology is evidenced in efforts to translate findings from treatments tested in research settings to actual clinical settings in the community (Newnham & Page, 2010). The challenge confronting clinical psychologist researchers and practitioners is the dissemination of findings for the benefit and welfare of clients. There is little doubt that a variety of factors affect the ability to do so competently. Systematic efforts to address critical issues related to the clinician, client, population, settings, problems, comorbidities, and the like can be found in the Beck Initiative's ACCESS model (Wiltsey-Stirman et al., 2010; Wiltsey-Stirman, Buchhofer, McLaulin, Evans, & Beck, 2009). The essential ingredients of this model include "intensive training and consultation, quality assurance, ongoing support, and innovative methods of implementing cognitive therapy in a variety of programs and settings" (Wiltsey-Stirman et al., 2009, p. 1302). This initiative, a project jointly sponsored by the Beck Institute and the Philadelphia Department of Behavioral Health and Mental Retardation Services, has given careful consideration to a variety of barriers and strategies to facilitate implementation. This project has both underscored and creatively addressed those factors impinging on the critical issues related to transportability.

Of course, the existence of empirically supported treatments in no way guarantees that they will be applied in a manner that is appropriate and as intended in clinical offices in the community. Treatment fidelity is not simply a matter of reading a handbook or attending a conference and presuming one has mastered the therapeutic strategy. Rather, transporting treatments requires a systematic and comprehensive effort including readings, training workshops, role-playing, viewing actual tapes of trainee sessions, providing feedback to trainees, and consultation. The implications for clinical psychologists, even empirically based ones, are clear.

Developing competency in the delivery of empirically grounded treatments requires a serious commitment to seeking and obtaining the training needed to develop, enhance, and refine skills. Clinical psychologists must internalize an identity that fosters continual growth and development in areas of direct application to clinical practice. The rationale underlying continuing education and supervised training is based on the assumption that the knowledge and skills of psychologists need updating to facilitate better outcomes. Failure to maintain a standard of best practices is an important professional and ethical concern. This issue raises significant professional, ethical, and competency issues for the clinician. To do otherwise risks the possibility that the clinical psychologist offers suboptimal versions of treatments that exclude or minimize critically potent treatment mechanisms.

Clinical psychologists have much to gain from the ACCESS Model of Wiltsey-Stirman and colleagues (2010), as its elements are relevant to the professional identification and refinement of the psychologist who is responsive to the literature. While this model was designed to facilitate quality training in the community, clinical psychologists would be wise to consider these same elements in their own attempts to incorporate empiricism into their daily practice. These elements (Wiltsey-Stirman et al., 2010) require clinicians to (a) engage in self-assessment and adaptation to the model; (b) seek to understand and assimilate the core basics of the therapeutic modality; (c) seek professional consultation with those experienced in the treatment model; (d) obtain expert opinion and feedback on one's clinical work; incorporate this feedback into clinical practice; (e) assess the impact of the treatment offered in one's practice through well-validated multimodal measures; and (f) arrange for means and methods to maintain the implementation and provision of high-quality services. Each of these elements is an essential component of shaping and maintaining competence in professional practice. The implications for professional identity are clear here. Clinical psychologists must adopt a value system that serves to motivate them to self-reflect, seek ongoing knowledge, learn from experts, desire feedback, assess quality, and develop plans for sustaining the quality of services offered.

Clinical Psychologist as Participant in Professional Organizations, Divisions, and Special Interest Groups. Professional identification also necessitates getting involved in groups that bring together large numbers of professionals for the ultimate purpose of advancing the field. Participating in professional organizations at national, state, and local levels is a public expression of one's identity. Organizations such as the APA and its specialty divisions (e.g., Society for Clinical Psychology) as well as organizations comprising individuals with special interests, such as the Association for Behavioral and Cognitive Therapies, the Society for Personality Assessment, and the Society for Psychotherapy Research, which may include special interest groups, serve many critical functions. These groups provide a social, educational, and political arena that serves to define professional identity; fulfill the professional interests and needs of its membership; offer numerous opportunities for sharing ideas; facilitate collegial interactions, professional networking, and relationship building; and afford the best in continuing education programs so that professionals can update and refine their skills and remain current. One's identity as a clinical psychologist hinges on keeping abreast of critical issues confronting the field, reinforcing the need to advocate for causes and issues that otherwise may undermine the roles and functions of the specialty.

Professional organizations often comprise rather large numbers of individuals who share a common vision and thereby can exert power through numbers to offset pressures and influences from outside bodies that may threaten the interests of the group as a whole. Likewise, these groups may preserve the identity of the specialty by fighting changes or trends and publicly addressing controversies that threaten the integrity of the professional role through public education and efforts to influence policy. Over the years there have been efforts by outside organizations to unfairly restrict the practice of clinical psychologists in hospitals, prevent psychologists from joining the professional staff of hospitals, undermine professional parity, oppose prescription privileges, threaten the role of clinical psychologists as independent practitioners, and even reserve the title of "doctor" to physicians. Left unopposed, these issues would otherwise threaten the very core upon which clinical psychologists identify and how they are viewed by the public.

Professional memberships allow clinical psychologists to contribute to the field and offer support and guidance on common professional, ethical, and legal issues. Professional organizations sponsor continuing education that fulfills the need for lifelong learning in the continually evolving knowledge base of the field. Those who avoid or ignore the many advantages of professional membership risk professional isolation, burnout, and perhaps even eventual impairment. Moreover, such individuals may lose valuable opportunities to express their professional identity. Clinical psychologists who are isolated and experiencing burnout and mental problems appear to be at higher risk for engaging in unethical practices.

Clinical Psychologist as Recipient of Postdoctoral Training, Licensure, and the ABPP Diploma. The training of clinical psychologists is designed to provide them with the knowledge, skills, attitudes, and ultimate competencies to ensure they are fully prepared to assume the role of the clinical psychologist. Inherent within the process of graduate and professional education is assuming an identity and assimilating the norms, mores, and values of the field. Doctoral education and training in psychology proceed in a developmentally graded, progressive, and sequential fashion by providing a solid undergirding in the scientific foundations of psychology and professional practice. Training follows a path from breadth to depth and may be viewed developmentally as progressing along a continuum from doctoral-level education, to practicum training, to internship training, to postdoctoral training, to licensure attainment, and to achieving specialty board certification (Rubin et al., 2007). Kaslow and colleagues (1992) have even elucidated a developmental perspective within postdoctoral training by describing early, middle, and late phases of development. Given that doctoral education is focused on creating competent generalists, the need for specialization and advanced skills emerges over time.

In further establishing a professional identity, the role of postdoctoral training has traditionally provided an important mechanism for achieving this end. Most states currently require 2 years of supervised professional experience under a licensed psychologist, 1 year of which must be post-doctoral, to sit for licensure (Kaslow et al., 1992). Nonetheless, it is likely that many individuals will complete postdoctoral training as a means to foster specialization, further solidifying and crystallizing their professional identity.

Undoubtedly, attaining professional licensure is the sine qua non of professional identity for psychologists. To be publicly considered a psychologist as well as to practice privately, one must achieve licensure. Psychology licensure is a professional mechanism for protecting the welfare of the public and monitoring the professional activities of those included under this title. Beyond licensure is the issue of professional certification in the specialty of clinical psychology, an achievement that further strengthens professional identity.

The American Board of Professional Psychology (ABPP), chartered in 1949, is an organization dedicated to creating specialists in professional psychology through maintaining quality standards and examination procedures through stages that may qualify an individual for the diploma. Despite the professional recognition associated with this diploma, relatively speaking, a small proportion of clinical psychologists seek to attain it. Efforts are under way to facilitate this process by encouraging clinical psychologists to sit for this examination and to achieve the distinction of practicing at an advanced level in their specialty. From the perspective of identity, the ABPP diploma in clinical psychology is a public declaration that the diplomate has met all the requirements of the board to certify that he or she is practicing as a competent professional at an advanced level.

Scope of Practice: Prescription Privileges. Scope of practice is also a factor influencing professional identity. The attainment of prescription privileges has a history in the field that spans the past decade or so, dating back to 1995 when the APA introduced the Prescription Privilege Initiative (Sowell2008; http://www.apa.org). Like many other factors associated with change, this issue has met with controversy (DeLeon & Graham, 1991). From a professional standpoint, a major concern is how prescription privileges will affect the identity, roles, and functions of the clinical psychologist of the future. An examination of these issues strikes at the very core of psychology as a behavioral science as opposed to a physical science. Inherent within this concern are the differences in paradigms that differentiate the two systems of thought, their methods, their approaches to studying problems, and their assessment strategies and interventions.

Some have been concerned that "medicalizing" psychology will undermine the field of psychology itself, possibly disenfranchise psychotherapy as a treatment modality, create a class system within the field of clinical psychology itself, and result in increased malpractice-related problems (DeLeon & Graham,1991). The reality is that clinical psychologists are independent practitioners, and as a field, professional psychology is well equipped to develop and create curricula, training experiences, and credentialing processes that will ensure the qualifications and quality of its practitioners. If anything, as a competency-based specialty, clinical psychology has the right to expand the scope of practice of its practitioners as long as they meet national standards of quality and develop and maintain the requisite competencies to do so. Under the scope of the label *clinical psychologist*, while practitioners identify with many different theoretical persuasions, the overarching descriptor defines the prototype. We suspect that prescribing clinical psychologists will form one more subgroup of specialists who practice within the specialty of clinical psychology. That being said, regardless of one's special distinguishing competencies, maintaining competence is a prerequisite to effective clinical practice. There are likely to be a number of critical attitudes that are relevant to maintaining competence in one's specialty and in acquiring new competencies. Central here are a commitment and willingness to obtain education and training and a willingness to learn essential skills related to practice (Fouad et al., 2009).

Clinical Psychologist as Maintaining and Refining Competencies through Continuing Education Activities. The development of professional foundational and functional competencies embodies a systematic, graduated educational and training process proceeding from practicum readiness, to internship readiness, and to readiness for entering into professional practice (Fouad et al., 2009). Following entry into clinical practice, the importance of engaging in and obtaining continuing education in clinical psychology goes without saying. The specialty of clinical psychology is growing at a rapid pace, and busy practitioners are challenged ethically and professionally by the challenge of remaining current in the field. Considering the many important issues confronting practitioners today, clinical psychologists have a duty and responsibility to maintain and refine their knowledge base, keep their skills crisp, remain healthy through self-care to avoid impairment, and hone their competencies and practice at the highest ethical, legal, and professional level. In essence, any factor that may affect the performance of the clinician and the clinical services he or she provides is a ripe area for continuing education. This process involves competence in practicing self-reflection and awareness, identifying areas in need of improvement, selecting high-quality continuing education activities, seeking out these important opportunities, and incorporating them into one's practice. Kaslow and colleagues (2004) have correctly called for the development of self-assessment tools as well as the education of students and practitioners in the use of such methods to promote a quality improvement process over one's professional life cycle.

In the area of continuing education, the APA Education Directorate has provided a list of standards that sponsoring organizations must meet to qualify as a sponsor of credits. While APA approves organizations to provide continuing education programs for psychologists, the organization assumes responsibility for the content of the program and the program itself. The professional consumer assumes responsibility for solidifying, enhancing, and expanding, when necessary, his or her skill mix to provide effective services as a professional practitioner. In some states, such as Pennsylvania, to maintain licensure, psychologists are required to earn 30 continuing education credits, 3 of which must be in professional ethics, every 2 years; others, such as New Jersey, have no such requirement.

There also is a movement afoot to require continuing education in the important domain of diversity and to enhance the evaluation process to demonstrate that learning has occurred. High-quality education, critical and timely topics, experienced presenters, experts in the content area, effective use of audiovisuals and handouts, carefully developed objectives, consideration of best teaching practices in program implementation, and effective use of evaluation tools are some of the hallmarks of high-quality continuing education. Psychologists must be aware of these criteria and choose high-quality opportunities that meet their needs.

Maintaining competency, however, involves more than simply taking required continuing education credits. Clinical psychologists need to develop a personal *professional development plan* based on a systematic process including continuing education classes/workshops, home study programs, peer supervision, reading relevant journals and books, obtaining consultation, and focused clinical supervision. The clinician would be wise, however, to first develop a set of professional goals and specific objectives for learning, consider available high-quality programs sponsored by reputable organizations, and seek educational experiences that fulfill an important professional need. Likewise, the clinician must be cognizant that taking a continuing education course or reading a manual rarely qualifies the individual to offer services. This issue borders on the important question about remaining aware of the limits of one's own competency and offering services in only those areas in which one is competent.

Clinical Psychologist as a Lifelong Learner in a World of Evolving Knowledge. The clinical psychologist must assume the identity of a lifelong learner to maintain competency. Lifelong learning implies a strong commitment to engaging in a long-term self-directed, educational process designed to enhance one's knowledge, skills, and attitudes in identified competency domains that underlie professional practice; these efforts must be sustained to ensure the effectiveness of the clinical psychologist over the professional life cycle. Lifelong learners embrace the continually emerging body of knowledge in clinical psychology and seek opportunities to understand the core areas that affect their professional effectiveness. Spring (2007) has argued that evidence-based practice encourages lifelong learning, while Kazdin (2008) elucidated the means through which both clinical research and practice can enhance one's knowledge base and yield information that can enhance clinical care. Clinical psychologists have a responsibility to know what they know and what they do not know and use learning processes as a means for building upon current strengths, reinforcing skills, creating new skills, and overcoming deficits in specific areas. Sound professional practice is built upon a solid foundation of professional identity that has internalized these values.

The alternative to lifelong learning is alarming and unethical at best. Failure to engage in learning may have a number of important risks and consequences for both practitioners and their clients. First, we examine the effect on clinicians. Clinical psychologists who fail to update their knowledge and skills run the risk of offering outdated services that may fall short of the standard of care in a given area. They may develop a false sense of security about the effectiveness of their services that precludes in their minds the need for further education. Prior training and experience do not necessarily guarantee continued competence on a given task (e.g., administering and interpreting the newest version of the WAIS). For example, as test updates are published, psychologists must seek opportunities for continued learning and skill development. Moreover, extensive experience in one area (e.g., private practice) does not qualify one to practice in another area (e.g., integrated healthcare setting). More specialized services require more specialized training. Finally, clinical experience with one population (e.g., adults) does not ensure competence in working with another population (e.g., children). Professional identification as a competent clinical psychologist demands a commitment to ongoing learning over the professional life cycle.

Clinical Psychologist as Seeker of Training Geared Toward Competency Development. Over the past years, developments in the training realm have emphasized competency-based education. The delineation of competency domains in professional psychology is justifiably credited with fostering and enhancing the quality of training today. Broadly defined competency domains, however, do little to identify precisely what it means to be competent within a given area. In clinical psychology, some critical competency domains include the relationship, assessment-diagnosis-conceptualization, intervention, research and evaluation, consultation and education, management and supervision, and diversity and ethics (Kaslow et al., 2004; Kenkel & Peterson, 2010). The specification of critical knowledge, skills, and attitudes categorized in a graduated, sequential fashion across timing benchmarks has set the stage for gearing training toward competency development. Specific criteria within each domain at each level of training have created important developmental milestones and criteria for determining the extent to which a budding psychologist has the potential to bloom into a professional. These criteria provide important opportunities for faculty and students to assess and self-assess respectively the progress achieved and the need for remediation. While having educational exposure to specific competency domains is necessary for competence, it is certainly not sufficient.

Benchmark Competencies for Professional Identification

In attaining and maintaining a professional identity, there are a number of benchmark competencies to be achieved as the trainee clinical psychologist proceeds from entry into the program to readiness for practicum experiences, to readiness for beginning internship, and to completion of the doctorate and being prepared to begin practice. Rodolfa and colleagues (2005) view professional development as a process proceeding along sequential milestones extending from doctoral education through maintaining ongoing competency. The Competency Benchmarks Work Group (Fouad et al., 2009) proposed that professionalism as a foundational competency comprises several components. including integrity-honesty, deportment, accountability, concern for others, and, of interest in the present context, professional identity. Professional identification, an important component of professionalism, then, proceeds in a developmental and incremental fashion.

Elman and colleagues (2005) view professionalism as the ultimate manifestation of an attained professional identity and argue that a critical aspect of professional development that is closely tied to professional identification is the ability to approach problems from the mindset of a psychologist. According to Elman and colleagues (2005), thinking as a psychologist thinks appears to be rooted in a number of factors: "(a) critical thinking and logical analysis; (b) being conversant with and utilizing scientific literature and professional literature; (c) being able to conceptualize problems and issues from multiple perspective (e.g., biological, pharmacological, intrapsychic, familial, organizational/systems, social (cultural)); and (d) being able to access, understand, integrate and use resources (e.g., empirical evidence, statistical approaches, technology, collegial consultation)" (p. 369). Fouad and colleagues (2009) view thinking as a psychologist as the threshold for performing competently at practicum, an unfolding of professional identity for doing so at internship, and consolidation of identity at practice entry.

To achieve a strong professional identity as a clinical psychologist from a developmental perspective warrants demonstration of a number of behaviorally based indicators. At the practicum readiness level, the student demonstrates affiliation with a professional organization (e.g., student member of APA), possesses information about his or her program and its training model and essential competencies, understands his or her limits of competence, and appreciates that knowledge extends past training (Fouad et al., 2009). At the internship readiness level, professional identity is manifested by attending professional presentations and conferences, seeking training workshops, and employing the professional literature as a basis for client care (Fouad et al., 2009). At the practice entry level, Fouad and colleagues (2009) see the individual keeping abreast of current developments in the specialty, making contributions to improve the specialty and one's peers, and assimilating scientific information into clinical practice. Elman and colleagues (2005) identified a number of methods for developing professional identity: "Peer interactions and socialization, Peer case consultation, Role modeling, Mentoring, Directed readings Discussions of controversies in field, Professional development conferences, Attendance at professional meetings, Participation in professional associations, Involvement with research and scholarly activities, and Representation of psychology in interdisciplinary activities" (p. 370).

Assessing Professional Identification

Kaslow and colleagues (2009) created a menu of measures for assessing Foundational and Functional Competencies. In the foundational area of professionalism they consider a variety of assessment methods that can be used to measure general competency domains as well as essential components of domains. The most useful strategies for assessing professional identity include annual performance reviews, ratings, portfolio reviews, self-assessment, standard oral examinations, and 360-degree evaluations (Kaslow et al., 2009). In a similar vein, Elman and colleagues (2005) proposed the use of self-assessment, ratings from peers, assessment of career satisfaction, assumption of leadership positions, and the use of "triple jump" evaluations.

The competent clinical psychologist is committed to attaining and maintaining a strong professional identity. A sound professional identification with the specialty and field is a hallmark of the competent clinical psychologist. To do so requires a commitment to ongoing self-assessment, openness to feedback from a variety of sources, and a commitment to assimilate this feedback as a means of consolidating one's professional identity.

Concluding Remarks

Identifying as a clinical psychologist continues to be shaped by a number of critical issues confronting the specialty today. Given the current climate regarding healthcare reform and the focus on integrated healthcare, the roles and functions of psychologists are changing dramatically. The face of clinical psychology is also changing rapidly and will necessitate adaptation to ensure survival in the marketplace. The clinical psychologist of tomorrow will spend much more time in a consultative role, providing much-needed expert guidance on handling patients in primary care settings (DiTomasso, Golden, & Morris, 2010). Yet, as Cook and Coyne (2005) noted, despite being trained in consultation (as well as education and research), clinical psychologists are not moving toward the assumption of these roles.

Clinical psychologists will also continue to face increasing accountability (Chwalisz, 2003). This pressure will require continued and sustained efforts to produce scientific evidence supporting effective clinical activities in the community, promoting cost savings in delivery of services, and providing added value. Incorporating science into clinical practice and relevant clinical practice issues into science will forge the way toward creating knowledge that has great potential for influencing practice. Clinical psychologists will need to lead the way toward producing relevant knowledge, consuming it, and translating and disseminating it into clinical practice (Cook & Coyne, 2005).

Given the current state of affairs, identifying new roles and applications is likely to expand professional opportunities. Considering the competency domains within which clinical psychologists are trained may foster new opportunities for practice. Diversification of roles may be one means for doing so but would require specification of requisite knowledge, skills, and attitudes.

In conclusion, professional identification as a clinical psychologist embodies a keen awareness of the relevant knowledge base in the specialty, sharpened skills in the application of this knowledge, and an overarching framework of attitudes and values that support professional development in the context of lifelong learning and advocacy for the specialty and profession. Maintaining professional identity is a multifaceted process that entails a commitment to accountability, empiricism, clinical effectiveness, and professional involvement as well as the attainment of designated milestone and capstone experiences and engagement in a number of behavioral indicators, all achieved within a context of ongoing self-awareness, self-reflection, self-direction, and lifelong learning.

REFERENCES

Ackerman, S. J., & Hilsenroth, M. J. (2001). A review of therapist characteristics and therapist characteristics and techniques negatively impacting the therapeutic alliance. *Psychotherapy, 38,* 171–185.

Ackerman, S. J., & Hilsenroth, M. J. (2003). A review of therapist characteristics and techniques positively impacting the therapeutic alliance. *Clinical Psychology Review, 23,* 1–33.

Agras, W., S., Walsh, B. T., Fairburn, C. G., Wilson, G. T., & Kraemer, H. C. (2000). A multicenter comparison of cognitive-behavioral therapy and interpersonal psychotherapy for bulimia nervosa. *Archives of General Psychiatry, 57,* 459–466.

Aiken, L. R. (1996). *Rating scales and checklists.* New York: Wiley & Sons, Inc.

Aiken, L. R. (1997). *Questionnaires and inventories.* New York: Wiley & Sons, Inc.

Ainsworth, M. D. S., Blehar, M. C., Walters, E., & Wall, S. (1978). *Patterns of attachment: Psychological study of the strange situation.* Hillsdale, NJ: Erlbaum.

Alexander, F., & French, T. M. (1946). *Psychoanalytic therapy.* New York: Ronald Press.

Allport, G. W. (1954). *The nature of prejudice.* Cambridge, MA: Addison-Wesley.

American Psychiatric Association. (1994). *Diagnostic and statistical manual of mental disorders (4th ed.).* Washington, D. C.: Author.

American Psychiatric Association. (2000). Practice guidelines for the treatment of patients with major depressive disorder (revision). *American Journal of Psychiatry, 157,* 1–45.

American Psychological Association. (1953). *Ethical standards of psychologists.* Washington, DC: Author.

American Psychological Association. (1975). Resolution on discrimination against homosexuals. *American Psychologist, 30,* 633.

American Psychological Association. (2000). *Minutes of APA Council of Representatives.* Washington, D. C.: Author.

American Psychological Association. (2002). Ethical principles of psychologists and code of conduct. *American Psychologist, 57,* 1060–1073.

American Psychological Association, Committee on Accreditation. (2002). Guidelines and principles for accreditation of programs in professional psychology. Washington, DC: Author.

American Psychological Association. (2003). Guidelines on multicultural education, training, research, practice, and organizational change for psychologists. *American Psychologist, 58,* 377–402.

American Psychological Association. (2005a). Continuing education sponsor approval system: Standards and criteria. Retrieved from http://www.apa.org/ed/sponsor/about/standards/manual.pdf

American Psychological Association. (2005b). *Policy statements on lesbian, gay, and bisexual concerns.* Retrieved from www.apa.org/pi/lgbc/policy/pshome.html.

American Psychological Association. (2006). *State provincial mandatory continuing education in psychology (MCEP) requirements—2006 survey results.* Washington, D. C.: Author

American Psychological Association. (2007). Record keeping guidelines. *American Psychologist, 62,* 993–1004.

American Psychological Association. (2009). *Report of the task force on gender identity and gender variance.* Retrieved from www.apa.org/pi/lgbc/transgender/2008TaskForce Report.pdf.

American Psychological Association, Committee on Accreditation. (2002). *Guidelines and principles for accreditation of programs in professional psychology.* Washington, D. C.: Author.

American Psychological Association, Ethics Committee (2010). Report on Ethics Committee, 2009. *American Psychologist, 65,* 483–492.

American Psychological Association, Ethics Committee (2011). Report on Ethics Committee, 2010. *American Psychologist, 66,* 393–403.

American Psychological Association Presidential Task Force on Evidence-Based Care. (2006). Evidence-based practice in psychology. *The American Psychologist, 61,* 271–285.

American Psychological Association (2012). *Benchmarks evaluation system.* Retrieved from http://www.apa.org/ed/graduate/benchmarks-evaluation-system.aspx

Anastasi, A. (1996). *Psychological testing* (7th ed.). London: The Macmillan Company.

Ano, G. G., & Vasconcelles, E. B. (2005). Religious coping and psychological adjustment to stress: A meta-analysis. *Journal of Clinical Psychology, 61,* 461–480.

Arredondo, P., & Arciniega, G. M. (2001). Strategies and techniques for counselor training based on the multicultural counseling competencies. *Journal of Multicultural Counseling and Development, 29,* 263–273.

Arredondo, P., Shealy, C., Neale, M., & Winfrey, L. L. (2004). Consultation and interprofessional collaboration: Modeling for the future. *Journal of Clinical Psychology, 60,* 787–800.

Artman, L. K., & Daniels, J. A. (2010). Disability and psychotherapy practice: Cultural competence and practical tips. *Professional Psychology: Research and Practice,* Advance online publication.

Asch, S. M., Kerr, E. A., Keesey, J., Adams, J. L., Setodji, C. M., Malik, S., & McGlynn, E. A. (2006). Who is at risk for receiving poor-quality health care? *New England Journal of Medicine, 354,* 1147–1156.

Ascher, L. M., & Esposito, C. (2005). Behavior therapy. In A. Freeman, S. H. Felgoise, A. Nezu, C. Nezu, & M. A. Reinecke (Eds.), *Encyclopedia of cognitive and behavior therapy* (pp. 68–70). New York: Springer Publishing Company.

Atkinson, D. R., Morten, G., & Sue, D. W. (1998). *Counseling American minorities* (5th ed.). New York: McGraw–Hill.

Axelson, J. A. (1999). *Counseling and development in a multicultural society* (3rd ed.). Pacific Grove, CA: Brooks/Cole.

Ayllon, T., & Azrin, N. H.. (1968). *The token economy: A motivational system for therapy and rehabilitation*. Englewood Cliffs, NJ: Prentice-Hall, Inc.

Azrin, N. H, & Foxx, R. (1974). *Toilet training in less than a day*. New York: Simon & Schuster.

Baker, D. C., & Bufka, L. F. (2011). Preparing for the telehealth world: Navigating legal, regulatory, reimbursement, and ethical issues in an electronic age. *Professional Psychology: Research and Practice, 42*(6), 405–411.

Barber, J. B., & Crits-Christoph, P. (1993). Advances in measures of psychodynamic formulations. *Journal of Consulting and Clinical Psychology, 61*(4), 574–585.

Barlow, D. H. (1981). On the relation of clinical research to clinic practice: Current issues. *Journal of Consulting and Clinical Psychology, 49,* 147–155.

Barlow, D. (2010a). Unified protocol for the transdiagnostic treatment of emotional disorders: Protocol development and initial outcome data. *Cognitive and Behavioral Practice, 17*(1), 88–101.

Barlow, D. H. (2010b). Negative effects from psychological treatments. *American Psychologist, 65(1),* 13–20.

Barlow, D. H. (2010c). The DoDo bird-again-and again. *The Behavior Therapist, 33*(1), 15–16.

Barnett, J. E. (2007). Seeking an understanding of informed consent. *Professional Psychology: Research and Practice, 38,* 179–182.

Barnett, J. E. (2008). The ethical practice of psychotherapy: Easily within our reach. *Journal of Clinical Psychology, 64,* 569–575.

Barnett, J. E., Erickson Cornish, J. A., Goodyear, R. K., & Lichtenberg, J. W. (2007). Commentaries on the ethical and effective practice of clinical supervision. *Professional Psychology: Research and Practice, 38,* 268–275.

Bartoli, E., & Gillem, A. R. (2008). Continuing to depolarize the debate on sexual orientation and religious identity and the therapeutic process. *Professional Psychology: Research and Practice, 39,* 202–209.

Beavers, R., & Hampson, R. B. (2000). The Beavers Systems Model of family functioning. *Journal of Family Therapy, 22,* 128–143.

Beck, A. T. (1964). Thinking and depression: 2. Theory and therapy. *Archives of General Psychiatry, 10,* 561–571.

Beck, A. T. (2005). The current state of cognitive therapy: A 40-year retrospective. *Archives of General Psychiatry, 62,* 953–959.

Beck, A. T., Rush, A. J., Shaw, B. F., & Emery, G. (1979). *Cognitive therapy of depression.* New York: Guilford.

Beck, J. (1995). *Cognitive therapy: Basics and beyond.* New York: Guilford Press.

Beckstead, L., & Isreal, T. (2007). Affirmative counseling and psychotherapy focused on issues related to sexual orientation conflicts. In K. J. Bieschke, R. M. Perez, & K. A. DeBord (Eds.), *Handbook of counseling and psychotherapy with lesbian, gay, bisexual, and transgender clients* (2nd ed., pp. 221–244). Washington, D. C.: American Psychological Association.

Belar, C., Deardorff, W., & Kelly, K. (1987). *The practice of clinical health psychology.* New York: Pergamon Press.

Belar, C., & Perry, N. W. (1992). National conference on scientific-practitioner education and training for the professional practice of psychology. *American Psychologist, 55,* 233–254.

Bellack, A. S., & Hersen, M. (1998). *Behavioral assessment: A practical guide.* Needham Heights, MA: Allyn & Bacon.

Benjamin, L. T., & Baker, D. B. (2000). The affirmation of the scientist-practitioner: A look back at Boulder. *American Psychologist, 55*(2), 241–247.

Bennett, B. E., Bricklin, P. M., & VandeCreek, L. (1994). Response to Lazarus's "How certain boundaries and ethics diminish therapeutic effectiveness." *Ethics and Behavior, 4,* 263–266.

Benson, N., Hulac, D. M., & Kranzler, J. H. (2010). Independent examination of the Wechsler Adult Intelligence Scale—Fourth Edition (WAIS-IV): What does the WAIS-IV measure? *Psychological Assessment, 22*(1), 121–130.

Bent, R. J., Schindler, N., & Dobbins, J. E. (1991). Management and supervision competency. In R. L. Peterson, J. D. McHolland, and R. J. Bent (Eds.), *The core curriculum in professional psychology* (pp. 121–126). Washington, D. C.: American Psychological Association.

Bersoff, D. N. (2008). *Ethical conflicts in psychology* (4th ed). Washington, D. C.: American Psychological Association.

Best, D. L., & Thomas, J. J. (2004). Cultural diversity and cross-cultural perspectives. In A. H. Eagly, A. E. Beall, & R. J. Sternberg (Eds.), *The psychology of gender* (2nd ed., pp. 296–327). New York: The Guilford Press.

Bieschke, K. J., Fouad, N. A., Collins, F. L., & Halonen, J. S. (2004). The scientifically-minded psychologist: Science as a core competency. *Journal of Clinical Psychology, 60*(7), 713–723.

Biggerstaff, M. A. (1994). Evaluating the reliability of oral examinations for licensure of clinical social workers in Virginia. *Research on Social Work Practice, 4,* 481.

Binder, J. L. (2004). *Key competencies in brief dynamic psychotherapy: Clinical practice beyond the manual.* New York: The Guilford Press.

Bishop, D., Epstein, N., Keitner, G., Miller, I., Zlotnick, C. (1980). *The McMaster Structured Interview for Family Functioning.* Providence, RI: Brown University Family Research Program.

Blackburn, I. M., James, I. A., Milne, D. L., & Reichelt, F. K. (2001). The revised cognitive therapy scale (CTSR): Psychometric properties. *Behavioural and Cognitive Psychotherapy, 29,* 431–447.

Blagys, M. D., & Hilsenroth, M. J. (2002). Distinctive activities of cognitive-behavioral therapy: A review of the comparative psychotherapy process literature. *Clinical Psychology Review, 22,* 671–706.

Bleiberg, K. L., & Markowitz, J. C. (2008). Interpersonal psychotherapy for depression. In D. H. Barlow (Ed.), *Clinical handbook of psychological disorders* (pp. 306–327). New York: Guilford Press.

Blum, D. (2002). *Love at Goon Park: Harry Harlow and the science of affection.* New York: Perseus Press.

Bohart, A. C., Elliott, R., Greenberg, L. S., & Watson, J. C. (2002). Empathy. In J. C. Norcross (Ed.), *Psychotherapy relationships that work: Therapist contribution and responsiveness to patients* (pp. 89–108). New York: Oxford University Press.

Boisvert, C. M., & Faust, D. (2003). Leading researchers' consensus on psychotherapy research findings: Implications for the teaching and conduct of psychotherapy. *Professional Psychology: Research and Practice, 34,* 508–513.

Boisvert, C. M., & Faust, D. (2006). Practicing psychologists' knowledge of general psychotherapy research findings: Implications for science–practice relations. *Professional Psychology: Research & Practice, 37*(6), 708–716.

Bolton, P., Bass, J., Neugebauer, R., Verdeli, H., Clougherty, K. F., Wickramaratne, P., ... Weissman, M. (2003). Group interpersonal psychotherapy for depression in rural Uganda: A randomized controlled trial. *Journal of American Medical Association, 289*(23), 3117–3124.

Borden, W. (2009). *Contemporary psychodynamic theory & practice.* Chicago: Lyceum Books, Inc.

Bordin, E. (1994). Theory and research on the therapeutic working alliance: New directions. In A. O. Horvath & L. S. Greenberg (Eds.), *The working alliance: Theory, research and practice.* New York: Wiley and Sons, Inc.

Borntrager, C., Chorpita, B., Higa-McMillan, C., & Weisz, J. (2009). Provider attitudes toward evidence-based practices: are the concerns with the evidence or with the manuals? *Psychiatric Services, 60*(5), 677–681.

Borresen, D. A., & Ruddy, N. B. (20). Colloaboration with medical professionals in the primary care settings. In R. A. DiTomasso, B. A. Golden, & H. J. Morris (Eds.), *Handbook of cognitive-behavioral approaches in primary care* (pp. 35–56). New York: Springer Publishing Company.

Borys, D. S. (1994). Maintaining therapeutic boundaries: The motive is the therapeutic effectiveness, not defensive practice. *Ethics and Behavior, 4,* 267–273.

Borys, D. S., & Pope, K. S. (1989). Dual relationships between therapist and client: A national study of psychologists, psychiatrist, and social workers. *Professional Psychology: Research and Practice, 20,* 283–293.

Bowen, M. (1978). *Family therapy in clinical practice.* New York: Jason Aronson

Bowlby, J. (1969). *Attachment and loss: Vol. 1. Attachment.* New York: Basic Books.

Bowlby, J. (1973). *Attachment and loss.* New York: Basic Books.

Bowlby, J. (1979). *The making and breaking of affectional bonds.* London: Tavistock.

Bowlby, J. (1988). *A secure base: Clinical applications of attachment theory.* London: Routledge.

Brody, A. L., Saxena, S., Schwartz, J. M., Stoessel, P. W., Maidment, K., Phelps, M. E., & Baxter Jr., L. R. (1998). FDG-PET predictors of response to behavioral therapy and pharmacotherapy in obsessive compulsive disorder. *Psychiatry Research: Neuroimaging, 84*(1), 1–6.

Brody, A. L., Saxena, S., Stoessel, P., Gillies, L. A., Fairbanks, L. A., Alborzian, S., ... Baxter, L. R. (2001). Regional brain metabolic changes in patients with major depression treated with either paroxetine or interpersonal therapy: Preliminary findings. *Archives of General Psychiatry, 58,* 631–640.

Bronfenbrenner, U. (1979). *The ecology of human development.* Cambridge, MA: Harvard University Press.

Brown, L. S. (1994). Concrete boundaries and the problem of literal-mindedness: A response to Lazarus. *Ethics & Behavior, 4,* 275–281.

Brownell, K. D. (2000). *The LEARN Program for weight management.* Dallas, TX: American Health Publishing Co.

Bruns, D., & Disorbio, J. M. (2009). Assessment of biopsychosocial risk factors for medical treatment: A collaborative approach. *Journal of Clinical Psychology in Medical Settings, 16,* 127–147.

Bruss, K. V., & Kopala, M. (1993). Graduate school training in psychology: Its impact upon the development of professional identity. *Psychotherapy, 30,* 685–691.

Burns, D. D. (1980). *Feeling good: The new mood therapy.* New York: Signet.

Burns, D. D., & Nolen-Hoeksama, S. (1992). Therapeutic empathy and recovery depression in cognitive-behavioral therapy. A structural equation model. *Journal of Consulting and Clinical Psychology, 60,* 441–449.

Butler, J. F. (2008). The family diagram and genogram: Comparisons and contrasts. *American Journal of Family Therapy, 36,* 169–180.

Caplan, G. (1970). *The theory and practice of mental health consultation.* New York: Basic Books.

Carr, A. (2009). Thematic review of family therapy journals in 2008. *Journal of Family Therapy, 31,* 405–427.

Carreira, K., Miller, M. D., Frank, E., Houck, P. R., Morse, J. Q., Dew, M. A., ... Reynolds, C. F. (2008). A controlled evaluation of monthly maintenance Interpersonal Psychotherapy in late-life depression with varying levels of cognitive function. *Journal of Geriatric Psychiatry, 23*(11), 1110–1113.

Carrère, S., Buehlman, K. T., Gottman, J. M., Coan, J. A., & Ruckstuhl, L. (2000). Predicting marital stability and divorce in newlywed couples. *Journal of Family Psychology, 14,* 42–58.

Carter, R. T. (1995). *The influence of race and racial identity in psychotherapy.* New York: John Wiley.

Carter-Pokras, O., & Baquet, C. (2002). What is "health disparity"? *Public Health Reports, 117,* 426–434.

Cassidy, J., & Kobak, R. R. (1988). Avoidance and its relationship with other defensive processes. In J. Belsky & T. Nezworsky (Eds.), *Clinical implications of attachment* (pp. 300–323). Hillsdale, NJ: Erlbaum.

Castonguay, L. G., & Beutler, L. E. (Eds.). (2005). *Principles of therapeutic change that works.* New York: Oxford University Press.

Castonguay, L. G., Constantino, M. J., & Holtforth, M. G. (2006). The working alliance: Where are we and where should we go? *Psychotherapy: Theory, Research, Practice, Training, 43,* 271–279.

Chambless, D. L., Baker, M. J., Baucom, D. H., Beutler, L. E., Calhoun, K. S., Crits-Christoph, P., ...Woody, S. R. (1998). Update on empirically validated therapies, II. *Clinical Psychologist, 51*(1), 3–16.

Chorpita, B. F., Brown, T. A., & Barlow, D. H. (1998). Diagnostic reliability of the DSM-III-R anxiety disorders. *Behavior Modification, 27,* 307–315.

Chun-Chung Chow, J., Jaffee, K., & Snowden, L. (2003). Racial/ethnic disparities in the use of mental health services in poverty areas. *American Journal of Public Health, 93,* 792–797.

Chwalisz, K. (2003). Evidence-based practice: A framework for twenty-first-century scientist-practitioner training. *The Counseling Psychologist, 31,* 497–528.

Claiborn, C. D., Goodyear, R. K., & Horner, P. A. (2002). Feedback. In J. C. Norcross (Ed.), *Psychotherapy relationships that work: Therapist contribution and responsiveness to patients* (pp. 217–234). New York: Oxford University Press.

Clark, D. M., Ehlers, A., Hackman, A., McManus, F., Fennell, M., Grey, N., Waddington, L., & Wild, J. (2006). Cognitive therapy versus exposure plus applied relaxation in social phobia: A randomized controlled trial. *Journal of Consulting and Clinical Psychology, 74,* 568–578.

Clark, R. A., Harden, S. L., & Johnson, W. B. (2000). Mentor relationships in clinical psychology doctoral training: Results of a national survey. *Teaching of Psychology, 27,* 262–268.

Clark, D. M., Layard, R., Smithies, R., Richards, D. A., Suckling, R., & Wright, B. (2009). Improving access to psychological therapy: Initial evaluation of two UK demonstration sites. *Behaviour Research and Therapy, 47,* 910–920.

Clark, D. M., Salkovskis, P. M., Hackmann, A., Middleton, H., Anastasiades, P., & Gelder, M. G. (1994). A comparison of cognitive therapy, applied relaxation and imipramine in the treatment of panic disorder. *British Journal of Psychiatry, 164,* 759–769.

Clougherty, K. F., Verdeli, H., Mufson, L. H., & Young, J. F. (2006). Interpersonal psychotherapy: Effectiveness trials in rural Uganda and New York City. *Psychiatric Annals, 36*(8), 566–573.

Cole, E. (2008). Navigating the dialectic: Following ethical rules versus culturally appropriate practice. *American Journal of Family Therapy, 36,* 425–436.

Collins, F. L., Kaslow, N. J., & Illfelder-Kaye, J. (2004). Introduction to the special issue. *Journal of Clinical Psychology, 60,* 695–697.

Constantine, M. G., & Sue, D. W. (Eds). (2005). *Strategies for building multicultural competence in mental health and educational settings.* Hoboken, NJ: Wiley & Sons.

Cook, J. M., & Coyne, J. C. (2005). Re-envisioning the training and practice of clinical psychologists: Preserving science and research orientations in the face of chance. *Journal of Clinical Psychology, 61,* 1191–1196.

Cooper, J. O., Heron, T. E., & Hewerd, W. L. (2007). *Applied behavior analysis (2*nd *ed.).* Upper Saddle River, NJ: Prentice-Hall.

Cornish, J. A. E., Gorgens, K. A., Monson, S. P., Olkin, R., Palombi, B. J., & Abels, A. V. (2008). Perspectives on ethical practice with people who have disabilities. *Professional Psychology: Research and Practice, 39,* 488–497.

Cos, T. A., DiTomasso, R. A., Cirilli, C., & Finkelstein, L. H. (2010). The consultation process in primary care. In R. A. DiTomasso, B. A. Golden, & H. J. Morris (Eds.), *Handbook of cognitive-behavioral approaches in primary care* (pp. 57–82). New York: Springer Publishing Company.

Crane, D. R. (2008) The cost-effectiveness of family therapy. A summary and progress report. *Journal of Family Therapy, 30,* 399–410.

Craske, M. G., & Barlow, D. H. (2008). Panic disorder and agoraphobia. In D. H. Barlow (Ed.), *Clinical handbook of psychological disorders* (4th ed., pp. 1–64). New York: Guilford Press.

Crits-Christoph, P., Connolly, M. B., Azarian, K., Crits-Christoph, K., & Shappell, S. (1996). An open trial of brief supportive-expressive psychotherapy in the treatment of generalized anxiety disorder. *Psychotherapy, 33*(3), 418–430.

Crits-Christoph, P., Wilson, G. T., & Hollon, S. D. (2005). Empirically supported psychotherapies: Comment on Westen, Novotny, and Thompson-Brenner (2004). *Psychological Bulletin, 131,* 412–417.

Dahl, H., Kächele, H., & Thomä, H. (Eds.). (1988). *Psychoanalytic process research strategies.* Berlin, Federal Republic of Germany: Springer-Verlag.

Dawes, R. (1996). *House of cards.* New York: Free Press.

De las Fuentes, C., Willmuth, M. E., & Yarrow, C. (2005). Competency training in ethics education and practice. *Professional Psychology: Research and Practice, 36,* 362–366.

DeLeon, P., Fox, R., & Graham, S. (1991). Prescription privileges: Psychology's next frontier? *American Psychologist, 46*(4), 384–393.

Department of Health and Human Services (2007). *Healthy people 2010: Midcourse review.* Retrieved Nov. 23, 2008, from http://www.healthypeople.gov/publications/html

Didato, S. V. (1971). Therapy failure: Price and/or prejudice of the therapist. *Mental Hygiene, 55*(2), 219–220.

DiNardo, P. A., Brown, T. A., & Barlow, D. H. (1994). Anxiety disorders interview schedule for DSM IV: Lifetime version. New York: Oxford University Press.

DiTomasso, R. A. (1999). *Cognitive model of primary care consultation.* Unpublished manuscript. Department of Psychology, Philadelphia College of Osteopathic Medicine, Philadelphia.

DiTomasso, R. A., Cahn, S. C., Cirilli, C., & Mochan, E. (2010). Evidence-based models and intervention in primary care. In R. A. DiTomasso, B. A. Golden, & H. J. Morris (Eds.), *Handbook of cognitive-behavioral approaches in primary care* (pp. 83–100). New York: Springer Publishing Company.

DiTomasso, R. A., & Colameco, S. (1982). Patient self-monitoring of behavior. *Journal of Family Practice, 15*(1), 79–83.

DiTomasso, R. A., & Gilman, R. (2005). Behavioral assessment. In A. Freeman, S. H. Felgoise, A. Nezu, C. Nezu, & M. A. Reinecke (Eds.), *Encyclopedia of cognitive and behavior therapy* (pp. 61–65). New York: Springer Publishing Company.

DiTomasso, R. A., Golden, B. A., & Morris, H. J. (Eds.) (2010). *Handbook of cognitive-behavioral approaches in primary care.* New York: Springer Publishing Company.

DiTomasso, R. A., & Gosch, E. A. (2002a). Anxiety disorders: An overview. In R. A. DiTomasso & E. A. Gosch (Eds.), *Comparative treatments for anxiety disorders* (pp. 1–31). New York: Springer Publishing Company.

DiTomasso, R. A., & Gosch, E. A. (2002b). *Comparative treatments for anxiety disorders.* New York: Springer Publishing Company.

DiTomasso, R. A., Knapp, S., Golden, B. A., Morris, H. J., & Veit, K. J. (2010). The cognitive behavioral clinician: Roles and function and ethical challenges in primary care. In R. A. DiTomasso, B. A. Golden, & H. J. Morris (Eds.), *Handbook of cognitive-behavioral approaches in primary care* (pp. 15–34). New York: Springer Publishing Company.

Doherty, W. J., & McDaniel, S. H. (2010). *Family therapy.* Washington, D. C.: American Psychological Association.

Donnelly, J. M., Kornblith, A. B., Fleishman, S., Zuckerman, E., Raptis, G., Hudis, C. A... Holland, J. C. (2000). A pilot study of interpersonal psychotherapy by telephone with cancer patients and their partners. *Psychooncology, 9*(1), 44–56.

Donovan, R. A., & Ponce, A. N. (2009). Identification and measurement of core competencies in professional psychology: Areas for consideration. *Training and Education in Professional Psychology, 3,* 46–49.

Dozier, M., Stovall, K. C., & Albus, K. E. (1999). Attachment and psychopathology in adulthood. In J. Cassidy & P. R. Shaver (Eds.), *Handbook of attachment: Theory research, and clinical applications* (pp. 497–519). New York: Guilford Press.

Drogin, E. Y., Connell, M., Foote, W. E., & Sturm, C. A. (2010). The American Psychological Association's revised "record keeping guidelines": Implications for the practitioner. *Professional Psychology: Research and Practice, 41*(3), 236–243.

Duncan, B. L., Miller, S. D., Wampold, B. E., & Hubble, M. A. (2010). *The heart and soul of change: Delivering what works* (2nd ed.). Washington, DC: American Psychological Association.

Dyson, R. G. (2004). Strategic development and SWOT analysis at the University of Warwick. *European Journal of Operational Research, 152,* 631–640.

Eells, T. D. (Ed.). (1997). *Psychotherapy case formulation: History and current status.* New York: Guilford Press.

Eells, T. D. (Ed.). (2007). *Handbook of psychotherapy case formulation* (2nd ed.). New York: Guilford Press.

Elkin, I., Shea, M. T., Watkins, J. T., Imber, S. D., Sotsky, S. M., Collins, J. F., …Docherty, J. P. (1989). National Institute of Mental Health Treatment of Depression Collaborative Research Program: General effectiveness of treatments. *Archives of General Psychiatry, 46*(11), 971–982.

Elman, N. S., & Forrest, L. (2007). From trainee impairment to professional competence problems: Seeking new terminology that facilitates effective action. *Professional Psychology: Research and Practice, 38,* 501–509.

Elman, N. S., Illfelder-Kaye, J., & Robiner, W. N. (2005). Professional development: Training for professionalism as a foundation for competent practice in psychology. *Professional Psychology: Research and Practice, 36,* 367–375.

Else-Quest, N. M., Hyde, J. S., Goldsmith, H. H., & Van Hulle, C. A. (2006). Gender Differences in temperament: A meta-analysis. *Psychological Bulletin, 132,* 33–72.

Engel, G. L. (1977). The need for a new medical model: A challenge for biomedicine. *Science, 196*(4286), 129–136.

Epstein, N. B., Baldwin, L. M., & Bishop, D. (1983). The McMaster Family Assessment Device. *Journal of Marital and Family Therapy, 9,* 171–180.

Epstein, R. M., & Hundert, E. M. (2002). Defining and assessing professional competence. *Journal of the American Medical Association, 287,* 226–235.

Eysenck, H. J. (1952). The effects of psychotherapy: An evaluation. *Journal of Consulting Psychology, 16,* 319–324.

Fairburn, C. G., & Cooper, Z. (2011). Therapist competence, therapy quality, and therapist training. *Behaviour Research and Therapy, 49,* 373–378.

Fairburn, C. G., Cooper, Z., O'Connor, M. E. (2008). Eating disorder examination (Edition 16.0D). In C. G. Fairburn (Ed.), *Cognitive behavior therapy and eating disorders.* New York: Guilford Press.

Falender, C. A., Cornish, J. A. E., Goodyear, R, Hatcher R., Kaslow, N. J., Leventhal, G.,…Grus, C. (2004). Defining competencies in psychology supervision: A consensus statement. *Journal of Clinical Psychology, 60,* 771–787.

Falender, C. A., & Shafranske, E. P. (2004). *Clinical supervision: A competency-based approach. Washington, D. C.:* American Psychological Association.

Farber, E. W., & Kaslow, N. J. (2010). Introduction to the special section: The role of supervision in ensuring the development of psychotherapy competencies across diverse theoretical perspectives. *Psychotherapy: Theory, Research, Practice, Training, 47,* 1–2.

Farber, B. A., & Lane, J. S. (2002). Positive regard. In J. C. Norcross (Ed.), *Psychotherapy relationships that work: Therapist contribution and responsiveness to patients* (pp. 175–194). New York: Oxford University Press.

Feder, J., Levant, R. F., & Dean, J. (2007). Boys and violence: A gender informed analysis. *Professional Psychology: Research and Practice, 38,* 385–391.

Fisch, L. (1996). *Ethical dimensions of college and university teaching: Understanding and honoring the special relationship between students and teachers.* San Francisco, CA: Jossey-Bass.

Fischer, A. R., Jome, L. M., & Atkinson, D. R. (1998). Reconceptualizing multicultural counseling: Universal healing conditions in a culturally specific context. *The Counseling Psychologist, 26,* 525–588.

Fiske, A. P., Kitayama, S., Markus, H. R., & Nisbett, R. E. (1998). The cultural matrix of social psychology. In D. T. Gilbert & S. T. Fiske (Eds.), *The handbook of social psychology* (Vol. 2, 4th ed., pp. 915–981). New York: McGraw-Hill.

Foa, E. B., & Emmelkamp P. M. G. (Eds.). (1983). *Failures in behavior therapy.* New York: John Wiley & Sons.

Fouad, N. A., Grus, C. L., Hatcher, R. L., Kaslow, N. J., Hutchings, P. S., Madson, M. B., Collins, F. L., Jr., & Crossman, R. E. (2009). Competency benchmarks: A model for understanding and measuring competence in professional psychology across training levels. *Training and Education in Professional Psychology, 3*(4), S5–S26.

Fraley, R. C., & Shaver, P. R. (2000). Adult romantic attachment: Theoretical developments, emerging controversies, and unanswered questions. *Review of General Psychology, 4,* 132–154.

Frank, J. D., & Frank, J. B. (1991). *Persuasion and healing: A comparative study of psychotherapy* (3rd ed.). Baltimore, MD: Johns Hopkins University.

Frank, E., Kupfer, D. J., Wagner, E. F., McEachran, A. B., & Cornes, C. (1991). Efficacy of interpersonal psychotherapy as a maintenance treatment of recurrent depression: Contributing factors. *Archives of General Psychiatry, 48*(12), 1053–1059.

Frank, K. A. (1993). Action, insight, and working through: Outlines of an integrative approach. *Psychoanalytic Dialogues, 3,* 535–577.

Freeman, A., Felgoise, S. H., & Davis, D. D. (2008). *Clinical psychology: Integrating science and practice.* Hoboken, NJ: Wiley & Sons, Inc.

Freud, S. (1905). Three essays on the theory of sexuality. *Standard Edition, 7,* 135–243.

Freud, S. (1923). The ego and id. *Standard Edition, 19,* 12–66.

Freud, S. (1940). An outline of psychoanalysis. *Standard Edition, 23,* 144–207.

Freud, S. (1953). Project for a scientific psychology. In J. Strachey (Ed. and Trans.), *The standard edition of the complete psychological works of Sigmund Freud* (Vol. 4, pp. 1–627). London: Hogarth Press. (Original work published 1900).

Froschl, M., & Sprung, B. (2005). *Raising and educating healthy boys: A report on the growing crisis in boys' education.* Washington, D. C.: Academy for Educational Development.

Fuertes, J. N., Bartolomeo, M., & Nichols, M. C. (2001). Future research directions in the study of counselor multicultural competency. *Journal of Multicultural Counseling & Development, 29*(1), 3–13.

Garfield, S. L. (1965). Research on client variables in psychotherapy. In S. L. Garfield & A. E. Bergin (Eds.), *Handbook of psychotherapy and behavior change* (pp. 213–256). New York: Wiley.

Gelso, C. J., & Carter, J. A. (1985). The relationship in counseling and psychotherapy: Components, consequences, and theoretical antecedents. *The Counseling Psychologist, 13,* 155–243.

Gelso, C. J., & Hayes, J. A. (2002). The management of countertransference. In J. C. Norcross (Ed.), *Psychotherapy relationships that work: Therapist contribution and responsiveness to patients* (pp. 267–284). New York: Oxford University Press.

Gelso, C. J., Lattas, M. G., Gomez, M. J., & Fassinger, R. E. (2002). Countertransference management and therapy outcome: An initial evaluation. *Journal of Clinical Psychology, 58*, 861–867.

Goldapple, K., Segal, Z., Garson, C., Beiling, P., Lau, M., Kennedy, S., & Mayberg, H. (2004). Modulation of cortical-limbic pathways in major depression: Treatment specific effects of cognitive behavior therapy compared to paroxetine. *Archives of General Psychiatry, 61*, 34–41.

Goldenberg, H., & Goldenberg, I. (2009). Revolution and evolution of family psychology. In M. Stanton & J. H. Bray (Eds.), *The Wiley-Blackwell handbook of family psychology* (pp. 21–36). Malden, MA: Blackwell Publishing Ltd.

Goldfried, M. R., Burckell, L. A., & Eubanks-Carter, C. (2003). Therapist self-disclosure in cognitive behavioral therapy. *Journal of Clinical Psychology, 59*, 555–568.

Goldstein, R. D., & Gruenberg, A. M. (2002). Interpersonal psychotherapy. In R. A. DiTomasso & E. A. Gosch (Eds.), *Comparative treatments for anxiety disorders* (pp. 206–222). New York: Springer.

Gosch, E. A., DiTomasso, R. A. & Findiesen, A. G. (2010). Behavioral strategies. In R. A. DiTomasso, B. A. Golden, & H. J. Morris (Eds.), *Handbook of cognitive-behavioral approaches in primary care* (pp. 247–264). New York: Springer Publishing Company.

Gottlieb, M. C. (1994). Ethical decision-making, boundaries, and treatment effectiveness: A reprise. *Ethics and Behavior, 4*, 287–293.

Gottman, J. M., & Notarius, C. I. (2002). Marital research in the 20th century and a research agenda for the 21st century. *Family Process, 41*, 159–197.

Gottman, J. M., Ryan, K. D., Carrere, S., & Erley, A. M. (2002). Toward a scientifically based marital therapy. In H. A. Liddle, D. A. Santisteban, R. F. Levant, & I. H. Bray (Eds.), *Family psychology: Science-based interventions* (pp. 147–174). Washington, D. C.: American Psychological Association.

Gouze, K. R., & Wendel, R. (2008) Integrative module-based family therapy. Application and training. *Journal of Marital and Family Therapy, 34*, 269–286.

Griffin, W. A. (1993). *Family therapy: Fundamentals of theory and practice.* New York: Brunner-Mazel.

Gross, B. H. (2001). Informed consent. *Annals of the American Psychotherapy Association, 4,* 24.

Grote, N. K., Spieker, S. J., Lohr, M. J., Geibel, S. L., Swartz, H. A., Frank, E., ... Katon, W. (2012). Impact of childhood trauma on the outcomes of a perinatal depression trial. *Depression and Anxiety, 29,* 563–573.

Groth-Marnat, G. (1997). *Handbook of psychological assessment* (3rd ed.). New York: Wiley & Sons, Inc.

Gustafson, K. E., & McNamara, R. (1987). Confidentiality with minor clients: Issues and guidelines for therapists. *Professional Psychology: Research and Practice, 18,* 503–508.

Gutheil, T. G., & Gabbard, G. O. (1993). The concept of boundaries in clinical practice: Theoretical and risk-management dimensions. *American Journal of Psychiatry, 150,* 188–196.

Guy, J. D., Poelstra, P., & Stark, M. (1989). Personal distress and therapeutic effectiveness: National survey of psychologists practicing psychotherapy. *Professional Psychology: Research and Practice, 20,* 48–50.

Haas, L. J., Malouf, J. L., & Mayerson, N. H. (1986). Ethical dilemmas in psychological practice: Results of a national survey. *Professional Psychology: Research and Practice, 17,* 316–321.

Haley, J. (1976). *Problem-solving therapy.* San Francisco, CA: Jossey-Bass.

Hall, G. C. N. (2001). Psychotherapy research with ethnic minorities: Empirical, ethical, and conceptual issues. *Journal of Consulting & Clinical Psychology, 69,* 502–510.

Halonen, J. S., Bosack, T., Clay, S., & McCarthy, M. (2003). A rubric for learning, teaching, and assessing scientific inquiry in psychology. *Teaching of Psychology, 30,* 196–208.

Handler, J. F. (1990). *Law and the search for community.* Philadelphia: University of Pennsylvania Press.

Hatcher, R. L. & Lassiter, K. D. (2007). Initial training in professional psychology: The Practicum Competencies Outline. *Training and Education in Professional Psychology, 1,* 49–63.

Hathaway, W. L., Scott, S. Y., & Garver, S. A. (2004). Assessing religious/spiritual functioning: A neglected domain of clinical practice? *Professional Psychology: Research and Practice, 35,* 97–104.

Hawton, K., Salkovskis, P., Kirk, J., & Clark, D. M. (Eds.). (1989). *Cognitive behaviour therapy for psychiatric problems: A practical guide.* Oxford, England: Oxford University Press.

Hayes, S. C. (2004). Acceptance and commitment therapy, relational frame theory, and the third wave of behavioral and cognitive therapies. *Behavior Therapy, 35,* 639–665.

Hayes, S. C., Pankey, J., & Gregg, J. (2002). Acceptance and commitment therapy. In R. A. DiTomasso & Gosch, E. A. (Eds.), *Comparative treatments for anxiety disorders* (pp. 110–136). New York: Springer Publishing Company.

Haynes, S. N., Leisen, M. B., & Blaine, D. D. (1997). Design of individualized behavioral treatment programs using functional analytical clinical case models. *Psychological Assessment, 9*(4), 334.

Haynes, S. N., & Williams, A. B. (2003). Case formulation and the design of behavioral treatment programs: Matching treatment mechanisms to causal variables for behavior problems. *European Journal of Psychological Assessment, 193,* 164.

Hecht, I. W. D., Higgerson, M. L., Gmelch, W. H., & Tucker, A. (1999). *The department chair as academic leader.* Phoenix, AZ: Oryx Press.

Helms, J. (1990). *Black and White racial identity: Theory, research, and practice.* Westport, CT: Greenwood.

Henggeler, S. W., Schoenwald, S. K., Borduin, C. M., Rowland, M. D., & Cunningham, P. B. (2009). *Multisystemic treatment of antisocial behavior in children and adolescents (2nd ed.).* New York: Guilford Press.

Henry, W. P., Schacht, T. E., & Strupp, H. H. (1986). Patient and therapist introject, interpersonal process, and differential psychotherapeutic outcome. *Journal of Consulting and Clinical Psychology, 58,* 768–774.

Herschell, A. D., Kolko, D. J., Baumann, B. L., & Davis, A. C. (2010). The role of therapist training in the implementation of psychosocial treatments: A review and critique with recommendations. *Clinical Psychology Review, 30,* 448–466.

Hoffman, S. G., & Smits, J. A. J. (2008). Cognitive-behavioral therapy for adult anxiety disorders: A meta-analysis of randomized placebo-controlled trials. *Journal of Clinical Psychiatry, 69,* 621–632.

Hoglend, P. (2004). Analysis of transference in dynamic psychotherapy: A review of empirical research. *Canadian Journal of Psychoanalysis, 12,* 280–300.

Hollon, S. D., & Beck, A. T. (1986). Cognitive and cognitive-behavioral therapies. In S. L. Garfield, & A. E. Bergin, (Eds.), *The handbook for psychotherapy and behavior change: An empirical analysis* (2nd ed., pp. 443–482). New York: Wiley.

Hollon, S. D., & Dimidjian, S. (2009). Cognitive and behavioral treatment of depression. In I. H. Gotlib & C. L. Hammen (Eds.), *Handbook of depression* (pp. 586–603). New York: The Guilford Press.

Horowitz, M. J. (1989). Relationship schema formulation: Role relationship models and intrapsychic conflict. *Psychiatry, 52,* 260–274.

Horowitz, L. M., Rosenberg, S. E., Ureno, G., Kalehzan, B. M., & O'Halloran, P. (1989). Psychodynamic formulation, consensual response method, and interpersonal problems. *Journal of Consulting and Clinical Psychology, 57,* 599–606.

Horvath, A. O., & Bedi, R. P. (2002). The alliance. In J. C. Norcross (Ed.), *Psychotherapy relationships that work: Therapist contribution and responsiveness to patients (pp. 37–70).* New York: Oxford University Press.

Horvath, A. O., & Symonds, B. D. (1991). Relation between working alliance and outcome in psychotherapy: A meta-analysis. *Journal of Counseling Psychology, 38,* 139–149.

Huprich, S. K. (2009). *Psychodynamic therapy: Conceptual and empirical foundations.* New York: Routledge

Hutton, J. M., & Williams, M. (2001). Assessment of psychological issues and needs in specialties of a large teaching hospital. *Psychology, Health, & Medicine, 6,* 313–319.

Hyde, J. S., Mezulis, A. H., & Abramson, L. Y. (2008). The ABC's of depression: Integrating affective, biological, and cognitive models to explain the emergence of the gender difference in depression. *Psychological Review, 115,* 291–313.

Jacobi, M. (1991). Mentoring and undergraduate academic success: A literature review. *Review of Educational Research, 61,* 505–532.

James, L. C., & Folen, R. A. (Eds.). (2005). *The primary care consultant: The next frontier for psychologists in hospitals and clinics.* Washington, D. C.: American Psychological Association.

Johnson-Greene, D. (2007). Evolving standards for informed consent: Is it time for an individualized and flexible approach? *Professional Psychology: Research and Practice, 38,* 183–184.

Jones, J. L., & Mehr, S. L. (2007). Foundations and assumptions of the scientist-practitioner model. American Behavioral Scientist, 50, 766–771.

Kabat-Zinn, J. (2005). *Guided mindfulness meditation.* Louisville, CO: Sounds True.

Kaslow, N. J. (2004). Competencies in professional psychology. *American Psychologist, 59,* 774–781.

Kaslow, N. J., Borden, K., Collins, F., Forrest, L., Illfelder-Kaye, J., Nelson, P., . . . Willmuth, M. E. (2004). Competencies conference: Future directions in education and training in professional psychology. *Journal of Clinical Psychology, 60,* 699–712.

Kaslow, N. J., Celano, M. P., & Stanton, M. (2009). Training on family psychology: A competencies-based approach. In M. Stanton & J. H. Bray (Eds.), *The Wiley-Blackwell handbook of family psychology* (pp. 112–128). Malden, MA: Blackwell Publishing.

Kaslow, N. J., Falender, C. A., & Grus, C. L. (2012). Valuing and practicing competency-based supervision: A transformational leadership perspective. *Training and Education in Professional Psychology, 6*(1), 47–54.

Kaslow, N. J., Grus, C. L., Campbell, L. F., Fouad, N. A., Hatcher, R. L., & Rodolfa, E. R. (2009). Competency assessment toolkit for professional psychology. *Training and Education in Professional Psychology, 3,* S27–S45.

Kaslow, N. J., McCarthy, S. M., Rogers, J. H., & Summerville, M. B. (1992). Psychology postdoctoral training: A developmental perspective. *Professional Psychology: Research and Practice, 23,* 369–375.

Kaslow, N. J., Rubin, N. J., Bebeau, M. J., Leigh, I. W., Lichtenberg, J. W., Nelson, P. D., ... Smith, I. L. (2007). Guiding principles and recommendations for the assessment of competence. *American Psychological Association, 38,* 441–451.

Kaslow, N. J., Rubin, N. J., Bebeau, M. J., Leigh, I. W., Lichtenberg, J. W., Nelson, P. D., ... Smith, I. L. (2007). Recognizing, assessing and intervening with problems of professional competence. *Professional Psychology: Research and Practice, 38,* 479–492.

Kazdin, A. E. (2001). *Behavior modification in applied settings (6th ed.).* Belmont, CA:

Kazdin, A. E. (2008). Evidence-based treatment and practice: New opportunities to bridge clinical research and practice, enhance the knowledge base, and improve patient care. *American Psychologist, 63,* 146–159.

Kazdin, A. E., & Weiss, J. R. (2003). *Evidence-based psychotherapies for children and adolescence.* New York: Guilford Press.

Kendall, P. C., Chu, B., Gifford, A., Hayes, C., & Nauta, M. (1998). Breathing life into a manual: Flexibility and creativity with manual-based treatments. *Cognitive and Behavioral Practice, 5*(2), 177–198.

Kendall, P. C., Hudson, J. L., Gosch, E., Flannery-Schroeder, E., & Suveg, C. (2008). Cognitive-behavioral therapy for anxiety disordered youth. A randomized clinical trial evaluating child and family modalities. *Journal of Consulting and Clinical Psychology, 76,* 282–297.

Kenkel, M. B., & Peterson, R. L. (Eds.) (2010). *Competency-based education for professional psychology.* Washington, D. C.: American Psychological Association.

Kenrick, D. T., Neuberg, S. L. & Cialdini, R. B. (1999). *Social psychology: Unraveling the mystery.* Boston: Allyn & Bacon.

Kent, R. N., O'Leary, K. D., Diament, C., & Dietz, A. (1974). Expectation biases in observational evaluation of therapeutic change. *Journal of Consulting and Clinical Psychology, 42,* 774–780.

Kernberg, O. F., Diamond, D., Yeomans, F. E., Clarkin, J. F., & Levy, K. N. (2008). Mentalization and attachment in borderline patients in transference focused psychotherapy. In E. Jurist, A. Slade, & S. Bergner (Eds.), *Mind to mind: Infant research, neuroscience and psychoanalysis* (pp. 167–201). New York: Other Press.

Kiesler, J. (1973). *The process of psychotherapy: Empirical foundations and systems of analysis.* Chicago: Aldine.

King, D. B., Viney, W., & Woody, W. D. (2009). *A history of psychology: Ideas and context* (4th ed.). New York: Pearson.

Klein, M. H., Kolden, G. G., Michels, J. L., & Chisholm-Stockard, S. (2002). Congruence. In J. C. Norcross (Ed.), *Psychotherapy relationships that work: Therapist contribution and responsiveness to patients* (pp. 195–216). New York: Oxford University Press.

Klerman, G. L., Weissman, M. M., Rounsaville, B. J., & Chevron, E. S. (1984). *Interpersonal psychotherapy of depression*. New York: Basic Books.

Kline, T. J. B. (2005). *Psychological testing: A practical approach to design and evaluation*. Thousand Oaks, California: Sage Publications.

Knapp, S., Gottleib, M., Berman, J., & Handelsman, M. M. (2007). When laws and ethics collide: What should psychologists do? *Professional Psychology: Research and Practice, 38,* 54–59.

Knapp, S., & Slattery, J. M. (2004). Professional boundaries in nontraditional settings. *Professional Psychology: Research and Practice, 35,* 553–558.

Knapp, S., & VandeCreek, L. (2004). A principle-based analysis of the 2002 American Psychological Association's Ethics Code. *Psychotherapy: Theory, Research, Practice, Training, 41,* 247–254.

Knapp, S. J., & VandeCreek, L. D. (2006). *Practical ethics for psychologists: A positive approach*. Washington, D. C.: American Psychological Association.

Koocher, G. (2008) Ethical challenges in mental health services to children and families. *Journal of Clinical Psychology, 64,* 601–612.

Koocher, G. P., & Keith-Spiegel, P. (2008). *Ethics in psychology and the mental health professions: Standards and cases (3rd ed.)*. New York: Oxford University Press.

Kram. K. E. (1988). *Mentoring at work- Developmental relationships in organizational life*. New York: University Press of America.

Kuyken, W., Padesky, C. A., & Dudley,R. (2009). *Collaborative case conceptualization*. New York: The Guilford Press.

Lamb, D. H., Catanzaro, S. J., & Moorman, A. S. (2004). A preliminary look at how psychologists identify, evaluate and proceed when faced with possible multiple relationship dilemmas. *Professional Psychology: Research and Practice, 35,* 248–254.

Lambert, M. J. (2010). Predicting negative treatment outcome. Methods and estimates of accuracy. In M. J. Lambert (Ed.), *Prevention of treatment failure: The use of measuring, monitoring and feedback in clinical practice* (pp. 83–105). Wahington, D. C.: American Psychological Association.

Lambert, M. J., & Barley, D. E. (2001). Research summary on the therapeutic relationship and psychotherapy outcome. *Psychotherapy, 38,* 357–361.

Lambert, M. J., & Barley, D. E. (2002). Research summary on the therapeutic relationship and psychotherapy outcome. In J. C. Norcross (Ed.), *Psychotherapy relationships that work: Therapist contribution and responsiveness to patients* (pp. 17–32). New York: Oxford University Press.

Lazarus, A. A. (1994). How certain boundaries and ethics diminish therapeutic effectiveness. *Ethics and Behavior, 4,* 255–261.

Lemma, A., Roth, A. D., & Pilling, S. (2008). The competencies required to deliver effective psychoanalytic/psychodynamic therapy. Retrieved from http://www.ucl.ac. uk/ clinical-psychology/CORE/Psychodynamic_Competences/Background_Paper. pdf

Lenington-Lara, M. (1999). Exploring the subjective experience of participants in multicultural awareness training course. *Dissertation Abstracts International, 60*(2-B), 085.

Lespérance, F., Frasure-Smith, N., Koszycki, D., Laliberté, M. -A., van Zyl, L. T., Baker, B.,... Guertin, M. C. (2007). Effects of citalopram and interpersonal psychotherapy on depression in patients with coronary artery disease: The Canadian Cardiac Randomized Evaluation of Antidepressant and Psychotherapy Efficacy (CREATE) Trial. *Journal of the American Meduical Association, 297,* 367–379.

Luebbe, A. M., Radcliffe, A. M., Callands, T. A., Green, D. & Thorn, B. E. (2007). Evidence-based practice in psychology: Perceptions of graduate students in scientist-practitioner programs. *Journal of Clinical Psychology, 63,* 643–655

Liddle, H., Santisteban, D., Levant, R. & Bray, J. (Eds.). (2002). *Family psychology: Science-based interventions.* Washington, D. C.: American Psychological Association.

Liddle, H. A. (2002). *Multidimensional Family Therapy for Adolescent Cannabis Users, Cannabis Youth Treatment (CYT) Series, Volume 5.* Rockville, MD: Center for Substance Abuse Treatment, Substance Abuse and Mental Health Services Administration.

Liddle, H. A., Dakof, G. A., Parker, K., Diamond, G., Barrett, K., & Tejeda, M. (2001). Multidimensional family therapy for adolescent drug abuse: Results of a randomized clinical trial. *American Journal of Drug and Alcohol Abuse, 27,* 651–688.

Lilienfield, M. J. (2007). Psychological treatments that cause harm. *Perspectives on Psychological Science, 2,* 53–70.

Linehan, M. M., & Korsland, K. E. (2003). *Dialectical Behavior Therapy Adherence Manual.* Seattle: University of Washington.

Lipinski, D. P., & Nelson, R. O. (1974). The reactivity and unrelaibility of self-recording. *Journal of Consulting and Clinical Psychology, 42,* 118–123.

Lock, J., Le Grange, D., & Crosby, R. (2008) Exploring possible mechanisms of change in family-based treatment for adolescent bulimia nervosa. *Journal of Family Therapy, 30,* 260–271.

Lowe, P. (2001, June 19). Therapists get 16 years. *Rocky Mountain News.* Retrieved from http://rockymountainnews.com/drmn/0,1299,DRMN_15_6750 52,00.html.

Luborsky, L. (1976). Helping alliances in psychotherapy: The groundwork of a study of their relationship to its outcome. In J. Claghorn (Ed.), *Successful psychotherapy* (pp. 92–116). New York: Brunner/Mazel.

Luborsky, L. (1977). Curative factors in psychoanalytic and psychodynamic psychotherapies. In J. P. Brady, J. Mendels, M. T. Orne, & W. Rieger (Eds.). *Psychiatry: Areas of promise and advancement* (pp. 187–203). New York: Spectrum.

Luborsky, L. (1984). *Principles of psychoanalytic psychotherapy. A manual for supportive-expressive treatment.* New York: Basic Books.

Luborsky, L., & Crits-Christoph, P. (1997) *Understanding transference: The cor conflictual relationship theme method.* Washington, D. C.: American Psychological Association.

Luborsky, L., Singer, B. A., & Luborsky, L. (1975). Comparative studies of psychotherapies: "Is it true that everbody has won and all must have prizes?" *Archives of General Psychiatry, 32,* 995–1008.

Luebbe, A. M., Radcliffe, A. M., Callands, T. A., Green, D., & Thorn, B. E. (2007). Evidence-based practice in psychology: Perceptions of graduate students in scientist-practitioner programs. *Journal of Clinical Psychology, 63,* 643–655.

Mahoney, M. J., & Arnkoff, D. B. (1978). Cognitive and self-control therapies. In S. L. Garfield & A. E. Bergin (Eds.), *Handbook of psychotherapy and behavior change* (pp. 689–722). New York: Wiley.

Malloy, K. A., Dobbins, J. E., Ducheny, K., & Winfrey, L. L. (2010). The management and supervision competency: Current and future directions. In M. B. Kenkel & R. L. Peterson (Eds.), *Competency-based education for professional psychology* (pp. 161–178). Washington, D. C.: American Psychological Association.

Mangione, L., & Nadkarni, L. (2010). The relationship competency: Broadening and deepening. In M. B. Kenkel & R. L. Peterson (Eds.), *Competency-based education in professional psychology* (pp. 69–86). Washington, D. C.: American Psychological Association.

Mannheim, C. I., Sancilio, M., Phipps-Yonas, S., Brunnquell, D. Somers, P., Farseth, G., & Ninonuevo, F. (2002). Ethical ambiguities in the practice of child clinical psychology. *Professional Research and Practice, 33,* 26–29.

Martin, D. J., Garske, J. P., & Davis, M. K. (2000). Relation of the therapeutic alliance with outcome and other variables: A meta-analytic review. *Journal of Consulting and Clinical Psychology, 68,* 438–450.

Masling, J. (2003). Stephen A. Mitchell, relational psychoanalysis, and empirical data. *Psychoanalytic Psychology, 4,* 587–608.

McFall, R. (1991). Manifesto for a science of clinical psychology. *The Clinical Psychologist, 44*(6), 75–88.

McGinnis, J. M., Williams-Russo, P., & Knickman, J. R. (2002). The case for more active policy attention to health promotion. *Health Affairs, 21,* 78–93.

McGoldrick, M., Gerson, R., & Shellenberger, S. (1999). *Genograms: Assessment and intervention.* New York: W. W. Norton.

McHolland, J. (1992). National Council of Schools of Professional Psychology Core Curriculum Resolutions. In R. L. Peterson, J. D. McHolland, R. J. Bent, E. Davis-Russell, G. E. Edwall, K. Polite, et al., (Eds.), *The core curriculum in professional psychology* (pp. 153–176). Washington, D. C.: American Psychological Association.

McHugh, R. K., & Barlow, D. H. (2010). The dissemination and implementation of evidence-based psychological treatments. *American Psychologist, 65,* 73–84.

McIntosh, V. V. W., Jordan, J., Carter, F. A. Luty, S. E., McKenzie, J. M., Bulik, C. M., …Joyce, P. R. (2005). Three psychotherapies for anorexia nervosa: A randomized, controlled trial. *American Journal of Psychiatry, 162,* 741–747.

McMinn, L. G. (2005). Sexual identity concerns for Christian young adults: Practical considerations for being a supportive presence and compassionate companion. *Journal of Psychology and Christianity, 24,* 368–377.

Messer, S., & Warren, S. (1995). *Models of brief psychodynamic therapy.* New York: Guilford Press.

Messer, S. B. (2004). Evidence-based practice: Beyond empirically supported treatments. *Professional Psychology: Research and Practice, 35,* 580–588.

Messer, S. B., & McWilliams, N. (2007). Insight in psychodynamic therapy: Theory and assessment. In L. G. Castonguay & C. Hill (Eds.), *Insight in psychotherapy* (pp. 9–29). Washington, D. C.: American Psychological Association.

Messer, S., & Warren, S. (1995). Models of brief psychodynamic therapy. New York: Guilford Press.

Mikulincer, M., & Shaver, P. R. (2003). The attachment behavioral system in adulthood: Activation, psychodynamics, and interpersonal processes. In M. P. Zanna (Ed.), *Advances in experimental social psychology* (pp. 53–152). San Diego, CA: Academic Press.

Miller, I. W., Bishop, D. S., Epstein, N. B., & Keitner, G. I. (1994). The McMaster Family Assessment Device: Reliability and validity. *Journal of Marital and Family Therapy, 11,* 345–358.

Miller, I. W., Ryan, C. E., Keitner, G. I., Bishop, D. S., & Epstein, N. B. (2000). The McMaster approach to families: Theory, assessment, treatment and research. *Journal of Family Therapy, 22,* 168–189.

Miller, J. K., Todahl, J. L., & Platt, J. J. (2010). The core competency movement in marriage and family therapy: Key considerations from other disciplines. *Journal of Marital and Family Therapy, 36,* 59–71.

Miller, N. E. (1975). Clinical applications of biofeedback: Voluntary control of heart rate, rhythm and blood pressure. In H. I. Russel (Ed.), *New horizons in cardiovascular practice* (pp. 239–249). Baltimore, MD: University Park Press.

Millon, T., Grossman S., Millon, C. Meagher, S., & Ramnath, R. (2004). *Personality disorders in modern life (2nd ed.).* Hoeboken, NJ: Wiley.

Minuchin, S. (1974). *Families and family therapy.* Cambridge, MA: Harvard University Press.

Mohr, D. C. (1995). Negative outcome in psychotherapy: A critical review. *Clinical Psychology: Science and Practice, 2*(1), 1–27.

Mufson, L., & Fairbanks, J. (1996). Interpersonal psychotherapy for depressed adolescents: A one-year naturalistic follow-up study. *Child & Adolescent Psychiatry, 35*(9), 1145–1155.

Muran, J., Safran, J., Samstag, L., & Winston, A. (2005). Evaluating an alliance-focused treatment for personality disorders. *Psychotherapy: Theory, Research, Practice, Training, 42*(4), 532–545.

Najavits, L. M., & Strupp, H. (1994). Differences in the effectiveness of psychodynamic therapists: A process-outcome study. *Psychotherapy, 31,* 114–123.

Nathan, P. E. (2000). The Boulder Model: A dream deferred or lost? *American Psychologist, 55*(2), 250–252.

National Council of Schools and Programs in Professional Psychology. (2007). *NCSPP competency developmental achievement levels.* Retrieved from htpp://www.ncspp.info/DALof%20NCSPP%209-21-07.pdf

National Institute of Mental Health (NIMH). (2000). *Child and adolescent violence research at the National Institute of Mental Health.* Retrieved from http://www.nimh.nih.gov/health/topics/child-and-adolescent-mental-health.

Needleman, L. D. (1999). *Cognitive case conceptualization: A guidebook for practitioners.* Mahwah, NJ: Lawrence Erlbaum.

Needleman, L. D. (2005). Case formulation. In A. Freeman, S. H. Felgoise, A. Nezu, & C. Nezu (Eds.), *Encyclopedia of cognitive and behavioral therapies* (pp. 98–102). New York: Springer.

Nelson, T. S., Chenail, R. J., Alexander, J. F., Crane, D. R., Johnson, S. M., & Schwallie, L. (2007). The development of core competencies for the practice of marriage and family therapy. *Journal of Marital and Family Therapy, 33,* 417–439.

Newman, C. F. (2010). Competency in conducting cognitive-behavioral therapy: Foundational, functional and supervisory aspects. *Psychotherapy: Theory Research Practice and Training, 47,* 12–19.

Newnham, E. A., & Page, A. C. (2010). Bridging the gap between best evidence and best practice in mental health. *Clinical Psychology Review, 30,* 127–142.

Nezu, A. M., & Nezu, C. M. (2010). Cognitive behavioral case formulation and treatment design. In R. A. DiTomasso, B. A. Golden, & H. J. Morris (Eds.), *Handbook of cognitive-behavioral approaches in primary care* (pp. 201–222). New York: Springer Publishing Company.

Nezu, A. M., Nezu, C. M., & Lombardo, E. R. (2004). *Cognitive behavioral case formulation and treatment design: A problem-solving approach.* New York: Springer Publishing Company.

Nichols, D. S. (2001). *Essentials of MMPI-2 assessment.* New York: Wiley.

Nichols, M. P. (1987). *The self in the system.* New York: Brunner/Mazel.

Norcross, J. C. (Ed.) (2002). *Psychotherapy relationships that work: Therapist contribution and responsiveness to patients.* New York: Oxford University Press.

Nunnally, J. C. (1994). *Psychometric theory.* New York: McGraw-Hill Book Company.

Nylen, K. J., O'Hara, M. W., Brock, R., Moel, J., Gorman, L., & Stuart, S. (2010). Predictors of the longitudinal course of postpartum depression following Interpersonal Psychotherapy. *Journal of Consulting and Clinical Psychology, 78,* 757–763.

O'Connor, M. (2001). On the etiology and effective management of professional distress and impairment among psychologists. *Professional Psychology: Research and Practice, 32,* 345–350.

O'Hara, M. W., Stuart, S., Gorman, L. L., & Wenzel, A. (2000). Efficacy of Interpersonal Psychotherapy for postpartum depression. *Archives of General Psychiatry, 57,* 1039–1045.

O'Kearney, R. T., Anstey, K. J., & von Sanden, C. (2006). Behavioural and cognitive behavioural therapy for obsessive compulsive disorder in children and adolescents. *Archives of General Psychiatry, 57*(11), 1039–1045.

Olkin, R., & Taliaferro, G. (2006). Evidence-based practices have ignored people with disabilities. In J. C. Norcross, L. E. Beutler, & R. F. Levant (Eds.), *Evidence-based practices in mental health: Debate and dialogue on the fundamental questions* (pp. 353–359). Washington, D. C.: American Psychological Association.

Ollendick, T. H., & King, N. J. (2004). Empirically supported treatments for children and adolescents: Advances toward evidence-based practice. In P. M. Barrett & T. H. Ollendick (Eds.), *Handbook of interventions that work with children and adolescents: Prevention and treatment* (pp. 3–26). New York: Wiley.

Olson, D. H. (2000). Circumplex model of marital and family systems. *Journal of Family Therapy, 22,* 144–167.

O'Neill, R. E., Horner, R. H., Albin, R. W., Sprague, J. R., Storey, K., & Newton, J. S. (1997). *Functional assessment and program development for problem behavior: A practical handbook.* Pacific Grove, OR: Brooks/Cole.

Orlinsky, D. E., Grawe, K., & Parks, B. K. (1994). Process and outcome in psychotherapy. In A. E. Bergin & S. L. Garfield (Eds.), *Handbook of psychotherapy and behavior change* (4th ed.). New York: Wiley and Sons, Inc.

Öst, L -G. (2008). Efficacy of the third wave of behavioral therapies: A systematic review and meta-analysis. *Behaviour Research and Therapy, 46,* 296–321.

Oyserman, D., Coon, H. M., & Kemmelmeier, M. (2002). Rethinking individualism and collectivism: Evaluation of theoretical assumptions and meta-analyses. *Psychological Bulletin, 128,* 3–72.

Paul, G. L. (1967). Strategy of outcome research in psychotherapy. *Journal of Consulting Psychology, 31*(2), 109–118.

PDM Task Force. (2006). *Psychodynamic diagnostic manual (PDM).* Silver Spring, MD: Alliance of Psychoanalytic Organizations.

Perez, J. E. (1999). Clients deserve empirically supported treatments, not romanticism. *American Psychologist, 54,* 205–206.

Pérez-Peña, R. (2003, September 27). Insurer seeks return of fees for therapy. *The New York Times.* Retrieved from http://www.nytimes.com/2003/09/27/nyregion/insurer-seeks-return-of-fees-for-therapy.html.

Perry, J. C., Augusto, F., & Cooper, S. H. (1989). Assessing psychodynamic conflicts. I. Reliability of the Idiographic Conflict Formulation Method. *Psychiatry, 52,* 289–301.

Persons, J. B. (1989). *Cognitive therapy in practice: A case formulation approach. (pp. 109–118).* New York: Norton.

Peterson, D. (1997). *Educating professional psychologists: History and guiding conception.* Washington, D. C.: American Psychological Association.

Peterson, D. (2003). Unintended consequences: Misadventures in training psychologists. *American Psychologist, 58,* 791–800.

Peterson, R. L., Peterson, D. R., Abrams, J. C., & Stricker, G. (1997). The National Council of Schools and Programs of Professional Psychology educational model. *Professional Psychology: Research and Practice, 28,* 373–386.

Piper, W. E., Ogrodniczuk, J. S., Joyce, A. S., McCallum, M., Rosie, J. S., & O'Kelly, J. G. & Steinberg, P.I. (1999). Prediction of dropping out in time-limited, interpretive individual psychotherapy. *Psychotherapy, 36,* 114–122.

Ponterotto, J. G., Gretchen, D., & Chauhan, R. V. (2001). Cultural identity and multicultural assessment: Quantitative and qualitative tools for theclinician. In L. A. Suzuki, J. G. Ponterotto, & P. J. Meller (Eds.), *Handbook of multicultural assessment: Clinical, psychological, and educational applications* (2nd ed., pp. 67–99). San Francisco: Jossey-Bass.

Pope, K. S., & Vasquez, M. J. T. (2005). *How to survive and thrive as a therapist: Information, ideas, and resources for psychologists in practice.* Washington, D. C.: American Psychological Association.

Pope, K. S., & Vasquez, M. J. T. (2007). *Ethics in psychotherapy and counseling: A practical guide (3rd ed.).* San Francisco, CA: John Wiley and Sons.

Pope, K. S., & Vetter, V. A. (1992). Ethical dilemmas encountered by members of the American Psychological Association: A national survey. *American Psychologist, 47,* 397–411.

Psychological Corporation (1997). *WAIS III, WMS III: Technical manual.* San Antonio, TX: Harcourt, Brace & Company.

Quintana, S. M., Troyano, N., & Taylor, G. (2001). Cultural validity and inherent challenges in quantitative methods for multicultural research. New York: Sage Publications.

Rachman, S. (1997). The evolution of cognitive behaviour therapy. In D. M. Clark & C. G. Fairburn (Eds.), *Science and practice of cognitive behaviour therapy* (pp. 1–26). Oxford, England: Oxford Press.

Rachman, S. (2000). Joseph Wolpe (1915–1997): Obituary. *American Psychologist, 55,* 431–432.

Rachman, S., & Wilson,G. T. (2008). Expansion in the delivery of psychological treatment in the United Kingdom. *Behavior Research and Therapy, 46*(3), 293–295.

Rae, W. A., Sullivan, J. R., Razo, N. P., George, C. A., & Ramirez, E. (2002). Adolescent health risk behavior: When do pediatric psychologists break confidentiality? *Journal of Pediatric Psychology, 27,* 541–549.

Rakovshik, S. G., & McManus, F. (2010). Establishing evidence-based training in cognitive behavior therapy: A review of current empirical findings and theoretical guidance. *Clinical Psychology Review, 30,* 496–516.

Raue, P. J., Goldfried, M. R., & Barkham, M. (1997). The therapeutic alliance in psychodynamic-interpersonal and cognitive-behavioral therapy. *Journal of Consulting and Clinical Psychology, 65,* 582–587.

Redfield, J., & Paul, G. (1976). Bias in behavior observation as a function of observer familiarity with subjects and typicality of behavior. *Journal of Consulting and Clinical Psychology, 44*(1), 156.

Reid, J. B. (1970). Reliability assessment of observation data: A possible methodological problem. *Child Development, 41,* 1143–1150.

Richard, D. C. S., & Huprich, S. K. (Eds). (2009). *Clinical psychology: Assessment, treatment and research.* Amsterdam: Elsevier.

Richards, M. M. (2009). Electronic medical records: Confidentiality issues in the time of HIPAA. *Professional Psychology: Research and Practice, 40,* 550–556.

Ridley, C. R., Li, L. C., & Hill, C. L. (1998). Multicultural assessment: Reexamination, reconceptualization, and practical application. *Counseling Psychologist, 26,* 827–911.

Roberts, M. C., Borden, K. A., Christiansen, M. D., & Lopez, S. J. (2005). Fostering a culture shift: Assessment of competence in the education and careers of professional psychologists. *Professional Psychology: Research and Practice, 36,* 355–361.

Robbins, M. S., Mayorga, C. C. & Szapocznik, J. (2003). The ecosystemic "lens" for understanding family functioning. In T. L. Sexton, G. R. Weeks, & M. S. Robbins (Eds.), *Handbook of family therapy: The science and practice of working with families and couples* (pp. 21–36). New York: Brunner-Routledge.

Robinson, T. L., & Howard-Hamilton, M. (2000). *The convergence of race, ethnicity, and gender.* Upper Saddle River, NJ: Prentice–Hall.

Rodolfa, E., Bent, R., Eisman, E., Nelson, P., Rehm, L., & Ritchie, P. (2005). A cube model for competency development: Implications for psychology educators and regulators. *Professional Psychology: Research and Practice, 36,* 347–354.

Rogers, C. R. (1951). *Client-centered psychotherapy.* Boston: Houghton-Mifflin.

Rogers, C. R. (1957). The necessary and sufficient conditions of therapeutic personality change. *Journal of Consulting Psychology, 21,* 95–103.

Rogler, L. H. (1999). Methodological sources of cultural insensitivity in mental health research. *American Psychologist, 54,* 424–433.

Roth, A., & Fonagy, P. (2005). *What works for whom? A critical review of psychotherapy research.* New York: Guilford Press.

Roth, A., & Pilling, S. (2008). The competences required to deliver effective cognitive and behavioural therapy for people with depression and with anxiety disorders. Retrieved from http://www.dh.gov.uk/en/Publicationsandstatistics/Publications/PublicationsPolicyAndGuidance/DH_078537

Rowe, C. L., & Liddle, H. A. (2008) Multidimensional family therapy for adolescent alcohol abusers. *Alcoholism Treatment Quarterly, 26,* 105–123.

Roysircar-Sodowsky, G., & Kuo, P. Y. (2001). Determining cultural validity of personality assessment: Some guidelines. In D. Pope-Davis & H. Coleman (Eds.), *The intersection of race, class, & gender: Implications for multicultural counseling* (pp. 213–239). Thousand Oaks, CA: Sage.

Rubin, N. J., Bebeau, M., Leigh, I. W., Lichtenberg, J., Nelson, P. D., Portnoy, S., ... & Kaslow, N. J. (2007). The competency movement within psychology: An historical perspective. *Professional Psychology: Research and Practice, 38,* 452–462.

Rudd, M. D., & Bryan, C. J. (2010). A CBT approach to assessing and managing suicide risk in primary care: Recommendations for clinical practice. In R. A. DiTomasso, B. A. Golden, & H. J. Morris (Eds.), *Handbook of cognitive-behavioral approaches in primary care* (pp. 399–418). New York: Springer Publishing Co.

Safran, J. D., Muran, J. C., Samstag, L. W., & Stevens, C. (2002). Repairing alliance ruptures. In J. C. Norcross (Ed.), *Psychotherapy relationships that work: Therapist contribution and responsiveness to patients* (pp. 235–254). New York: Oxford University Press.

Samstag, L. W., Muran, J. C., Wachtel, P. L., Slade, A., Safran, J. D., & Winston, A. (2008). Evaluating negative process: A comparison of working alliance, interpersonal behavior, and narrative coherency among three psychotherapy outcome conditions. *American Journal of Psychotherapy, 62,* 165–194.

Sanchez, L. M., & Turner, S. M. (2003). Practicing psychology in the era of managed care: Implications for practice and training. *American Psychologist, 58,* 116–129.

Sanderson, W. C. (2003). Why empirically supported psychological treatments are important. *Behavior Modification, 27*(3), 290–299.

Schloss, P. J., & Smith, M. A. (1994). *Applied behavior analysis in the classroom.* Boston: Allyn and Bacon.

Schwartz, A., & Crits-Christoph (2002). Supportive-expressive therapy. In R. A. DiTomasso & E. A. Gosch (Eds.), *Comparative treatments for anxiety disorders* (pp. 238–263). New York: Springer Publishing Company.

Schwartz, J. M. (1998). Neuroanatomical aspects of cognitive-behavioural therapy response in obsessive-compulsive disorder. An evolving perspective on brain and behaviour. *British Journal of Psychiatry Supplement, 35,* 38–44.

Schwartz, J. M., Stoessel, P. W., Baxter, L. R. Jr., Martin, K. M., & Phelps, M. E. (1996). Systematic changes in cerebral glucose metabolic rate after successful behavior modification treatment of obsessive-compulsive disorder. *Archives of General Psychiatry, 53,* 109–113.

Sexton, T. L., & Alexander, J. F. (2002). Family-based empirically supported interventions. *The Counseling Psychologist, 30,* 236–261.

Sexton, T. L., Alexander, J. F., & Mease, A. L. (2004). Levels of evidence for the models and mechanisms of therapeutic change in family and couple therapy. In M. J. Lambert (Ed.), *Bergin and Garfield's handbook of psychotherapy and behavior change* (5th ed.) (pp. 543–589). New York: Wiley

Sexton, T. L., Coop-Gordon, K., Gurman, A. S., Lebow, J. L., Holtzworh,-Munroe, A., & Johnson, S. M. (2007). *Task force report recommendations form the Division 43: Family Psychology Task Force on Evaluating Evidence-Based Treatments in Couples and Family Psychology.* San Francisco: American Psychological Association.

Sexton, T. L., Hanes, C. W., & Kinser, J. C. (2010). Translating science into clinical practice. In J. C. Thomas & M. Herson (Eds.), *Handbook of clinical psychology competencies* (pp. 153–180). New York: Springer.

Shaver, P. R., & Mikulincer, M. (2005). Attachment theory and research: Resurrection of the psychodynamic approach to personality. *Journal of Research in Personality, 39,* 22–45.

Shelton, J. L., & Rosen, G. M. (1980). Self-monitoring by patients. In G. M. Rosen, J. P. Geyman, & R. H. Layton (Eds.), *Behavioral science in family practice* (pp. 171–188). New York: Appleton-Century-Crofts.

Siegle, G. J., Cameron, S. C., & Thase, M. E. (2006). Use of fMRI to predict recovery from unipolar depression with cognitive behavior therapy. *American Journal of Psychiatry, 163,* 735–738.

Skinner, H., Steihauer, P., & Sitarenios, G. (2000). Family Assessment Measure (FAM) and process model of family functioning. *Journal of Family Therapy, 22,* 190–210.

Slade, A. (1998). Attachment theory and research: Implications for the theory and practice of individual psychotherapy with adults. In J. Cassidy & P. Shaver (Eds.), *The handbook of attachment theory and research* (pp. 575–594). New York: Guilford Press.

Smith, T. B., McCullough, M. E., & Poll, J. (2003). The association between religiousness and depressive symptoms was examined with meta-analytic methods across 147 independent investigations (N = 98,975). *Psychological Bulletin, 129,* 614–636.

Smith-Bell, M., & Winslade, W. J. (1994). Privacy, confidentiality and privilege in psychotherapeutic relationships. *Journal of Orthopsychiatry, 64,* 180–193.

Sowell, M., Kahn, D., Youngman, A., Lawrence, K., Rae, W., & Jensen-Doss, A. (2008). *Prescription privileges for psychologists: Views of pediatricians and pediatric psychologists.* Presented at American Psychological Association 2008 Convention, Boston, MA.

Spending Review. (2008). 11 of top 15 brands increase advertising spending in 2007's Q1-Q3. *DTC Perspectives, 7*(1), 10.

Spiegler, M. D., & Guevremont, D. C. (2003). *Contemporary Behavior Therapy* (4th ed.). Belmont, CA: Wadsworth.

Spring, B. (2007). Evidence-based practice in clinical psychology: What it is, why it matters; what you need to know. *Journal of Clinical Psychology, 63*(7), 611–631.

Stanos, J. F. (2004). Test review: Wechsler Abbreviated Scale of Intelligence. *Rehabilitation Counseling Bulletin, 48,* 56–57.

Stanton, M. (2010). The consultation and education competency. In M. B. Kenkel & R. L. Peterson (Eds.), *Competency-based education in professional psychology* (pp. 105–124). Washington, D. C.: American Psychological Association.

Sternberg, R. J., & Detterman, D. K. (Eds.). (1986). *What is intelligence?* Norwood, NJ: Ablex Publishing.

Strunk, D., Brotman, M., DeRubeis, R., & Hollon, S. (2010). Therapist competence in cognitive therapy for depression: Predicting subsequent symptom change. *Journal of Consulting and Clinical Psychology, 78*(3), 429–437.

Strupp, H. S., & Binder, J. L. (1984). *Psychotherapy in a new key: A guide to time-limited dynamic psychotherapy.* New York: Basic Books.

Stuart, S., & Roberston, M. (2003). *Interpersonal psychotherapy: A clinician's guide.* London: Edward Arnold.

Stuart, S., Robertson, M., & O'Hara, M. W. (2006). The future of interpersonal psychotherapy. *Psychiatric Annals, 36*(8), 578–588.

Sturmey, P. (Ed.) (2007). *Functional analysis in clinical treatment.* Burlington, MA: Academic Press.

Sue, D. W. (2001). Multidimensional facets of cultural competence. *The Counseling Psychologist, 29,* 790–821.

Sue, D. W, Arredondo, P., & McDavis, R. J. (1992). Multicultural counseling competencies and standards: A call to the profession. *Journal of Counseling and Development, 70,* 477–486.

Sue, D. W., Ivey, A. E., & Pedersen, P. B. (1996). *A theory of multicultural counseling and therapy.* Pacific Grove, CA: Brooks/Cole.

Sue, S. (1999). Science, ethnicity, and bias: Where have we gone wrong? *American Psychologist, 54,* 1070–1077.

Sullivan, J. R., Ramirez, E., Rae, W. A., Razo, N. P., & George, C. A. (2002). Factors continuing to breaking confidentiality with adolescent clients: A survey of pediatric psychologists. *Professional Psychology: Research and Practice, 33,* 396–401.

Sumerall, S., Lopez, S. J., & Oehlert, M. E. (2000). *Competency-based education and training in psychology.* Springfield, IL: Charles C. Thomas.

Summerfeldt, L. J., & Antony, M. M. (2002). Structured and semi-structured interviews. In M. M. Antony & D. H. Barlow (Eds.), *Handbook of assessment and treatment planning* (pp. 3–37). New York: Guilford.

Summers, R. F., & Barber, J. P. (2010). *Psychodynamic therapy: A guide to evidence-based practice.* New York: Guilford.

Svinicki, M., & McKeachie, W. J. (2011). *McKeachie's teaching tips: Strategies, research, and theory for college and university teachers* (13th ed.). Belmont, CA: Wadsworth.

Tajfel, H., & Turner, J. C. (1986). The social identity theory of intergroup behavior. In S. Worchel & W. G. Austing (Eds.), *Psychology of intergroup relations* (pp. 7–24). Chicago: Nelson-Hall.

Tarasoff vs Board of Regents of the University of California, Cal. Rptr. 14, No. S. F. 23042 (Cal. Sup. Ct., July 1, 1976), 131.

Teasdale, J. D. (1988). Cognitive vulnerability to persistent depression. *Cognition and Emotion, 2,* 247–274.

Thoresen, C. E., & Plante, T. G. (2005). Spirituality, religion, & health: What we know and what should you know. *Clinician's Research Digest,* Supp 32, American Psychological Association.

Thorndike, E. L. (1905). *The elements of psychology.* New York: A. G. Seiler.

Trierweiler, S. J., Stricker, G., & Peterson, R. L. (2010). The research and evaluation competency: The local clinical scientist—Review, current status, future directions. In M. B. Kenkel & R. L. Peterson (Eds.), *Competency-based education for professional psychology* (pp. 125–142). Washington, D. C.: American Psychological Association.

Tryon, G. S., & Winograd, G. (2002). In J. C. Norcross (Ed.), *Psychotherapy relationships that work: Therapist contribution and responsiveness to patients* (pp. 109–128). New York: Oxford University Press.

Tryon, W. W. (2010). Professional identity based on learning. *The Behavior Therapist, 33*(1), 9.

Turner, E. H., Matthews, A. M., Linardatos, E., Tell, R. A., & Rosenthal, R. (2008). Selective publication of antidepressant trials and its influence on apparent efficacy. *New England Journal of Medicine, 358,* 252–260.

United Nations Enable. (2006). *Frequently asked questions regarding the Convention on the Rights of Persons with Disabilities.* Retrieved from http://www.un.org/disabilities/default.asp?id_151.

U. S. Census Bureau. (2010). *2010 Census of Population and Housing.* Retrieved from http://www.census.gov/prod/cen2010/

U. S. Department of Health and Human Services. (2001). *Mental health: Culture, race, and ethnicity—A supplement to Mental Health: A Report of the Surgeon General.* Retrieved from http://www.surgeongeneral.gov/library/reports/

Vaillant, G. E. (1977). *Adaptation to life.* Boston, MA: Little, Brown.

VandeCreek, L., Miars, R. D., & Herzog C. E. (1987). Client anticipations and preferences for confidentiality of records. *Journal of Counseling Psychology, 34,* 62–67.

Van Windenfelt, B. (1995). *The prediction and prevention of relationship distress and divorce.* Nijmegen, The Netherlands: Quickprint.

Van Zandt, C. E. (1990). Professionalism: A matter of personal initiative. *Journal of Counseling and Development, 68,* 243–245.

Wade, W. A., Treat, T. A., & Stuart, G. L. (1998). Transporting an empirically supported treatment for panic disorder to a service clinic setting: A benchmarking strategy. *Journal of Consulting & Clinical Psychology, 66,* 231–239.

Walters, S. T., Matson, S. A., Baer, J. S., & Ziedonis, D. M. (2005). Effectiveness of workshop training for psychosocial addiction treatments: A systematic review. *Journal of Substance Abuse Treatment, 29,* 283–293.

Wampold, B. E. (2001). *The great psychotherapy debate: Models, methods, and findings.* Mahwah, NJ: Lawrence Erlbaum.

Wampold, B. E. (2005). Do therapies designated as empirically supported treatments for specific disorders produce outcomes superior to non-empirically supported treatment therapies? In J. C. Norcross, L. E. Beutler, & R. F. Levant (Eds.), *Evidence-based practices in mental health* (pp. 299–328). Washington, D. C.: American Psychological Association.

Wampold, B. E. (2007). Psychotherapy: The humanistic (and effective) treatment. *American Psychologist, 2,* 857–873.

Weiss, J., Sampson, H., & the Mount Zion Psychotherapy Research Group (1986). *The psychoanalytic process. Theory, clinical observation and empirical research.* New York: Guilford Press.

Weissman, M. M. (2006). A brief history of interpersonal psychotherapy. *Psychiatric Annals, 36*(8), 553–557.

Weissman, M. M., Markowitz, J. C., & Klerman, G. L. (2000). *Comprehensive guide to interpersonal psychotherapy.* New York: Basic Books.

Westen, D. (1998). The scientific legacy of Sigmund Freud: Toward a psychodynamically informed psychological science. *Psychological Bulletin, 124,* 331–371.

Westen, D., Novotny, C. M., & Thompson-Brenner, H. (2004). The empirical status of empirically supported psychotherapies: Assumptions, findings, and reporting in controlled clinical trials. *Psychological Bulletin, 130*(4), 631–663.

Wheeler, D. W., Seagren, A. T., Becker, L. W., Kinley, E. R., Mlinek, D. D., & Robson, K. J. (2008). *The academic chair's handbook* (2nd ed.). New York: Jossey-Bass.

Williams, S. (2002). Person-centered therapy. In R. A. DiTomasso & E. A. Gosch (Eds.), *Comparative treatments for anxiety disorders* (pp. 223–238). New York: Springer Publishing Company.

Wilson, G. T. (1997). Treatment manuals in clinical practice. *Behaviour Research and Therapy, 35*(3), 205–210.

Wilson, G. T., Grilo, C., & Vitousek, K. (2007). Psychological treatment of eating disorders. *American Psychologist, 62*(3), 199–216.

Wilson, G. T., Wilfley, D. E., Agras, S., & Bryson, S. W. (2010). Psychological treatments of binge eating disorder. *Archives of General Psychiatry, 67*(1), 94–101.

Witsey-Stirman, S., Bhar, S. S., Spokas, M., Brown, G. K., Creed, T. A., Perivoliotis, D.,... Beck, A. T. (2010). Training and consultation in evidence-based psychosocial treatments in public mental health settings: The ACCESS model. *Professional Psychology: Research and Practice, 41,* 48–56.

Witsey-Stirman, S., Buchhofer, R., McLaulin, J. B., Evans, A. C., & Beck, A. T. (2009). The Beck Initiative: A partnership to implement cognitive therapy in a community behavioral health system. *Psychiatric Services, 60,* 1302–1304.

Wolpe, J. (1958). *Psychotherapy by reciprocal inhibition.* Stanford, CA: Stanford University Press.

Wolpe, J. (1990). *The practice of behavior therapy* (4th ed.). New York: Pergamon Press.

Wolpe, J., & Turkat, I. D. (1985). Behavioral formulation of clinical cases. In I. D. Turkat (Ed.), *Behavioral case formulation* (pp. 144–213). New York: Plenum.

Worthington, E. L., & Sandage, S. J. (2001). Religion and spirituality. *Psychotherapy: Theory, Research, Practice, and Training, 38,* 473–478.

Yarhouse, M. A. (2008). Narrative sexual identity therapy. *American Journal of Family Therapy, 39,* 196–210.

Zimmerman, M. (1994). *Interview guide for evaluating DSM-IV psychiatric disorders and the Mental Status Examination.* Greenwich, RI: Psych Press Products.

ACCESS Model: A systematic effort to address critical issues related to the clinician, client, population, settings, problems, and comorbidities through intensive training and consultation

Accountability: An emphasis on implementing brief, evidence-based practice and monitoring outcomes

American Board of Professional Psychology (ABPP): The predominant body overseeing competency-based credentialing in 13 specialty areas of clinical psychology

Assessment: A higher-order, detailed, highly complex and sophisticated process of integrating, synthesizing, and deriving meaning about a client from a number and variety of sources. Assessment can be used to infer characteristics and traits about an individual, develop a formal diagnosis, aid in the development of a case conceptualization, create a treatment plan, determine prognosis, make professional recommendations, and answer a referral question

Attachment theory: Maintains that human beings are born with an innate psychobiological system (the attachment behavioral system) necessary for survival, instinctually driving them to seek proximity toward significant others (attachment figures)

Automatic thoughts: Immediate, reactionary, and situationally specific perceptions

Behavioral assessment: An empirical, multimodal, multimethod, multi-informant approach that places a premium on the specification of observable behavior and time-related causal factors

Behavioral model: A model of case formulation that emphasizes stimulus–response relationships from a classical conditioning perspective

Behavioral sex differences: Differences in behaviors among males and females that may have a biological basis

Benchmarking studies: Establish the effectiveness of psychotherapeutic interventions in outpatient settings with minimal exclusion criteria

Biological assessment: The evaluation of physiological parameters

Biopsychosocial assessment: Proposed by Engel (1977), who convincingly argued for a more comprehensive evaluation of patients in medical settings. This multimodal assessment approach addresses key domains, including the biological or physical, cognitive, affective, social, behavioral, environmental/familial, and cultural aspects of the individual, and the many factors included within each domain

Boulder model: The first curriculum for clinical psychology training programs, which emphasized training in science over training in clinical work. The Boulder model informs training in PhD programs

Case formulation/case conceptualization: A hypothesis or series of hypotheses about the causes, precipitants, and maintaining influences of an individual's psychological, interpersonal, and behavioral problems

Catharsis: The expression or release of painful emotions

Clinical curiosity: An attitude and desire to understand clients intimately through direct inquiry, with goals of understanding each client's individuality and distinct culture

Clinical interview: A formalized professional interaction between a clinical psychologist and client that provides a context or backdrop against which other information about the client can be understood

Clinical psychology: A field of professional psychology that focuses on providing specialty services, such as assessment, treatment, and prevention of psychological and behaviors disorders, to individuals across the lifespan

Coalitions: A problematic interaction pattern where some family members develop a bond and contradict another family member

Cognitive assessment: The systematic measurement of a number of characteristics that affect the functioning in the everyday lives of our clients, including attention, memory, learning, decision-making, language, and problem-solving

Cognitive-behavioral therapy (CBT): A problem-focused, psychoeducational, time-limited, present-oriented treatment

Cognitive model: Posits that individuals' feelings and behaviors are guided by their perceptions and interpretations of events

Communication skills: The ability of clinical psychologists to convey information to their clients

Congruence: The concept that the therapist presents himself or herself as a real and genuine person without a façade, is free and open to his or her own experience, and is himself or herself in the relationship

Conscious mind: Part of Sigmund Freud's structure of the mind, which contains awareness at the moment

Consultation: A collaborative endeavor between the consultant and the consultee in which the consultant intervenes in an indirect manner without assuming responsibility for the direct delivery of the service

Consultee-Centered Case Consultation (CCCC): The process of working in situations when the focus of the consultation is the consultee. The reason for the consultation is embedded within the reaction of the consultee to a patient or group of patients

Continuing education: Formal learning activities that are necessary for maintaining licensure and allow psychologists to keep pace with relevant and emerging issues in the field and increase competencies

Core Conflictual Relationship Theme (CCRT): A psychodynamic model that employs patient narratives to elucidate relationship patterns and conflicts by considering the patient's wishes, anticipated or real responses obtained from others, and reactions to the responses obtained from others

Corrective Emotional Experience: A psychodynamic technique in which the patient is re-exposed, under more favorable circumstances, to emotional situations he or she could not handle in the past

Countertransference: Comprises (a) the therapist's reaction to the client in the form of positive or negative attitudes, beliefs, assumptions, feelings, and behaviors that (b) is triggered by the client, the circumstances of the therapy, or events in the therapist's life that (c) are related to past relationships in the therapist's life and that (d) serve to meet the needs of the therapist as opposed to the client

Culturally sensitive research: Research designed to respect the value of culture and ethics by conducting research with ethnically, linguistically, and racially diverse populations

Defenses: Described by Sigmund Freud as patients' use of various strategies to avoid experiencing upsetting unconscious material

Developmental Achievement Levels: A means of assessing relationship competence on a continuum from novice to expert that was developed by the National Council of Schools and Programs of Professional Psychology

Diagnosis: A formal, standardized means of communicating information about an individual by describing his or her constellation of symptoms as meeting the diagnostic criteria for a particular disorder

Disengagement: A problematic interaction pattern where there seems to be little connection between family members

Diversity: Dimensions of identity and culture that differ from person to person, such as gender, age, sexual orientation, disability, religion/spiritual orientation, education, and socioeconomic status

Drive theory: Proposed by Sigmund Freud, who felt that the most fundamental human motives are rooted in biology, and ongoing efforts to regulate sexual and aggressive impulses are paramount in human development, shaping adult personality

Duty to warn: The ethical obligation to warn an intended victim of violence if the psychologist is privy to this information, regardless of whether it was discovered in the context of therapy

Dynamic formulation: A systematic attempt to determine each patient's unique problem and to develop an intervention plan that resolves it

Ego functioning: A broad domain reflecting various psychological abilities, such as reality testing, affect regulation, impulse control, judgment, thought processes, defensive functioning, and object relations

Empathy: Refers to the capacity to fully understand and appreciate the manner in which the client perceives the world

Enmeshment: A problematic interaction pattern where a person is not allowed to think differently or to individuate from the family system

Ethical competency: A concept that reflects positive ethics, risk management, best practices, and defensive practice

Examination for Professional Practice of Psychology (EPPP): The national licensing examination for clinical psychologists in the United States

Exosystem: In Bronfenbrenner's model, the outer layer, which encompasses aspects of the individual's life that are not direct influences or a part of everyday life, but nevertheless play a role in influencing the person's environment and development

Family systems assessment: A systematic means of measuring family functioning

Feedback: A process in which the therapist delivers information to the client about his or her thoughts, feelings, behaviors, attitudes, and assumptions with the intent of promoting personal growth in the context of a safe environment

Functional Analytic Model: A model of case conceptualization that places primary emphasis on environmental factors that occur before, during, and contingent upon the emission of a target response. The most basic assumption of this model is, then, that a client's behavior is learned as a result of his or her unique history of consequences associated with the individual's behavior

Gender socialization: The learning of behaviors and attitudes considered appropriate for a given sex

Gender stereotypes: Working templates for how men and women *should* behave

Grief: A loss of a relationship or loss of a healthy self

Health disparities: The unequal distribution of disease and mortality across different groups

Hollon and Dimidjian's Model: A cognitive model of case formulation for depression that emphasizes conditional and unconditional beliefs and underlying assumptions that are characterized by negative cognitive content

Individual differences: Refers to the endless number of ways in which people can differ, and how these differences often account for the differences in observable behaviors across individuals

Informed consent: The process of providing the client with all the information he or she needs to decide whether or not to participate in research, assessment, and/or psychotherapy

Intermediate beliefs: Thoughts activated by schemata; they represent the rules and assumptions that guide everyday functioning and decision-making

International Society for Interpersonal Psychotherapy (ISPT): The dominant organization associated with interpersonal therapy; established criteria for levels of accreditation in interpersonal therapy in 2003

Interpersonal skills: The ability to understand the client and his or her needs, creating a sound basis for responding to the client at a deeper level and fostering a sense of hope that change is possible

Interpersonal skill deficits: The default problem of focus in interpersonal therapy when the individual reports no significant life events or relationship problems coinciding with depression. Patients in this category are typically socially isolated and have either a pattern of unrewarding relationships or chronic difficulty establishing and maintaining significant social bonds

Interpersonal inventory: A comprehensive, semistructured interview about the patient's interpersonal functioning and current and past relationships

Interpersonal therapy (IPT): An empirically supported, time-limited, present-focused psychotherapy, originally developed for depression, that conceptualizes patients' current problems within an interpersonal context

J. Beck's Model: A cognitive model of case formulation that emphasizes the client's present diagnosis; factors leading to the emergence and maintenance of current problems; maladaptive cognitions and their relationship to the client's feelings, behaviors, and physical symptoms; impact of early learning events; underlying beliefs; coping mechanisms; the cognitive triad; and current stress factors

Kuyken, Padesky, and Dudley's Model: A cognitive model of case formulation that emphasizes how the integration of the patient's experience, relevant theory, and empirical research provides a descriptive and explanatory model of the client's problems through a process of collaboration

Lifelong learning: A strong commitment to engaging in a long-term, self-directed, educational process designed to enhance one's knowledge, skills, and attitudes in identified competency domains that underlie professional practice; must be sustained to ensure the effectiveness of the clinical psychologist over professional life cycle

Local clinical scientist: A way to bridge the gap between science and practice

Medical model: A characterization of psychological disorders as medical illnesses, so that the patient cannot be blamed for being sick

Mentor: A trusted, experienced professional who guides the development of a less experienced individual in his or her quest to acquire the requisite knowledge, skills, and attitudes in critical competency domains that define the specialty

Mesosystem: In Bronfenbrenner's model, the middle layer created by the relationships that exist between members of the microsystem

Microsystem: In Bronfenbrenner's model, the inner layer system, which consists of family, school/work, neighborhood, religious affiliations, and all that is in the immediate surroundings of the individual

Multicultural competence: Involves the dimensions of (1) awareness of one's own attitudes and beliefs, (2) knowledge about cultural differences, and (3) skills in working with diverse groups

Multiple relationships: When a psychologist is in a professional role with a person and (1) is in another relationship with the same person, (2) is in another relationship with a person closely associated with or related to the person with whom he or she has the professional relationship, or (3) may in the future enter into another relationship

National Council of Schools and Programs in Professional Psychology (NCSPP): An organization that advocates for graduate programs to offer comprehensive training in areas in which psychologists are expected to be competent and delineates the skills necessary for competent practice that should be included in the core curriculum of education and training programs

Needleman's Model: A cognitive model of case formulation that incorporates several key components: demographic information; a description of the client's presenting problem; the circumstances that led to the emergence of the presenting problem; a comprehensive list of problems, concerns, and behaviors of relevance to treatment; DSM-IV-TR diagnoses and personality traits; core beliefs; sources of core beliefs; vicious cycles and factors that maintain problems; treatment goals; factors expected to interfere with therapy; and a treatment plan

Nezu and Nezu's Model: A model of case formulation that emerged from a problem-solving perspective and is designed to bridge the gap that often exists between the art and science of clinical practice in professional psychology

Patient-Centered Case Consultation (PCCC): Focuses on a patient who is being seen by a mental health professional and about whom the consultee has important questions and seeks answers to one or more questions of significance

People with disabilities (PWD): People who have long-term physical, mental, intellectual, or sensory impairments that may hinder their full and effective participation in society on an equal basis with others

Personality assessment: The selection, administration, scoring, and interpretation of a variety of different devices designed to tap one or more areas of a person's stable and relatively enduring patterns of thinking, perceiving, and behaving that characterize his or her transactions with the environment

Persons' Model: A cognitive model of case formulation that incorporates six key elements: the problem list; the hypothesized core mechanism underlying the problems; how the hypothesized mechanism accounts for the problems on the client's list; the relationship between the mechanism and the problems; the precipitants of the client's presenting problems; origins of the mechanism; and predicted roadblocks to treatment

Positive ethics: Refers to a psychologist's responsibility and desire to uphold the General Principles as delineated by the American Psychological Association's Ethical Principles of Psychologists and Code of Conduct

Practitioner-scholar model: Otherwise known as the Vail model; focuses primarily on training master clinicians who use the professional literature as a basis for solving questions relevant to their clinical practice

Preconscious mind: Part of Sigmund Freud's structure of the mind that contains acceptable feelings and thoughts accessible to awareness through focus and attention

Prescription privilege: A political movement in certain state legislatures to allow prescriptive authority for properly trained psychologists; this would enable them to prescribe psychotropic medications

Primary prevention: Initiatives aimed at preventing mental health problems, typically in children and adolescents

Professional development plan: A plan for maintaining competency that includes continuing education classes/workshops, home study programs, peer supervision, reading relevant journals and books, obtaining consultation, and focused clinical supervision

Professional identity: Comprises the acquisition of attitudes essential to one's role as a clinical psychologist coupled with a deep sense of responsibility and duty to the specialty, respect for its mores and value system, and a sense of honor and fulfillment in performing its roles and functions in society

Psychodynamic Diagnostic Manual (PDM): Was developed in response to concerns with the DSM system of classification and diagnosis of psychiatric disorders; articulates a common terminology among psychoanalytic and psychodynamic clinicians. The PDM aims at providing a more extensive description of the patient's internal life and provides a deeper understanding of naturally occurring patterns.

Psychodynamic model: A case formulation model that describes the patient's presenting problem in the context of central conflicts in the patient's life

Psychosexual development: Sigmund Freud's theory of development that identified a course of maturation from infancy and early childhood as critical in later adult personality formation

Reciprocal inhibition: Theory that inducing a relaxed state would inhibit the experience of fear, as relaxation and fear states were believed to be mutually exclusive

Reframing: A therapeutic technique in which a therapist presents an individual or family with an alternate way of viewing the situation, problem, or behavior

Relational fitness: The inherent capacity to engage in those facilitative behaviors that are requisite to the daily functioning of the clinical psychologist

Relationship competency: The capacity to develop and maintain a constructive working alliance with clients

Reliability: The stability of the diagnoses derived from interviews by the same clinician over time (test–retest), between clinicians (interrater reliability), and the overall homogeneity and internal consistency of the item pool

Religion: Beliefs, rules, practices, symbols, and rituals with a relationship to God or a higher power as its centerpiece

Role dispute: A conflict with a significant other

Role-plays: Artificial interactions or skits where people play different roles to learn or practice a skill

Role transitions: Involve a significant life change such as relocating, having a baby, divorcing, or retiring

Schemata (or core beliefs): Enduring patterns of evaluating and interpreting one's world, which are global and inflexible

Scientist-practitioner model: A training model intended to bridge the gap between science and practice. The ideal realization of the scientist-practitioner model is a professional who uses systematic scientific methods to develop, guide, and enhance his or her practice, with the client's best interest of paramount importance

Secondary prevention: Initiatives or screening measures that allow for early identification of at-risk or maladaptive behaviors, such as binge drinking in college students

Self-assessment: Examining one's own inner attitudes, beliefs, assumptions, feelings, and behaviors in the role of the professional psychologist as a participant-observer

Self-awareness: Knowledge of one's strengths, limitations, blind spots, outcomes, and areas in need of further improvement

Self-care: The activities individuals undertake to enhance their health and emotional functioning

Self-determination: Each individual's right to control the course of his or her own life

Self-disclosure: Revealing personal information to a client

Self-monitoring: A behavioral assessment technique in which client is actively and collaboratively employed as a data collector

Social categorization theory: Explains how people make sense of their social world in an effort to accurately strategize appropriate behaviors and predict potential harm (emotional or physical)

Spirituality: Refers to one's personal relationship with God (or higher power or universal spirit); a desire to find personal meaning and direction in life; and a promotion of classic virtues such as love, compassion, and forgiveness

Standardized patient: A trained actor who represents a mock patient/case

SWOT analysis: An approach to program development that addresses four major areas of consideration: the strengths of an organization, its weaknesses, and opportunities and threats in the environment

Systems approaches: Focus not on the individual, but on the system of which the individual is a part

***Tarasoff* case:** A Supreme Court ruling that the protection of individual privacy must end when danger to the public begins

Tertiary prevention: Otherwise known as crisis management; interventions, rehabilitation, and psychoeducation designed to improve coping or to enhance social support among individuals with psychological disorders

Third wave therapies: Cognitive therapies developed over the past 20 years that include emphasis on mindfulness, the client's personal values, cognitive defusion, relationships, the importance of the therapeutic relationship, and treatment rationale

Transference: Involves (a) a form of stimulus generalization of past experience (or conflicts) and displacements in the form of positive or negative attitudes, beliefs, assumptions, feelings, and behaviors toward the therapist that is (b) triggered in response to the therapist's characteristics and that (c) involves a misperception or distortion on the part of the client

Transtheoretical model: A model of case formulation that captures the inherent competencies required to perform a case conceptualization

Triangulation: A type of interaction occurring between family members where two people's interaction patterns are problematic and a third person becomes involved in an attempt to stabilize the relationship

Unconditional positive regard: A construct that captures the unconditional acceptance, respect, and prizing of the client by the therapist and is modestly associated with positive outcome by creating a platform for interventions or in and of itself

Unconscious mind: Part of Sigmund Freud's structure of the mind that contains instinctual urges, impulses, and desires containing unacceptable feelings and thoughts

Vail model: Otherwise known as the practitioner-scholar model; emphasizes clinical practice over research skills. The Vail model informs training in PsyD programs

Validity: The extent to which a psychological test measures what it has been designed to measure

Working alliance: Otherwise known as therapeutic or helping alliance; a collaboration that includes agreement on treatment goals, consensus on therapeutic tasks, and a bond between the client and therapist

INDEX

ABOUT THE AUTHORS

Robert A. DiTomasso, PhD, ABPP, is Professor of Psychology and Chairman of the Department of Psychology at the Philadelphia College of Osteopathic Medicine (PCOM). He is a Diplomate in Clinical Psychology of the American Board of Professional Psychology, a Fellow of the Academy of Clinical Psychology, a Founding Fellow of the Academy of Cognitive Therapy, and a licensed psychologist in Pennsylvania and New Jersey. He obtained his doctoral degree from the University of Pennsylvania and completed an internship at Temple University School of Medicine, Department of Psychiatry, Behavior Therapy Unit, Eastern Pennsylvania Psychiatric Institute. He completed extensive postdoctoral training and supervision in cognitive therapy and primary care psychology. He previously served as Adjunct Associate Professor at the University of Pennsylvania and as Associate Director of Behavioral Medicine at West Jersey Health System Family Practice Residency for many years. He teaches and provides clinical supervision and research mentorship to students in the APA-accredited doctoral program in clinical psychology at PCOM. Dr. DiTomasso is a Consulting Editor of the *Journal of Clinical Psychology.*

Stacey C. Cahn, PhD, is Associate Professor in the Department of Psychology at the Philadelphia College of Osteopathic Medicine (PCOM) where she mentors and supervises PsyD students in the APA-accredited PsyD program in Clinical Psychology. Dr. Cahn received her BA from the University of Michigan, and her PhD in Clinical Psychology from Rutgers University. She completed her internship at the University of Medicine and Dentistry of New Jersey (UMDNJ) and post-doctoral fellowships at Rutgers University and UMDNJ. Dr. Cahn is a licensed psychologist in both New Jersey and Pennsylvania. Her clinical and research interests include the treatment and study of eating and weight disorders. Dr. Cahn is a Consulting Editor of the *Journal of Clinical Psychology.*

Susan M. Panichelli-Mindel, PhD, is Assistant Professor and Director of Research in the PsyD program in Clinical Psychology at the Philadelphia College of Osteopathic Medicine (PCOM). She teaches and provides clinical and research mentorship to students in the APA-accredited PsyD program in Clinical Psychology at PCOM. She received her PhD in Clinical Psychology from Temple University and completed an internship at the Behavioral Therapy Service of the Institute of Pennsylvania Hospital. She is a licensed psychologist in Pennsylvania with extensive experience in the delivery of cognitive-behavioral empirically supported treatments to children and adolescents. Her research and clinical interests include issues related to child psychopathology and treatment, with an emphasis on the prevention and treatment of anxiety disorders.

Roger K. McFillin, PsyD, ACT, is the Co-Founder of the Center for Integrated Behavioral Health in Bethlehem, PA. He is a Diplomate of the Academy of Cognitive Therapy and a licensed psychologist in Pennsylvania and New Jersey. He received his PsyD in Clinical Psychology from Philadelphia College of Osteopathic Medicine, where he was the recipient of the Dean's Award for Academic Excellence.

ABOUT THE SERIES EDITORS

Arthur M. Nezu, PhD, ABPP, is Professor of Psychology, Medicine, and Public Health at Drexel University and Special Professor of Forensic Mental Health and Psychiatry at the University at Nottingham in the United Kingdom. He is a fellow of multiple professional associations, including the American Psychological Association, and board-certified by the American Board of Professional Psychology in Cognitive and Behavioral Psychology, Clinical Psychology, and Clinical Health Psychology. Dr. Nezu is widely published, is incoming Editor of the *Journal of Consulting and Clinical Psychology*, and has maintained a practice for three decades.

Christine Maguth Nezu, PhD, ABPP, is Professor of Psychology and Medicine at Drexel University and Special Professor of Forensic Mental Health and Psychiatry at the University at Nottingham in the United Kingdom. With over 25 years' experience in clinical private practice, consultation/liaison, research, and teaching, she is board-certified by the American Board of Professional Psychology (ABPP) in Cognitive and Behavioral Psychology and Clinical Psychology. She is also a past President of ABPP. Her research has been supported by federal, private, and state-funded agencies and she has served as a grant reviewer for the National Institutes of Health.